Political Change in Britain

Also by David Butler

THE BRITISH GENERAL ELECTION OF 1951
THE ELECTORAL SYSTEM IN BRITAIN SINCE 1918
THE BRITISH GENERAL ELECTION OF 1955
THE STUDY OF POLITICAL BEHAVIOUR
ELECTIONS ABROAD (*editor*)
THE BRITISH GENERAL ELECTION OF 1959 (*with Richard Rose*)
BRITISH POLITICAL FACTS, 1900–1974 (*with Anne Sloman*)
THE BRITISH GENERAL ELECTION OF 1964 (*with Anthony King*)
THE BRITISH GENERAL ELECTION OF 1966 (*with Anthony King*)
THE BRITISH GENERAL ELECTION OF 1970 (*with Michael Pinto-Duschinsky*)
THE CANBERRA MODEL
THE BRITISH GENERAL ELECTION OF 1974 (*with Dennis Kavanagh*)

Also by Donald Stokes

THE AMERICAN VOTER (*co-author*)
ELECTIONS AND THE POLITICAL ORDER (*co-author*)

Political Change in Britain

The Evolution of Electoral Choice

Second edition

DAVID BUTLER
Fellow of Nuffield College, Oxford

DONALD STOKES
Dean of the Woodrow Wilson School
Princeton University

ST. MARTIN'S PRESS   NEW YORK

AFFILIATED PUBLISHERS: Macmillan Limited, London –
also at Bombay, Calcutta, Madras and Melbourne

Preface to the Second Edition

THIS book is a reconstruction and expansion of *Political Change in Britain*, which we published in 1969. The new analyses we offer here were made possible by the extension of our studies considerably beyond the period treated in the earlier book. The conclusions we drew there were based primarily on the analysis of interview data gathered from representative samples of the electorate in 1963, 1964 and 1966. Repeated observations of political behaviour over even so short a period as three years could reveal many of the sources of political change. Moreover we exploited our respondents' recollections of their own and their parents' politics over a much longer period.

But we were anxious to continue our observations and to span a wider interval of contemporary politics. We wanted especially to include in our work periods in which each of the two main parties was in the ascendant. Therefore, even as we published our earlier results from 1963–6 we were preparing for additional surveys of our continuing panels and of new samples of electors in 1969 and in 1970 when the Conservatives returned to power. The materials of this book are drawn from the full period 1963–70.

Although in the pages that follow we have preserved much of the initial argument intact, this book differs substantially from its predecessor in both form and content. Because we wished to introduce new material without lengthening the book we have omitted certain chapters (notably those on trade union influence, on the mass media and on the Liberals) to which we had little to add. More important, we have drastically reordered the surviving chapters, transferring many of their parts in order to emphasize the continuity of political alignments and to underline three main types of change. For the convenience of those familiar with the previous book we have listed these changes in an Appendix (C). In another Appendix (A) we describe at length our sample design and response rates. We have also (Appendix B) listed all the questions asked in our five surveys and the percentage distributions of the replies to the 'closed' questions. We have relied on the presence of these percentage distributions in the Appendix to simplify the empirical content of the main text in one important respect. In many cases we have omitted a description of the sub-sample sizes from our tables when these can be reconstructed from a knowledge of the total sample and of the distribution of responses given in the text of the questionnaires in the Appendix. We have also omitted frequencies from the tables for the sake of clarity of exposition whenever a frequency is approximately the same as the total sample size.

The authors of a book of this sort are faced by the problem of multiple audiences. We have written with a view to the interests of readers both inside and outside the universities in Britain and elsewhere, whether professionally concerned with politics or not. We have no illusions that we shall satisfy them all. Some readers will find the book needlessly abstract; others will wish that there could have been more theoretical modelling. Some will find the book too heavily quantitative; others will be impatient because we have reduced so much to prose or contingency tables, reserving to footnotes the more elaborate statistical models that underlie some of our findings. Some will find the book too remote from the day-to-day politics of Britain; others will sigh for a more general and comparative framework. From all these readers we invite a degree of sympathy for a dilemma that has been with us through all the successive drafts of these pages.

March 1974   David Butler
                                                     Donald Stokes

Acknowledgments

Two authors appear on the title-page of this book and we bear sole responsibility for its contents. But we could not have begun to produce it without the assistance of many people and institutions. We are indebted first and foremost to the Warden and Fellows of Nuffield College, Oxford, and to the Institute for Social Research and the Department of Political Science of the University of Michigan. Nuffield College not only found the bulk of the funds for the initial British fieldwork but provided a home for the enterprise and encouragement throughout its long course. The University of Michigan forgave one author his protracted absence waiting for the 1964 British election to take place, and the Institute for Social Research supplied the facilities for analyzing the data as well as the roof under which the bulk of the book was written. Many other institutions contributed in different ways to our undertaking. In addition to Nuffield College, funds for our research came from the Nuffield Foundation, the Rockefeller Foundation, the John Simon Guggenheim Foundation, the National Science Foundation and the British Social Science Research Council. We are very grateful to the British Market Research Bureau for the way in which they carried out our exacting fieldwork requirements, and in particular to Timothy Joyce and Charles Channon. We should also like to thank Mrs Wise of the Tabulating Research Center, and the staff of the Atlas Computing Laboratory, especially Paul Nelson. Our interviews were coded with great zeal and efficiency by various helpers in Oxford.

A devoted band of helpers worked at one period or another full-time on this enterprise and we must express our very deep gratitude to Don Aitkin, John Francis, Martha Ion, Michael Kahan, Thomas Mann, Ron May, Stella Moyser, Virginia Nye, Douglas Scott, Audrey Skeats, Margaret Squires, Arthur Stevens, Ann Taylor, Margaret Thomas, Phyllis Thorburn, Robert Travis and Julie Larson Wurglitz.

We want to make special mention of our obligation to Ralph Brookes, Angus Campbell, Philip Converse and Warren Miller for their intellectual stimulus and their penetrating and exact reading of our text. We must reserve a pantheon for Anthony King who laboured through successive drafts of our manuscript, offering searching but always constructive criticisms.

We wish to thank Leslie Kish and Percy Gray for their kind advice on sample design and Irene Hess and Thomas Tharackan for organizing the computation of our sampling errors.

The Gallup Poll, National Opinion Polls and the Opinion Research Centre were most generous in allowing us to see and quote their findings, and Paul Duncan-Jones was indefatigable in helping us to analyze a vast body of N.O.P. data.

Others whom we should thank for their diverse and often very substantial help and criticism include:

Mark Abrams	Jean Nicholls
Paul Abramson	Dipak Nandy
Michael Adler	Keith Ovenden
George Anderson	Clive Payne
George Bain	Michael Pinto-Duschinsky
Brian Barry	Peter Pulzer
Stephen Beackon	Robert Putnam
Jay Blumler	Graham Pyatt
Susan Brooks	Don Rawson
Ronald Butt	David Robertson
Richard Crossman	Garry Runciman
David Deans	Patricia Ryan
James Douglas	Ed Schneider
Henry Durant	Kleri Smith
Sir Michael Fraser	Michael Steed
Alan Gelb	Leigh Stelzer
John Goldthorpe	Humphrey Taylor
Peter Hyett	Stan Taylor
Gudmund Iversen	Frank Teer
Gary Katzmann	Ailsa Walker
William Miller	Nigel Walker
Austin Mitchell	William Wallace
Louis Moss	Philip Williams

We must also thank those forbearing British citizens whose answers in thousands of hours of interviews made this book possible.

Our greatest debt, however, is to our wives and to our children for ten years of long-suffering support as they endured the repeated separation and uprooting that transatlantic collaboration involves.

D.B.
D.S.

Contents

PART II: REALIGNMENT

PART III: REPLACEMENT

PART IV: CONVERSION

CONCLUSION

Introduction

1 Approaches to Change

THE possibility of rulers being constitutionally driven from office in a free election is relatively new in the history of government. The voters who now hold this power in the liberal democracies can, of course, exercise it only by selecting between alternatives that have been defined by competing leaders or groups. In Britain it is the political parties that provide the focus of choice. Indeed, in the longer historical view, parties antedate the mass electorate since it was the parties who enfranchised the voters and mobilized their support. But the public is not the creature of the parties, and the ebbs and flows of popular favour affect, often in quite unexpected ways, the whole conduct of British government.

The unpredictable quality of electoral change emphasizes the complexity of its sources. When the lives of governments were decided purely within the Houses of Parliament, those who sought power could well understand the motives and forces upon which its transfer depended. But when the ultimate decision moved outwards to thousands of polling stations across the country, these forces became vastly more complex and difficult to fathom. Every government in recent years has at times felt its support in the country ebbing away without warning. Indeed, these rises and falls of party strength are often incomprehensible both to those whose fortunes most plainly depend upon them and to those whose profession it is to explain them.

This is a book about such changes. It is based on detailed and repeated interviews with British electors over seven years. But we have tried to look behind the fluctuations of party support in the 1960s and the half century before and to explore their sources systematically. We are limited by the historical context in which we gathered our data, but since it was a time of exceptional political instability we have the electors' testimony from two periods of Labour ascendency, from two periods where the parties were evenly balanced, and from one when the Conservatives were handsomely ahead. The fact that the long-term forces shaping party strengths were little affected by these transient fluctuations emphasizes that in most of this book we are looking at phenomena which are not bounded by the specific circumstances of British political life in the 1960s.

While we aim to contribute to an understanding of that period in British history, we also aim to clarify some more general problems of political change.

Since the sources of change are many, and systematic analysis must deal with a wide variety of considerations, we have deliberately forgone the theoretical and empirical neatness that could be achieved by confining our view to the interplay of a few key factors, preferring instead a ruthless eclecticism. The full series of British election results reflects the overlay of a number of distinct processes of change, just as the single groove of a recording disc represents the overlay of the many instruments in a symphony orchestra. Any analysis of change must distinguish and treat separately its various components.

Types of Change

We shall find it convenient to think of the processes of change as being of three fundamental kinds. The first of these are changes which involve the physical replacement of the electorate. Even in a few short years, some millions of electors die and others come of age; the longer our historical view the greater the extent of the replacement. Of course immigration and emigration also yield some turnover in the electorate, as do many changes in the legal requirements for the franchise. But the effects of these in recent years have been small by contrast with the inexorable processes of birth and maturation on the one hand and of aging and death on the other.[1]

The importance of this sort of change is obvious. In any era the young will be unlike the old in many of their attitudes, and some of these differences will extend to politics. Therefore, replacing one with the other will alter the political complexion of the electorate a little every year; over time these effects will be cumulative. A man of seventy-five who died after voting in 1959 once had to choose between the competing claims of Asquith and Balfour. But a man who first became entitled to vote in 1964 was not born until the Second World War. The transition from the Macmillan triumph of 1959 to the Wilson victory of 1964 was in some part the result of the replacement of the first type of elector by the second. And if we consider the transition from Baldwin to Wilson the role played by the electorate's physical renewal must be far more extensive.

[1] The granting of votes at 18 in 1970 was by far the largest change since 1928 when the franchise was finally granted to all women.

A second type of change is that which involves the electorate's enduring party alignments. Support comes to any party for the most astonishing variety of reasons. But some of these will be general enough and enduring enough to be considered as bases of party alignment. Since the rise of the Labour Party the foremost of these in Britain has been social class. But other cleavages have cut across the electorate in modern times. During the years of Conservative–Liberal rivalry the issue of Home Rule produced one lasting realignment of party strength while the conflict of church and chapel provided another basis of enduring political cleavage. Furthermore, the role of social class itself has altered a good deal with the passage of time.

There is a very close connection between the renewal of the electorate and changes of party alignment. As we shall see, once an elector has acquired an allegiance to party he is unlikely again to be so open to political conversion. Therefore, he will be less responsive than a younger and previously unaligned elector when any new grounds of party cleavage develop. As a result the renewal of the electorate may have to proceed for many years before a changing alignment is fully reflected in party support. We shall in fact argue that such an evolutionary process has applied to the relationship between social class and party alignments.

The third type of change is that which involves the electors' response to the immediate issues and events of politics. Although, as we shall show, such stimuli have a greater effect on younger voters, the rise and fall of party strength between general elections – and even more the fluctuations expressed in local and by-elections and in the regular opinion polls – cannot be due mainly to the physical replacement of the electorate. These changes are due rather to the variability of behaviour among people who remain in the electorate. Most changes of this kind do not presage a lasting shift of party alignment. A hard budget, an unpopular prime minister, a severe winter, a sense that the Government has grown tired in power – influences such as these are overlaid on the more enduring bases of party support and produce the fluctuations which are displayed in the many indicators of the state of the parties, including general elections. The ease with which these more ephemeral influences deflect the party balance depends on how deeply the more basic cleavages cut through the electorate. We shall develop this point as we interpret the increased volatility of the electorate in the 1960s. But these immediate and short-run influences must be clearly separated from changes in the country's lasting partisan alignments.

The distinctions among these types of change have helped to give structure to this book. We shall distinguish among them in our analysis, but they of course do not operate in isolation in the real world. It is all too easy to lose sight of all but one type of explanation and to be disappointed when it proves inadequate to account fully for political change. An example of this lies in the evidence which we offer that at this period of history long-term change through deaths and comings of age is working continuously in favour of the Labour Party. This finding attracted the attention of a number of readers of our first edition, and when the political commentators soon thereafter searched for reasons that might explain Labour's resurgence in the six months prior to the 1970 election, our demographic analysis was often cited. It seemed to us a poor candidate for such an explanatory role, since the effects traceable to deaths and comings of age were much longer-term than Labour's recovery. Nonetheless, when the Labour Party failed to win the 1970 General Election, there were those who felt that our thesis had somehow failed. In view of the ease with which such long-term trends can be offset by short-term changes, the outcome of a single election threw no real light on the validity of our thesis about the electorate's replacement. Indeed, in the pages that follow we contend that, if anything, we underestimated Labour's gains through deaths and comings of age – not to mention immigration. Yet in saying this we are not predicting future Labour victories but merely pointing out that the Conservatives have to make converts in order to stand still. To list the handicaps which the horses carry to the starting-point is not to forecast the result of the race: it is merely to point out one of the complex factors that should be taken into account.

Our stress on different types of change is only one of the distinctions which is fundamental to this book. Of the several others on which we rely none is more important than the difference between viewing change from the standpoint of the individual elector and from the standpoint of the full electorate or of the political system.

Elector and Electorate

A duality of focus, on the one hand on individual electors and on the other on the full electorate of which they are part, runs throughout this book. We give sustained attention to individual citizens, to the place of politics in their everyday world, to their changing political responses as they age, to the imagery by which they interpret the link between politics and social class, to the conditions which make them accessible to the influence of political issues, and to their views of the political parties and their place in a party system. If we are to fathom the sources of electoral change we must learn a good deal about each of these things.

Yet the whole of electoral analysis must not be focused on the individual citizen. The reasons for his behaviour often lie in a wider political or social milieu. Moreover, the consequences of individual change can be known only by aggregating the behaviour of individual electors to see what is true of the electorate as a whole. Electoral analysis demands both the reduction or disaggregation of mass phenomena to individual terms and also the aggregation of individual phenomena to explore effects in the full electorate. Both of these intellectual processes are essential to almost every one of the chapters that follow.

The need for disaggregation or analytic reduction is heightened by the fact that so much of our electoral data comes in aggregated form. Public officials conscientiously count the votes to determine what constitutes the collective choice of the electorate. But in Britain the regulations govern-ing the secret ballot prevent these results from being disaggregated in the official or unofficial returns. Because voting papers are shuffled together on a constituency-wide basis before they are counted, the smallest units for which general election figures are available contain on average 60,000 electors.

Constituency totals for turnout and party preference do hold many keys to understanding what is in the individual voter's mind. For example, the remarkable uniformity of swings in party support across all constituencies offers persuasive evidence of the importance of national political issues and events as opposed to more local influences on the choice of the individual elector.[1] Constituency figures also provide useful clues to the nature of regional variations, the effect of the presence of a third party and similar questions.

Yet there will always be barriers to our discerning individual changes from statistics of this kind. We may deduce from the uniformity of swings that voters respond more to national issues and leaders than to local factors. But their uniformity tells us nothing about which issues have been in the voter's mind and what their effect has been. This is of course the principal justification for the use of interview methods in electoral studies. The sample survey provides an additional tool for those who feel, with Namier, that they 'must search for such evidence as they can find of the roots of human behaviour'.

---

[1] For a discussion of the paradoxical sense in which the uniformity of party swings argues *against* a full nationalization of electoral forces the reader may, however, consult Chapter 6.

We have no illusions that our efforts at analytic reduction have met with full success. In many cases we shall at the most have clarified what needs to be known. Critics of voting studies, particularly those based on surveys, sometimes seem to assume that the investigators suppose that their methods are omnicompetent, offering a key to all mysteries. Nothing could be farther from our view.

Perhaps we can help to make clear our position with a flight of fancy. Suppose there existed a body of information about the views and attitudes of the British electorate in the 1860s comparable to that which we have collected for the 1960s. Surely no one would question that such materials would be a priceless boon to any historian analyzing electoral politics at the beginning of the Gladstone–Disraeli era. But equally no one would suggest that such data would explain all aspects of electoral change in the period. Indeed, if the survey's design had been limited by what could then have been known about the evolution of British society and politics, it would certainly have overlooked factors that have emerged as important only in the perspective of time. Nonetheless, with all its limitations, such a cache of materials could not help but modify historical interpretations of the 1860s.

The Electorate and Political Leaders

We must equally avoid focusing the whole of electoral analysis on the electorate itself. The changes of party support that result from summing individual preferences at successive elections depend in the most immediate sense on attitudes and beliefs that the electorate has carried to the polling-station. We must give sustained attention to these social-psychological factors in individual preference if we are to understand electoral change. In view of the difficulty of knowing in detail the attitudes and beliefs of a mass citizenry, it is not surprising that electoral research should expend its major empirical effort in penetrating the voters' minds. But the sources of electoral change are to be found in the electorate itself only in the most proximate sense. If we are to develop a comprehensive account of change we must look beyond the electorate to its environment; beyond the immediate social-psychological factors in the electorate's 'response' and consider the changing 'stimuli' to which it is successively exposed. For example, the economic motives that are so prominent in the electorate's behaviour are not free creations of the voters' minds. They depend on actual experiences of being out of work or on short time, of receiving a rise in wages, of having to pay more in the market place – factors which can often be summed up for the country as a whole by various macro-economic indicators, such as the unemployment rate or the cost of living index. To understand the relationship between these economic inputs and the outputs of party support we must examine individual perceptions and attitudes: do voters think their condition has improved or worsened under the present Government? do they think it would change under a new Government? and so on. These introduce considerable slippage into the relationship of economic indicators to party support, as we shall see. But our account of economic influences would be limited indeed if we were to confine our attention solely to what is in the voters' minds and fail to consider the objective economic context of perceptions and behaviour, including the efforts of the Government to manipulate the economy for electoral reasons and to time elections for economic reasons.

An immensely important element of the environment in which the electorate behaves is of course provided by the parties and leaders who seek the public's support. So important are the parties in giving meaning to contests in the individual parliamentary constituencies in Britain that for many voters candidates have no identity other than their partisan one. Any developed analysis of electoral change must therefore take account of the behaviour of parties and leaders as well as of the electorate itself. Of course it is also true that the electorate is an exceedingly salient element of the environment in which political leaders behave; the past or the expected behaviour of voters is at the bottom of much of what governments and parties do or say, as they appeal for the public's support. Indeed, an interplay of elites and mass is so obviously at the heart of the electoral process that it must be central to any analysis of electoral change.

This is true not only of changes in response to immediate issues and events but also to those involving basic realignments of party strength. A modern example of the decisive importance that events at a level of *haute politique* can have for changes of mass alignments is the emergence of social class as the dominant line of electoral cleavage in Britain. As in many other countries of Western Europe, the enfranchisement of the industrial working class in Britain created circumstances favourable to the rise of a working class party and a greater polarization of electoral alignments along class lines. Yet it is impossible to account for this development in Britain without giving full weight to the events at an elite level which helped establish Labour as one of the leading parties. Were it not for the First World War and the resulting split between the Lloyd George and Asquithian Liberals, electoral alignments today might owe rather less to class, and rather more to those religious cleavages which had previously been so important in determining party support.

The interplay of elite and mass in electoral realignments is plain when there is a displacement of parties, but it may be of equal importance when the identity of the leading parties remains unchanged. This viewpoint is sometimes neglected in American commentaries which have sought to identify the 'critical elections' that have brought lasting shifts of Republican and Democratic strength. An election may of course be called 'critical' in the wholly descriptive sense of marking the appearance of a new pattern of support that persisted in subsequent elections.[1] But such elections have sometimes been seen as those in which there is an abrupt and profound change of the electorate's loyalties, establishing a new pattern of partisan dispositions sufficiently stable to endure irrespective of the changing conditions of future elections. Such a view almost certainly understates the importance of the choices and appeals subsequently presented to the electorate in deciding whether a new electoral pattern is to survive. If the issues and leaders that evoked the pattern persist in future elections, the pattern will tend to persist. If they do not, it may prove highly transient. One may at least imagine the Democratic Party, having suffered the disaster of 1896, retreating from Bryan's leadership and policies as rapidly as the Republican Party, having suffered the disaster of 1964, retreated from Goldwater's leadership and policies.[2] Under these circumstances the sectional realignment of the 1890s might not have survived into the new century, and 1896 might not have come to be seen as a 'critical' election at all. Similarly, one may at least imagine the split among the British Liberals having been healed by the middle twenties and Labour having been overtaken by sufficient troubles for it to accept once again a subordinate role within a Lib–Lab coalition. Under these circumstances the trend towards the alignment of party support by class might have been retarded or even reversed.

To regard realignments of party strength as resulting from the survival of elite appeals does not involve any challenge to the importance of those processes within the electorate itself which conserve past displacements of party support. If the 'primary' issues that alter electoral alignments are allowed time to operate, their immediate effects will be conserved or even

[1] The late V. O. Key, who originated this term, used it almost wholly descriptively. See 'A Theory of Critical Elections', *Journal of Politics*, **17** (1955), 3–18.

[2] The election of 1964 indeed exhibited a sectional pattern of alignment hauntingly like that of 1896, although the roles of the parties had been completely reversed. See W. D. Burnham, 'American Voting Behavior and the 1964 Election', *Midwest Journal of Political Science*, **12** (1968), 1–40.

amplified by a number of 'secondary' processes within the electorate. Some of these are internal to voters themselves. The longer individuals hold to a new position, the more likely they are to develop a view of politics that makes it difficult to shift back; the working man who switches to the Conservatives as the party more likely to bring prosperity may well revise his hitherto unfavourable opinions of other aspects of the party. Some 'secondary' processes have to do with the formation of political attitudes in the family and other face-to-face groups. Indeed, the recruitment of children (and their children in turn) into their parents' party can maintain an electoral alignment long after its 'primary' issues have spent their force. In later chapters we shall speak of the 'age' of an existing alignment in terms of whether it rests more on 'primary' or such 'secondary' forces.

What we have said about transient displacements of the party balance implies that short-run changes of party strength must also be seen in terms of the interaction of parties and leaders with the electorate. This focus on interaction is explicit in much of the recent theorizing about competitive party systems. For example, the interactional models of Downs and others can equally be interpreted as theories of the behaviour of electors or as theories of the behaviour of the political leaders who seek their support.[1] The state of the economy is increasingly recognized as the strongest factor affecting short-term party switches. But it conditions the conduct of governments as much as of voters – and the reactions of voters to prosperity or its absence influence the way in which governments try to manipulate the level of the economy. This emphasis on interaction is an essential element in our treatment of the issues and leader images that altered the strength of the Conservative and Labour Parties during the period of our studies. Although we have spent more effort on the behaviour of electors, our analysis deals at a number of points with the nature of the appeals and issues that confronted them.

The Context of Research

This book reflects the merging of two traditions of electoral research. The Institute for Social Research at the University of Michigan, building

[1] See, for example, A. Downs, *An Economic Theory of Democracy*, New York, 1957, pp. 114–41; G. Tullock, *Toward a Mathematics of Politics*, Ann Arbor, 1967, pp. 50–61; and O. Davis and M. Hinich, 'A Mathematical Model of Policy Formation in a Democratic Society', in J. L. Bernd, ed., *Mathematical Applications in Political Science, II*, Dallas, 1966, pp. 175–208.

on the expansion of political science that flowed from the arrival of opinion polling in the 1930s, had by the mid-1950s developed a special interest in the aggregation of individual behaviour to explain the electorate's collective decision and the place of the mass public within the total political system.[1] Nuffield College, Oxford, had since 1945 employed a more historical approach treating elections as comprehensive political events; by recording and analyzing the activities of the politicians, the party machines and the media before and during a campaign, the Nuffield Studies have sought, in an increasingly detailed way, to explore the forces brought to bear on the voter.[2]

Although this is a book about the changing strength of British parties, and our work is bounded in a variety of ways by the politics of Britain, it is not narrowly British either in origin or intention. The analytic frameworks that we use draw heavily on earlier investigations in America and Europe. And, in the case of some of our findings, we have been helped in choosing between conflicting interpretations of British data by findings from other nations. This is true, for example, of the interpretation we give to the strengthening of party allegiance with age. Moreover, our findings from Britain throw light on problems affecting other party systems – indeed on democratic politics as a whole. From classical times those seeking a systematic understanding of politics have been obliged to sift the varieties of political experience found in the actual world.

The area of our research has limits in time as well as space. The fact that the primary data on which this book is based were collected between 1963 and 1970 inevitably gives our work a temporal context. We have consulted election returns and other evidence pertaining to a much longer interval of time, indeed the whole of this century. And we have relied on our respondents' memories to recall information about the past, as, for example, the class, partisan and religious identifications of their parents when they themselves were young. But our investigations are inevitably anchored in the detailed evidence from a specific seven-year period.

[1] This trend is apparent in the closing chapters of A. Campbell, P. E. Converse, W. E. Miller and D. E. Stokes, *The American Voter*, New York, 1960, and even more clearly in *Elections and the Political Order*, New York, 1966, by the same authors.

[2] R. B. McCallum and A. Readman, *The British General Election of 1945*, Oxford, 1947; H. G. Nicholas, *The British General Election of 1950*, London, 1951; D. E. Butler, *The British General Election of 1951*, London, 1952; D. E. Butler, *The British General Election of 1955*, London, 1955; D. E. Butler and R. Rose, *The British General Election of 1959*, London, 1960; D. E. Butler and A. King, *The British General Election of 1964*, London, 1965; D. E. Butler and A. King, *The British General Election of 1966*, London, 1966; David Butler and Michael Pinto-Duschinsky, *The British General Election of 1970*, London, 1971.

It is not a simple matter to say what limitations these temporal bounds have imposed on our findings. In our original work we felt most keenly the constraints due to one of the parties having a preponderant lead over most of the three years on which we were focusing. Although party fortunes fluctuated, 1963–6 was a period of exceptional Labour strength. The difficulty that this put in the way of our analysis was not primarily that of a Labour 'bias', although allowances had certainly to be made for the very pro-Labour readings of many of our measures of the country's mood and allegiance. The difficulty lay much more in the limited extent of many of the changes we were able to analyze, even though the party tide did turn at least twice during that period. However, by continuing our studies we have been able to examine the electorate's behaviour in an era of Conservative predominance and to observe a very much sharper change in mood than had occurred in 1963–6. We conducted interviews with a nation-wide sample at a time in 1969 when the Conservatives were handsomely ahead of Labour by every measure of electoral mood, and our final survey was in the wake of the Conservative victory in 1970 – a narrow victory after a Labour recovery that shifted the strength of the parties more sharply than any change we had previously had the chance to record.

As the temporal context of this sort of research widens, its findings are less the prisoners of a specific period. The varied circumstances of succeeding periods can give a surer understanding of the importance of various factors in electoral change. The number of elections and of distinct periods of change must always remain small, and the nature of the evidence provided by the unfolding of political history sets bounds to the discovery and testing of hypotheses. But these bounds become less severe as the temporal span of our observations lengthens.

Elements of Design

We felt from the beginning that the objectives of this research would require a large-scale survey of British electors, nationwide in scope, and involving two or more contacts with our sample of electors at widely separated points of time. The fact that at least one of these approaches was to follow directly after a general election introduced a degree of uncertainty into our plans, given the prime minister's freedom to choose a date. We were clear, however, that one of the contacts with our sample should be outside the context of an election, and we went ahead in the summer of

1963 with an interview survey of 2009 randomly selected electors in 80 randomly selected constituencies of England, Scotland and Wales. The exclusion of Northern Ireland was due solely to the prohibitive outlay of resources that would have been required to enlarge our Ulster sample so as to do justice to the special political circumstances of the area.

In the event, almost a year and a half separated this first round of interviews and the dissolution of Parliament. Following the General Election of 1964, however, we re-interviewed as many of those contacted in the summer of 1963 as could be found, as well as a number of additional respondents selected to enhance the sample's representativeness in the autumn of 1964. The result of the 1964 election suddenly posed a fresh problem. After an unexpectedly long wait for one election, it was now clear that we were likely to have another sooner than anyone had thought. Therefore, we laid plans to contact our panel of electors a third time whenever Mr Wilson might dissolve Parliament, and immediately after the election in March 1966 we re-interviewed as many of these people as we could, in addition to a number of new respondents drawn to enhance the representativeness of the sample.

Those who were interviewed on all these three occasions gave on average more than three hours of conversation over this thirty-four-month period. What they told us over a very wide range of questions served as the main basis for what appeared in the First Edition of *Political Change in Britain*. But as we wrote our first edition, we knew that deeper insights could be gained from a longer-term study and we planned a new approach to the electorate at the end of the 1966 Parliament. In the summer of 1969 we approached an entirely new, though smaller, sample of the electorate (but in the same 80 constituencies) and obtained 1114 interviews. After the June 1970 election we conducted interviews with three separate groups: 1355 respondents from our 1963–6 surveys whom we could still manage to contact; 799 respondents from our 1969 survey whom we could still manage to contact; and an additional sample of 1088 electors.[1]

This book therefore is based, first, on evidence drawn from interviews with a fairly exact microcosm of the electorate at five separate points of time between 1963 and 1970, and second, upon evidence about the changes in attitude of one group of electors between 1963, 1964, 1966 and 1970 and of another group between 1969 and 1970.

The form of our interviews allowed us to explore a very wide range of questions, as well as to observe the evolution of thought and behaviour over a lengthening interval in the lives of these individuals. These inter-

[1] For full details of our samples and their supplementation see Appendix A.

views differed from the more familiar newspaper opinion survey not only in their length but also in their emphasis on letting the respondent express his attitudes or perceptions or recollections in terms of his own choosing. Many of the questions we put to our sample invited one of several alternative responses, fixed in advance. But many were 'open-ended' or 'free-answer' questions which gave the respondents full latitude to express their ideas in their own words, and some of our most important findings – for example, as to the links that are thought to connect class and party – came from examining the terms that voters used spontaneously.

Although our interview surveys furnish much of the evidence used in this book, we have not intended to provide a conventional survey report. On the one hand, we have raised issues not covered by the questionnaires on which our interviews were based[1] and have drawn extensively on many other sources of evidence. On the other hand, we have set forth very much less than an exhaustive report of the replies given by our respondents.

Plan of the Book

This book takes its shape from the contrast of continuity and change and from the different components of change. Part One tries to separate out the main factors associated with enduring party allegiance, the elements in national and social life that induce and reinforce those links between individuals and their parties which may last throughout their lives. It looks in turn at the way in which political attitudes are shaped by family, by class, by neighbourhood and by region. Part Two examines the broad forces of social and political change which in a cumulative way have changed the balance of party strength over the century, exploring the changing religious and class attitudes associated with the decline of the Liberals and the rise of Labour. Part Three turns to those changes in party strength that arise inevitably with the turnover of the electorate through deaths and comings of age, as well as through migration, measuring just how far from politically neutral are the consequences of demographic trends. It is only in Part Four that we come to the short-term causes of change, the reactions to the day-to-day stimulus of political propaganda and events, measuring how many voters actually altered their allegiance during the 1960s and assessing in succession the role of issues, of ideology, of images of leaders and of economic changes in fostering such shifts.

[1] For the questions used in all the surveys see Appendix B of this edition.

PART ONE

Continuities of Alignment

2 Parties in the Voter's Mind

THE role played by the parties in giving shape and direction to the be-haviour of voters is so taken for granted that its importance is easily missed. Without it, however, the mass of the people could scarcely participate in regular transfers of power. Individual electors accept the parties as lead-ing actors on the political stage and see in partisan terms the meaning of the choices which the universal franchise puts before them. British govern-ment would be fundamentally changed if parties were absent from the voter's mind.

The service performed by the parties in giving meaning to politics for a remote electorate may indeed be one main explanation for the flourishing of party systems in the modern world. Since Britain so obviously has a one-party Cabinet and a Parliament operating strictly on party lines, it might seem natural for the British elector to accept parties as leading actors and accord them support simply because they are there. But it might equally be argued that the parties are there because they have been able to win support from electors who accept their role as leading actors. In the evolution of British democracy the parties were fostered as elite cadres by their ability to become objects of universal awareness. Party government is partially a tribute to the politicians' success in appealing for mass support in their parties' names.

Indeed, the factors which induce voters to see the parties as the main figures of politics probably lead them to see the parties as more unitary objects than in fact they are. An inside observer, knowing the actual ten-sions within the parties over policies and personalities, might wonder that the elector can give the parties so definite an identity. The public indulges in a similar sort of gentle reification in regard to churches and firms and other organizations. But in few of these are the heterogeneous elements in what is perceived so open to view. The seeing of parties as single entities is the more remarkable in places where parties are still more fissiparous; for example, the electorate sees the parties as leading actors in the United States in spite of the frequent cross-voting in both houses of Congress and in spite of the fragmented nature of the parties' national and local structure.

The sources of this simplification in the public's mind have fascinated writers on political psychology. Graham Wallas, that pioneer exponent of so many political concepts, suggested half a century ago that the parties loomed large in popular perceptions of politics because the electorate required 'something simpler and more permanent, something that can be loved and trusted, and which can be recognized at successive elections as being the same thing that was loved and trusted before; and party is such a thing'.[1]

Why should the parties have such a definite identity in the public's mind? Part of the answer lies in the remoteness of the citizen from the affairs of government. Whatever may once have been possible in Athens or Venice, nations of the size and social complexity of Britain have all developed a political division of labour that reserves most governmental decisions to a relatively small elite. As we look for the sources of the hold of party on popular thinking about politics, it is well to begin with the remote and marginal nature of politics for the British voter.

The Remoteness of Politics

Individual responses to politics are wonderfully varied. There is no single elector, no archetypal citizen who epitomizes the British voter's condition. The Welsh miner with a political tradition based on pit and chapel, the London shop assistant who glances occasionally at a political headline after gutting the sports pages, the Manchester businessman who sees his interest as affected by day-to-day decisions in Westminster and Whitehall, the widow in Bournemouth who is cut off from any contact with the outer world – each would differ fundamentally in the degree and kind of his interest in politics. Yet we could hardly overlook the limited extent of political involvement across the whole electorate.

Certainly playing the role of voter is unlikely to inspire any deep involvement in political affairs. Voting for Parliament ordinarily requires only a few minutes of time every fourth or fifth year. If electors also use their franchise at the annual local elections, the visits which they pay to the polling booth will still be a negligible part of their lives. The behaviour demanded of those who play this role is hardly sufficient to bring politics to the centre of the voter's consciousness.

Few voters, moreover, engage themselves in any deeper involvement in the party system. A profile of the electorate's participation in several types

[1] G. Wallas, *Human Nature in Politics*, London, 1910, p. 83.

of activity is drawn in Figure 2.1. Our detailed evidence suggests that these forms of political behaviour comprise a cumulative hierarchy; those in the small minorities most involved in politics, the active campaigners or the meeting goers, tended also to be part of the larger groups performing less demanding acts such as voting in local elections. But what is most notable

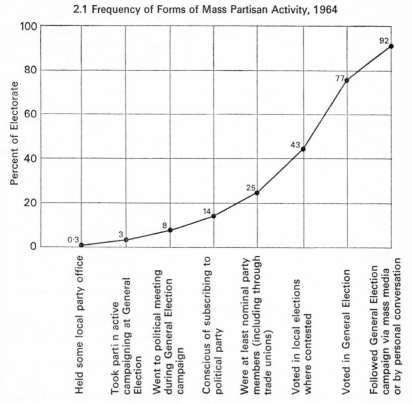

2.1 Frequency of Forms of Mass Partisan Activity, 1964

here is the small number who do anything at all beyond voting in General Elections. Only one in two voted in local elections and only one in ten went to an election meeting. Only one in fifty took an active part in the campaign, and the number engaged in party activities between campaigns was altogether negligible.

Although we did not gather evidence on all these points in 1970, there is no doubt that this profile of involvement would have been very similar in shape for that year, but the levels would have been slightly lower. The proportion conscious of subscribing to a local party had fallen from 14 per cent to 10 per cent; the proportion voting in local elections from 43 per cent to 37 per cent; the proportion voting in the General Election from 77 per cent to 72 per cent; and the proportion following the campaign in the mass media from 92 per cent to 91 per cent.[1]

Nor are the mass of people engaged in political behaviour outside the party system. The networks of interest groups linked to Westminster and Whitehall are operated by elites that are as restricted in size as those that play continuously active roles in the party system. The survey undertaken in Britain by Almond and Verba, looking beyond the closed circle of interest group politics, found only one elector in twenty who recalled ever having sought to influence any matter before Parliament.[2] In rare moments of social and political upheaval, such as the General Strike of 1926 or the Chartist demonstrations of a century before, larger numbers engaged in political acts outside the party system. By contrast the numbers taking part in demonstrations against nuclear arms or the Vietnam war have been relatively small.

The limits of the public's overt political activity are matched by the limits of its political information. Over the past thirty years survey studies in various countries have demonstrated how limited is the mass electorate's information about policy issues, or the structure and processes of government, or the identity of leading political figures. Such findings are surprising only against a naïve or idealized conception of political democracy. Large portions of the electorate may indeed be ignorant of things which are taken completely for granted by knowledgeable observers. For example, the vast majority of West German electors has repeatedly been found to be unaware of the role of the Bundesrat, while two-thirds of Americans do not know that members of the House of Representatives are elected every two years.[3]

Glimpses of similar political innocence have been given by surveys in Britain. The Gallup Poll indicated in 1963 that several million electors thought that Britain already belonged to the European Common Market.

[1] For the remarkable Australian parallel with this profile see D. Aitkin, *Stability and Change in Australian Politics* (forthcoming).

[2] G. A. Almond and S. Verba, *The Civic Culture*, Princeton, 1963. The question 'Have you ever done anything to try to influence an act of Parliament?' elicited these replies: 'often' (0·8 per cent); 'once or twice' or 'a few times' (5 per cent), 'never' (92 per cent); and 'don't know' (2 per cent).

[3] An excellent summary of studies disclosing the limits of the public's information about politics and government appears in John Wahlke, 'Policy Demands and System Support', *British Journal of Political Science*, **1** (1971), pp. 271–90.

National Opinion Polls found a sizeable fraction of the electorate in 1964 supporting the idea that it would be right to nationalize the mines and the railways. The majority of a sample interviewed for the *Sunday Times* in 1962 could not name any political figure in either party other than the party leaders themselves, while in 1971 an Opinion Research Centre Survey found 30 per cent of people picking out Roy Jenkins as a member of the Government one year after Labour had lost office (they also found that 51 per cent cherished the illusion that Enoch Powell was a minister). We shall see in Chapter 13 evidence of how little our own sample had formed stable opinions on major policy issues confronting the Government and in Chapter 15 how few voters placed any such opinions within a more embracing ideological framework, such as that of left and right. Indeed, in 1963 we encountered respondents who were unable to identify Harold Macmillan after he had been Prime Minister seven years; one even believed that Mr Attlee was still at the head of government.[1]

Yet the electorate's response to politics in modern democracies is far from one of blank incomprehension. However complex and distant the realm of government may seem, voters are capable of behaving in a purposive way and of seeking goals they value. Indeed, the parties would never have succeeded in harnessing the allegiance of the electorate if they had not been seen as a partial means to such ends. The parties have achieved their prominence as political actors in the public's mind by linking themselves to goals that matter to the electorate whose support they seek.

Parties and the Voter's Goals

The ends to which the parties have sought to link themselves have to do with the things that governments are thought to have an influence upon –

[1] The low salience of political leaders and institutions for the ordinary voter does not necessarily betray alienation. In 1970 we asked our respondents to say how warm or cold they felt about a number of groups, people or institutions on a thermometer ranging from 0° to 100°, suggesting that 50° would indicate neutral feeling. The average rating of Parliament was 73°, of the Queen and Royal Family 78°, of the police 82°. The great bulk of respondents felt extremely warmly towards at least one of the parties; indeed, the four-fifths of the sample which held a Conservative or Labour self-image gave an average thermometer rating of 80° to their own party and rated the opposite party not much less than 50°. Moreover, these ratings were consistent with the placements of the parties on a bad–good scale described in the Appendix. Conservative and Labour partisans on average rated their own parties as distinctly 'good' and the opposite parties as no worse than midway from good to bad.

in a word, the 'outputs' of government, a term that we shall use very broadly. There is of course nothing distinctively modern about the belief that governments affect the world in ways that their peoples, whether enfranchised or not, care deeply about. The Tudors won support by ending the disorders of the Wars of the Roses, just as the Roman imperium was widely accepted for the improved conditions of life that it brought. Although traditional societies can still be found in which the mass of people remains largely unaware of the role of central political authority, this has not been true of western communities for a very long time.

What is quite new is the immense scope of governmental activity and the ever wider range of outputs of which the public may be aware. Asked in the 1960s what problems they thought the Government should do something about, our sample of the British electorate unleashed a flood of replies which spread over a remarkably wide terrain.[1] Many of the matters touched by these replies were economic – reducing unemployment, creating jobs in depressed areas, increasing exports, containing the cost of living, fostering economic growth; many dealt with welfare and the social services – raising pensions, altering family allowances, providing free medicine and other health services, building more houses, keeping rents down, improving schools; others dealt with transport, with crime and punishment, with industrial peace, with immigration and race, with defence and Britain's place in the world, and with an astonishing number of other matters ranging from the lifeboat service to the control of bingo.

The increase in government outputs gives considerable importance to the ability of political leaders to form links between what the government does and what the public values. Indeed, the party battle is often fought in essentially these terms, and big rewards have gone to the leaders who managed to persuade large numbers of electors to see these links in a particular way. A striking example of this was provided by Lloyd George with his insight in 1918 that the public could be made to see that housing should be a major goal of government policy. What bonds the public will accept are, of course, not entirely in the province of political elites to determine. Indeed, in some cases the correspondence between what the Government is thought to affect and what it actually can affect is remarkably weak. We shall have reason to note that governments were generally held to account for the country's prosperity long before the advance of economic understanding had put into the hands of governments the tools required for the pursuance of rational economic policies.

[1] The series of questions asked about problems government might affect is to be found in Appendix B (question 10).

The enlargement in the role of government has also greatly complicated the public's problem in connecting effect with cause. The technical difficulties of assigning responsibility for past government action or inaction, and of calculating probabilities of future action has increased far more rapidly than the political sophistication of the general public, despite the spread of education and of mass communications. Probably it was easier for the country in the sixteenth century to know how order had been restored than in the 1960s to know why Britain's balance of payments had gone wrong.

Modern electorates tend to 'solve' the problem of causal reasoning by assuming that certain causal relationships must exist rather than by discerning what they are. Electors focus their attention primarily on certain conditions which they value positively or negatively and simply assume that past or future governments affect them. The public can call for a government's dismissal in economic hard times just as it calls for a team manager's dismissal in a losing season, in each case concluding that causal relationships must exist without knowing in detail what they are.

The goals or the conditions that governments are thought to affect may be quite specific and concrete – raising pensions, abolishing the 11-plus examination and the like. But they are often defined in terms that are diffuse or general. Indeed, goals of overwhelming importance in modern British politics have been the interests or welfare of the middle and working classes. Electors looking back on a government's performance may be quite unsure how in practice it has affected these ends and they may be even less clear how future governments might affect them. But the belief that government action influences the welfare of different social classes is nonetheless enormously important in the behaviour of many voters. Similarly the belief that actions of government affect peace or economic prosperity or national prestige or other diffuse goals may enter the voters' calculations without their having undertaken more than the most rudimentary reasoning as to how the government has done so. The country's satisfaction or dissatisfaction with the achievement of general and even semi-conscious goals probably lies behind many of the changes of electoral 'mood' which seem so evident to the political observer. The generality of the goals that matter to the electorate is a theme we shall often touch on in later chapters.

The perceived link between government and the fulfilment of conditions which the public values is only one part of the chain that links goals to electoral choices in the voter's mind. The distinctive place of party in forging this chain involves two main additional links.

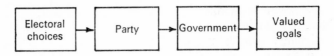

The three arrows in this sketch offer a key to much that follows later in the book. We have commented already on the last of these arrows, a link that is very real in the public's mind even if the electorate rarely has a very developed understanding of the causal relationships that lie beneath it. There can equally be no doubt that the middle of these arrows is real to the public. The electorate accepts the partisan nature of British government, and the identity of the party 'in power' is one of the few facts that are almost universally known. Indeed the true extent of knowledge of something so taken for granted is not easily checked in a survey without putting respondents off. Nonetheless in mid-1964 we did ask a pilot sample a question designed to ascertain whether they knew the identity of the governing party. In this little test every respondent knew that the Conservatives were in office and almost all had a reasonably accurate view of how long they had been there.[1]

The partisan character of governments tends to associate the parties in the public's mind with the effects that government is thought to have. With the machinery of the state in party hands the outputs of government become the responsibility of the ruling party, and electors can hold the party in office to account for the conditions which the Government has permitted to exist. They can also try to get a party into office in the belief that it will be able to use the power of government to change these conditions in a given way. Once again, the voters' perception of the causal relationships between government actions and changing conditions may be remarkably unformed. The fact that a party is in power when what they want actually happens may serve well enough; they may indeed have extraordinarily little understanding of how long an output of government has normally been in the making. In this sense, party government serves to institutionalize *post hoc ergo propter hoc* reasoning on a grand scale.

With more than one party seeking their support, the voters' judgments about values and party control will often be comparative ones. They may contrast the performance of the party that has held office with what they think its rivals would have done, just as they may contrast the probable performance in the future of the rival claimants on power. But these judg-

---

[1] Our pilot survey was with fifty-two randomly selected respondents from four constituencies, two urban and two rural. To each respondent we put the question 'Can you tell me which party is in power and how long it has held office?'

ments need not be comparative. Given the fundamental asymmetry between being in and out of power, it is inevitable that the ruling party should receive the closer scrutiny. There is for example evidence that the public tends to reward the party in power for good times and punish it for bad without attempting to say whether times might have been better, or worse, under an alternative government. In politics, too, the team manager may be sacked even though he has done better than his potential successors in keeping setbacks from turning into utter disaster.

Illustrations of the degree to which the electorate associates the parties with the putative outputs of government that it values positively or negatively appear in many chapters of this book. Some of these links have to do with the bases of enduring party alignments, especially the values represented by the interest of the social classes. But these connections are also formed in terms of goals or conditions to which the public gives more varied and individual valuations or concerning which it sees the parties as more sharply set apart at some times than at others. We shall develop each of these points when we set out a framework for the analysis of political issues.

The partisan character of governments is not an immutable feature of the British constitution. There have been periods of coalition rule and the opinion polls periodically report wide support for its return – suggesting that awareness of party government is more widespread than acceptance of its desirability. The plainly visible tenure of power by single parties sets Britain apart from countries where coalition rule is the norm and where constitutional arrangements make the question of control more complex. It would be interesting to know more about the perceptions of the electorate in these contrasting situations. Survey evidence suggests that the American public has a much fuzzier sense of party control in national government.[1] Beliefs about the partisan identity of coalition government would justify comparative study; how, for example, do the electorates of Holland or Finland see their Governments in party terms?

The leftmost arrow of our sketch on p. 26 suggests the final contribution of party in linking the electoral act to outputs of government in the voter's mind. The parties, being thought capable of affecting the world in ways that matter, in effect organize the voter's choice at the polling station. The

---

[1] The proportion of the American public that can reliably say which party is in control of the Congress has at times been less than half. See D. E. Stokes and W. E. Miller, 'Party Government and the Saliency of Congress', *Public Opinion Quarterly*, **26** (1962), 531–46. Plainly one of the factors that has affected the size of this fraction is whether the Presidency and the houses of Congress are in the hands of the same party.

only candidates with a hope of succeeding are those who carry a party's designation. Before party labels were placed on the ballot paper in 1970, virtually every voter was able to make the link between candidate and party, even though many knew nothing else about him: they perceived that to vote for a candidate was to vote for a government of his party, one which he would sustain in power throughout the life of a Parliament.

Moreover, the electorate's response to the partisan choices it faces in the constituencies can be expected to produce a single-party government. Under the prevailing electoral system, the sum of individual choices has in almost all cases given possession of the government machine to one party. Even the closest of contests usually produces a decisive result. No process of bargaining between parties is ordinarily interposed between the voter's act and the formation of an administration; the electorate is able to see a clear and immediate relation between its collective judgment and party control.

It would be wrong to suppose that this full chain is sharply defined in the electors' mind. We have drawn it for analytical purposes and not as a literal description of their categories of thought; we have tried to be clear about the crudeness of several links, especially the limits to many voters' understanding of how the parties guide the actions of government and of how the actions of government may affect the conditions they value. Moreover, there can be little doubt that the electorate feels at times that the chain is a frail one and that the choices at the polls, as defined by the parties, are fairly irrelevant to the problems facing the country. But there is equally little doubt that, whatever the degree of its ignorance or confusion, the electorate attempts to use the ballot to achieve things it cares about.

There is no reason to expect the mass of people to be particularly introspective about this process. Nonetheless, we did probe the extent of the public's awareness of the relation of its behaviour to the actions taken by government. In 1963 and again in 1969 we put to our sample this series of questions:

Over the years how much do you feel the Government pays attention to what the people think when it decides what to do?

Why is that?

How much do you feel that having political parties makes the Government pay attention to what the people think?

Why is that?

And how much do you think that having elections makes the Government pay attention to what the people think?

Why is that?

By any test this sequence of questions proved extraordinarily difficult for the ordinary respondent to cope with; it was clear, whatever the defects of our question wording, that we were on difficult ground. It was also clear that many voters felt that the Government did most things without any reference to the public's views. Fully half our sample replied to the first of these questions by saying that they didn't think the Government paid much attention to what the people thought, and less than one in ten felt that the Government paid a great deal of attention. The replies to the succeeding questions gave, however, a somewhat different balance of views, as Table 2.2 shows. The influence attributed to elections is the more im-

2.2 Perceptions of Popular Influence on Actions of Government

		Good deal	Some	Not Much	Don't Know	Total
Over the years how much do you feel the Government pays attention to what the people think when it decides what to do?	1963	8%	20	50	22	100%
	1969	9%	19	61	11	100%
How much do you feel that having political parties makes the Government pay attention to what the people think?	1963	21%	29	16	34	100%
	1969	23%	25	26	26	100%
And how much do you think that having elections makes the Government pay attention to what the people think?	1963	46%	26	9	19	100%
	1969	46%	26	16	12	100%

pressive in view of the fact that these conversations were held outside the context of an election campaign. With governments of different party complexions in power in 1963 and 1969 and with many indications of a widespread change in public mood, the proportion believing in government responsiveness to elections remained virtually unaltered at the end of these six years, although the number of sceptics was swelled by a diminution in the 'don't knows'.

Of equal interest is the insight into the public's image of party government offered by our respondents in amplification of their answers to the three root questions. Many of our respondents had a clear, if weakly developed, sense of the importance of parties and elections in linking the people to actions of government. A housewife in Uxbridge explained the Government's attention to the people by observing 'They would never get into power otherwise'; an estate agent in Blackpool, 'If they wish to remain in power it is very necessary'. A painter in Bridgwater explained his answers this way:

> (Why Government pays attention?) They've got to take notice of the people.
> (Why parties help Government pay attention?) They've got to have a party to get the views of the people.
> (Why elections help Government pay attention?) The people feel they have a chance of altering things.

A widow in Leek said:

> (Why Government pays attention?) I think they try their best to run the country properly, so they have to pay attention.
> (Why parties help Government pay attention?) Because they need the people's votes and having several parties keeps them on their toes.
> (Why elections help Government pay attention?) For the same reason. Support is needed to keep them in power.

And a clerical officer in Bermondsey said:

> (Why parties help Government pay attention?) The whole parliamentary system ensures that they take notice through the Opposition.
> (Why elections help Government pay attention?) It's obvious that if they want power they must show interest.

From a full reading of our 1963 replies, we attempted to classify our respondents into three general groups. The first of these was made up of those who showed a relatively developed sense of popular control through a competitive party and election system, mentioning especially the dependence of parties on electoral support even before being prompted by the third of our questions. The second group was made up of those who voiced some belief in the public's influence on government but did not mention control through competitive elections until prompted. The third group was made up of those who showed no sort of belief in popular influence. Some of them indeed expressed a contrary view, saying that governments dupe the people and make election promises only to break them. 'It's too easy to talk and promise things – they don't have to carry them out' was the view of a machinist in Hexham. But the largest element in this third group were those who simply failed to express any generalized belief in the influence of the people over the actions of government.

Such a classification gives an interesting profile of the extent to which the idea of influence has crystallized in the electorate's mind. We have no illusion that this typing of belief is more than suggestive, but the figures set out in Table 2.3 do indicate, however roughly, the existence in the minds of

2.3 Beliefs about Popular Influence, 1963

Respondent held well-developed understanding of popular control through a competitive party and election system, to which he felt British politics conformed	13%
Respondent held at least a partial understanding of popular control through a competitive party and election system and saw elements of such a system in British politics	47
Respondent had not crystallized a general belief in popular control through a competitive party and election system	40
	100%

many voters of a generalized belief in the role of parties and elections in linking the electorate to government outputs. What we are tapping here is primarily the degree to which the voter has formed *generalized* beliefs about popular influence. In addition many voters who perceived a more specific focus of influence have fallen into the last category of Table 2.3; this was true, for example, of a number of respondents who saw the parties as drawing electoral strength by representing class interests.[1]

The idea that the party system serves as an instrument of popular control is closely linked with the idea that the parties should alternate in control of the government. A circulation of governments is the inevitable consequence of the electorate's using the competition of parties to achieve its goals. But the electorate could force this result without developing more generalized beliefs about the desirability of a circulation of governments, and we have probed our samples to see whether such beliefs have in fact taken root and have helped guide the electorate's behaviour.

[1] It should also be noted that we had focused on the respondent's sensitivity to the influence that electors may achieve by the Government's anticipating the electoral consequences of its acts. But electors may also have influence by choosing between rival governments on the basis of policies to which they are committed to give effect in office. The distinction between influence that involves governments' anticipating the behaviour of the electorate and influence that involves the electorate's anticipating the behaviour of governments is of course not a clear one in the public's own mind. But by placing a heavier accent on the first of the two processes of influence we may understate somewhat the extent of the public's generalized beliefs about the links between their electoral choices and the outputs of government.

The Alternation of Governments

There is little doubt that the possibility of alternating in power is central to the outlook of the party leaders. This possibility sustains the 'out' party, shaping both its recruitment of parliamentary talent and its style of conducting the business of opposition. The desirability of such transfers of power is in fact overwhelmingly accepted by the leaders of both the main parties, and is a standard argument ('it's time for a change') available to the opposition in pressing its case before the mass electorate.

How much influence has this belief on the electorate itself? Our studies embraced a period in which there were two turnovers of party control. The government in power at the beginning of the 1960s was very old, indeed the oldest in a century. Its successor returned for a mandate from the people while it was still very young and was denied a second mandate after its tenure of power had lengthened. We had therefore an unusual opportunity to test whether the public held quite general beliefs about the transfer of power which affected the choices it reached in these years.

Some familiar problems of opinion analysis stand in the way of any simple assessment of the importance of such beliefs. In particular, two sorts of responses can overlay real convictions as to the desirability of the alternation of governments. On the one hand, party allegiance may bias the elector's response to the idea that the parties should alternate in power: those whose party is for the moment out of office will be more likely to endorse such a view than those whose party provides the government. On the other hand, some of the responses given to the idea of alternation in power will be the uncertain and transient views of those who do not hold a genuine belief on the matter. Here, as in Chapter 13 and elsewhere, we have to be alert to the way that response uncertainty can blur our measurement of well-rooted attitudes.

The fact that power was actually transferred in the midst of our research provides, however, the means of separating party bias and response uncertainty from genuine belief. Let us first of all consider the detection of the biasing effect of party allegiance. It would be reasonable to suppose that Conservatives whose allegiance remained fixed throughout 1963 to 1966 would become more receptive to the desirability of alternation once Labour was in power and that constant Labour supporters would be more enthusiastic about the idea while their party was still in opposition. Our evidence shows this to have been the case. The responses to a question about the desirability of alternating governments given in the early years of our research by those who were steadfastly Conservative or Labour throughout the period make it plain that opinion shifted markedly according to whose ox would be gored; Table 2.4 shows that perceptible, and opposite, shifts took place among these two groups of party stalwarts at a time when a Labour Government replaced a Conservative one. It is interesting to note

2.4 Belief in Turnover of Party Control Among Stable Conservative and Labour Partisans, 1963–6[a]

	Beliefs Held by Those Who Were Consistently			
	Conservative		Labour	
	1963	1966	1963	1966
Control of the Government should pass from one party to another every so often	43%	53%	64%	51%
It's all right for one party to have control for a long time	46	38	26	40
Don't know	11	9	10	9
	100%	100%	100%	100%
	(n = 334)		(n = 410)	

[a] This analysis is limited to those whose partisan self-image was consistently Conservative or consistently Labour in 1963, 1964 and 1966. Beliefs as to the desirability of turnover of party control are based on the replies to question 32d in the Appendix.

that Labour partisans were more united in their belief in the virtues of party turnover in 1963 than were the Conservatives in 1966. This may reflect the fact that in 1963 the Conservative Government was very old, while in 1966 the Labour Government was still quite young. But it may also reflect the fact that Conservatives are more used to seeing their party in power. A general belief in the virtues of alternation is more likely to spring up in those who are accustomed to their party being in opposition.

The detailed shifts of individual belief over the period of the transfer of power give insight into the presence of pure uncertainty of response. Table 2.5 on the next page shows the turnover among constant Conservative and Labour supporters between a period when their party was in power and a period when it was not. The percentages set at the row and column margins of this table show once again the greater attractiveness of the idea of alternation when one's own party is out of power, and this change of marginal percentages is reflected in the relative size of the figures in the interior cells of the table that lie above and below the main diagonal of constant opinion from upper left to lower right. But the figures in the cells

2.5 Changes of Belief in Turnover of Party Control
Among Stable Conservative and Labour Partisans, 1963–6[a]

Report When Own Party Held Government

		Should Be Turnover	Long Control All Right	Don't Know	
	Should Be Turnover	30	21	7	58
Report When Opposite Party Held Government	Long Control All Right	13	17	3	33
	Don't Know	4	4	1	9
		47	42	11	100%

(n = 744)

[a] This analysis is limited to those who remained supporters of the Conservative or of the Labour Party during three interviews from 1963 to 1966. Conservatives are classified by columns according to their answers in 1963 and by rows according to their answers in 1966. Labour supporters are classified by rows according to their answers in 1963 and by columns according to their answers in 1966.

below this diagonal show that there were substantial movements of opinion in a direction *opposite* to the trend that party bias would suggest. It is reasonable to conclude that these contrary movements reflect pure uncertainty of response, the tendency of respondents to give more or less random answers in successive interviews in the absence of any true belief.

In view of the actual turnover of party control midway in our work, each of these forms of 'false' report implies a change of the respondent's position between successive interviews.[1] We can therefore examine the effects which generalized attitudes towards the turnover of party control may have on party choice by selecting from our panel sample those who remained constant in their views at all three interviews, either endorsing the idea of turnover or saying that the long retention of power was quite all right.

The evidence provided by these two groups makes clear that generalized beliefs about the desirability of periodic transfers of control do play a role in the behaviour of the mass electorate and that they had a decisive effect in this period on the fortunes of a Conservative Government that had been in

[1] We must make allowance for the fact that someone who gave a completely random reply at each interview can have given the same reply by chance at all three interviews. But these will constitute only a small element of those in our panel who remained constant in their views in three successive interviews. See Chapter 15, pp. 316–19.

2.6 Support for Conservatives in 1964 Among 1959 Conservative Voters
By Beliefs About Desirability of Turnover of Party Control[a]

	Control of government should pass from one party to another every so often	It's all right for one party to have control of government for a long time
Voted Conservative in 1964	63%	89%
Did not vote Conservative in 1964	37	11
	100% (n = 93)	100% (n = 42)

[a] This analysis is limited to respondents within our panel who endorsed the same position about the desirability of circulation of governments at all three interviews and reported that they had voted Conservative at the 1959 General Election.

power since the early 1950s. Evidence of this is set out in Table 2.6, which contrasts the stability of Conservative preferences between 1959 and 1964 among those who held a generalized belief in the desirability of the circulation of governments and those who did not hold such a belief. The erosion of Conservative strength was substantially greater among the first of these groups. Moreover, this finding is consistent with those for each category of 1959 voters. The movement of prior Labour supporters towards the Conservatives was much weaker among those who expressed a generalized belief in the turnover of party control. Furthermore, Labour's relative share of support in 1964 from those who had been Liberal or who had not voted or who had been too young to vote in 1959 was substantially larger among those who thought the circulation of governments desirable. Given the closeness of the result in 1964 the numbers involved in these differences were quite enough to show that general beliefs in favour of alternation in power supplied the last margin needed to dismiss from office the aging Conservative Government.[1]

This conclusion rests on movements over the whole period of the 1959 Parliament, the greater part of which occurred prior to our first interview in 1963. Those of our respondents who expressed a belief in the circulation of governments were not, however, merely justifying a shift from the Conservatives they had already made. The tendency seen in Table 2.6 was also evident in shifts away from the Conservatives between 1963 and 1964,

[1] The swing to Labour between 1959 and 1964 among all those who held stable beliefs as to the desirability of the circulation of governments was 6·1 per cent, whereas those who accepted the idea of the long tenure of a single party actually recorded a swing of 3·6 per cent to the Conservatives.

after we had taken one measurement of the voter's belief in turnover of power.

Moreover, this pattern is matched, in reverse, six years later by the contrast in the stability of Labour preferences between 1966 and 1970 among those who did and those who did not hold a generalized belief in the desirability of the circulation of governments, as Table 2.7 shows.

2.7 Support for Labour in 1970 among 1966 Labour Voters by Beliefs About Desirability of Turnover of Party Control[a]

	Control of government should pass from one party to another every so often	It's all right for one party to have control of government for a long time
Voted Labour in 1970	73%	85%
Did not vote Labour in 1970	27	15
	100%	100%
	(n = 120)	(n = 25)

[a] This analysis is limited to respondents within our panel who endorsed the same position about the desirability of circulation of governments in 1964, 1966 and 1970 and reported that they had voted Labour at the 1966 General Election.

The likelihood that a Labour supporter would shift away from the party because of a belief in alternation was less after six years of Labour rule than was the likelihood that a Conservative would switch after thirteen years of Tory rule. But it seems clear that we were tapping a concept which was real to part of the electorate and that the concept had an impact on the survival of governments.

The Intrinsic Values of Party

All great realignments of party strength have involved values that the electorate attaches to the outputs of government, and the same may usually be said of the larger short-run fluctuations in party strength. But it is inevitable that the parties should develop values of their own in the elector's mind. As long-established actors on the political stage it is natural that the parties should have become objects of mass loyalty or identification. As a result, the success of a given party and the confounding of its enemies has a value in its own right for many electors, quite apart from the uses which the party might make of power. The dramatic idiom is not misplaced. A protagonist in the political drama can evoke from the electoral audience a response at the polling station which has mainly to do with the values of having one's heroes prevail. The same point is suggested by other idioms that are often applied to the electoral contest, especially those of games. Commentaries on politics are rich with sporting metaphors, and the values of partisan loyalty may be as intrinsic to the contest as the values of loyalty to a team.

The intrinsic appeal of a party may indeed rest on inclinations that lie deep within the personality of the individual elector. We shall not probe very far into the realms of personality in this book, but we have no doubt that such factors supply part of the motives of electors who find intrinsic values in supporting a given party.[1] Of course it is also true that personality factors can be part of the reason why an elector values certain outputs of government and hence the party that seems likely to achieve them; a voter's desire for Britain to brandish nuclear weapons may be a projection on to government of aggressive tendencies that go back deep into childhood. But it seems likely that such factors are more often involved in the intrinsic values that the elector finds satisfied in party allegiance.

Our view of the 'intrinsic' values of party should be broad enough to include a number of psychic or social utilities that party may have for the voter that are distinct from the values government may supply. The intrinsic values of partisanship may, for example, be those of preserving harmony in the friendship group or the home or the nuptial bed. Or they may be those of reducing the costs to individuals of obtaining the information they need to discharge their civic duty as electors, as we shall note later. We shall indeed speak of a variety of such personal and social uses of party allegiance as 'intrinsic' values to set them off from the utilities which may flow from the actions of government. There is no doubt that these residual values are often in the voter's mind.

This aspect of party support is more easily understood when it is seen how early in life partisan inclinations may appear. Children who know nothing of the uses of power may still absorb a party preference from their home, as we shall see in the next chapter. This early role of the family has its counterpart in the influence of a succession of associations in adolescence or adulthood. Many of the groups found at work or church or public house may foster a common political inclination among their members, perhaps

[1] Exceedingly suggestive studies of factors of this kind are H. J. Eysenck, *The Psychology of Politics*, London, 1954; R. E. Lane, *Political Ideology*, New York, 1962; A. F. Davies, *Private Politics*, Melbourne, 1955; and F. I. Greenstein, *Personality and Politics*, Chicago, 1969.

through reinforcing values associated with specific governments' outputs, but still more through reinforcing the intrinsic values of party.

There is indeed an important interplay between these two kinds of values in the shaping of long-term party strength. The great changes of alignment in the British party system in the 1840s, the 1880s, the 1920s and in the early 1940s were plainly linked to things that large sectors of the public wanted of government. But the 'primary' changes induced by forces of this kind will subsequently be amplified by 'secondary' changes that have relatively more to do with intrinsic values of party support that the individual discovers within his family and small group, or within his own mind, after supporting the same party for some while. We shall see evidence in Chapter 8 that the class realignment of modern politics took a generation and more to complete and also that this realignment, as time has passed, has depended less and less on the primary forces that first created it – with the probable consequence that preferences have come to move more fluidly across class lines.

Electoral history suggests that strong new primary forces can sweep away political attachments that depend mainly on the intrinsic values of party. Yet it would be unwise to discount the importance of accustomed loyalties. Among other things, they enter in at least two ways into the motives that induce citizens to go to the polling station. Despite the limited demands on time and energy made by voting, the act is not costless to the individual, as various commentators have noted, and the problem of explaining why people take the trouble to vote, when a single vote can make so little difference, is a real one.[1] Much of the answer is supplied by the several kinds of value we have been discussing. Electors have the *instrumental* motive of voting: the casting of their ballots may contribute to the election of a government whose outputs they value. They may also have the *expressive* motive of voting: the casting of their ballots shows support for the party they identify themselves with, and has an intrinsic value of its own.

Yet we must also allow for the *normative* motive of voting; the casting of the voter's ballot may reflect primarily a sense of civic obligation. Indeed, the democratic ethos creates a strong presumption that electors will use their franchise, and this idea is heavily reinforced by the mass media as well as by everyday conversation as polling day approaches. Blurred ideas of

[1] An influential statement of the costs, indeed of the 'irrationality' of voting, appears in A. Downs, *An Economic Theory of Democracy*, New York, 1957, pp. 260–76. For an interesting alternative theoretical argument, see W. H. Riker and P. C. Ordeshook, 'A Theory of the Calculus of Voting', *American Political Science Review*, **62** (1968), 25–42.

popular sovereignty and universal suffrage are so interwoven in the prevailing conceptions of British government that the obligation to vote becomes almost an aspect of the citizen's national identity. As a result, a number of people are drawn to the polling place who would be unlikely to get there otherwise.

But those who are drawn to the polling station in this way must support some party when they are there. The democratic ethos has obliged them to take action about a distant and complex realm of affairs, one that is not clearly enough defined to give them a motive for voting but for their sense of civic obligation. The result is to create yet another intrinsic value in having a tie to party. The elector who possesses a firm attachment has a basis for preferring one party programme, one set of political leaders, and indeed one interpretation of current political reality to its rivals. The psychological convenience of such a habitual tie adds to the values that are intrinsic to being a party supporter.

Partisan Self-Images and Electoral Choices

The values which the individual sees in supporting a party usually extend to more than one general election. There may be strong continuity in the outputs of government, such as the welfare of a class, which provide the individual with the same basis for his choice over successive contests. Moreover, the values involved in party support of the intrinsic sort tend by their very nature to be enduring ones. As a result, most electors think of themselves as supporters of a given party in a lasting sense, developing what may be called a 'partisan self-image'.

This phenomenon is a familiar one in many party systems. Writing of 'party identification' in their book on Norwegian parties Valen and Katz ask:

> Why is such a concept necessary? Why not simply use voters' reports on their voting behaviour with which party identification is of course correlated? The reason is that we need a more generalized measure of the individual's orientation to take account of a variety of behaviours.[1]

The United States has produced the most intensive studies of such dispositions towards party; these have demonstrated that there is a remarkable degree of independence between electors' generalized identification

[1] H. Valen and D. Katz, *Political Parties in Norway*, Oslo, 1964, p. 187.

with party and their behaviour in particular elections, especially in the choice of a President.[1] From the time when comparable measurements of these identifications began to be taken on a nationwide scale in the early 1950s, the distributions of party loyalty have fluctuated only modestly from sample to sample despite massive swings in the presidential vote.

There is no doubt that the partisan dispositions of British voters tend to be generalized ones. Looking back over their own past voting in general elections, in 1963 well over four-fifths of our respondents said that they had always supported the same party. These recollections probably exaggerate the true extent of continuity, but the report is nonetheless impressive. Moreover, our repeated measurements of the preferences of our panel showed the majority holding fast to the same party from 1963 to 1970, although, as we shall show, the minority whose partisanship fluctuated was of a size that some will find surprising.

To study more closely the nature of our respondents' partisan self-images, we asked them at each interview, quite separately from questions about their voting, to describe their partisan inclinations in a more general way and we were able to divide the sample into those who described themselves as Conservative, Labour or Liberal in this more general sense.[2] At least 90 per cent of the sample accepted such a generalized partisan designation at each interview, except in 1969, when at a time of extreme government unpopularity the figure fell to 85 per cent.

One of the clearest evidences for the generalized nature of partisan dispositions in Britain comes from local government elections. In 1963, for example, those who went to the polls in local elections that were fought on a party basis voted to an overwhelming degree in line with their expressed party self-image, as Table 2.8 shows.[3] Some small deviations are apparent. Almost certainly the lesser solidarity of Conservatives shown here reflects the disillusion which affected the party's supporters in the spring of 1963. But the most central fact is that well over 90 per cent of our respondents stayed with their generalized tie to the national parties, though local elections might be thought to be fought on entirely special local issues. This dominant role of a more general partisan tie is entirely consistent with the

[1] The most extended discussions of the concept of party identification appear in *The American Voter*, pp. 120–67 and in *Elections and the Political Order*, pp. 9–157.

[2] See question 36 in Appendix B.

[3] Many local elections were not fought on a party basis and in many more one or more of the national parties were not represented. We checked from external sources the pattern of candidatures in each ward where we conducted interviews. An interesting proof of the veracity of our respondents is that none claimed to have voted for a party which had not in fact put up candidates in their ward.

2.8 Local Election Vote in May 1963 by Partisan Self-Image[a]

| | Partisan Self-Image | | |
	Conservative	Labour	Liberal
Local election vote			
Conservative	85%	1%	2%
Labour	3	95	4
Liberal	6	2	88
Independent[b]	4	1	6
Other[b]	2	1	0
	100%	100%	100%

[a] This analysis is limited to people identifying themselves with one of the three main parties who were also qualified electors in wards where candidates of their 'own' parties contested the local council elections in May of 1963.

[b] A candidate whose ties to one of the main parties were a matter of general knowledge was classified as partisan rather than as 'independent' or 'other'.

evidence our sample gave of their lack of involvement in local issues. When we asked those who voted in the May 1963 elections whether there were any issues that had especially concerned them, four out of five said 'no' without hesitation; the remainder mentioned matters that were in fact more often the concern of Westminster than of the Town Hall.

The significance of generalized party ties is further illustrated by their link with participation in local elections. We asked each of those who expressed a generalized partisan self-image how strong the tie was.[1] Table 2.9 shows that the chance that an elector would vote increased sharply

2.9 Local Election Turnout by Strength of Partisan Self-Image, 1963

| | Strength of Partisan Self-image[a] | | |
	Very Strong	Fairly Strong	Not very Strong
Proportion voting in local council elections[b]	64%	54%	39%

[a] Classification based on question 36a.

[b] This tabulation is based on respondents identified from external sources as living in wards which had partisan local government contests in May of 1963.

with the strength of his general attitude to the parties. These findings are wholly consistent with the growing tendency to interpret local government elections as referenda on the national parties.

In view of the generality and continuity of partisan dispositions it is natural to wonder whether a partisan self-image may not survive in the

[1] See question 36a in Appendix B.

elector's mind during a temporary defection to non-voting or even to support of another party. This sort of tenacity of generalized partisan identifications is one of the most central findings in American studies. Large numbers of voters have defected to the presidential candidate of the opposite party in every recent election. But their proclaimed party allegiance has remained remarkably undisturbed during such defections; in fact, it continues to be a better predictor of what the voter will do in future elections than is his current presidential vote. In the Eisenhower elections of 1952 and 1956 millions of traditional Democrats voted Republican for President, just as millions of traditional Republicans voted Democratic in the Johnson–Goldwater contest of 1964. But many of these defectors maintained their normal loyalties in voting for other offices in the same year and the great majority of them returned to the fold in subsequent presidential elections.[1]

Has this pattern any parallel in Britain? The answer is that, in the main, partisan self-images and electoral preferences travel together in Britain far more than in America. We may draw this contrast in terms of a continuum extending from the extreme case in which no changes of electoral preferences are matched by shifts of partisan self-image to the opposite extreme in which all changes of electoral preference are so matched. The American pattern falls considerably short of the first of these extremes and the British considerably short of the second. But the divergence of the two is clear, as the placement of the two countries on such a continuum in Figure 2.10 shows. In the American case, shifts of partisan self-image

2.10 Changes of Vote and Party Self-Image in America and Britain[a]

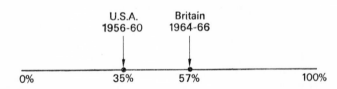

[a] The data for America are drawn from the University of Michigan panel study of the 1956 and 1960 presidential elections. The British data are drawn from our 1964–6 panel.

[1] Moreover, the role that a partisan self-image is found to play in shifts of electoral preference is consistent with the evidence that it links the electoral preferences of the American voter with more remote sociological influences, especially the identifications of religion and class. In other words, party identification seems in America to supply the link by which sociological identifications have an enduring influence on electoral choice. See A. S. Goldberg, 'Discerning a Causal Pattern among Data on Voting Behavior', *American Political Science Review*, **60** (1966), 913–22.

accompanied only 35 per cent of changes in presidential vote between the elections of 1956 and 1960, whereas in the British case such shifts accompanied 57 per cent of changes of vote between the elections of 1964 and 1966.

This Anglo-American difference in the stability of partisan self-images in the presence of changing vote preferences is sharply evident when we examine a series of elections. Table 2.11 compares the stability of self-image and vote in the American congressional elections of 1956, 1958 and 1960 and British parliamentary preferences in the summer of 1963 and the elections of 1964 and 1966. The contrast is clear. Although roughly

2.11 Stability of Partisan Self-Image and Voting Preference Between Three Points in Time in America and Britain[a]

		Party Preference in Voting for Congress			Party Preference in Voting for Parliament		
		Stable	Variable		Stable	Variable	
Partisan Self-Image	Stable	76	16	92	75	8	83
	Variable	2	6	8	4	13	17
		78	22	100%	79	21	100%

[a] The American data are drawn from the University of Michigan panel study of the 1956, 1958 and 1960 elections. The British data are drawn from our 1963–64–66 panel.

three-quarters of each of these national electorates held to their established (and consistent) party loyalties and vote preferences over the three points in time, the dominant mode of change in America was for party self-image to remain fixed while vote preference changed. In Britain, by contrast, the dominant mode of change was for party self-image and vote preference to change in tandem. Indeed, half as many British electors changed their partisan self-image while keeping to the same vote preference as the other way round, whereas in America only one-eighth as many did so.

The more durable nature of the individual's party self-image when voting for the opposite party in America must largely be due to the different challenges faced by the elector in the two countries. On polling day the British elector votes only for a single office at a single level of government.

The American has to cope simultaneously with a vast collection of partisan candidates seeking a variety of offices at federal, state and local levels: it is small wonder that voters are conscious of generalized beliefs about their ties to party, although some of their individual choices are not guided by these. They will tend to develop a generalized conception about ties to party even if they come to feel that they are 'Independent' voters free of such ties. It is indeed revealing that in the American political vernacular the term 'Independent' is used by a substantial section of the electorate to assert their freedom from a party. There is no real British equivalent. British political commentators use 'floating voter' as a term of art for electors who change their preferences, while candidates who stand for office without party backing call themselves 'Independents'. But there is no term by which ordinary voters are accustomed to declare their party irregularity. The electoral system has not provoked them to find one.[1]

Without this prompting from the electoral system, British voters are less likely than the American to make distinctions between their current electoral choices and more general partisan dispositions. The majority of voters do in fact have general dispositions towards party which give continuity to their behaviour in a succession of specific choices. But in transferring their vote from one party to another they are less likely to retain a conscious identification with a party other than the one they currently support.[2]

The contrast we have drawn between Britain and America held throughout our studies. Yet the slippage between self-images and votes was enough for the British pattern to look increasingly like the American as the shifts of strength between the Labour and Conservative Parties became more and more massive in the later 1960s. Figure 2.12 charts these movements across the five points of the decade for which we have readings. The figure makes plain that electoral preferences swung much more widely

[1] When in August 1966 the Gallup Poll asked British electors the question 'In politics, as of today, do you consider yourself as Conservative, Labour, Liberal or Independent?' only 3 per cent, given this explicit prompting, chose Independent. An equivalent question in the United States has consistently drawn an 'Independent' response from more than 25 per cent of the sample.
[2] The different role played by partisan self-images in Britain and the United States is also reflected in how well they link electoral preference to background social characteristics, such as religion and class. In America these background influences have an enduring effect on the vote by forming very long-lived identifications with party. The distinctiveness of the American pattern is attested by evidence from several western European countries. See U. Schleth and E. Weede, 'Causal Models on West German Voting Behavior', in R. Wildenmann, ed., *Sozialwissenschaftliches Jahrbuch für Politik*, Vienna, 1971.

2.12 Labour's Share of Partisan Self-Images and Vote Preferences, 1963–70

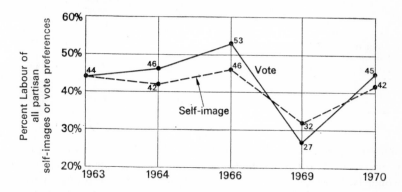

than did party self-images. Labour never reached the deep trough in partisan identifications that it had in vote preferences in its darkest days of the late sixties.[1] The fact that it did not must be counted among the factors which prepared the ground for the party's remarkable recovery in the six months prior to the election of 1970. Indeed, its astonishing resilience with the electorate in the first months of 1970, a phenomenon which seemed to many observers much more difficult to explain than Labour's shortfall on the eve of the election, becomes less puzzling if this background pattern of partisan self-images is kept in view.

The changing pattern of relationship between self-image and vote is perhaps clearest when we contrast the slippage between the two at different points in the decade. Table 2.13 sets out the joint distribution of self-images and vote preferences in the summer of 1963. It is clear from the table that the two were linked exceedingly closely and that neither party held an advantage in votes beyond what might have been expected from the then-current distribution of party loyalties.

During the period of Labour's greatest disarray later in the decade a very different pattern emerged. When we examine in Table 2.14 the joint distribution of self-images and preferences in the summer of 1969 we find a

[1] Indeed, the Conservative Research Department, having appreciated the value of consulting partisan self-images as well as current vote preferences, never found Labour running behind the Conservatives in partisan loyalties, in a series of private surveys in 1967 to 1969, despite the Conservatives' wide lead in current choices. We are inclined to think that this was due to accidents of timing. Labour was well behind the Conservatives both in party self-images and vote preference in our own survey in 1969, but not nearly so far behind in one as in the other. See *The British General Election 1970*, p. 346.

2.13 Vote Preference by Partisan Self-Image, 1963

| | Partisan Self-Image | | | |
	Conservative	Labour	Liberal	None
Vote preference				
Conservative	86%	2%	4%	11%
Labour	4	91	2	14
Liberal	4	2	88	11
None, don't know[a]	6	5	6	64
	100%	100%	100%	100%

[a] Includes 'other'.

much greater disparity between the two. We also see at once that the Conservative Party did far better in 1969 in terms of vote preferences than would be expected simply from the division of the electorate's partisan self-images. In particular, the party won support from 8 per cent of Labour's

2.14 Vote Preference by Partisan Self-Image, 1969

| | Partisan Self-Image | | | |
	Conservative	Labour	Liberal	None
Vote preference				
Conservative	95%	8%	11%	26%
Labour	1	71	9	10
Liberal	1	5	67	7
None, don't know[a]	3	16	13	57
	100%	100%	100%	100%

[a] Includes 'other'.

partisans, while giving away to Labour only 1 per cent of its own. Moreover, only 3 per cent of Conservative identifiers were unsure how they would vote, while fully 16 per cent of Labour identifiers were unsure. As a result, the Conservatives outmatched Labour by almost two to one in vote preferences in 1969 but by less than nine to seven in terms of party self-images.

But the gap between self-images and votes was very much narrower by the time of the election in 1970. Labour's recovery was reflected in self-confessed loyalties as well as votes. Indeed, the party's gain in partisan self-images was large enough for it to have won a clear victory in 1970 if the country had divided purely in these terms. It did not win such a victory because the Conservatives continued to draw more votes than Labour from the opposite party and the politically unaligned and lost fewer of their partisans to abstention, as Table 2.15 shows. But the table also indicates that the alignment of party self-images and vote preferences was much closer in 1970 than it had been a year before in the season of Labour's deepest despair.

2.15 Vote Preference by Partisan Self-Image, 1970

	Partisan Self-Image			
	Conservative	Labour	Liberal	None
Vote preference				
Conservative	85%	12%	27%	26%
Labour	4	68	12	23
Liberal	2	4	50	8
Didn't vote, other	9	16	11	43
	100%	100%	100%	100%

Hence, the evidence from the 1960s emphasizes both the similarity and dissimilarity of the role played by partisan self-images in Britain and the United States. In the decade's later years an increasing portion of the British electorate seemed capable of retaining partisan self-images to which their electoral choices returned after a period of disenchantment. But this pattern was much less marked in Britain than in America. We suspect that the distinctiveness of the American pattern is derived from the distinctiveness of the American electoral system, especially the frequency of elections and the presence on the American ballot of candidates for many offices at several levels of government. This is at least a reasonable hypothesis until the British and American patterns can be compared with evidence from still other party systems in Europe and the Commonwealth.

Whatever the role of party loyalties in guiding the behaviour of those who shift their preferences, it is clear that millions of British electors remain anchored to one of the parties for very long periods of time. Indeed, many electors have had the same party loyalties from the dawn of their political consciousness and have reinforced these loyalties by participating in successive elections. The manner in which partisan self-images take root and strengthen is an essential aspect of the individual's experience over the political life cycle, which we shall now examine.

3 The Political Life Cycle

THERE has been a natural inclination in electoral studies to consider single elections. While the focus is a useful one, it is important to see that one election with all its preliminaries is but a moment in the life of the nation or the individual citizen and that much is to be gained by taking a longer view. The processes of change are hardly to be understood without doing so. We begin here with the development of political attitudes during the lifetime of the individual voter, identifying several phases of the political 'life cycle' and the characteristics of political attitudes and behaviour that are distinctive to each phase.

The concept of a political life cycle involves a certain licence. Against the background of the twentieth century's political changes it may seem absurd to discuss a systematic pattern of individual development that can be likened to the biological life cycle. Why should the evolution of attitudes in a man born in 1884, who grew up in the gentlemanly world of the Conservative–Liberal struggle, resemble that in a man born in 1924, who grew up under the conditions that culminated in the Labour landslide of 1945? Why should either resemble that of a member of the age cohort first voting in the 1960s? We shall argue that there are, in fact, common aspects to the way in which each of these political generations absorbed its political ideas. Indeed, the very concept of a 'political generation' – of there being a common pattern in the behaviour of those entering the electorate in the same period – implies that the young show a common susceptibility to political ideas during their years of growing awareness.

Taking some liberties, we may distinguish four ages of political man – his infant innocence of the existence of politics (the likelihood of his having been born at all has significance for political change, as we shall see); his childhood, adolescent, or early adult years when he first becomes aware of politics; his later adult years in which political interest increases and party attitudes harden; and his old age when, though his partisan allegiance probably remains unchanged, his attention to politics declines towards relative indifference (once again, the timing of his ultimate demise is politically significant). Of these, the second and third provide our main concern. We shall consider first the formative years, the period of what is often called the individual's 'socialization' into politics, and then the years in which political attitudes are less susceptible to change.

The Impressionable Years

W. S. Gilbert's quatrain about everyone's being born 'either a little Liberal or else a little Conservative' is often cited in acknowledgment of the deep childhood roots of partisanship in Britain, amounting to the inheritance of party allegiance. But inheritance in this case is social rather than biological and Lamarckian rather than Darwinian: it is acquired political characteristics that are transmitted, however imperfectly, from parent to child.[1]

In most human societies the impressions made on the young are first of all the work of parents and the immediate family. But we should be clear about the complexities of the link between the political outlook of the family and the outlook developed in the young. Parental influence may indeed be direct, if uncoercing: the child may accept the political norms of

[1] Interest in political socialization has spread so rapidly that the political development of the young is by now almost a standard subject of empirical studies in a number of countries. In Britain the most systematic attention has been given the subject by Richard Rose. See his *Politics in England*, London, 1965. See also Paul Abramson, 'The Differential Political Socialization of English Secondary School Students', *Sociology of Education*, **40** (1967), 246–74; Jack Dennis and others, 'Political Socialization to Democratic Orientations in Four Western Systems', *Comparative Political Studies*, **1** (1968), 71–101; Jack Dennis and others, 'Support for Nation and Government among English Children', *British Journal of Political Science*, **1** (1971), 25–48, with rejoinders by Ian Budge, ibid., 389–92, and A. H. Birch, ibid., 519–20; and R. E. Dowse and J. A. Hughes, 'The Family, the School and the Political Socialization Process', *Sociology*, **5** (1971), 21–46, and the same authors' 'Girls, Boys and Politics', *British Journal of Sociology*, **22** (1971), 53–67. See also R. P. Kelvin, 'The Non-Conforming Voter', *New Society*, 25 November 1965, 8–12. In America works such as Herbert H. Hyman's *Political Socialization*, Glencoe, Illinois, 1959, and Fred I. Greenstein's *Children and Politics*, New Haven, 1965, have become classics, and extensive empirical studies have been done on the influence of the family, peer groups, the school and other socializing agencies. See, for example, Robert Hess and Judith Horney, *The Development of Political Attitudes in Children*, Chicago, 1967, and M. Kent Jennings and Richard G. Niemi, 'The Transmission of Political Values from Parent to Child', *American Political Science Review*, **62** (1968), 169–84. Political socialization has also been a fundamental process in the influential conceptual frameworks authored by Gabriel Almond and David Easton and their associates. See Gabriel A. Almond and James S. Coleman, *The Politics of Developing Areas*, Princeton, 1960, Chapter 1; Gabriel A. Almond and Sidney Verba, *The Civic Culture*, Princeton, 1963; and David Easton, *A Framework for Political Analysis*, New York, 1965.

his family group, which will be pre-eminently those of his parents. But parental influence may work in less direct ways and the child may accept from his parents modes of outlook which, although not immediately political, must inevitably colour his later political judgments. For example, a family pessimism about human nature may lead both father and son to shun reformist parties.

Moreover, the family must be the carrier of the beliefs and values of a wider culture. Obviously this is true in terms of the whole nation; to have been brought up as an Englishman (or Welshman or Scot) must have immense consequences for a man's approach to politics. Equally clear, and more important for our present theme, are the consequences of being part of one of the sub-cultures of the nation, particularly those defined by class. The child's place in the social structure, acquired from family, would have a profound influence on political attitudes even if the family itself did little to socialize the child into the norms of a sub-culture. This influence stands revealed when the norms of family and social milieu conflict; the son of a Conservative working man, as we shall see, may put aside his inherited partisanship for that of his working class friends. But equally these instances of conflict reveal the deep impress of the childhood home; the survival of the parents' norms in a class environment whose norms are different testifies to the family's influence on the young.

The family may help form the child's impression of other aspects of politics than the virtues of the parties. There is, for example, evidence that the interest which politics hold for adult electors is influenced by the degree of interest it held for their parents. Only one in three of our respondents who remembered both parents as interested in politics said that politics was of 'not much' interest to themselves, whereas nearly 60 per cent of respondents who said that neither parent was interested in politics said that they too were not interested.[1] The same traces are to be seen in our respondents' memory of how early in life they first became aware of poli-

---

[1] Our dependence on the child's recall introduces obvious problems of interpretation which should be borne in mind at many places in this chapter. Cautionary evidence as to the frailties of recall is supplied by studies of the young which have also obtained data on the political attitudes of parents. See, for example, Richard H. Niemi, 'Collecting Information About the Family' in *Socialization to Politics: a Reader* ed. J. Dennis (New York, 1973) pp. 464–90. It is far from obvious, however, whether these errors of recall will in a particular case inflate or diminish the correlation observed between parent and child. The tendency to remember one's parents as having one's own beliefs will of course magnify the relationship falsely. But more random errors of memory will tend to understate the real strength of these ties. There is indeed evidence that in some cases these opposite effects are substantially offsetting; however, any of our findings that involve the child's recall should be read with a degree of caution.

tics. Of those still in their twenties and therefore least removed from their childhood years, the number remembering themselves as politically interested by the age of ten is twice as large among those who recall both parents as interested in politics as it is among those who recall neither parent as interested.

But it is the direction of the child's partisanship that is the foremost legacy of the early years. A child is very likely indeed to share the parents' party preference. Partisanship over the individual's lifetime has some of the quality of a photographic reproduction that deteriorates with time: it is a fairly sharp copy of the parents' original at the beginning of political awareness, but over the years it becomes somewhat blurred, although remaining easily recognizable. The sharpness of the first reproduction is shown by Table 3.1, which examines the early preferences of those who

3.1 Earliest Party Preference by Parents' Conservative or Labour Preference, 1963

Respondent's Own First Preference	Both Parents Conservative	Parents' Partisanship Parents Divided Con/Lab	Both Parents Labour
Conservative	89%	48%	6%
Labour	9	52	92
Liberal	2	—	2
	100%	100%	100%

remembered each of their parents as either Conservative or Labour partisans. Children of parents who were united in their party preference were overwhelmingly likely to have absorbed the preference at the beginning of their political experience. We shall shortly return to the legacy of parents whose preferences were divided.

The progressive blurring of this first reproduction can be seen by examining the current preferences of the same respondents (those who remembered each of their parents as Conservative or Labour). The preferences of these respondents as adults in the mid-1960s are shown in Table 3.2 on the next page. The imprint of the family's partisanship is still clear but it is more blurred than it was in Table 3.1. The greater erosion of Conservative preferences among those of divided parentage reminds us that the forces which have intervened in the adult years may not favour the parties in equal measure.

When the direction of mother's preference is distinguished from father's it is plain that each parent, and not the father only, helps to form the

3.2 Present Party Preference by Parents' Conservative or Labour Preference, 1963

Respondent's Own Present Preference	Both Parents Conservative	Parents' Partisanship Parents Divided	Both Parents Labour
Conservative	75%	37%	10%
Labour	14	49	81
Liberal	8	10	6
Other	—	—	—
None	3	4	3
	100%	100%	100%

nascent partisanship of their children. Table 3.3 shows the proportions of our adult respondents whose first preferences were Conservative according to the various patterns of their parents' preference. This array is a remarkable testament to the joint influence of mothers and fathers. Nor would the figures differ in any substantial way if they were presented separately for men and women. Apparently both sons and daughters were equally susceptible to this joint influence and not only sons to father or daughters to mothers.

Fathers, however, have had much more to do with the partisanship of

3.3 Proportion of Earliest Preferences Conservative by Pattern of Parents' Preference[a]

		Father was		
		Conservative	Neither[b]	Labour
Mother was	Conservative	89%	46%	50%
	Neither[b]	68%	27%	16%
	Labour	41%	8%	6%

[a] Each entry of the table gives the proportion of respondents within a given pattern of parental preferences whose own first preference was Conservative.
[b] The 'Neither' category includes those whose parents were of Liberal or changing preference or of no remembered preference.

their children since their own partisanship was so much more likely to have been visible in the family. Table 3.3 indicates that when the mother was partisan, and agreed with the father, she strongly reinforced his influence on the child, and that when the mother was partisan, and disagreed with the father, she was, if anything, a little more likely to carry the child with her.[1] But the case of the partisan father and the neutral or non-political mother was a far commoner one in the childhood experience of the present electorate. Indeed, all but a quarter of our respondents recalled a clear partisanship for their fathers, but nearly half were unable to attribute a partisanship to their mothers.

Table 3.4 shows how, largely as a result of this, there is a greater tendency

3.4 Agreement of Elector's Party with Party of Father and Mother[a]

		Whether Elector's Party Is Same as Father's		
		Yes	No	
Whether Elector's Party Is Same as Mother's	Yes	39	9	48
	No	21	31	52
		60	40	100%

[a] This tabulation is limited to respondents who were themselves self-described Labour or Conservative supporters and who remembered at least one of their parents as being Labour or Conservative.

for electors' partisanship to agree with their fathers'. The table, which classifies all respondents who were themselves Conservative or Labour and who remember at least one of their parents as being Conservative or Labour, shows more than twice as many fathers having supplied a lead independent of mother as the other way round. But we can see from the prior table that this is entirely the result of the greater likelihood that fathers had a party allegiance that was known to their children.

This difference reflects the greater politicization of men in British society.

[1] A recent nationwide study of American high school seniors and their parents showed these adolescents as more likely to be influenced by their mothers than their fathers when the two parents disagreed as to party. See M. Kent Jennings and Kenneth P. Langton, 'Mothers *versus* Fathers: the Formation of Political Orientations among Pre-Adults', *American Political Science Review*, **62** (1968), 169–84.

Involvement in political affairs was by no means equalized at a stroke (or two strokes) with the coming of a fully equal franchise in the 1920s.[1] Even in the 1960s the interest which the men in our sample took in politics was greater: three-fifths of our women respondents said they had 'not much' interest in politics, as against only one-third of our men. An interesting additional characterization of the relative political weight of mothers and fathers as remembered by the present electorate is found in our respondents' account of the main reasons why their parents held the party allegiance they did. Fewer than a fifth mentioned the influence of some other member of the family on their fathers. But nearly three-fifths attributed their mother's party allegiance to the influence of her husband or someone else in the household.

In politics as in so much else the family's influence is large because the child's opinions are unformed. But the family is not the sole influence in the impressionable years, especially those of adolescence and early adulthood. The plasticity which renders the young open to so deep an impress from their parents also renders them more open to influences from other quarters than they will be later, when set in their adult ways. Many of these influences are lodged in a wider social milieu of school or work. In particular, the widening contacts of the young must often bring them the values and norms which connect party to class.

Such a process is reflected in the entries of Table 3.5, which have been

3.5 Agreement of Earliest Preferences with Parents' Partisanship Among Children from Conservative or Labour Families by Whether Parents' Partisanship was Aligned with Class, 1963

| Respondent's earliest party preference[a] | Parents Supported[b] | |
	Party Dominant in Class	Opposite Party
Agreed with parents' preference	91%	70%
Differed from parents' preference[c]	9	30
	100%	100%

[a] See question 34c.
[b] Includes cases in which one parent was remembered as favouring the party dominant in the class (or the opposite party) and the other as having no preference.
[c] Includes all cases in which the earliest preference of the child was remembered as differing from that of the parents.

[1] Most women over 30 were given the vote in 1918, but it was not until 1928 that the age of women's voting was reduced to 21 and the franchise became effectively equal for men and women.

built up by comparing the first remembered party preferences of children from Conservative and Labour homes with those of their parents and comparing their parents' party preferences with the dominant political tendencies of their class – Conservative in the case of middle class families, Labour in the case of working class families. The table shows a greater erosion of family political traditions where they are inconsistent with those of class. But the table shows equally the strong continuity of these traditions even when dissonant with a class milieu. The first preferences of fully 70 per cent of respondents whose families were not aligned with the majority of their class agreed with their parents' preference.

Indeed, the survival value of these minority political views was still very evident at the point of our respondents' adult lives when we first interviewed them. The evidence of this is set out in Table 3.6, which has the same structure as the prior table but substitutes our respondents' current

3.6 Agreement of Present Preference with Parents' Partisanship Among Children from Conservative or Labour Families by Whether Parents' Partisanship was Aligned with Class, 1963

Respondent's present party preference[a]	Parents Supported[b] Party Dominant in Class	Opposite Party
Agrees with parents' preference	85%	58%
Differs from parents' preference[c]	15	42
	100%	100%

[a] See questions 36a and 36c.
[b] Includes cases in which one parent was remembered as favouring the party dominant in the class (or the opposite party) and the other as having no preference.
[c] Includes all cases of respondents who did not hold their parents' party preference.

preferences for those they remember holding when they first became aware of politics. It is seen that the present allegiance of fully 58 per cent of respondents whose families were not aligned with the majority of their class continued to coincide with the preference to which they were exposed in the home as children.

We would expect the individual's class milieu to play a greater role in forming the allegiance of the young in cases where the parents were of mixed political views or held no clear views as to party. The evidence of this is set out in Table 3.7 on the next page, which shows the proportions of earliest and present party preferences consistent with those dominant in the child's class among children of parents who were of mixed allegiance or held

3.7 Agreement of Earliest and Present Party Preferences with Partisanship
Dominant in Respondent's Class Among Children of Parents with Mixed or
No Party Allegiance, 1963[a]

| | Among Children of Parents | |
	Of mixed party allegiance	Of no party allegiance
Proportion of respondents whose earliest preferences agreed with those dominant in their class	65%	70%
Proportion of respondents whose present preference agrees with those dominant in their class	74%	73%

[a] This analysis is limited to children who have remained in their parents' social class.

no clear party allegiance. Indeed, evidence from other countries indicates
how extraordinary a role is played in Britain by the individual's class milieu
in forming a partisan allegiance in those who have not experienced a clear
partisan influence from their parents. Table 3.8 contrasts the British findings
with those from comparable interview studies in France, the United States
and Japan. The data available from these other studies make it necessary
for us to confine our attention to the influence of the father. It is clear from
the table that a very sharp contrast indeed is found between the incidence of
adult partisanship among those from relatively non-political homes in
Britain and these other lands. We do not suggest that influences related to
class are wholly responsible for the allegiances formed by electors from

3.8 Extent of Partisanship in Adults Not Associating a Party Preference
with Their Father, in Four Nations

	Great Britain	France[a]	United States[b]	Japan[c]
Per cent holding a party preference among adults who do not associate a party preference with their fathers	89·5	47·7	50·7	61·1

[a] From a nationwide survey undertaken in France in 1958 and reported in P. E. Converse and G.
Dupeux, 'Politicization of the Electorate in France and the United States', *Public Opinion Quarterly, 26*
(1962), pp. 578–99.
[b] From the nationwide surveys undertaken in the United States by the Survey Research Center.
Reported in P. E. Converse and G. Dupeux, ibid.
[c] From a nationwide survey undertaken in Japan in 1967. Data kindly furnished by Professor R. E. Ward
and Dr. A. Kubota.

such homes. But the formative role of class is strongly implied by the preceding table, 3.6. The individual who begins life without a partisan lead from parents tends to accept the lead that is so clearly given in Britain by a class milieu, with the consequence that the British electorate is far more politicized in a partisan sense than are most democratic electorates.

The relative impressionability of the young also means that they will be unusually open to the influence of issues and events which dominate national politics at the time of their entry into the electorate. If strong forces move the country towards one of the parties we can expect these forces to be most clearly evident in the behaviour of the youngest electors, on whom the weight of prior loyalties sits most lightly. The effects of such forces are vividly illustrated in our own sample by the reported first votes of those who entered the electorate in the Labour years after the Second World War. But the profile of the main parties' support among new voters over a generation suggests in a remarkable way the ebbs and flows of party fortune. These proportions are reconstructed from the reported first votes of our sample in Figure 3.9, which plots the Labour Party's share of new votes for the two main parties in each election from 1935 to 1970. This profile of the behaviour of the youngest electors indicates clearly the surge

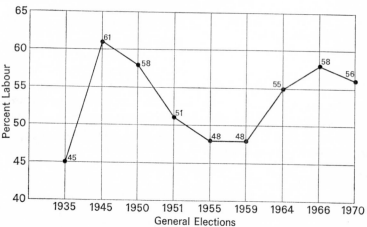

3.9 Labour's Share of Support for the Two Main Parties from New Electors, 1935–70[a]

[a] The 1970 figure refers to new electors who would have been qualified under the law as it stood in previous contests. Electors aged between 18 and 20 who were enfranchised by the 1969 Act are excluded. If all new voters were included the figure for 1970 would be 59 per cent.

in Labour's strength during the Second World War and its aftermath, the decay of its strength during the Conservative years of the 1950s, and the fresh Labour surge in the early and middle 1960s.

These formative influences have carried over into later voting. The greater Labour feeling of the Second World War and its aftermath could still be seen in the support for the two leading parties in the mid-sixties. Among those who first voted in the Labour years of 1945 and 1950 the proportion voting Labour in the General Election of 1964 stood at 60 per cent; among those who first voted in the Conservative years of 1951, 1955 and 1959, at only 53 per cent. With the aging of the voter the relatively plastic attitudes of youth tend to harden and the acquired habits of the early voting years begin to become more deeply fixed.

The Later Years

The hardening of partisanship in the mature elector is a tendency which has been very generally observed in various countries and party systems. The strengthening of the British elector's partisan self-image with age is suggested by the entries of Table 3.10, which shows the proportions within

3.10 Strength of Partisan Self-Image by Age, 1970

	17	18–24	25–30	31–40	41–50	51–60	61–70	71–
				Age				
Percent describing selves as 'very strongly' attached to party[a]	17	23	35	43	47	52	63	64

[a] See question 37b in 1970 questionnaire.

successive age groups describing themselves as very or fairly strongly attached to a party.[1] The increase seen here is too regular to be explained in

[1] A survey undertaken by the Opinion Research Centre in 1968 tended to confirm this finding as to the strengthening of party allegiance with age. The replies to the question 'How strongly Conservative, Labour or Liberal do you feel?' within three age groups were these:

	21–34	35–54	55+
Very strongly	21%	36%	49%
Fairly strongly	40	34	30
Not very strongly	24	19	14
Don't know	1	1	—
Without party allegiance	15	10	7
	101%	100%	100%

terms of a greater politicization among those who grew up in an earlier era, and we shall see additional evidence in a moment that the period in which the elector first became politically aware is less important in this connection than the length of time the voter has held to the same partisan belief.

A comparable pattern is found in actual behaviour. Since strongly felt ties are less likely to be displaced, the strengthening of partisanship in the aging voter implies that older electors will be less changeable in their voting. Such a trend is shown by Table 3.11 in terms of the constancy of party choice between the General Elections of 1966 and 1970 within four age cohorts.[1] The strong political tides during the 1966 Parliament affected

3.11 Constancy of Party Choice 1966–70 by Cohort

	Pre-1918	Interwar	1945	1951–66
Proportion supporting same party in the 1966 and 1970 elections	71%	67%	61%	55%

the several cohorts very unequally; the young were much more prone to desert a prior party choice.

There is evidence that what determines the strength and unchangeability of partisan ties is not so much the voter's age in years as the duration of his attachment to one party. Younger voters tend to be more plastic because their party preferences tend to be more recent. But older voters who have supported a party for as brief a time prove to be just as weak and changeable in their partisanship. When the strength and duration of partisanship are examined within age-levels, it is quite clear that what counts is the duration of the party tie and not the age reached by the elector.

[1] Since we shall often use these cohorts in the course of our analysis, it is well to set out their definition in some detail. The oldest group, the 'Pre-1918' cohort, is comprised of those who came of age soon enough to have qualified to vote in the General Election of 1918. We include in this group women who were by then of age, despite the fact that they had yet to receive the vote. The next oldest group, the 'Interwar' cohort, is comprised of those who came of age between the General Elections of 1918 and 1935. Once again, we shall overlook the fact that women between the ages of 21 and 30 were not enfranchised until the General Election of 1929. The third group, the '1945' cohort, is comprised of those who came of age between the General Elections of 1935 and 1950. The '1951–66' cohort is comprised of those who did not come of age until after the General Election of 1950 but who were able to vote in 1966. The 'Post-1966' cohort includes not only those who reached 21 between 1966 and 1970 but also those who, having reached 18 by June 18, 1970, were entitled to vote by the Representation of the People Act of 1969. But this last grouping constitutes only a half cohort: the 1970 contest was the first General Election for new voters born over a seven-year period.

This finding is reflected in Table 3.12, where each of three age levels is divided into people who in the mid 1960s had supported the same party for 13 or more years and those who had not. It is plain from the table that it is duration of party support rather than age itself which strengthens party loyalty. Among those with long-established partisanship, age made no difference to its strength. Among those with a more fickle voting record, the old were, if anything, more weakly attached to their current party than the young. The same pattern is found if these data are examined by comparing changeableness in voting with age and duration of partisanship.

3.12 Proportion Strongly Partisan by Age and by
Duration of Party Tie, 1964[a]

| | | Age | | |
		25–39	40–59	60+
Duration of Present Party Tie	13 years or more	81%	80%	82%
	Less than 13 years	64%	70%	54%

[a] Each entry of the table shows the proportion describing themselves as very or fairly strongly attached to party within a group jointly defined by age and duration of present partisanship.

That psychological attachments become stronger the longer they are held is a fairly general finding in the social sciences,[1] as we have noted; furthermore it is easy to sense how the recurrence of election campaigns can progressively deepen the partisanship of the committed voter. We observed in the previous chapter that each general election confronts the voters once again with the necessity of acting on distant and complex matters about which they are very imperfectly informed. In this situation an established partisanship provides voters with a simple means of sorting political leaders into the worthy and less worthy, and of making judgments on the merits of conflicting party claims whose full evaluation could require a lifetime of study. Moreover, a partisan commitment simplifies their choice between rival candidates for Parliament whose party label may be their most salient or their sole characteristic. Every time a partisan tie functions in this way it is likely to become stronger. The voter's experience

[1] Comparable American evidence of the deepening of partisanship with time is given by *The American Voter*, pp. 161–4.

over a series of campaigns can indeed be regarded as a kind of 'learning', in which the rewards of increased clarity and simplicity reinforce the party ties that supply them.

The psychological processes that underlie the strengthening of partisanship with time must be fairly complex. Some writers have found the concept of 'immunization' a useful one; electors whose partisanship is new, as the youngest electors' will always be, are more susceptible to the contagion of political change, whereas those of a longer partisan history have been immunized by their repeated experience of party politics.[1] Our view is that these processes must involve the increasing experience that the partisan voter gains over time in accommodating new political information within his existing partisan frameworks. The longer a given tie with party is held and the more experience the elector has in coding new messages consistently with it, the less likely is it that information about new issues and events will lead him to revalue the parties. We might indeed think of the committed voter as a kind of information processing device whose circuitry for receiving and interpreting messages in a given way becomes increasingly effective as additional information is received and stored. But the elector whose partisan circuitry is still undeveloped has a higher probability that messages about new political issues or events or leaders will cause him to revalue the parties.

Certainly it is plain that committed voters are likely to interpret many political events in a partisan fashion. Those who study the political effects of the mass media report frequent examples of such party bias. One of the nicest is the tendency for the television viewer to score highly on the 'appreciation index' measuring response to a party political broadcast if he already sympathizes with the party.[2] An equally clear example from our own interviews is the tendency of the committed voter to see the personal qualities of his own party leader in a particularly favourable light. The Labour stalwarts in our sample were especially prone to discover purely personal deficiencies in Harold Macmillan, Sir Alec Douglas-Home and Edward Heath alike, just as steadfast Tories remained disenchanted with Harold Wilson through four interviews. There were of course differences in the degree of esteem felt for the different party leaders by these voters,

[1] Those who first gave currency to this image asserted that 'we mean not a metaphor, but the literal logic of the immunity idea: resistance to disturbances is built up by disturbances; lack of resistance to disturbances is due to lack of disturbances'. See W. N. McPhee and J. Ferguson, 'Political Immunization', in W. N. McPhee and W. A. Glaser, eds., *Public Opinion and Congressional Elections*, New York, 1962, pp. 155–79.

[2] Evidence on this point may be found in *The British General Election of 1964*, p. 162 and p. 182 and *The British General Election of 1966*, p. 144.

and we shall consider these in some detail in Chapter 17. But the biasing effects of party allegiance were evident in perceptions of every leader in these years.

It is worth while mentioning a process which is often attributed to the aging elector but for which there is in fact little evidence. Both academics and journalists have thought that many voters begin their political lives on the left and move rightward as they grow older. A theory of political 'senescence', as it is sometimes called, fits comfortably the more general belief that the attitudes of youth are naturally liberal or radical, while those of age are naturally conservative. Empirical support for such a theory is thought to be supplied by the fact that Conservative strength is greater among older electors than it is among younger. The profile of party support by age seems at first glance to lend the theory a good deal of credence.

Such a process evidently contributes to political change in some party systems but its importance in Britain seems limited. One indication of this can be seen in some further irregularities of party strength by age. When the age profile of party support is examined more closely, it is seen that in the 1960s Conservative strength tended to be weakest among those in early middle age, i.e. those born in the 1920s and just before. Electors younger than this tended actually to be a little *more* Conservative than those who lay within the precincts of early middle age.

This irregularity, although an embarrassment to any simple theory of conservatism increasing with age, can readily be reconciled with the concept that the *conservation* of established political tendencies is what increases with age. The profile of age support in the mid-1960s can be accounted for in terms of the impress of early political forces on the young and the preservation of these forces in the hardening allegiances of later years. We must ask not how old the elector is but when it was that he was young. Figure 3.9 on p. 57 showed how electors' first votes varied with the year in which they first voted. Voters who were of early middle age in this period, among whom Conservative support was weakest, were too young to have voted before the Second World War but entered the electorate in the postwar Labour flood. Electors who were older than this came of age when Labour was far weaker; indeed, many reached maturity before the Labour Party could establish any serious claim to power. We would expect electors who were younger than the 1945 cohort to be most variable in their party support, since they were still, in the 1960s, in their impressionable years.

More detailed empirical evidence on these points is supplied by profiles of party support by age drawn from the data of National Opinion Polls. In each of several periods in the mid-1960s N.O.P. massed the evidence of several successive samples, permitting unusually reliable estimates to be made of the division of party support within successive age groups. Figure 3.13 shows the profile of party strength by ten-year age groups during the election campaign of 1964. This curve confirms the slight peaking of Labour support among the 35–44 group, which came of age in the years from 1941 to 1950. A fairly sharp decline of Labour strength is seen in the older age groups, while a somewhat lower level of Labour support is seen among the younger.

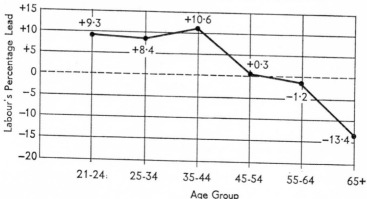

3.13 Labour's Lead Over Conservatives by Age, 1964 Election[a]

Source: National Opinion Polls; per cents based on total sample.

Additional insight into the elector's differing susceptibility to change at different ages is gained by comparing this profile for the autumn of 1964 with one from the prior winter of 1963–4, when the country's mood was a good deal more Labour. This comparison is given by Figure 3.14 on the next page. The pattern that stands out is the relationship between age and extent of change. The movement towards the Conservatives in fact diminishes monotonically in successive age groups.

The pattern of Figure 3.14, although far from a conclusive test, is not very kind to the senescence hypothesis. If we were to suppose that the political movements of this period were the result, first, of a general weakening of Labour's strength for reasons which were likely to affect any elector and, second, of a movement of aging voters towards a Conservative position, we should expect a stronger rightward movement at higher ages or at the very least a more uniform shift to the Conservatives at all ages. The pattern that is in fact observed is more consistent with the alternative

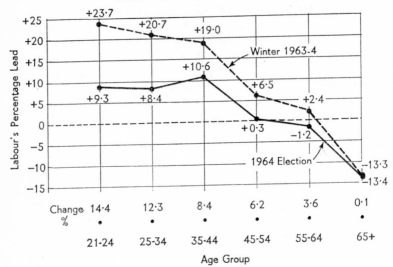

3.14 Labour's Lead Over Conservatives by Age,
Winter 1963–4 and 1964 Election[a]

[a] Source: National Opinion Polls; per cents based on total sample.

hypothesis that the conservation of established tendencies rather than Conservatism as such, is what increases with age. There is about these data more of immunization than of senescence.[1]

The descriptions given by our respondents of their own partisan histories were no kinder to the view that senescence has been a major element of change. In the mid-1960s the proportion of early Labour sympathizers who had gone over to the Conservatives was no larger than the proportion of early Conservatives who had turned to Labour. And the proportion of Conservatives who had become Liberals was a good deal larger than the proportion of Labour supporters who had become Liberals.

Moreover, the great majority of those who had changed in a given direction remembered doing so when the dominant tides of politics were

[1] Similar comparisons over the period of Labour's spectacular slump of 1966–8 show a similar profile of volatility. Change was less marked in each successive age group. But the period from 1964–6 yields conflicting evidence: while our own sample shows the same pattern as the N.O.P. figures for the other periods, N.O.P. suggests a fairly massive swing to Labour among older voters, supposedly won over by the substantial pension increase of 1965. It is beyond our present scope to reconcile this difference, although it may be partly attributable to the universal survey problem of getting a representative sample of older people. Certainly this deviant case does not vitiate our general contention that the changeableness of electors tends to diminish with age.

moving that way. Shifts from Labour were mainly linked to the period of Conservative ascendancy in the 1950s. And shifts away from the Conservatives were in most cases linked either with the great Labour era after the Second World War or with the years of Conservative decline in the early 1960s. We shall see in Chapter 11 that the shifts from Labour to the Conservatives seen in our long-term panel from 1959 to 1970 were not much greater than the shifts from the Conservatives to Labour over the same eleven years.

The fact that those who are young in a given period are exposed to common political influences, which are conserved as a cohort ages, gives rise to the phenomenon of political generations. The differences among generations that have been exposed to different influences and different problems is a recurring theme of political commentary. The importance of generational differences at the level of political leadership was indeed one of Bagehot's most eloquent themes. But such differences are equally a key to understanding changes at the level of the electorate. In Chapter 10 we extend our discussion of the individual's life cycle and consider the framework that might be needed to analyze in these terms changes in the electorate as a whole.

But it would obviously be wrong to portray all attachments as due to inheritance reinforced by time and modified by political events. Life chances, such as marriage or change of job or house or skills, may also shape allegiance. A small percentage of our sample – almost all of them women – said that they changed their party when they got married, and there is a fair presumption that the domestic influence of spouse and in-laws accounts for many more switches.

But other social influences are at work, reinforcing or weakening party allegiance. We shall consider the wider impact of a class milieu in later chapters. Here we can only suggest how often unconscious and unperceived pressures of neighbourhood, workplace or daily paper can affect partisanship. We asked our respondents to characterize the partisanship of their neighbourhood and of their workmates and to name the daily paper they read. Those whose environment was politically homogeneous (i.e. those who saw their spouses, neighbours and workmates as of the same party as their parents were and who read a like-minded newspaper) almost never seem to have deserted their parents' party. But if one or more of these potential influences were in conflict, the possibility of a change of preference became much greater.

That most people do adhere to the party of their parents therefore attests to the fact that most voters are exposed to influences later in life that are generally consistent with the party into which they were born. In recent decades the most important of these have been the life experiences associated with class. We now turn to the political role of class, examining in Chapter 4 the pervasive links of class to party and in Chapter 5 several of the influences in the voter's social environment which are related to class.

4 The Dominant Class Alignment

CLASS has long been pre-eminent among the factors used to explain party allegiance in Britain – and not just by academic observers. The Labour canvasser is warned away from the suburban villas lest he 'stir them up' while some Conservative agents can be heard dismissing council estates as '90 per cent socialist'. There is, in fact, evidence that partisanship has followed class lines more strongly in Britain than anywhere else in the English-speaking world.[1] Yet, as we shall see, the links between class and party are more complex than is often supposed and their extent and nature have changed substantially over the years. Indeed, considering the large amount of attention focused upon these links, the evidence about their nature remains oddly limited. The analysis of class alignments is incomplete in two main respects. First, too little attention has been paid to the beliefs that link class to party in the voter's mind. The fact of partisan differences between classes is documented in a wealth of statistical evidence; the system of ideas, the attitudes, motives and beliefs which lie behind the observed differences have been largely neglected. Second, treatments of class alignment have tended to be static in their approach. Class has supplied the dominant basis of party allegiance in the recent past; but within living memory the alignments were less clear and even in recent years they have shifted noticeably. This chapter considers some problems in the measurement of class and explores the links between class and party, including the beliefs that give meaning to politics in terms of class. The chapters that follow consider the changing nature of this relationship.

[1] An excellent comparative survey of Britain, Canada, Australia and the United States appears in R. R. Alford, *Party and Society*, Chicago, 1963. Alford's examination did not extend to New Zealand where class differences in party support approach British levels. See A. Robinson in S. Lipset and S. Rokkan, ed., *Party Systems and Voter Alignments* New York, 1967, pp. 95–112.

The Bases of Class

The subtleties of the class system and its delicate evolutions have not only provided the most obsessive theme in English novels for the last two centuries; they have also been at the centre of sociological studies since the days of Marx and Weber. No one who has read Hoggart's brilliant essay, for example, or Bott's enlightening study, or who has followed the refinement of the concepts of class and status in the writings of Runciman and of Goldthorpe and Lockwood can fail to appreciate how varied and subtle are class phenomena.[1] The identity and number of classes, the attributes characterizing classes, the relationship between classes, the openness of classes to individual movements up and down between generations or within one adult lifetime – these are all matters that are seen very differently in different parts of society.

We, therefore, sought to interpret the class system in the light of our respondents' own perceptions of it. In view of the wide currency of 'class' we kept the term while allowing our respondents to define the class categories in their own words.[2] We began in our first survey by asking whether respondents thought of themselves as belonging to a class. Those, about half the sample, who said that they did were then asked in a completely unprompted way to name their class. The replies offer remarkable evidence of the primacy of the 'middle' and 'working' class designations; only one in twenty-five of such respondents failed to make use of one or other of the two. Those who did offer something else were mainly scattered among the 'upper' class, the 'lower middle' class, the 'upper working' class categories with only a small residue.[3]

Those who had replied to the initial question by saying that they did not

---

[1] See A. M. Carr-Saunders and D. Caradog Jones, *A Survey of the Social Structure of England and Wales*, 2nd ed., Oxford, 1937; D. V. Glass, ed., *Social Mobility in Britain*, London, 1954; W. G. Runciman, *Relative Deprivation and Social Justice*, London, 1966; Margaret Stacey, *Tradition and Change*, *A Study of Banbury*, London, 1960; R. Hoggart, *The Uses of Literacy*, London, 1957; E. Bott, *Family and Social Network*, London, 1957; and J. H. Goldthorpe and D. Lockwood, 'Affluence and the British Class Structure', *Sociological Review*, n.s. **11** (1963), 133–63.

[2] The series of questions we describe here was put to a random half of the sample interviewed in the autumn of 1964. For the text of the questions see 44b on p. 479.

[3] Some of this residue – which amounted to less than 4 per cent of those questioned – in effect offered a synonym for the more frequent categories. Several described themselves as being of the 'professional class', one said he was of the 'labour class' and one placed himself in the 'miners' class'. One cheerful eccentric, a very fat publican, said he belonged to the 'sporting class'.

think of themselves as belonging to a class were then asked whether they would place themselves in the middle or working class if pressed to do so. The overwhelming majority said that they would; indeed, we were left with only one respondent in twelve who neither volunteered nor accepted a middle or working class identification. The hold of these two broad categories on popular thought was underlined by the fact that less than a quarter of those who had described themselves as middle or working class chose, under probing, to qualify their answer by saying that they were in the upper or lower rather than the average part of their class.

When in 1970 we asked respondents to name the main social classes, two-thirds spontaneously offered a framework using the terms 'upper', 'middle', 'lower', 'working', alone or in combination. A sixth said 'don't know' and only a sixth used other types of categories such as rich and poor or capitalists and the rest. When we asked them what class they put themselves in, 77 per cent spontaneously described themselves as 'middle class' or 'working class' while a further 5 per cent only added a slight qualification such as 'upper middle', 'lower middle' or 'upper working' while 1 per cent described themselves as 'upper class'. When the remaining 17 per cent were prompted,[1] all but 1 per cent were willing to assign to themselves a middle or working class label. In short, virtually everyone accepted the conventional class dichotomy between middle and working class. It is difficult not to see this as evidence of the acceptance of the view that British society is divided into two primary classes. This is much more than a sociologist's simplification; it seems to be deeply rooted in the mind of the ordinary British citizen.[2]

In view of the extraordinary hold of this dichotomy we sought to explore the characteristics that people attributed to members of the middle and working class. Once again we found wide agreement. As Table 4.1 on the next page shows, occupation provided the main basis for characterizing the classes. When our respondents described the kind of people who belong to the middle class, references to occupation outnumbered references to wealth or income by three to one and references to education or manners or shared attitudes by twelve to one. When they described the kinds of people

---

[1] See question 44b.

[2] F. M. Martin found that four out of five respondents chose 'middle' or 'working' as class designations. See his chapter 'Some Subjective Aspects of Social Stratification', in D. V. Glass, ed., *Social Mobility in Britain*, London, 1954, p. 55. The results of a number of other surveys show that a greater dispersion of answers can be produced by presenting a sample initially with a more elaborate set of categories, but this does not qualify our inferences from the replies to a less structured series of questions.

who belong to the working class the primacy of occupation was even more striking.[1]

The role of occupation in perceptions of class was matched by its primacy as a predictor of the class with which people identified themselves. There is overwhelming evidence that occupational status is the best guide to whether individuals place themselves in the middle or working class.

4.1 Descriptions of Class Characteristics, 1963

	% of responses
What sort of people would you say belong to the middle class?	
Occupation – non-manual, white collar, skilled, professional, self-employed	61%
Income and level of living – rich, wealthy, comfortably off	21
Attitudes and hierarchical location – snobbish, superior, aristocratic	5
Manners and morals – social graces, moral standards, attitudes towards work	5
Educational level or intelligence – well educated, intelligent, public school, university	5
Family background, breeding	1
Political – supporters of Conservatives, of right wing, of centre	1
Other	1
	100%
What sort of people would you say belong to the working class?	
Occupation – manual, semi-skilled and unskilled, people who work for a living, employees	74%
Income and level of living – poor, low income, people who live in poor housing, in slums	10
Manners and morals – social graces, moral standards, behaviour, attitudes towards work	7
Attitudes and hierarchical location – humble, subservient, people without airs, lower classes	5
Educational level or intelligence – poorly educated, left school early, unintelligent	3
Other	1
	100%

[1] The presence of the term 'working' in the designation of the class may well raise the suspicion that the frequency of occupational replies has been inflated by nominal answers which do not really distinguish the working from middle class in occupational terms. Detailed inspection of the evidence, however, showed this not to be the case. Those who characterized the working class in terms such as 'people who work for a living' were found in almost every case to have in mind the manual/non-manual distinction or comparable occupational criteria.

There is, of course, a circular element in such observations; 'occupational status' is measured by sorting a very large number of individual occupations into a hierarchy that is based on judgments about their relative status made by census officials or academics, or even by the public itself. Yet a subjective element is involved in treating almost any 'objective' social characteristics in hierarchical terms. This is true, for example, of education; whether people of more education are to be accorded higher status than those of less, other things being equal, depends ultimately on the values that the society in question happens to hold at the time.[1]

The measurement of occupational grade necessarily involves the investigator in some intricate problems of assessment.[2] We have relied in our own coding of occupational level on a detailed classification of occupations

[1] This subjective element in the relationship of education and social status is plain enough at the top of the educational range on both sides of the Atlantic. Anyone who has observed the matter at close hand knows, for example, how irrelevant the earning of a doctorate is in raising the class position of an Oxbridge graduate beyond where it was when he received his first degree, not to mention where it had been when he left Eton.

[2] The complexities of occupational status are faithfully recorded in the evolution of measures of social grade in Britain. Stevenson's original index, prepared in 1911, consisted of five hierarchical grades – professional, intermediate, skilled, partly skilled and unskilled – to which he assigned occupations on the basis of his own and others' estimates of relative prestige. See the *Annual Report of the Registrar-General for England and Wales, 1911* and the *Proceedings of the Royal Statistical Society*, 1928, pp. 207–30. This ranking was incorporated in the decennial Census Classification of Occupations and has persisted with some modifications up to the 1961 census.

Later investigators became increasingly dissatisfied with the large and exceedingly heterogeneous Class III of the census grades. Until the 1961 census this middle group contained actors, aircraft pilots and laboratory assistants, among others, as well as skilled manual tradesmen. Hall and Jones improved the discrimination between middle-range occupations by introducing seven hierarchical grades, basing their classification in part on judgments of occupational prestige elicited from a sample of the general population. See J. Hall and D. Caradog Jones, 'Social Grading of Occupations', *British Journal of Sociology*, 1 (1950), 21–49. The Government Social Survey uses seven grades, distinguishing clerical workers from skilled operatives, By the later 1950s most market research organizations had come to use a sixfold classification (with the widely-known designations A, B, C1, C2, D and E) which was first employed by Research Services Limited when that firm had responsibility for the national readership survey of the Institute of Practitioners in Advertising (I.P.A.). The distinction between C1 and C2 was intended to separate lower non-manual from skilled workers. Classification of respondents was normally done by interviewers on the basis of the occupation of the head of the household, supplemented at times by data on income or on the physical condition of the dwelling. The problems of comparing doorstep classifications made by interviewers of very different training and practices led to a desire within the market research agencies for the existing categories, A to E, to be explicitly defined in terms of the Registrar General's Classification of Occupations and for the coding of occupational grade to be done by central office staffs on the basis of these definitions. This is the approach we have adopted here.

into social grades proposed by a working committee of the Market Research Society, using the occupational categories of the 1961 Census Classification of Occupations. We have, however, modified these definitions to divide the lowest group of non-manual workers, those designated as C1 in conventional market-research terms, between those who have skilled or supervisory role and those who do not.[1] Thus the categories we have used are given in Table 4.2.

4.2 Social Grades of Occupation

Our Designation	Market Research Designation	
I	A	Higher managerial or professional
II	B	Lower managerial or administrative
III IV	C1	{ Skilled or supervisory non-manual { Lower non-manual
V	C2	Skilled manual
VI	D	Unskilled manual
VII	E	Residual, on pension or other state benefit

How do self-placements into the middle and working class differ across these occupational categories? Table 4.3 shows the relationship between the respondent's subjective class identification and the occupational level

4.3 Class Self-Image by Occupational Status of Head of Household, 1970

	Higher managerial I	Lower managerial II	Supervisory non-manual III	Lower non-manual IV	Skilled manual V	Unskilled manual VI
Middle class	80%	60%	57%	46%	26%	20%
Working class	20	40	43	54	74	80
	100% (96)	100% (166)	100% (170)	100% (122)	100% (568)	100% (358)

[1] Examples of our assignment of occupations to social grades and a discussion of the reliability of our measurement of social grades appear in M. J. Kahan, D. E. Butler and D. E. Stokes, 'On the Analytical Division of Social Class', *British Journal of Sociology*, **17** (1966), 127. We should make special acknowledgement of our great debt to Michael Kahan for his contribution here and throughout this chapter.

of the head of the respondent's household.[1] The proportion of respondents identifying themselves with the middle class falls continuously from 80 per cent in group I to 20 per cent in group VI.

The close alignment of occupational level and class self-image accords well with our evidence that occupation is the most important of the elements that characterize the classes in the public's mind. There are other elements, of course – education, income, style of living and the like. These are not independent of occupation – income and occupation are, for example, closely linked – but they are not wholly dependent on it; we would therefore expect them to make some distinct contribution to the individual's image of his own class.[2]

The images which people have of themselves as middle or working class therefore depend on a variety of life circumstances and are much more than an empty verbal response to a survey question. Tracing the full set of 'objective' influences on these 'subjective' images would draw us beyond the political concerns of this book. Because of the pre-eminent importance of occupation we shall use it in most cases as a measure of class location, although we shall often consult the individual's image of his own class and occasionally turn to other 'objective' influences. Although such simplifications are unavoidable, the complexities of the underlying relationships must be kept in mind throughout our analysis of the ties of class to party.

[1] We have followed the practice of categorizing respondents on the basis of the bread-winner's occupation even where the respondent is working, on grounds that the occupant of the major figure in the family group tends to give the family as a whole its position in the class system. In this and what follows we have excluded group VII, a residual category comprised mainly of state pensioners without other means of support, on grounds that these people lie somewhat outside the occupational stratification order. Less than 3 per cent of our respondents fell into this category.

[2] As one example of this we examined the extent to which middle class identification varies by income within four levels of occupation. At every level the higher the income

Proportion Identifying with Middle Class by Income Level and Occupational Grade, 1963[a]

		Occupational Grade			
		I–II	III	IV–V	VI
Annual Income	£1200+	72%	71%	54%	—
	£750–1199	63%	64%	24%	15%
	£350–749	66%	51%	15%	8%
	£349 or less	62%	42%	16%	7%

[a] Occupation and Income are those of the head of household.

the more people feel middle class, but this is especially apparent in the intermediate levels, III, IV and V, where the cues lent by occupational status are presumably less clear. Indeed, in the highest and lowest grades, where these cues are sharper, the rise is only slight, although the absence of unskilled workers who are very highly paid makes it impossible to trace this relationship for grade VI over the full income range.

Appraising the Relationship of Class and Party

Even the most straightforward description of the alignment of class and party holds subtleties to trap the unwary. Let us set out the relationship in the simplest form, allowing for the two classes and the two parties which have dominated British life and politics in recent decades; the electorate can be classified thus within a four-fold table.

	Middle class	Working class
Conservative	a	b
Labour	c	d

This sort of table is thoroughly familiar in the literature on social class, but its simplicity is deceptive. First, a caution must be offered about the separation of Conservative from Labour.[1] The table necessarily treats this separation as a stationary one. But if there are flows of support between the two parties, the same table at different times can give a different account of the relationship between class and party. If, for example, there is a strong swing to the Conservatives for reasons which are felt in both classes, entries *a* and *b* will be larger and *c* and *d* smaller than would be true of a period less favourable to the Conservatives. The effect of such a contrast may be illustrated in this way:

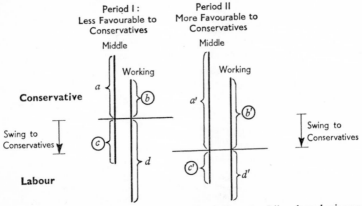

[1] Of course, the table also simplifies the situation by ignoring Liberals and minor party supporters, as well as those without a current preference.

We may think of the change between the first and second period as having the effect of moving downwards the dividing line between Conservative and Labour in both columns of our four-fold table, that is, within both the middle and the working class. As our figure suggests, *b* and *c*, which were equal in period I, become markedly unequal in period II; the Conservatives' share of the working class vote has become much larger than Labour's share of the middle class vote for reasons which may have little to do with class *per se* – as we shall do well to remember when we contrast the data from 1963–6 with that from 1969–70.

A second, albeit similar, caution is necessary about the way in which the separation of the middle and working class can alter the description of the relationship of class and party given by our four-fold table. Although the division of the population into two social classes has ample warrant, the actual point at which the division should be made is far from certain. We have been particularly aware of this in our own use of occupation as a distinguishing attribute. The orthodox view has been that the occupational distinction between middle and working class should follow the distinction between manual and non-manual. But, as we showed above, a drop in middle-class self-images occurs before the lowest level of non-manual occupations is reached.[1]

This issue deserves more attention than it has received. Its implications may once again be suggested visually by a figure which shows the consequences of two alternative decisions about the handling of a notional marginal group; this is set out at the head of the next page. Under the first of these decisions the proportions supporting the Conservatives in the middle class and Labour in the working class are nearly equal. But under the second decision the proportions are notably different. When one considers the pattern of past discussions of class voting, it becomes plain how much the argument must have depended on the conscious or implicit coding decisions by which voters were divided between classes.

A third caution about descriptions of the relationship of class and party can be illustrated by our four-fold table. It is essential to distinguish between the class *source* of each party's support and the party *destination* of each class's support. Answering the questions whence each party's vote has come and where each class's support has gone requires quite different operations with the four entries in our table. To say how much each class

[1] In the First Edition of this book we often grouped these lowest white-collar people with the working class, for the reasons set out in M. J. Kahan, D. E. Butler and D. E. Stokes 'On the Analytical Division of Social Class', *British Journal of Sociology*, **17** (1966), 123–30. In this Edition we have, with some hesitation, normally reverted to the more conventional dichotomy between manual and non-manual.

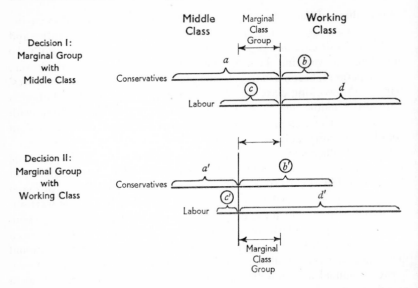

has contributed to a given party's support we would want to divide a and b by $(a + b)$ so as to express each as a proportion of all Conservative voters, or alternatively c and d by $(c + d)$ so as to express each as a proportion of all Labour voters. But to say how much of a given class has supported each of the parties we would want to divide a and c by $(a + c)$ so as to express each as a proportion of all middle class voters and b and d by $(b + d)$ so as to express each as a proportion of all working class voters. Each of these calculations has its uses but they are not the same. Indeed, the failure to distinguish the question of the class source of party support from the question of the party destination of class support has led to serious misinterpretation of poll findings, as we shall see in Chapter 8 when we consider the basis of working class Conservatism.

	Middle class	Working class	Totals
Conservative	a	b	$a + b$
Labour	c	d	$c + d$
Totals	$a + c$	$b + d$	

Class Cleavages in Party Support

Our findings on the strength of links between class and partisanship in Britain echo broadly those of every other opinion poll or voting study.[1] Here, for example, are the figures from our interviews in the summer of 1963. Table 4.4 makes plain that there were strong enough cross-currents

4.4 Party Support by Class Self-Image, 1963

| | | Class self-image | |
		Middle	Working
Partisan	Conservative	79%	28%
Self-Image	Labour	21	72
		100%	100%

in each class for partisanship not to have been determined entirely by class. Yet its pre-eminent role can hardly be questioned.

The tie of party to class is in fact still more impressive if we distinguish in these data the preferences of electors who qualified their middle or working class identification. The support for the two parties across the full range of class self-placements is shown in Table 4.5. Apart from the Conservative

4.5 Party Self-Image by Extended Class Self-Image, 1963

| | | Class Self-Image | | | | | | |
		Upper Class	Upper Middle	Middle Class	Lower Middle	Upper Working	Working Class	Lower Working
Partisan	Conservative	100%	84%	79%	76%	48%	28%	23%
Self-Image	Labour	0	16	21	24	52	72	77
		100%	100%	100%	100%	100%	100%	100%

unanimity of the tiny minority who described themselves as upper class, the greatest departure here from the percentages of Table 4.4 is the 48 per cent supporting the Conservatives among those who described themselves as 'upper working class'.

It is not surprising to find that the profile across our six occupational

[1] The full Gallup figures on this from 1945 to 1964 are set out in an article by Dr Henry Durant in R. Rose, *Studies in British Politics*, London, 1966, pp. 122–8. The National Opinion Poll figures for 1964 are set out in *The British General Election of 1964*, p. 296, and for 1966 in *The British General Election of 1966*, p. 260.

4.6 Party Self-Image by Occupational Status, 1963

	Higher Mana-gerial I	Lower Mana-gerial II	Super-visory Non-manual III	Lower Non-manual IV	Skilled manual V	Un-skilled manual VI
Conservative	86%	81%	77%	61%	29%	25%
Labour	14	19	23	39	71	75
	100%	100%	100%	100%	100%	100%

grades is very similar. Table 4.6 shows the continuous fall of Conservative strength down the occupational scale. Once again the figure which seems most discrepant from the strong pattern of the array is that for lower non-manual (IV), the highest occupational group which still tends to identify itself with the working class (as Table 4.3 showed); the Conservatives gathered in much more than half the support of this group.

The intermediate partisanship of the 'highest' working class group in both the self-rated and the occupational profile suggests that it constitutes an intermediate social group occupying a somewhat ambiguous position in a class system of two primary groupings. There is indeed a great overlap between those who are in the lowest non-manual occupations and those who describe themselves as 'upper' working class, even though the correspondence is far from complete. A full discussion of the class position and party inclinations of these people would draw us fairly deeply into questions of industrial organization, social mobility and perceived status that lie beyond our scope.[1] These electors, drawn in conflicting directions by their ambiguous location in the social hierarchy, stand out from those solidly on one side or the other. Table 4.7 shows the Labour proportion at each occupational level among those who saw themselves as middle class and those who saw themselves as working class. This table has three main regions. The four left-hand cells in the upper row constitute a firmly Conservative region: among non-manual workers who identified themselves with the middle class, the Conservatives attracted on average nine out of ten of those who supported a major party. The two right-hand cells in the lower row constitute a firmly Labour region: among the great body of skilled and unskilled manual workers who identified themselves with

[1] See D. Lockwood, *The Black-Coated Worker*, London, 1958, J. Goldthorpe, D. Lockwood, F. Bechhofer and J. Platt, *The Affluent Worker: Political Attitudes and Behaviour*, London, 1968, and W. G. Runciman, *Relative Deprivation and Social Justice*, London and Berkeley, 1966.

4.7 Proportion Labour Among Major Party Supporters
by Occupational Level and Class Self-Image, 1963

		Higher Managerial I	Lower Managerial II	Supervisory Non-Manual III	Lower Non-Manual IV	Skilled Manual V	Unskilled Manual VI
Class Self-Image	Middle	10%	11%	9%	17%	46%	55%
	Working	43%	42%	43%	48%	76%	79%

the working class nearly eight out of ten supported Labour in preference to the Conservatives. The other six cells in the table form a middle region in which party support was fairly evenly divided: among non-manual workers who called themselves working class and among manual workers who called themselves middle class the balance of partisanship was remarkably equal. It is interesting that lower non-manual workers, whether they identified themselves with the middle or the working class, differed little in their level of Labour support from those of similar identification among supervisory or higher occupations. In other words the higher Labour preference of the lowest non-manual group, as shown in the earlier table, 4.6, can be seen as overwhelmingly linked to their greater tendency to identify themselves with the working class.

In marked contrast to the intimate ties between class and Conservative and Labour support, support for the Liberals was remarkably unrelated to class self-image and to occupational grade. The Liberals indeed constitute a standing challenge to any over-simple account of class and party. The level plateau of Liberal strength, shown for 1963 (when the party's fortunes stood relatively high) in Table 4.8 on the next page, is very unlike the ridges and valleys of major party support that we saw in Table 4.7. The middle class element, so dominant in Liberal leadership, is just evident in their mass support, the party faring least well in the lower region of the working class. But the main impression conveyed by these figures is of the breadth and evenness, in class terms, of the Liberals' appeal.

These varying patterns of class support for the main parties draw us back to the question of the basis of the ties between class and party. This is a

4.8 Proportion Liberal by Occupation Level and Class Self-Image, 1963

		Higher Mana-gerial I	Lower Mana-gerial II	Super-visory Non-Manual III	Lower Non-Manual IV	Skilled Manual V	Un-skilled Manual VI
Class Self-Image	Middle	12%	20%	16%	24%	12%	10%
	Working	22%	14%	13%	14%	10%	5%

question that may scarcely seem to need an answer. One of the most perceptive students of class in Britain has remarked:

> There is nothing, in a sense, that needs to be explained about a South Wales miner voting Labour or an executive of General Motors voting Republican. The simplest model of rational self-interest is enough to explain these cases . . .[1]

Although such a view catches an important aspect of the truth, it can easily lead to the neglect of worthwhile questions. At the very least, we may wonder whether 'rational self-interest' should be construed in wholly individual terms, or whether some who belong to a common class may not perceive a more general class interest even when they would have difficulty particularizing it in terms of their own individual interest. We may also wonder whether some class voting may not have less to do with perceived interests, either individual or general, than with the influence of distinctive class norms. Some who vote Conservative in the stockbroker belt, like some who vote Republican among General Motors executives, may simply be complying with the norms of their subculture; they may mark their ballots with no more thought of governmental consequences than they have when they mow their lawns or go to church. Here we begin to touch on questions which, to a peculiar degree, elude definitive answers; yet we feel it is worthwhile to outline three distinct models of the nature of class

[1] W. G. Runciman, *Social Science and Political Theory*, Cambridge, 1963, p. 94.

partisanship and to set out evidence for their validity and their relative importance.

Politics as Class Conflict

The first of these models involves the conception of politics as a conflict of *opposed* class interests, with the parties attracting their support by representing those interests. It is easy to associate such an intellectual view with Marx, although conceptions of class conflict go back as far as Aristotle and the playing out of this conflict in the parliamentary arena involves a thoroughly non-Marxist acceptance of the rules of the constitutional game.

Seen in terms of class conflict, the game of politics will benefit one class at the expense of the other. In the language of game theory, we might indeed say that the distinguishing feature of the class conflict model is that politics is seen as a 'zero-sum' game, in which the gains of one class are matched by the losses of the other. More is involved than a simple belief that the parties 'look after' class interests: these interests are seen as opposed and their opposition is what the party battle is thought to be about.

The voter who holds strongly to such a view will tend to sort his perceptions of various social and political relationships into a distinctive pattern. Let us consider first his probable view of the triad comprised by himself, his own class and the opposite class.

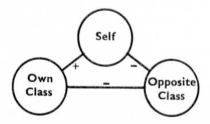

The individual whose party support is rooted in beliefs about class conflict will tend to form a strong positive identification with his own class and a negative identification with the opposite class – and will tend to see the relationship between the classes as one of necessary conflict. When we extend this approach to include the parties as well as the classes it is not difficult to assign to each of the relationships within it a positive or negative value, on the basis of a class-conflict view of politics:

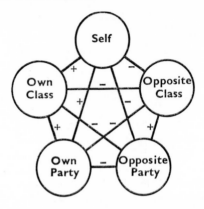

The bond between the voter's class and his party is seen as one of positive representation of interests, and so too is the bond between the opposite class and its party. The distinctive aspects of this intellectual view are, however, the negative 'cross-relationships' perceived between the classes and the parties. The projection of class conflict into the political arena arrays each party against the 'other' class.

This ideology of conflict consists therefore of a complex of 'balanced' triads of attitude and belief – 'balanced' in the sense that the individual will perceive a supporting relationship between any two objects when he likes or dislikes them both and a hostile relationship when he likes one and dislikes the other. To use the language of academic psychology we would say that the entire configuration was balanced.[1] The pattern of positive and negative bonds shown here may indeed be regarded as a social psychological representation of politics seen in terms of class conflict.

In our search for evidence that such a system of beliefs does in fact underlie at least some class voting, we have focused on the most distinctive elements of the configuration: the negative cross-relationships between the voter's own class and the opposite class and between his own class and the opposite party and his response to the perceived positive relationship between the opposite class and party.

[1] The property of balance was first given systematic attention by Fritz Heider in 'Attitudes and Cognitive Organization', *Journal of Psychology*, **21** (1946), 107–12, but Festinger, Osgood, and many other writers have since considered this aspect of cognitive organization. An admirable statement of the relevance of theories of cognitive balance or dissonance to political analysis is given by R. E. Lane and D. O. Sears in *Public Opinion*, Englewood Cliffs, New Jersey, 1964, pp. 44–53. The formal property which gives 'balance' to our configuration representing a class conflict belief system is the fact that it is impossible to find within it a triad including an odd number of negative bonds.

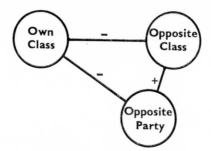

We have looked for evidence of these psychological ties in the extended replies our panel sample gave in several interviews to a very free set of questions concerning their likes and dislikes about the parties.[1]

A well-developed example of beliefs in which conflict plays an important part was given by the replies of a retired porter in South Shields. Asked in the summer of 1963 what he disliked about the Conservatives, he said,

> Their representation of unearned capital. Their disregard for the working classes. They are solely a money class representing high finance, which is detrimental to the prosperity of the country and people.

Asked what he liked about the Labour Party he said,

> They represent my standard of living and are endeavouring to achieve many things that are more essential to the working people.

In the autumn of 1964 this respondent's answers to the same questions were as follows:

> (Dislikes about Conservatives) They are absolutely class biased. They have no room for the working class, and their whole attitude is in support of the capitalists.

> (Likes about Labour) They are seventy-five per cent for the uplifting of the working classes.

[1] The questions are 4a–f in Appendix B. We have in addition searched for beliefs linking class to party in the replies to this series of questions: 'Do you think that (middle/working) class people vote mainly for one party or are they fairly evenly divided between the parties?' (If mainly for one) 'Which party is that? Why do you think they vote mainly for that party?' (See question 44p.).

And in the spring of 1966:

> (Dislikes about Conservatives) They are controlled by national and international capital. I hold them responsible for every war Great Britain has been in. I blame them for subjecting the working class to a mean, bare living. Their whole interest is self-interest.

> (Likes about Labour) They are the proper party to look after the working classes in respect of the social services and education and the welfare state generally. I like their guidance of the trade union movement.

Evidence that the negative cross-relationships shown in our diagram of a conflict belief system do exist appeared in the replies of a number of less articulate respondents. For example, a Barnsley housewife whose husband was a repairman for the National Coal Board said:

> (Dislikes about Conservatives, 1963) They don't help the working class. They're out to make money on anything.

> (Likes about Labour, 1963) More for the working class. They believe in helping those who need it – like old people and people with large families.

> (Likes about Labour, 1964) More realistic. More for everybody. A lot of them are from the working class and have a better idea of things and what people need.

> (Dislikes about Conservatives, 1966) I don't like them at all; they are more for the money people than the working class.

> (Likes about Labour, 1966) They are better for the working class. They do more for us. They have a better idea of what does us most good and they understand our problems better.

Some respondents had a developed sense of the way a zero-sum game between classes is played in the political or governmental arena, particularly the significance of the Budget. For example, a middle-aged Glasgow hosiery knitter, a crane-driver's wife, said this in the summer of 1963:

> (Dislikes about Conservatives) Well, I think when they are in power and there is any Budget it is usually the better class people who come off the best; like income tax benefits.

(Likes about Labour) As far as the working class families are concerned, they are more liberal with income tax reliefs. I have always believed that Labour is for the working class.

But the bulk of respondents who expressed ideas about class conflict in the political arena used more general or diffuse images. For example, a domestic servant in Stoke-on-Trent spoke in these terms:

(Dislikes about Conservatives, 1963) They are not good to the workers. They would squash you down if they could; would have you work for nothing if they could.

(Likes about Labour, 1963) They are more for the workers. They would be good for the workers. They are giving you a fair deal.

(Dislikes about Conservatives, 1966) They would squash you if they had the chance. They wouldn't give you any help.

Beliefs in the existence of conflict were more often expressed in working class responses, as we shall see in a moment. But a number of middle-class respondents also voiced the sense of opposed class interest distinctive to such a system of ideas. The wife of a textile technician in Paisley, for example, gave clear evidence that she perceived the Labour Party as representing an opposed class interest:

(Dislikes about Labour, 1963) This attitude towards money. They seem to think they can rob the rich to save the poor.

(Dislikes about Labour, 1966) I don't like their attitude towards the richer people – that they are the ones who should pay for all the extras and help that the poor people get.

It would, however, be wrong to assume that anything like a majority of electors saw the tie of class to party in terms of conflict between classes. When laid against a fully developed model of such a belief system, the beliefs actually expressed by most of those in our sample who voted in 'accord' with their class were fragmentary and incomplete. If we are to account for the bulk of class voting we must take account of other belief systems as well.

The Simple Representation of Class Interest

One alternative conception of the ties between class and party is a variant of the conflict model. Politics may be seen as an arena in which the parties do indeed represent class interests – but interests which are not necessarily seen as opposed. The absence of a sense of conflicting interests may reflect a belief that, in the language of game theory, politics is a *positive-sum* (and *variable-sum*) rather than a *zero-sum* game; such a belief is strongly embedded in the theory of representation which, nearly two centuries ago, Burke applied to the interests of his day. Alternatively, it may simply reflect the fragmentary nature of the perceptions of electors able to see clearly enough that their party looks after the interest of their class, but not much beyond that.

Such a relatively unadorned conception of a party as representing the interest of a class was apparent in the comments of many of our respondents. For example, a miner's wife in Don Valley spoke of the main parties in these terms in the summer of 1963:

(Likes about Conservatives) No, I don't take much notice.

(Dislikes about Conservatives) No, I tell you I'm not interested in them.

(Likes about Labour) Well, I think we'd be better off if they got in. They would do more for the working classes.

A belief that one of the parties looks after the interest of a particular class is not in this case coupled with hostility towards, or even any very developed ideas about, the opposite party or class. The same fairly unelaborated belief in Labour's role as representative of working class interest was expressed by the same woman three years later:

(Likes about Conservatives, 1966) Nothing.

(Dislikes about Conservatives, 1966) They promise all sorts of things; but they don't carry them out.

(Likes about Labour 1966) They haven't had much chance yet, but I think now they will really get down to things. They are for the working people.

Asked why working class people vote mainly for Labour, she replied simply, 'It's their party'.

A belief in the simple representation of class interest, unaccompanied by a strong sense of class conflict, is similarly evident in the replies given over three interviews by a bricklayer's wife in Central Ayrshire:

(Likes about Conservatives, 1963) I wouldn't really know how to answer this question. I wouldn't know what to say.

(Dislikes about Conservatives, 1963) Nothing.

(Likes about Labour, 1963) I like them because they're for the working class people. That's the only real point there is about them.

(Dislikes about Labour, 1963) There's nothing I don't like about them.

(Why do working class people mainly vote Labour?) Because they think Labour will do things for them and get them things to suit their income.

(Likes about Conservatives, 1964) Nothing.

(Dislikes about Conservatives, 1964) They seem to go back on what they say sometimes.

(Likes about Labour, 1964) I think they try their best to keep what they promise for working class people and the old folks; that is the main thing, the old folks.

(Dislikes about Labour, 1964) Nothing.

(Main reason she voted Labour, 1964) To me Labour is for the working class. It is only right to vote for people who will try to help you.

(Likes about Conservatives, 1966) No, nothing.

(Dislikes about Conservatives, 1966) I don't like their attitude towards the Labour Party. (Didn't like their attitude?) I didn't like some of Mr Heath's remarks about them.

(Likes about Labour, 1966) Mr Wilson is a man who will stand by his word. They are really out to help the working class.

(Main reason she voted Labour, 1966) It is for the working class.

For such a respondent the element of the larger system that is overwhelmingly important is the simple triad between the elector, his own class and his class's party:

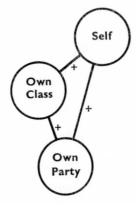

The individual, identifying with a particular class, forms a positive bond to the party which looks after the interest of the class, without necessarily forming any of the negative bonds that are distinctive of the conflict model of the relationship of class to party.

It would, however, be remarkable if perceptions of class interest were involved in all cases of individual behaviour consonant with the dominant partisan tendencies of the middle and working class. Many who vote 'with' their class do so for reasons that do not directly involve class interest. Many middle class voters, for example, believe that the education and business experience of Conservative leaders give them greater general skill in governing, especially in handling the country's finances. Although this belief is shared by a number of working class voters as well, its greater incidence in the middle class adds to the distinctiveness of middle class voting without directly involving class interest.

Partisanship in the Class Culture

The individual's response to the political norms of his class milieu can also help to keep the classes politically distinct without perceptions of class interest necessarily being involved. However important the perception of interests may have been in creating the political divergence of classes in the first place or in sustaining them in the longer run, anything so pervasive as the norm of Labour voting in the working class or Conservative voting in the middle class is likely to be accepted by many members of the class simply because it is there. Within the British nation there are distinct class subcultures which differ as to dress, speech, child rearing and much else.

The processes by which individuals accept the norms of these cultures are quite general, and it would be as absurd to see perceived class interests in all class voting as it would be to infer such interests from class differences in the time of dinner or the rituals of mourning.

Party choice as a reflection of a class norm involves a triad similar to that associated with the model of politics as the simple representation of class interests. The individual supports a party because he perceives a positive bond between the party and his own class. But in this case the bond may be formed of nothing more than the individual's perception that the party is positively valued by his class. There can be no doubt that

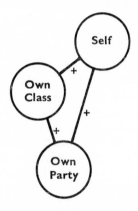

the bonds between the classes and the parties are widely perceived in the electorate. A belief in such a normative bond ran through a number of our respondents' free descriptions of the parties and the reasons for their own allegiance. A labourer's wife in Stirling, for example, explained her support of Labour by saying simply that 'I always vote for them; it's the working man's place to vote Labour'. A clerical officer in Bermondsey said he voted for the Conservatives because 'I feel they are more in keeping with my station in life'. The wife of a Durham miner explained working class support for Labour in these terms: 'The area itself has a lot to do with it; it's a lot of working class together, like around here.' The influence of class in determining the partisanship of a local environment is a theme to which we return in Chapter 5.

The closeness of the association of class and party in the public's mind is attested to by two other kinds of evidence in our studies. The first is the way our respondents placed the parties on a simple scale extending from middle class to working class. As part of a wider assessment of party 'images' we asked a random half of our sample at each interview to place the Conservative and Labour parties on twelve scales, of which this was one.[1] Fully 90 per cent of our respondents placed the Conservatives towards the middle class end of the scale, and 83 per cent put Labour towards the working class end. Indeed, the separation of the parties in class terms exceeded their distinctness on all the other scales by a very wide margin.[2]

The diffusion of political norms, especially in the working class, is also reflected in the proportion of our respondents who perceived their own class as giving its preponderant support to a particular party. Among our middle class respondents a third said that most of the middle class voted Conservative; among working class respondents fully three-fifths maintained that their class mainly supported Labour. Despite the fact that many of these people themselves supported the party of the 'opposite' class, almost no one said that the middle class supported Labour or the working class the Conservatives. It is noteworthy that those who saw their class as dividing its support were less one-sided in their own partisan alignments. Both in the middle and working class those who said that their class divided its support between the parties were less likely themselves to adhere to the party which attracted dominant support from their class. Some ambiguity surrounds such a difference, since the observed pattern may also reflect the tendency of those who deviate from the class to lessen any psychological tension or dissonance by failing to acknowledge the class norm. Yet such an alternative interpretation would also assume that the norm has a motive power for the individual, a power which in other cases has aligned the voter with the perceived norm.

A Profile of Beliefs about Class and Party

Although the difficulties are formidable, it is worth attempting some tentative estimate of the extent to which the approaches to class and party described in our three models are manifest in the electorate. We base our

[1] The format of these scales followed the lines of the 'semantic differential' technique due to Charles Osgood and his associates. See C. E. Osgood, G. J. Suci and P. H. Tannenbaum, *The Measurement of Meaning*, Urbana, 1957.

[2] By treating each party's ratings as a separate group of observations we may formalize the distinctness of the parties' placements on these scales in terms of ω^2, the proportion of the total variance of these ratings that is attributable to the difference of the mean party placements. For the middle class/working class scale ω^2 achieved a value of 0·71. On none of the other eleven scales (see question 8a) did it achieve a value exceeding 0·37; indeed, the average value for the eleven was 0·12.

judgment on the evidence furnished by respondents whom we interviewed three times from 1963 to 1966 and who held throughout the period consistent class and party allegiances – either Conservative and middle class or Labour and working class. The questions were those which yielded the quotations earlier in the chapter. First, we inspected our respondents' verbatim comments on their likes and dislikes about the parties at each of the interviews. Second, we examined their descriptions of the reason for their party preference at each of the interviews. Third, we looked at the reasons given by respondents in the first interview to explain why their class accorded preponderant support to a given party.

Respondents who gave evidence in any interview of perceiving class interests as opposed fell into our first category. Respondents who referred only to class benefits were classified as believing in a simpler representation of class interests. Among those who did not speak of class interests at all, we sorted into a separate category those who gave some indication of seeing support for a particular party as a norm appropriate to their class.

Such a categorization is far from including every elector whose vote conforms to the dominant political tendency of his class. Many happen to vote 'with' the majority of their class for reasons that have nothing to do with class interests or norms. The differing net effect of such influences in the middle and working classes helps to keep the classes politically distinct without any explicit belief in class interests or norms having to be present in the voter's mind. And the traditional character of voting means that some electors vote 'with' their class to reward or punish a party which they value positively or negatively for reasons having little to do with contemporary interests of any kind.

Our classification of beliefs yields a very different profile for the middle and working classes, as Table 4.9 shows. This table makes clear how very

4.9 Beliefs About the Relation of Class and Party
Held by Middle Class Conservatives and Working Class Labour Voters

Nature of Beliefs	Conservative Middle Class	Labour Working Class
Politics as the representation of opposing class interests	13%	39%
Politics as the representation of simple class interests	12	47
Politics as an expression of class political norms	10	5
No interest-related or normative content	65	9
	100% (n = 96)	100% (n = 301)

much more salient to the working class are the ideas of class interest and class conflict. Seven in eight of our working class Labour supporters gave evidence of seeing politics as the representation of class interests, and almost half of these regarded such interests as opposed. Among middle class Conservatives fewer than one in three gave evidence of seeing politics in terms of the representation of class interests.

The meaning of this profile of working class beliefs depends a good deal on one's expectations. The theme of class conflict is a muted one, affecting less than half the working class Labour electors – yet, in terms of numbers, they are a formidable body. What is mainly notable in Table 4.9, however, is the contrast between the middle and working classes. This contrast fits what a number of writers have said about the images of the social order held by those in different class locations. In particular, Dahrendorf, after reviewing the empirical work of Centers, Popitz, Willener and Hoggart in a variety of national settings, noted the 'strange and important fact' that

> those 'above' visualize society as a comparatively ordered continuous hierarchy of positions; those 'below' are, above all, struck by the gap between them and 'the others'.[1]

He associates with this divergence a markedly different tendency to see society in terms of conflict:

> It would seem that the dominant groups of society express their comparative gratification with existing conditions *inter alia* by visualizing and describing these conditions as ordered and reasonable; subjected groups, on the other hand, tend to emphasize the cleavages that in their opinion account for the deprivations they feel . . . The integration model, the hierarchical image, lends itself as an ideology of satisfaction and conservation; the coercion model, the dichotomous image, provides an expression for dissatisfaction and the wish to change the *status quo*. Even at a time at which the revolutionary ideologies of the Marxist type have lost their grip on workers everywhere, there remains an image of society which, in its political consequences, is incompatible with the more harmonious image of those 'above', whether they be called 'capitalists', 'ruling class', or even 'middle class'.[2]

[1] R. Dahrendorf, *Class and Class Conflict in Industrial Society*, rev. ed., Stanford, 1959, p. 284.
[2] Ibid., p. 284.

Our evidence certainly shows that the working class is much more prone than the middle class to see politics in class terms, whether including conflict or not. The words of a factory bench worker in Nuneaton – 'it's a case of us and them' – rarely had a counterpart in the comments of our middle class respondents. Indeed, the summary of reasons given for the partisanship of Conservative middle class fathers and Labour working class fathers in Table 4.10 suggests that the appropriateness of a particular party to a particular class was for working class children the main explanation as to why their parents voted as they did.

4.10 Reasons Recalled for Party Preference of Fathers
Who Voted with Majority of Their Class

Main reason recalled for party preference	Of Conservative middle-class fathers	Of Labour working-class fathers
Class-related	32%	69%
Traditional feeling	19	6
Influence of others in family	16	7
General approval of party	33	18
	100% (n = 107)	100% (n = 419)

This difference of outlook between middle and working class accords well with differences of party ideology. The Conservatives can style themselves as the representatives of a more national interest, one that includes the interests of all classes within a hierarchical social order. The middle class elector can therefore identify his party with an existing social order which preserves the interest of the upper and middle classes without relying on concepts of class interest and conflict that are so evident in working class thought.[1]

[1] Some observers have wanted to see the values associated with the Conservatives, aligned with the most prestigious institutions of British society, as a dominant national pattern, from which all Labour support ought to be seen as 'deviant'. Parkin, for example, has written: 'In other words, the values and symbols which have historically attached to the Labour Party and other parties of the Left, are in a sense deviant from those which emanate from the dominant institutional orders of this society. Examples of such institutions would include the Established Church, the public schools and ancient universities, the elites of the military establishment, the press and the mass media, the monarchy and the aristocracy, and finally and most importantly, the institutional complex of private property and capitalist enterprise which dominates the economic sector – the post-war innovations in public ownership notwithstanding.' F. Parkin, 'Working Class Conservatives: A Theory of Political Deviance', *British Journal of Sociology*, **18** (1967), 280.

The Conservatives' appeal as a 'national' party, the governing agent of an integrated if stratified social order, has helped keep the middle class strongly Conservative since the rise of the Labour Party. This image is indeed one that holds considerable appeal for working class voters as well, as a number of Labour politicians ruefully note; the Conservatives' ability to see their party as above politics – indeed, as above class interest in any narrow sense – is often mentioned wryly by their opponents. But in the main the working class held to a more dichotomous view of the social order; Labour's image in the period of our work still reflected the party's explicitly working class origins and trade union connections.

We do not suggest that middle class Conservatives fail to see reasons of self-interest for supporting their party. On the contrary, millions of middle class electors do in fact identify their own interests with the tax and distributive policies of the Conservative Party. What our evidence does suggest is that they are less likely than working class electors to see these interests in class terms. For the working class, on the other hand, ideas of class interest loom far larger. Indeed, for millions of working class electors the cleavage of interest between 'us' and 'them' gives the clash of the parties its basic meaning.[1]

The relation of class to party is not, however, a static one. Conceptions of the social order have changed in an age of relative affluence, and the balance of beliefs about class and party has inevitably been modified as older electors have died and younger ones have come of age. These processes are continuing ones and we shall examine in Chapters 8 and 9 several aspects of change that involve class, tracing the historical evolution of the class alignment. In Chapter 5 we examine several aspects of the individual's class environment.

[1] See Runciman, *Relative Deprivation and Social Justice*, p. 34, for the useful distinction between the 'egoism' of the middle class and the 'fraternalism' of the working class.

5 Class, Generation and Social Milieu

WE must look outward to the voters' environment as well as inward to their attitudes and beliefs if we are to explain the links of class and party. There is a sociological as well as a psychological reality to these connections, and we must move beyond our analysis of the beliefs linking class and politics in the voter's mind to consider aspects of the social milieu which forge a link between class and party. We shall first examine the transmission of social and political identifications in the initial social group, the childhood family. We shall then extend this analysis to consider ways in which this inheritance is aided or inhibited by education and the social environments of the later years. Such a discussion poses interesting questions about the political effects of broad changes in the structure of the economy and in Britain's social policies for education and housing. At the end of the chapter we shall extend the treatment of the social milieu to include other sources of the political information and political cues to which the voter is exposed.

Our analysis of class would be incomplete without some consideration of how class and party allegiances take root and change over the life cycle. Both class and party are acquired characteristics which parents may pass on to their children. Yet each is imperfectly inherited, and each can be altered over the individual's lifetime. Bringing the perspective of Chapter 3 to the matter of Chapter 4 will lead us to ask how the social environments of the adolescent and adult years may reinforce or diminish the continuity between generations.

Social Mobility and Political Mobility

We begin with a broad attempt to characterize the class location of successive generations in the same family and to examine the effects of change.[1] For this purpose we collected details of the occupational tasks

[1] An extensive literature treats the political effects of occupational mobility. See in

performed by the fathers of our respondents comparable to the details we gathered about the occupations of respondents themselves (or of the heads of the households within which they lived at the time of our interviews). In Table 5.1 we set out a full comparison of the change in occupational grades between generations.

We can greatly simplify the analysis of changes of class location if, as in

5.1 Occupational Grade of Father and of Head of Household, 1970

		Father's Occupation						
		I	II	III	IV	V	VI	
	I	2·5	0·8	1·0	0·7	1·3	0·7	7·0
	II	1·2	2·5	1·7	0·7	3·1	1·6	10·8
Head of Household's	III	0·8	0·8	2·9	1·1	4·1	2·9	12·6
Occupation	IV	0·5	0·9	1·5	1·1	3·5	1·9	9·4
	V	0·6	1·5	2·9	1·8	18·1	12·8	37·7
	VI	0·1	0·2	1·4	1·0	6·6	13·2	22·5
		5·7	6·7	11·4	6·4	36·7	33·1	100%

particular S. M. Lipset and R. Bendix, *Social Mobility in Industrial Society*, Berkeley and Los Angeles, 1959; S. M. Lipset, *Political Man: The Social Bases of Politics*, Garden City, N.Y., 1960; J. A. Barber, *Social Mobility and Voting Behavior*, Chicago, 1970; P. R. Abramson and J. W. Brooks, 'Social Mobility and Political Attitudes', *Comparative Politics*, **3** (1971), 403–28; B. G. Stacey, 'Inter-Generation Mobility and Voting', *Public Opinion Quarterly*, **30** (1966), 33–9; J. H. Goldthorpe, D. Lockwood, F. Bechhofer and J. Platt, *The Affluent Worker; Political Attitudes and Behaviour*, Cambridge, 1968, pp. 49–72; W. G. Runciman, *Relative Deprivation and Social Justice*, London and Berkeley, 1966; and K. H. Thompson, Jr, 'Class Change and Party Choices: A Cross-National Study of the Relationship between Intergenerational Mobility and Political Party Preference', Ph.D. dissertation, University of Wisconsin, 1967.

Chapter 4, we look at the two broad class groupings of the manual working class and non-manual middle class and consider the individuals who have crossed the threshold between the two. This simplified comparison of father's and respondent's social grade is set out in Table 5.2. Those who have moved upward between generations are included in the cell in the upper right-hand corner of Table 5.2; those who have moved downward

5.2 Intergenerational Occupational Mobility, 1970

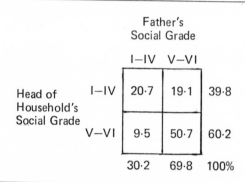

in the cell in the lower left-hand corner. The figures show that by this test slightly less than one-fifth of the electorate had experienced upward mobility and slightly less than one-tenth had experienced downward mobility. The imbalance between these two proportions is consistent with the upward bias of occupational structure in Britain over the last two generations, under which the ratio of non-manual to manual occupations has become progressively larger.[1]

There can be little doubt that movement of this kind has political effects. Let us first compare the Conservative and Labour preferences among upwardly mobile voters whose parents were Conservative or Labour. As Table 5.3 on the next page shows, the legacy of a Conservative parentage was

[1] Moreover, the imbalance has become more marked in our data over time. A comparable table from our sample for 1964 showed 18·8 per cent of the electorate as upwardly mobile and 10·8 per cent as downwardly mobile. For evidence on the fall in the proportion of the work-force engaged in manual occupations from 1950 to 1965 see G. S. Bain, *The Growth of White Collar Unionism*, Oxford, 1970. For a comprehensive account of changes in the composition of the work-force in the period 1931–61, based upon the Registrar-General's social classifications, see R. Knight, 'Changes in the Occupational Structure of the Working Population', *Journal of the Royal Statistical Society*, Part 3 (1967), 408–22.

5.3 Conservative and Labour Preferences among Middle Class Electors with Conservative or Labour Working Class Parents, 1970

Upwardly mobile Offspring are	Parents were : Conservative	Labour
Conservative	90%	43%
Labour	10	57
	100%	100%

clearly apparent in the preferences of upwardly mobile children, whereas the legacy of a Labour parentage was substantially eroded, though not blotted out. The fact that among those who come from a working class Labour background 57 per cent were Labour – a proportion vastly greater than the Labour percentage among the middle class as a whole – is a tribute to the influence of early socialization in the family. But the difference of 33 per cent between the proportion of Labour supporters among children of Conservative parents and the proportion of Conservatives among the children of Labour parents can be regarded as a measure of the conversion rate associated with moving from working to middle class.

We should beware of reading too simple a view of the nature of social and political change into Table 5.3. Undoubtedly the processes underlying these figures are very diverse. We presume that in many cases political conversion does follow a change of class location as the individual is exposed to different class-related beliefs about politics. In other cases changes of party may be an early, anticipatory, response to a change of social location which is far from complete. The office boy may not take long to adopt the political views that will suit him for the boardroom.

There must also be cases where Conservative partisanship was one of a cluster of ideas and values within the childhood family that predispose an individual to move upwards. It is not only that children rising into the middle class were liable to switch away from their parent's partisanship to Conservatism. It also appears that those who rose into the middle class were drawn to a disproportionate extent from children of working class Conservatives. When we compare the rate of upward mobility among those born into the working class according to the party of their parents, we find more than twice as many children from Conservative than from Labour homes moving into the middle class.

The key to this difference probably lies in the family's aspirations for the child's success in education and in other pathways to higher status such as marriage.[1] It is plausible to suppose that working class parents who were Conservative often had some middle class antecedents and were less likely to view the social order as a conflict between 'us' and 'them' and more likely to believe in a functional division of labour which values the higher social strata positively, or at least in neutral terms. Such parents would also be more likely to encourage, or at least not to oppose, their children's moving into the middle class, through education, marriage or choice of job. In view of the extent to which a child's educational attainment is determined by motives absorbed from his family, it may well be that the additional opportunities provided for working class children by the reform of the educational system have benefited to a disproportionate extent those from Conservative homes. Evidence of a higher rate of upward mobility in children from such homes is given by Table 5.4.

5.4 Rate of Upward Mobility from Working Class to Middle Class by Party of Parents, 1970

	Parents were:		
	Conservative	Labour	Other[a]
Proportion of offspring now middle class	55%	24%	36%

[a] Includes Liberals, mixed Conservative and Labour, and non-political parents.

But it is also possible that some upward as well as downward mobility between generations simply restored the *status quo ante* by returning the child to the class of his grandparents. Although we felt there was no hope of getting enough details about the jobs of our respondents' grandfathers to assign them an occupational grading, we discovered that the overwhelming bulk of our respondents had a clear idea of whether their parents had grown up in working class or middle class homes. Two-fifths of those with middle class grandfathers but working class fathers rose to the middle class whereas only 25 per cent of those with a purely working class background rose to the middle class. Equally, just over a third of those with middle class parents but working class grandparents slipped down to a manual occupation whereas only a quarter of those who had two generations of the middle class behind them did so. These figures shed additional light on the differing rates of recruitment of working class children into the middle class according to the party of their parents.

[1] See B. Jackson and D. Marsden, *Education and the Working Class*, London, 1962.

The advantage to the Conservatives of the long-term rise of non-manual occupations is therefore partly diminished by the fact that some upward mobility between generations simply made middle class adults out of working class children who were already disposed to be Conservative. However, this diminution may in turn have been partly offset by the lower rate of downward mobility and by the weaker tendency of those who slipped down the social scale to be converted to the working class party. The contrasting effects of upward and downward social mobility have been widely commented on in Britain and elsewhere.[1]

The reluctance of the downwardly mobile to accept working class norms can be seen in the fact that even among those who admitted to becoming working class only a minority supported Labour. The contrast in conversion rates among those who saw themselves as above their parents' class and those who saw themselves as below it is shown in Table 5.5. In order to remove the effect of the relationship between mobility and parents' party, this comparison is given only for parents who had supported the party of their class. Whereas 43 per cent of middle class children of working class Labour parents had become Conservatives, only 32 per cent of working class children of middle class Conservative parents had become Labour.

5.5 Party Preference of Upward and Downward Mobile Electors

Present Party Preference	Middle Class Electors with Working Class Labour Parents	Working Class Electors with Middle Class Conservative Parents
Conservative	43%	68%
Labour	57	32
	100%	100%

Because inherited party allegiances so often survive in those who cross the threshold between manual and non-manual occupations, social mobility offers a partial explanation of why middle and working class voters are

[1] Abramson and Brooks did not find stronger conversion among the upwardly than among the downwardly mobile in their re-analysis of Gallup Poll data on the attitudes of British youth. See 'Social Mobility and Political Attitudes', *Comparative Politics*, **3** (1971), 403–28.

not more perfectly aligned behind the class parties. Some of the 'cross-voting' in each class can be seen as a carry-over of family allegiances to which the socially mobile elector had been exposed early in the life cycle. This effect of social mobility is evident if we compare the relationship of class to party among those whose class position is similar to their fathers' and grandfathers' with this relationship among those who have a different position from their fathers. The comparison is set out in Table 5.6, where the greater extent of 'cross-voting' among socially mobile electors is immediately apparent. Indeed, a party cleavage by present class virtually disappears among the socially mobile.

5.6 Conservative and Labour Support by Class among
Socially Stable and Socially Mobile Electors, 1970[a]

	Socially Stable Electors[b] Social Grade		Socially Mobile Electors[c] Social Grade	
	I–IV	V–VI	I–IV	V–VI
Conservative	87%	29%	56%	50%
Labour	13	71	44	50
	100%	100%	100%	100%

[a] This analysis is limited to respondents whose partisan self-images were Conservative and Labour in 1970.
[b] Socially stable electors are defined as those whose social grade is I to IV, whose fathers' social grade was also I to IV, and who remember their fathers as having grown up in middle class homes; and those whose social grade is V or VI, whose fathers' social grade was also V or VI, and who said their fathers grew up in working class homes.
[c] Socially mobile electors are defined as those whose social grade is I to IV and whose fathers' social grade was V or VI; and those whose social grade is V or VI and whose fathers' social grade was I to IV.

A similar set of points can be made about the manner in which social mobility can blur the relationship between occupational status and class self-image. We shall not present the evidence on these points here. But we find a weaker alignment of class image and occupational grade among those who crossed the manual/non-manual threshold between generations than among those who did not. Therefore, some of the 'mis-identification' of those in the non-manual grades with the working class and of manual workers with the middle class reflects the survival of class images learned by the socially mobile elector early in life.

These generational considerations call attention to other aspects of the individual's experience that fix or alter social and political identifications over the life cycle. Here we shall consider two, the individual's educational experience and the influence of the residential neighbourhood. Each of these can broaden the generational aspect of the relationship of class and party, although each has a significance for party choice that transcends the generational perspective. Indeed, their significance is sufficient to make clear how much the far-reaching changes of educational and housing policy in Britain during this century must be involved in the balance of strength between the parties.

The Schools and Party Allegiance

The rise of mass education and the educational streaming of the population for occupational roles have made the schools a principal agency for conserving or changing social status.[1] They are not the sole means. Marriage, especially for women, and economic success or failure unheralded by education continue to be important. But few would doubt the increasingly central role played by education.

Educational streaming preserves the occupational *status quo*. Children tend to have educational experiences that will lead to a social status for themselves that is not widely different from that of their parents. This tendency is very marked in our own data for those in our 1970 sample who received their education after the sweeping changes introduced by the Education Act of 1944.[2] Table 5.7 shows a steep drop in the proportion of children educated in a public or grammar school as we move down the father's social grade. Among those whose fathers were professional or

---

[1] See A. H. Halsey and J. Floud, *Social Class and Educational Opportunity*, London, 1956.
[2] Categories applicable before the implementation of the 1944 Act cannot be exactly matched with those afterwards. This is only one of the difficulties in classifying schooling. The categories in Scotland and overseas are barely comparable with those in England and Wales. The gradual coming of comprehensive education in the 1960s further confused the picture; however, since only 12 per cent of our respondents in the 1951–66 and post-1966 cohorts actually went to comprehensive schools we have excluded such schools from our analysis.

5.7 Type of Secondary Schooling by Social Grade of Father[a]

| | | Social Grade of Father | | | | | |
		I	II	III	IV	V	VI
Type of secondary school	Grammar or fee-paying	82%	51%	49%	55%	18%	17%
	Secondary modern	18	49	51	45	82	83
		100%	100%	100%	100%	100%	100%

[a] This analysis is limited to respondents from our 1970 sample who fell in the 1951–66 and post-1966 cohorts and who therefore received their secondary schooling after the reforms instituted by the Education Act of 1944.

higher managerial over four-fifths went to a grammar or fee-paying school, whereas among those whose fathers were unskilled manual workers less than one-fifth did so.

It is equally plain that educational experience is strongly related to the individual's subsequent social status. This pattern is set out by Table 5.8

5.8 Social Grade by Type of Secondary Schooling and by Social Grade of Father[a]

| | | Father Social Grade I–IV | | Father Social Grade V–VI | |
| | | Respondent attended | | Respondent attended | |
		Grammar or fee-paying	Secondary modern	Grammar or fee-paying	Secondary modern
Respondent's social grade	I–IV	93%	50%	42%	19%
	V–VI	7	50	58	81
		100%	100%	100%	100%

[a] This analysis is limited to respondents in our 1951–66 and post-1966 cohorts. It also excludes respondents who still lived within their father's households.

separately for those with manual and non-manual fathers. Children both from middle and working class homes who went to a grammar school or fee-paying school were more likely to have achieved non-manual social status than were those who went to a secondary modern school. Therefore the educational system tended to conserve the status of those who went to grammar or fee-paying schools from middle class homes or to secondary modern schools from working class homes. But it was a means of upward social mobility for those who went to the first type of school from working class homes, and of downward mobility for those who went to the second type from middle class homes.

What effect these patterns might have on the party preferences of the young depended on the partisanship of the childhood home. The educational system might change party allegiance while conserving social status if the child were drawn from a home that was politically out of step with the dominant norms for the father's class.

Equally, the education system might conserve party allegiance while changing social status if the child were drawn from a home that was politically in step with the dominant norms of the class into which the child would move. The most notable instance of this is the case of the children from working class Conservative homes who have used grammar school education as a pathway to non-manual social status. Our evidence clearly shows that working class children were more likely to go to grammar schools if their parents were Conservatives. This interesting pattern is evident in the figures of Table 5.9, which divides the respondents in our

5.9 Type of Secondary Schooling by Party of Childhood Family among Children of Fathers with Manual Occupations[a]

| | | Childhood family was[b] | | |
		Conservative	Other	Labour
Type of respondent's school	Grammar or fee-paying	40%	18%	13%
	Secondary modern	60	82	87
		100%	100%	100%

[a] This analysis is limited to respondents from our 1970 sample who fell in the 1951–66 and post-1966 cohorts.
[b] Conservative or Labour homes are those in which both parents had this partisanship or one did and the other had none. 'Other' homes are those of mixed, Liberal, or no partisanship.

youngest cohorts whose fathers were of manual status according to whether their families were Conservative, or Labour, or of no clear partisanship.

This pattern is consistent with, and indeed partially explains, the finding set out earlier in Table 5.4 that working class children from Conservative homes were more likely to be upwardly mobile than were other working class children. Presumably aspirations for children's advancement, greater tolerance of the middle class and of middle class status, appreciation of education as a means of getting ahead, and Conservative allegiance were often parts of a broader cluster of values and beliefs. One of the main consequences of the 1944 Education Act may indeed have been to provide a means by which the children of the Conservative working class could better realize the social aspirations held for them by their parents.

The schools therefore played a more limited role in political conversion than would have been true if educational experiences had not so closely followed the individual's social and political background. We may summarize in Table 5.10, separately for children from non-manual and manual

5.10 Proportion Labour of Supporters of Two Main Parties by Type of Secondary School and Partisanship of Childhood Family[a]

		Children from middle class families which were[b]		
		Conservative	Other	Labour
Type of respondent's school	Grammar or fee-paying	11%	30%	70%
	Secondary modern	18%	62%	90%

		Children from working class families which were[b]		
		Conservative	Other	Labour
Type of respondent's school	Grammar or fee-paying	19%	50%	81%
	Secondary modern	22%	56%	74%

[a] This analysis is limited to respondents from our 1970 sample who were in the 1951–66 and post-1966 cohorts.

[b] Middle class families are those in which the father's social grade was I to IV, working class families those in which the father's social grade was V or VI. Conservative or Labour homes are those in which both parents had this partisanship or one did and the other had none. 'Other' homes are those of mixed, Liberal, or no partisanship.

homes, how the proportion Labour of those who support one of the two main parties varied with the partisanship of the childhood family and with the type of school attended. The table makes clear that family political inheritance still mattered far more than education in determining partisanship. Yet there is a discernible difference in the present allegiances of those who attended grammar or fee-paying schools and of those who attended secondary modern schools, especially among children from middle class homes.

The social environments of the adult elector include more than the occupational roles to which education is a partial gateway. Two individuals of identical occupational grade and income may experience differences of social milieu that are of great importance for their political outlooks. Some of these differences lie in the realm of occupation itself. The world of the skilled worker in one of the large and heavily unionized car-manufacturing plants is very different indeed from the world of the skilled craftsman employed in a small shop in a market town. But differences are also found outside the workplace. Although some of these will depend on occupation and the income it brings, an independent role can be played by the social environments of family, friendship groups and residential neighbourhood.

Party and Residence

A great deal has been written in recent years about the political significance of economic life styles. Indeed, during the 1950s, when a rising curve of prosperity coincided with a rising curve of Conservative strength, it was thought that the prosperous working class might be acquiring the social and political self-images of the middle class as it acquired middle class consumption patterns. This process of 'embourgeoisement' through consumer affluence was seen as quite distinct from upward mobility through changes of occupational role. Particularly in the wake of the Conservatives' third successive victory in 1959 it was thought that middle class consumption levels might be eroding the industrial worker's identification with the working class and, with it, his commitment to the Labour Party.[1] During the 1950s real incomes had risen on average by almost 3 per cent per annum. The number of private cars had jumped from 2 million in 1950 to 5 million in 1959. Refrigerators, washing machines and television sets all ceased to be middle class luxuries and appeared on the mass market. Even before the 1920s, when Neville Chamberlain launched his housing plans, the Conservatives had espoused the dream that a property-owning democracy would be a Conservative democracy. Was that dream now being realized?

[1] See M. Abrams and others, *Must Labour Lose?*, London, 1960, and C. A. R. Crosland's lecture 'Can Labour Win?', reprinted in his *The Conservative Enemy*, London, 1962, pp. 143–63.

The collapse of Conservative strength in the early 1960s dealt a rude blow to the embourgeoisement hypothesis. If the Conservative gains of the 1950s were really the result of prosperous workers coming to think of themselves as middle class, these gains should surely not have been so abruptly swept away. The reversal of party fortunes suggested that economic expansion had benefited the Conservatives more as the governing party during a prosperous period than as the party of an expanding middle class. Since the early 1960s the embourgeoisement idea has come under increasingly sharp attack from those who are sceptical whether anything so deeply rooted as identifications with class will be transformed merely by changes in consumption.[1]

We have in the main been equally sceptical and have paid scant attention to the role of washing machines, refrigerators and the like in shaping social and political identifications. But one sort of economic life style – housing – seems to us largely exempt from such scepticism and deserving closer scrutiny. Indeed, housing may rival occupation in the extent to which it expresses social aspirations, creates social self-images and economic self-interests, and exposes the individual to political information within a face-to-face environment. In a word, housing probably has more to do with defining the sub-cultures of social class than all else but occupation itself.[2]

Patterns of residential housing are so extraordinarily varied that some categorization is again necessary. We may distinguish broadly between three types of dwellings according to whether they are owner-occupied, are rented from private landlords, or are rented from local housing authorities. Each of these types covers a wide range of housing. But the range is especially broad in the case of private rental housing, which extends from luxury flats to dwellings marked for slum clearance. The distribution of Britain's housing stock over the three types varies widely between areas and has shifted markedly for the country as a whole in twenty years. We will

[1] See in particular J. H. Goldthorpe and D. Lockwood, 'Affluence and the British Class Structure', *Sociological Review*, **11** (1963), 133–63, and J. H. Goldthorpe, D. Lockwood, F. Bechhofer and J. Platt, *The Affluent Worker: Political Attitudes and Behaviour*, London, 1968. For a recent critique of their theses, see I. Crewe, 'The Politics of Affluent and Traditional Workers in Britain', *British Journal of Political Science*, **3** (1973), 29–52.

[2] For an interesting effort to use sociometric methods to study the effects that neighbourhoods may have on individual voting by being units of social or political identification and by providing arenas of interpersonal persuasion see M. Fitton, 'Neighbourhood and Voting: a Sociometric Examination', *British Journal of Political Science*, **3** (1973), pp. 445–72.

return to these variations when we assess the political significance of housing policy.

The range within each type of housing cautions us against too unwary a belief in the hierarchical arrangement of the three. But if we keep in mind the necessary reservations, especially as to the very wide range of housing rented from private landlords, we may accept a rough social ordering from council housing to owner-occupied dwellings. This view is quite consistent with the occupations and class self-images of those who live in each type of housing, as Figure 5.11 makes clear. There is a difference of 33 per cent in the proportion non-manual between council housing and owner-occupied dwellings, and a difference of 30 per cent in the pro-

5.11 Proportion Non-Manual and Proportion Identifying with Middle Class by Type of Housing, 1970

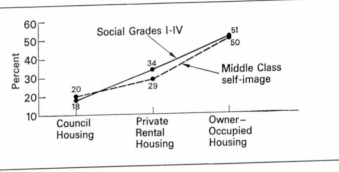

portion thinking of themselves as middle class between those who live in these two types of housing.

A clear pattern can also be seen in the party preferences of those living in the three housing groups. In 1970 the proportion Conservative of those identifying with one of the two main parties was 31 per cent among council housing tenants, 46 per cent among those who lived in private rental property, and 59 per cent among those who owned their own homes. We would expect fairly large party differences in view of the very different occupational composition of the three housing groups, although the culture of the local neighbourhood may help to support the party differences of occupational groups rather than the other way round. But we may ask whether there are differences in the partisanship of those living in these three types of housing which reach beyond what we would expect on the basis of occupational composition.

Evidence that party differences are not simply explicable by occupational status is presented by Table 5.12. The table shows that within each of the non-manual and manual occupational groups in 1970 there remained measurable differences in the party allegiance of those who lived in council housing, private rental housing and owner-occupied dwellings.

5.12 Proportion Conservative by Social Grade and Type of Housing, 1970[a]

		Council housing	Private rental housing	Owner-occupied housing
Social Grade	I–IV	51%	63%	76%
	V–VI	28%	38%	42%

[a] This table is confined to those who have either Conservative or Labour Self-Images.

A large number of values are associated with house ownership or council tenancy (and with some types of private tenancy). The house-owner has 'a stake in the country', something material to count on against his old age. He needs to manage his finances to keep up his mortgage payments and he has a special interest in maintaining the value of his property. The council tenant may be just as conscientious a householder and he too has to keep up the regular payments for his rent. But his interests and his association with his neighbours are likely to be quite distinct from those of an owner-occupier.

The politicians have recognized this. One of the staple issues of postwar argument has been the balance in government housing policy between the private and the council sector. Labour has been much more sympathetic to council building, quite heavily subsidized; the Conservatives have tried to foster private building, subsidized only indirectly through tax remissions on mortgage payments. Neither party has taken a wholly one-sided position but there can be no doubt that the Conservatives are seen as the friends of the owner-occupier and the Labour Party as the friends of the council tenant.

We have seen the strong links of type of occupancy with both social class and with party. The values that lead a voter into one type of housing are likely to be reinforced by the very fact of living where he does. One characteristic of council housing is that it tends to be grouped in large estates. The council tenant is overwhelmingly likely to have council tenants as neighbours all around him. The owner-occupier is only slightly less likely to be surrounded by other owner-occupiers.

When we asked our respondents about the social class of their neighbours we found, as Table 5.13 shows, that council tenants were much more likely to see their neighbours as working class. Similarly, when we asked working class respondents about their neighbours' politics we found that

5.13 Proportion Viewing Neighbours as Mainly Working Class

| | | Social Grade | |
		I–IV	V–VI
Type of House	Owner-occupied	32%	66%
	Council housing	82%	77%

81 per cent of council tenants saw them as mainly Labour but among owner-occupiers and private tenants the figure was only 66 per cent.

If the neighbourhood social milieu can have pervasive effects on party allegiance, we would expect it to reinforce or inhibit the transmission of party norms between generations. We may illustrate this role by extending our earlier analysis of the children of manual working class parents who have non-manual occupations themselves. Table 5.14 describes the current party allegiances of these upwardly mobile respondents according to the partisanship of their parents and the type of housing in which they now live. Although this comparison reduces several of our groupings to fairly small size and thereby introduces an additional degree of chance variability, the general pattern is clear. Upwardly mobile children of Conservative parents were scarcely more likely to have held to their inherited party if they now lived in owner-occupied homes. But upwardly mobile children of mixed or non-partisan parents and, still more, of Labour parents were much likelier to have become Conservatives if they now lived in homes of this kind.

The political importance of the residential milieu finds further support

5.14 Proportion Conservative of Upward Mobile Respondents Identifying with the Two Main Parties by Type of Housing and Partisanship of Childhood Family, 1970[a]

		Childhood family was[b]		
		Conservative	Other	Labour
Type of Housing	Owner-occupied	91%	74%	46%
	Private rental	88%	60%	26%
	Council housing	89%	56%	9%

[a] This analysis is limited to those in our 1970 sample whose fathers belonged to occupational grades V or VI and who belonged themselves to occupational grades I to IV.
[b] Conservative or Labour homes are those in which both parents had this partisanship or one did and the other had none. 'Other' homes are those of mixed, Liberal, or no partisanship.

when we examine movements in party preference among those who changed their level of housing during the period of our research. As Table 5.15 shows, the vast majority of our respondents remained at the same level from 1963 to 1970. But seven years were long enough for 10 per cent of the panel to have moved 'upward' between levels and for another 5 per cent to have moved 'downward'.

5.15 Turnover of Level of Housing, 1963 to 1970

Stayed at same level:		85%
In council housing	27%	
In private rental housing	11%	
In owner-occupied housing	47%	
Moved upward:		10%
From council to private rental housing	3%	
From private rental to owner-occupied housing	4%	
From council to owner-occupied housing	3%	
Moved downward:		5%
From private rental to council housing	3%	
From owner-occupied to private rental housing	1%	
From owner-occupied to council housing	1%	
		100%

Voters who had experienced these alternative housing histories exhibited marked differences in the continuity of party support. Among those who had stayed at the same level there was little change; the proportion having Labour self-images diminished from 1963 to 1970 by only 2 per cent. Among the small group that had moved to a lower level of housing, there was a modest swing against Labour; the proportion having Labour self-images was 6 per cent less in 1970 than in 1963. But among those who had moved to a higher level of housing Labour's support fell away much more sharply. In this group as a whole the proportion with Labour self-images was 19 per cent lower in 1970 than in 1963. The reduction was 12 per cent among those moving from council to private rental housing, 20 per cent among those moving from private rental to owner-occupied housing, and 23 per cent among those moving the greatest distance, from council housing to owner-occupied dwellings.

The formative role which housing may play is further emphasized if we consider changes in Labour strength from 1963 to 1970 among those who began in council housing. Labour's support in 1963 was greatest among those who would remain council-house tenants throughout the decade; of these 62 per cent identified with Labour. But Labour's strength in 1963 was not much less among council-house tenants who would move to private rental or to owner-occupied housing; of these 53 and 56 per cent thought of themselves as Labour. By the end of the decade, however, Labour enjoyed a very different degree of support among these three groups. Of those who still lived in council housing, 56 per cent thought of themselves as Labour. But of those who had moved to private rental or owner-occupied housing only 41 and 33 per cent did so.

The political differences by housing level focus our attention on the evolution of housing policy over this century. Although we cannot say with precision how much the political impact of housing is due to the formation of class self-images, or to economic interests linked with type of housing, or to the flow of political information and influence to the voter within a neighbourhood milieu, the residence of an elector must be regarded as a background factor of great political significance. Electoral change is partly explained by a model that is, in the econometrician's phrase, 'housing-driven', one which implies that changes in the 'exogenous' housing variable have direct and indirect effects on the strength of the parties.

The housing stock available to the electorate has varied both spatially and temporally. The differences by area are very wide. In 1970 more than half the dwellings in Scotland were rented from public housing authorities, against an average of 30 per cent for Britain as a whole. According to the 1966 census the Ladywood division of Birmingham was the constituency with the highest concentration, with 87 per cent; the Woodside division of Glasgow was the lowest, with 3 per cent. The differences by area in the concentration and quality of owner-occupied housing were, if anything, greater.[1]

Equally impressive are the changes over twenty years' time in the fractions of the nation's housing stock contributed by the three types of dwellings. These are summarized in Figure 5.16, which also gives official

5.16 Evolution of Britain's Housing Stock, 1951–81[a]

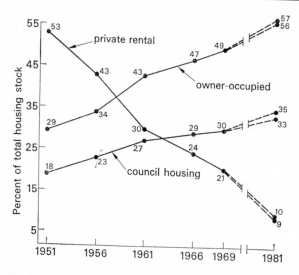

Source: *Social Trends*, 1971 (H.M.S.O.).

[a] The higher estimate of council housing and the lower estimates of private rental and owner-occupied housing for 1981 are based on a more vigorous programme of slum clearance.

projections to 1981. These series show that private rental housing, which made up more than half of Britain's housing stock in 1951, dropped to little more than a fifth by 1969 and was expected to contribute no more than a tenth by 1981. This decline was accompanied by a rise both in owner-occupied and in council housing. From just over a quarter of the total in 1951 owner-occupied dwellings rose to almost half the total by

[1] See *The British General Election of 1970*, pp. 358–79, for a full tabulation.

1969 and were expected to comprise nearly three-fifths by 1981. But these years also brought a marked increase in council housing – from 18 per cent in 1951 to 30 per cent in 1969, with an added rise expected over the next decade.

There is nothing inevitable about these changes. They reflect market forces that were allowed to operate. And they reflect conscious decisions of government on housing, land use and transport. The evolution of housing policy in Britain parallels the development in several European countries. But the course taken in Britain differs sharply from the experience of several of the older Commonwealth countries. We might in particular imagine a recent past in which less emphasis had been placed on the provision of high-density public housing by local government councils. The mass construction of council housing, typically in large concentrations, has probably done much to preserve the solidary feeling of parts of the working class. It is of course difficult to gauge the effects of actual housing policy against alternatives without knowing more about the world to which alternative policies might have led. But it seems hardly arguable that the housing policies first articulated in the aftermath of the First World War, later accepted by both main parties at the national level, and strongly pursued by local government councils, especially those dominated by Labour, have provided a residential milieu for part of the electorate which has had marked effects on political allegiance.

Political Information and Party Cleavage

The residential milieu helps form and conserve party preference partly because it helps define the social networks through which there is a continued flow of informal information about politics. The content and partisan angling of what the voter hears about politics are quite different on the council housing estate and the suburban housing estate. Because these differences tend to follow class lines and because residential environments are notably stable in class terms, the residential milieu tends to reinforce the class alignment.

We have cited reasons, apart from the flow of informal political information, why party preference should go with type of housing. In particular, housing may create economic self-interests which draw the voter towards one party or the other. But it is equally true that political information may flow in other channels than the informal networks of the residential neighbourhood – or the workplace.[1] Indeed, one of the most important additional channels, the mass media, can provide political information to the voter that is not linked to any social network.[2] If we broaden the search for factors which help sustain the cleavage between parties, the remarkable stability of the readership of a partisan national press must surely be included.

Ten or so national morning newspapers are available at breakfast time to the overwhelming bulk of British households.[3] In 1964 eight of them provided 92 per cent of the 18 million morning newspapers sold each day and they reached over 80 per cent of households – a higher proportion than in any other country.[4] Because of this centralization, fully established for a couple of generations, Britain has a smaller total of independent morning newspapers than any comparable nation.[5] On the other hand, the individual citizen, with at least eight different papers reaching his locality, has an unusual range of choice. One consequence of the centralization of the press is that the market tends to be divided up, each paper angling its presentation to a limited segment of the population. And since each paper has its own independent newsgathering and editorial resources, each

[1] We regard the family as a special element of the neighbourhood environment, although it is one of great importance because of the amount of political information which can circulate in the family and the strength of the affective bonds among its members. Only 14 per cent of our married respondents who had a party preference reported that their spouses definitely preferred another party.

[2] Although it is a commonplace among students of media effects that information may move from the media to the individual via a 'two-step' (or several-step) process. The 'two-step' hypothesis was first discussed in P. F. Lazarsfeld, B. Berelson and H. Gaudet, *The People's Choice*, New York, 1944, although it was treated more fully in E. Katz and P. F. Lazarsfeld, *Personal Influence*, Glencoe, Ill., 1955. See also E. Katz, 'The Two-Step Flow of Communications: an Up-to-Date Report on a Hypothesis', *Public Opinion Quarterly*, **21** (1957), 61–78.

[3] Throughout the 1960s there were in fact ten serious national dailies produced in London. But because of the specialist nature and the size of their circulation we do not deal here with the *Financial Times* (150,000) or the *Daily Worker/Morning Star* (65,000). The *Daily Sketch* was submerged into the *Daily Mail* in 1971.

[4] In 1964 there were seventeen provincial morning newspapers (in no case with a circulation of more than 130,000). There were seventy evening newspapers, with a total circulation of over eight million, which tended to be primarily local in their coverage. There were also eight Sunday morning newspapers, with a total circulation of 24 million. The circulation of newspapers per head of population is 66 per cent greater in Britain than in the United States. For morning newspapers it is three times as great.

[5] One reason for our special focus on the morning press in this chapter is that electors give it precedence over the other newspapers. While 60 per cent of our respondents claimed to have followed the campaign in their morning newspaper only 11 per cent mentioned a Sunday paper as a political source and only 6 per cent an evening news-paper.

manages to be fairly strongly differentiated from its rivals in style and in politics.

The mass circulation papers are all explicit in their partisanship, and all to some degree carry their partisanship from their editorial to their news columns. Throughout the 1960s, though seldom slavish in their party orthodoxy, the *Daily Express*, *Daily Mail*, *Daily Telegraph* and *Daily Sketch* were Conservative while the *Daily Mirror* and *Daily Herald/Sun*[1] were Labour. The 'elite' papers, *The Times* and the *Guardian*, are harder to place. In 1964 and 1966 *The Times*, in the end, gave very qualified advice to vote Conservative while the *Guardian* abandoned its traditional Liberalism to ask support for the Labour Party.

A newspaper's readers tend to be remarkably faithful to it. Most people read only one morning newspaper and go on buying it for very long periods. Morning newspaper circulations, despite vast promotion efforts, only edge up or down by, at most, a few per cent a year. In 1964 the circulation of every national daily was within 10 per cent of where it had been four years earlier, apart from the *Daily Sketch* (down 20 per cent) and the *Guardian* (up 20 per cent). Although it is a simple thing to change one's delivery order at the newsagent or pick up a different paper at the station bookstall, few people do so. Less than 4 per cent of our sample admitted to ever having switched morning newspapers. Indeed, over successive interviews only the distribution of characteristics such as age and sex showed greater stability than readership of the morning dailies.

What bearing does the partisanship of a newspaper have on the partisan preferences of its readers? It is clear, to begin with, that the partisan bias of the newspapers is reflected fairly faithfully in the biases of their readers. In every case, as Table 5.17 shows, a preponderant group of readers of the

5.17 Partisanship of Newspaper Readers, 1963

Readers' Partisanship	Conservative				Labour		Less Committed	
	Tele-graph	Sketch	Mail	Express	Mirror[a]	Herald/Sun	Times	Guardian
Conservative	78	54	48	48	18	9	60	23
Labour	9	29	28	38	66	83	20	33
Liberal	6	13	18	10	11	3	10	37
Other or none	7	4	6	4	5	5	10	7
	100%	100%	100%	100%	100%	100%	100%	100%
	(n = 111)	(n = 48)	(n = 190)	(n = 434)	(n = 445)	(n = 128)	(n = 10)	(n = 30)

[a] This figure includes *Daily Record*, the Glasgow version of the *Daily Mirror*.

[1] The *Daily Herald* was transmuted into the *Sun* on September 15, 1964.

mass circulation dailies shared the paper's traditional partisanship – overwhelmingly in the case of the *Telegraph* and the *Sun* and by a substantial margin in every other case except that of the *Guardian* (which has a long Liberal tradition). If only those who had read their paper for ten years or more were considered, the proportion of readers favouring the paper's choice of party was higher in almost every case. The proportion of Conservative-minded *Express* readers rose from 48 per cent to 52 per cent; and for the *Telegraph* from 77 per cent to 82 per cent. The proportion of Labour-inclined *Sun* readers rose from 83 per cent to 86 per cent. The two exceptions are not surprising: the veteran readers of the *Guardian* appeared unpersuaded by the paper's switch to Labour support – even more of them were Liberal. The veteran readers of the *Mirror* were not more Labour-inclined than the new young readers the paper had won in the last ten years.

The coincidence between a paper's partisanship and that of its readers is not, of course, simply ascribable to the paper's stimulus and the reader's response; it may equally be due to the opposite process. The problem of the press's partisan influence is made more difficult by the fact that readership and partisanship may both reach far back into the past. The distinctive partisan colouring of those who read the morning dailies could be taken as evidence of the press's influence only if it is clear that the choice of a newspaper preceded the choice of a party. But it is, of course, quite possible either for a paper to be chosen for its partisanship or for the choice of both paper and party to reflect the influence of a family or class milieu. In such a case, the press might play a role in conserving a party tie; it would not have created it.

These alternative possibilities supply the only plausible explanations for the way in which parents' partisanship is echoed in their children's adult choice of newspaper, as shown by Table 5.18. The reflection of early

5.18 Partisanship of Present Newspaper by Party of Childhood Family, 1963

| | | | Family was[a] | |
		Conservative	Other	Labour
Respondent	Conservative newspaper	66%	55%	35%
Now	Labour newspaper	22	36	55
Reads[b]	Other	12	9	10
		100%	100%	100%
		($n = 393$)	($n = 589$)	($n = 405$)

[a] 'Conservative' or 'Labour' homes are those in which both parents had this partisanship or one did and the other had none. 'Other' homes are those of mixed, Liberal or no partisanship.
[b] 'Conservative' or 'Labour' readers are those seeing only newspapers from one partisan group. 'Other' readers are those who see newspapers from both or neither party group.

family partisanship in newspapers taken by voters from politicized homes casts a new light on the political distinctness of those who read the morning dailies, since the correlation seen here is the work of factors that will also increase this distinctness without any need for newspapers to have influenced their readers. The correlation shown in Table 5.18 cannot result from the voter's family having influenced the paper's editors. And today's editors cannot have influenced the family in the voter's childhood. The correlation is most likely to have been produced by the family's passing on a partisanship which the child has matched by his choice of paper, or by its passing on a more general social location to which both paper and party are appropriate. If the voter's report on his family is accepted, it is clear that newspapers often profit from, rather than shape, their readers' party ties.

We should not, however, discount the press's role in conserving partisanship. When the agreement of child with parent is examined separately for those who read a paper consistent with their parent's party and those who do not, as is done in Table 5.19, we see an impressive difference in the

5.19 Party Support by Partisanship of Respondent's Family and
Respondent's Present Newspaper, 1963

		Family was[a]			
		Conservative		Labour	
		Respondent's newspaper is[b]		Respondent's newspaper is[b]	
		Conservative	Labour	Conservative	Labour
Respondent's	Conservative	79%	44%	25%	5%
Own	Labour	13	42	62	86
Party	Other[c]	8	14	13	9
		100%	100%	100%	100%
		($n = 259$)	($n = 85$)	($n = 141$)	($n = 221$)

[a] See fn. a, Table 5.18.
[b] See fn. b, Table 5.18.
[c] Includes Liberals, other parties and voters without a party.

survival of parental partisanship according to the child's current reading habits. Too simple a view ought not to be taken of these findings; once again the adult may have kept or changed his partisan reading habits to accord with his evolving partisan beliefs or his changed social conditions. Nonetheless, it is difficult to think that the conserving and reinforcing effect of the partisan press has nothing to do with these differences.

What is more, the formative role of the press may be somewhat larger in the case of voters whose political legacy from their family was mixed or relatively weak. Table 5.20 divides such people by whether they now read a Conservative or Labour newspaper. The cleavage in the current partisanship of these two groups is at least suggestive of the influence of the press in forming or sustaining a party tie.

5.20 Party Support by Partisanship of Newspaper Among Persons from Other than Conservative and Labour Families, 1963

		Partisanship of Newspaper[a]	
		Conservative	Labour
Respondent's Own Partisanship	Conservative	48%	14%
	Labour	28	66
	Other[b]	24	20
		100% (n = 321)	100% (n = 231)

[a] 'Conservative' or 'Labour' readers are those who see no morning paper except one or more from their own partisan group.
[b] Includes Liberals, other parties and voters without a party.

The national press need not be seen solely as conserving party ties. In periods of great disenchantment with a government its natural supporters among the national papers may help to feed the public's discontent. This was undoubtedly true for the Labour Party and the *Daily Mirror* in the later sixties. We set out evidence in our first edition of a similar relationship between the Macmillan Government and the Conservative press in the 1963–4 period.[1] Moreover, television, without the enduring editorial alignments of the press, is a much more variable influence. We shall indeed argue in Chapter 9 that television's rising importance helps to account for the increasing volatility of the electorate in the period in which television has successfully challenged the primacy of the printed media.

But our evidence nonetheless suggests that the national press, faithfully read by millions of partisans each morning, has helped conserve the established party alignments. If a politically more neutral or variable medium such as television had held sway for most of this century, the dominant party cleavage might not have been so deep or lasting. As it is, this cleavage has been remarkably durable, not only by class but also by region and more local areas, as we shall now see.

[1] See pp. 234–44 of the first edition.

6 The Geography of Party Support

THE pre-eminence of class in electoral alignments is not a universal fact of modern politics. There are many countries and party systems where race, or religion, or region, or other lines of potential cleavage are more important than class in defining electoral support. We can indeed imagine a very different electoral history for modern Britain. The Irish question in particular might have influenced the pattern of party politics even more radically than it did. This issue, which so clearly cut across class lines, led to a drastic realignment of parties in the 1880s, with Joseph Chamberlain leading a large body of the industrial working class over to the Conservatives. To this day it leaves a major mark on the politics of Clydeside and Merseyside. It is not beyond possibility that if Europe had escaped a general war in August 1914 the United Kingdom would have slipped into civil war over the position of Ulster under Dublin Home Rule. The resulting conflict might have left scars on the British body politic comparable to those imposed on the United States for a hundred years by its own civil war. In such a situation the place of class would have been very different.

Certainly there are variations in British electoral behaviour which cannot be attributed to class in any simple way. Some of these variations reflect traditions and interests which reach far into the past, well before the present manifestations of the class or party system, and some reflect current particularities, such as the differing economic make-up of different parts of the country. This chapter is concerned with such variations. The discussion will not lead us away from class so much as towards an understanding of additional ways in which social structure is reflected in electoral behaviour.

National Uniformity and Regional Variations

Behind a good deal of contemporary comment on British electoral behaviour lies an exceedingly simple image of political alignment and change. It is often assumed that enduring allegiance to party is based on class and that changeability is a response to the transient issues of national politics. In its crudest form this image is a simple model with two factors, the first factor, class, explaining the continuities of electoral support and the second factor, the national issues of the moment, explaining the short-term fluctuations of party strength which are seen in all parts of the country. The model envisages two quite different kinds of homogeneity of electoral behaviour between areas. On the one hand, the class basis of enduring allegiance is everywhere the same; on the other hand, electoral change, being a response to common national issues, is also everywhere the same.

Such a model has at least the virtue of highlighting the contrasting ways in which different parts of the country actually behave. Of course, the generally uniform pattern of swings between the parties has always been broken by regional and local variations; we shall moreover argue that even very uniform swings may conceal a paradoxical lack of uniformity. But, by any measure, swing is far more uniform across the regions than is class support for the parties. Any idea that class provides a universal ground for party allegiance is difficult to reconcile with the extraordinarily uneven spread of party support between regions, continuing decade after decade. These differences are sometimes neglected because of the attention focused on the impressive evenness of swing.[1] But the scale and endurance of the

---

[1] The relative uniformity of British swings emerges when we look at comparable American figures. The standard deviation of swings from the national average is almost three times as great in the United States as in Britain.

	Britain				United States		
Year	Seats Included	Mean Swing	Standard Deviation of swing	Year	Seats Included	Mean Swing	Standard Deviation of swing
1950–51	224	0·7	1·4	1952–54	318	4·3	5·2
1951–55	349	1·8	1·4	1954–56	333	2·2	5·1
1955–59	455	1·1	2·2	1956–58	324	6·9	5·5
1959–64	370	3·5	2·4	1958–60	227	2·7	5·6
1964–66	429	3·2	1·7				
1966–70	468	4·4	2·1				
1970–74	175	0·9	2·9				

The constituencies included in this table are those whose boundaries were not significantly altered and whose patterns of major party candidature were the same at both elections.

The congressional districts included in this table are those which had major party candidates at both elections.

basic regional differences can be shown by comparing the results in two evenly balanced elections fifteen years apart. Figure 6.1 shows the relative strength of the two main parties in 1955 and 1970 in 26 sub-regions of the country.

Two points stand out from this figure. First, the electoral tides that swept over the nation made few sharp changes in the ordering of the regions. The lines remain broadly parallel, although Conservative strength did decline a bit in all the regions north of the line from the Mersey to the Humber while it increased in all regions to the south of it, with Scotland moving most clearly towards Labour and East Anglia most clearly in the other direction. But second, and more important for our present argument, are the wide, enduring disparities between regions. The extreme contrast is between Wales where in 1970 as in 1955 Labour was more than 20 per cent ahead of the Conservatives, and South East England where the Conservatives continued almost 20 per cent ahead of Labour.[1]

Such contrasts are a challenge to any simple class explanation of party allegiance, although in part they merely reflect differences in the class composition of regions. The social classes are not evenly distributed over the country, and some of the regional differences of party support may be due simply to this uneven distribution of class make-up between different regions. Variation of this sort is evident in our own samples from the North of England and from the South East. As shown by Table 6.2 on page 124, the ratio of working class to middle class was roughly two to one in the North but less than three to two in London and the South East, whether class is measured by occupational grade or class self-image. But this difference of class composition does not fully explain the difference of party allegiance between our Northern and South Eastern samples. In 1970 Labour's share of the support given to the two main parties was 9 percentage points higher in the North than it was in London and the South East, and the working class proportion of the population was 8 or 9 percentage points higher in the North than in the South East, as we see

---

For an extended discussion of this difference between the two countries see D. E. Stokes, 'Parties and the Nationalization of Electoral Forces', in W. N. Chambers and W. D. Burnham, eds., *The American Party Systems*, New York, 1968, pp. 182–202.

[1] Of course, in one important respect we have exaggerated the political homogeneity of the United Kingdom in this chart and throughout the book. As a matter of research strategy we confined our sampling to the 618 constituencies of England, Scotland and Wales, excluding twelve seats in Northern Ireland; these are therefore omitted from Figure 6.1 as well. But we recognize that by so doing we have excluded the most outstanding element of diversity within the nation.

6.1 Regional Differences in Conservative Percentage Lead over Labour in 1955 and 1970

1955

Conservative Lead   Labour Lead

20% — Rest of Scotland
S.E. England
Highlands
S.W. England
Merseyside
10% — Outer London
Rest of N.W.
E. Anglia
S.E.Lancs.
Rest of W.Midlands
0% — Forth
West Midlands
Clydeside
E.Midlands
10% — Yorks
Inner London
N. England
Rest of Yorks
Rural Wales
20%
30%
40% — Industrial Wales

1970

Labour Lead   Conservative Lead

S.E. England — 20%
S.W. England
Rest of Scotland
E.Anglia
Outer London — 10%
Rest of West Midlands
W.Midlands
Highlands
Rest of N.W.
S.E.Lancs — 0%
Yorks
Merseyside
E.Midlands
Rural Wales — 10%
Inner London
Rest of Yorks
Forth
N.England
Clydeside — 20%
— 30%
Industrial Wales
— 40%

6.2 Class Composition of North and South East England, 1970[a]

	North	London and South East
Occupational Grades		
I–IV	35%	43%
V–VI	65	57
	100%	100%
Class Self-Image		
Middle	33%	42%
Working	67	58
	100%	100%

[a] In Tables 6.2 and 6.3 we have defined the North as including Cheshire, Cumberland, Durham, Lancashire, Northumberland, Westmorland and Yorkshire; and London and the South East as including Berkshire, Buckinghamshire, Dorset, Essex, Hampshire, Hertfordshire, Isle of Wight, Kent, London, Surrey and Sussex.

in Table 6.2. But this arithmetic would be enough to explain the party difference between regions only if all working class voters supported Labour and all middle class voters supported the Conservatives.

The part of the political difference between regions that cannot be explained in terms of class composition must be reflected in differences of party support by class between regions. The different rates at which the middle and working class give their support to the parties in the North and South East is shown in Table 6.3. In the North the proportion of the middle

6.3 Party Support by Class Self-Image in the North and South East, 1970[a]

		North of England				South East	
		Class Self-Image				Class Self-Image	
		Middle	Working			Middle	Working
Partisan Self-Image	Con.	72%	**b** 29%		Con.	71%	**b** 40%
	Lab.	**c** 28%	71%	Partisan Self-Image	Lab.	**c** 29%	60%
		100%	100%			100%	100%
		b − c = 1%				b − c = 11%	

[a] For definitions of regions see footnote to Table 6.2.

class supporting the Conservatives is nearly the same as the proportion of the working class supporting Labour. But in the South East the Conservatives' strength in the middle class exceeds Labour's strength in the working class by 11 percentage points as reflected by our measure of cross-support. Plainly the electoral differences between these large areas involve more than the simplest facts of their class composition. Indeed, when we examine the relative contribution of both kinds of differences we find that the overall difference of party strength between the North and South East is due more to variations of party support by class than it is to the differing class makeup of the regions.[1]

[1] To make clear the basis of this comparison let us denote by P the proportion Labour among middle class major-party supporters in the South East (hence $1 - P$ is the proportion Conservative among such electors in this region), by Q the proportion Labour among working class electors in the South East (hence $1 - Q$ is the proportion Conservative among working class electors in this region), by W the proportion working class among electors supporting one of the two main parties in the South East (hence $1 - W$ is the proportion middle class among major-party supporters in the South East), by ΔP the difference between P and the proportion Labour among middle class electors in the North, by ΔQ the difference between Q and the proportion Labour among working class electors in the North, and by ΔW the difference between W and the proportion working class among major-party supporters in the North. It follows from these definitions that Labour's proportion of major-party supporters in the South East is

$$\text{Lab (S.E.)} = P(1 - W) + QW$$

and in the North is

$$\text{Lab (N)} = (P + \Delta P)(1 - W - \Delta W) + (Q + \Delta Q)(W + \Delta W)$$

It is easily shown that the overall difference of Labour's proportion of major-party support in the two regions can be represented as a linear combination

$$\text{Lab (N)} - \text{Lab (S.E.)} = \underbrace{\Delta W(Q - P)}_{\substack{\text{class} \\ \text{composition} \\ \text{effect}}} + \underbrace{(\Delta Q - \Delta P)W + \Delta P}_{\substack{\text{class} \\ \text{support} \\ \text{effect}}} + \underbrace{(\Delta Q - \Delta P)\Delta W}_{\substack{\text{interaction} \\ \text{effect}}}$$

whose components can be associated with differences of class composition and of the pattern of party support by class by seeing how each of the components depends on the values of ΔP, ΔQ and ΔW. The left-hand component is seen to involve only ΔW and may therefore be interpreted as the portion of Labour's greater strength in the North which is due to the difference of class composition between North and South East. Of course the value of this component depends also on P and Q, but not on the extent to which P and Q differ from the corresponding rates of party support in the North. The middle component is seen to involve only ΔP and ΔQ and may therefore be interpreted as the portion of Labour's greater strength in the North which is due to differences in the pattern of party support by class between the two regions. The right-hand component is seen to involve both types of differences between the regions and may therefore be regarded as an 'interaction' term. Since ΔP and ΔQ are of roughly equal magnitude, however, their difference almost vanishes and this interaction term is in this case

The size of our sample precluded us from pursuing this analysis to smaller sub-regions of the country. For this purpose we aggregated a great many nationwide samples interviewed by National Opinion Polls over the 1963–66 period. By this means we were able to assemble enough cases to speak with some confidence about the varying relation of class to party in eleven regions into which the country has often been divided for statistical purposes. We set out in Table 6.4 the results of this detailed regional analysis.

6.4 Regional Patterns of Party Support by Social Class, 1963–6

South and Midlands

West Midlands	All	AB	C1	C2	DE
Con	43·3	77·7	61·5	36·1	32·6
Lab	49·7	13·8	29·6	57·1	61·4
Lib	6·9	8·0	8·8	6·7	5·9
Other	0·1	0·5	0·1	0·1	0·1
	100%	100%	100%	100%	100%
n =	10,611	914	2,007	5,061	2,629
	100%	8·6	18·9	47·7	24·8

East Midlands	All	AB	C1	C2	DE
Con	40·4	83·2	60·4	33·5	28·7
Lab	51·9	8·9	30·3	59·0	64·3
Lib	7·6	7·7	9·0	7·5	6·9
Other	0·1	0·2	0·3	—	0·1
	100%	100%	100%	100%	100%
n =	8,529	560	1,631	3,838	2,500
	100%	6·6	19·1	45·0	29·3

South Central	All	AB	C1	C2	DE
Con	50·1	78·3	62·2	42·5	36·6
Lab	39·5	10·5	25·3	46·8	55·8
Lib	10·3	10·9	12·5	10·6	7·3
Other	0·1	0·3	—	0·1	0·3
	100%	100%	100%	100%	100%
n =	6,284	779	1,459	2,495	1,551
	100%	12·4	23·2	39·7	24·7

East Anglia	All	AB	C1	C2	DE
Con	44·2	75·1	59·1	35·1	28·9
Lab	44·4	13·0	27·2	53·9	61·5
Lib	11·2	11·7	13·5	10·7	9·6
Other	0·2	0·2	0·2	0·3	—
	100%	100%	100%	100%	100%
n =	8,603	1,144	1,984	3,095	2,380
	100%	13·3	23·0	36·0	27·7

South-West	All	AB	C1	C2	DE
Con	47·0	77·4	63·8	38·2	28·2
Lab	38·2	9·9	21·6	46·9	56·1
Lib	14·6	12·6	14·5	14·6	15·6
Other	0·2	0·1	0·1	0·3	0·1
	100%	100%	100%	100%	100%
n =	8,738	1,141	2,115	3,315	2,167
	100%	13·1	24·2	37·9	24·8

London and South-East	All	AB	C1	C2	DE
Con	45·1	74·1	58·5	33·6	28·5
Lab	44·1	13·0	28·8	56·0	63·8
Lib	10·6	12·7	12·5	10·1	7·4
Other	0·2	0·2	0·2	0·3	0·3
	100%	100%	100%	100%	100%
n =	20,939	3,115	5,609	7,488	4,727
	100%	14·9	26·8	35·8	22·5

negligible. Indeed, since ΔP and ΔQ tend to vary together, we have found this to be true in most applications we have made of this method, and we have been able to decompose an overall political difference between regions into a term that reflects the difference of class composition and a term that reflects variations of the pattern of class support. In the case of our comparison of the North and South East, an overall difference of 8·9 per cent decomposes into 2·3 per cent due to differences of class composition. 5·7 per cent due to differences of class support, and 0·9 per cent due to the interaction of the two.

6.4 Regional Patterns of Party Support by Social Class (continued)

Scotland, Wales and North of England

Scotland	All	AB	C1	C2	DE
Con	40·7	79·8	61·6	30·5	28·9
Lab	50·8	10·8	29·4	60·6	63·6
Lib	6·0	7·2	6·7	5·7	5·3
Other	2·5	2·2	2·3	3·2	2·2
	100%	100%	100%	100%	100%
$n =$	12,803	1,354	2,329	3,901	5,219
	100%	10·6	18·2	30·5	40·7

North East	All	AB	C1	C2	DE
Con	35·0	72·7	60·6	26·5	25·2
Lab	59·4	18·6	31·0	69·2	69·5
Lib	5·5	8·5	8·2	4·2	5·2
Other	0·1	0·2	0·2	0·1	0·1
	100%	100%	100%	100%	100%
$n =$	8,385	590	1,392	3,758	2,645
	100%	7·0	16·6	44·8	31·6

Lancashire and Cheshire	All	AB	C1	C2	DE
Con	41·1	74·1	57·3	34·6	29·6
Lab	50·1	14·8	30·6	57·3	63·2
Lib	8·5	10·8	11·9	7·7	6·9
Other	0·3	0·3	0·2	0·4	0·2
	100%	100%	100%	100%	100%
$n =$	18,932	1,853	3,584	7,186	6,309
	100%	9·8	18·9	38·0	33·3

Yorkshire	All	AB	C1	C2	DE
Con	38·6	78·9	56·9	28·0	26·3
Lab	52·0	10·0	30·7	63·6	65·9
Lib	9·2	11·0	12·2	8·3	7·7
Other	0·2	0·1	0·2	0·1	0·1
	100%	100%	100%	100%	100%
$n =$	9,159	966	1,814	3,936	2,443
	100%	10·5	19·8	43·0	26·7

Wales	All	AB	C1	C2	DE
Con	22·2	58·0	41·9	15·2	13·5
Lab	71·7	30·8	46·0	79·9	82·9
Lib	5·0	9·5	10·1	4·0	2·9
Other	1·1	1·7	2·0	0·9	0·7
	100%	100%	100%	100%	100%
$n =$	7,565	715	1,278	3,126	2,446
	100%	9·5	16·9	41·3	32·3

Source: National Opinion Polls

National Opinion Polls allowed us access to all the data on voting intention, social grade, age, sex and marital status, union membership and certain other items collected by them between October 1963 and December 1966. This cumulatively amounted to a probability sample of 120,000 interviews. We have drawn on this vast body of data in our analyses of age-cohorts and of union voting, as well as in the regional analysis presented here. N.O.P. used the Registrar General's (Old) Standard Regions in classifying respondents from these surveys. They also used the normal market research coding of social grade based on occupation and interviewers' assessment. For these reasons it is not possible to match their findings comprehensively with our own.

The uniformity in the relationship of class and party is far greater across the regions of Britain than it is in many countries. Yet Table 6.4 shows substantial variation both of class composition and class support for the parties in these eleven regions. The distributions of social grade appearing at the foot of each table show how much the social composition of regions varies. In London and the South East 41·7 per cent had non-manual occupations (A, B or C1). In Wales the proportion was only 26·4 per cent; in the North East only 23·6 per cent. But the political differences between regions involve also marked variations of party support by class. In the South Central region 42·5 per cent of skilled manual workers (C2) gave their support to the Conservatives; in Wales 15·2 per cent did so. Labour's share of the lower white collar group (C1) ranged from 21·6 per cent in the South West to 46·0 per cent in Wales.

We may indeed see how much more than simple differences of class composition is involved in the partisan differences of regions by grouping these data roughly into the 'two nations', the depressed North and the expanding South, that gave rise to so much political comment in the early 1960s. The figures of Table 6.5, which arrange the regions into these two broad groupings, reveal marked differences of party strength: Labour's proportion of the support for the two leading parties was on the average 10 per cent higher in the massed samples of Scotland, the North East, Lancashire and Cheshire, Yorkshire and Wales than it was in the samples of the West and East Midlands, the South Central region, East Anglia, the South West, and London and the South East.

Some part of this difference is due to the varied class composition of these 'two nations'. Among those supporting the two main parties, the working class proportion voting Labour was 7·5 percentage points higher in the North and Wales than it was in the Midlands and South. But this difference would not by itself account for the partisan difference separating these two halves of the country even if every manual worker were Labour and every non-manual worker Conservative, which was by no means the case. The political cleavage between the two nations was also due to their differing patterns of party allegiance within the classes, as Table 6.5 makes clear. In the North of England, Scotland and Wales Labour's strength among working class electors in this period was as high as the Conservatives' strength among middle class electors; the level of 'cross-support' in the two class groupings was virtually identical. But in the Midlands and South, Labour's share of the working class vote was decidedly less than the Conservatives' share of the middle class vote; the balance of cross-support was 11·7 per cent in the Conservatives' favour.

We can in fact estimate what proportion of the difference in behaviour between the two areas is the result of basic differences in the way the classes allocated their support and what proportion is the result simply of differences in the relative size of the classes. Such an analysis shows that the first kind of difference is more than twice as important as the second; more than

6.5 Party Support by Class in Two Regional Groupings, 1963–6[a]

North of England, Scotland and Wales				South and Midlands		
	Middle Class	Working Class			Middle Class	Working Class
Conservative	70·3%	[b] 29·5%		Conservative	74·7%	[b] 37·0%
Labour	[c] 29·7	70·5		Labour	[c] 25·3	63·0
	100·0%	100·0%			100·0%	100·0%
	b − c = −0·2%				b − c = 11·7%	

[a] This table is formed by recombining the National Opinion Polls data given by Table 6.4. Liberal and 'other' preferences have been excluded. 'Middle class' is formed of occupational grades A, B and C1, 'working class' of occupational grades C2, D and E.

two thirds of the overall difference of 9·3 percentage points in Labour's strength in the two areas was due to the contrasting patterns of party support within class while less than a third was due to the simple difference of the relative size of the classes.[1] The key to the two nations politically lies largely in factors that have produced the contrast of party strength within classes.

The quest for such factors would cover a very broad terrain of social and political history. Certainly the scale and type of industrialization and the experience of economic distress – in the 1960s, the interwar period, and before – have been very different in the two nations. And there are historical patterns of alienation from established authority in the peripheral regions, most notably in the case of Wales. In one respect, however, we should see class as an explanatory factor in a slightly more complicated way than is involved in simple differences of class composition.

A good deal of empirical support can be found for the principle that once a partisan tendency becomes dominant in a local area processes of opinion formation will draw additional support to the party that is dominant. If

[1] The basis of these claculations is set out in the footnote to p. 125 above. The overall difference of 9·3 per cent in Labour's proportion of support for the two main parties in North and South divides into a component of 2·8 per cent representing the 'class composition' effect, a component of 6·4 per cent representing the 'class support' effect, and a component of 0·1 per cent representing the 'interaction' effect (which is once again altogether negligible).

this is true, perceptions of class interest may impart to an area a political tendency that is exaggerated still further by the processes that form and sustain a local political culture, thereby altering the pattern of party support within classes. The effects of a local political environment are plainly relevant to the regional variations we have examined, as well as being of interest in their own right.

The Influence of a Local Political Environment

The tendency of local areas to become homogeneous in their political opinions has attracted the attention of many observers and been described in many ways.[1] We may see evidence of this tendency in Britain by examining two contrasting types of local areas, each of which is likely to have a strong social and political ethos. On the one hand, the mining areas are traditionally seen as the archetypal strongholds of solidary working class support for Labour. On the other, the seaside resorts, even more than the suburbs, seem to stand out as communities permeated by the Conservatism of the middle class. We had several areas of each kind in our sample, and we have examined our samples of each for evidence of the influence of the local political environment.

These two kinds of areas differ immensely in their class composition. Table 6.6 shows that only 23 per cent of our sample in mining seats called themselves middle class and only 19 per cent performed occupational tasks within our categories I–IV. But the comparable proportions of our sample in the resort areas were 51 and 55 per cent. These facts of class composition would be enough to assure a marked divergence of party support in the

---

[1] The earliest statement of this phenomenon is Herbert Tingsten's enunciation of the 'theory of the centre of political gravity'. See his *Political Behaviour*, London, 1937. Several American authors have used the term 'breakage effect' to describe the tendency of a locally dominant party to get more support than it might expect to receive on the basis of class or other factors, on the analogy of the way those who organize horse-race betting keep the odd pennies when winnings are rounded off. See B. R. Berelson, P. F. Lazarsfeld and W. N. McPhee, *Voting*, Chicago, 1954, pp. 98–101; P. Cutright and P. Rossi, 'Grassroots Politics and the Vote', *American Sociological Review*, **23** (1958), 171–9, and D. Katz and S. J. Eldersveld, 'The Impact of Local Party Activity Upon the Electorate', *Public Opinion Quarterly*, **25** (1961), 1–24. For comparable evidence in Britain see F. M. Martin in 'Social Status and Electoral Choice in Two Constituencies', *British Journal of Sociology*, **2** (1952), 231–41, and F. M. Bealey, J. Blondel and W. McCann, *Constituency Politics*, London, 1965, pp. 154–65.

6.6 Class Composition of Mining and Resort Areas 1970

	Mining	Resorts
Occupational Grade		
Grades I–IV	19%	55%
Grades V–VI	81	45
	100%	100%
Class Self-Image		
Middle Class	23%	51%
Working Class	77	49
	100%	100%

two kinds of areas. But the much more spectacular difference has to do with the behaviour of the classes, as Table 6.7 shows. The Conservatives actually outran Labour among the working class of resort areas. In fact,

6.7 Partisan Self-Image by Class in Mining Seats and Resorts, 1970

Mining Seats

	Class Self-Image	
	Middle Class	Working Class
Conservative	50%	b 21%
Labour	c 50	79
	100%	100%
	b − c = −29%	

Resorts

	Class Self-Image	
	Middle Class	Working Class
Conservative	80%	b 52%
Labour	c 20	48
	100%	100%
	b − c = +32%	

if we were to take account of Liberal support as well, Labour would be found to have attracted the support of only a third of the working class in the seaside resorts.[1] The Conservative advantage in the cross-support

[1] We are indeed reminded of the ancient story still told in Labour circles of the Bournemouth elector who entered the polling station and timidly enquired where servants voted for Brigadier Page-Croft.

proportions was 32 per cent. In the mining seats, however, the picture is almost reversed. The Labour Party received fully 50 per cent of the middle class vote and lost only a fifth of the vote of the working class. Indeed, the balance of cross-support in the mining areas was 29 per cent in favour of Labour. The difference of this balance in the two types of areas is as large as any we have seen.

But if we take areas that have less self-evident single occupational characteristics than mining areas and resorts, we find an equally spectacular difference. The special census of 1966 presented its findings on a constituency basis and it is possible to use their official data to rank constituencies from the most to the least in terms of many basic census characteristics, for example in terms of the proportion of council tenants, or Commonwealth-born, or agricultural workers, or, more relevant to our purpose, manual workers.[1] If we consider those of our respondents living in constituencies which were among the 10 per cent with the lowest proportion of manual workers and the 10 per cent with the highest, we can discover whether the same difference in political pattern is to be observed.

As Table 6.8 shows, the contrast is enormous. A voter who sees himself

6.8 Partisan Self-Image by Class in Most Manual and Most Non-Manual Seats, 1970

		Most Manual 10% of Seats		Most Non-Manual 10% of Seats	
		Class Self-Image		Class Self-Image	
		Middle Class	Working Class	Middle Class	Working Class
Partisan Self-Image	Con.	46	**b** 21	78	**b** 50
	Lab.	**c** 54	79	**c** 22	50
		100%	100%	100%	100%
		b − c = −33%		b − c = +28%	

[1] See *1966 Census and Parliamentary Tables*, H.M.S.O., 1969. For constituency percentages of the more significant categories see *The British General Election of 1970*, pp. 358–82.

as working class is as likely to be Conservative as Labour if he lives in a very middle class constituency. In a very working class constituency the odds are 4 to 1 that he will be Labour. Equally, the man who feels middle class is more likely than not to be Labour if he lives in a very working class constituency while in a very middle class constituency it is 4 to 1 that he will be Conservative.

These differences ought not to be assigned too readily to any single explanatory principle. Several processes can have helped to exaggerate a partisan tendency that had already been imported to the middle and working class areas by perceptions of class interest. Some writers have argued that a local electorate will perceive and conform to local political norms.[1] Others have suggested that this tendency reflects the persuasive influences of informal contacts on the shop floor, in the public house and other face to face groups of the elector's world.[2] These processes will draw those who hold a minority opinion towards the view that is dominant in their local milieu, exaggerating the strength of a leading party and altering the pattern of party support by class. We shall shortly offer evidence of these persuasive effects when we consider the remarkable uniformity of partisan change throughout widely differing constituencies.

Evidence that these processes are much more extensively at work emerged when we divided our cumulated file of National Opinion Polls into distinct constituencies. The 120,000 interviews taken by the N.O.P. organization over the period from 1963 to 1966 were conducted in 184 constituencies, giving an average of more than 600 respondents in each, a sample that is quite large enough for reliable estimates to be formed of the class composition of each constituency and of the Conservative and Labour proportions within each of the classes. Figure 6.9 on the next page exhibits, first, the relationship between the proportion that the middle class constituted in each constituency and the proportion Conservative among middle class voters who supported one of the two main parties in each constituency. It can be seen at once that the constituencies of higher middle class concentration tended to have a higher level of Conservative support within the middle class. This relationship is not a linear one; the underlying processes of opinion formation do not aggregate in this simplest way. We have drawn on

[1] A Yorkshire miner's daughter among our respondents explained her vote simply: 'We lived in a Labour district.'
[2] Excellent reviews of alternative explanations of this phenomenon are given in R. Putnam, 'Political Attitudes and the Local Community', *American Political Science Review*, **50** (1966), 640–54, and K. R. Cox, 'The Voting Decision in a Spatial Context', in R. J. Chorley and P. Haggett, eds., *Progress in Geography*, London, 1969.

6.9 Conservative Proportion of Middle Class Support for Two Main Parties by Proportion of Constituency That is Middle Class^a

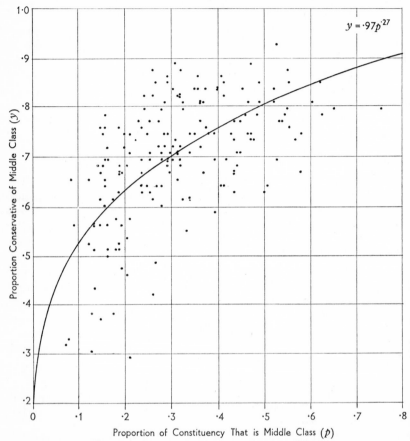

^{a} This figure is based on data from 184 constituencies in which the National Opinion Polls interviewed more than 120,000 respondents from 1963 to 1966. The analysis shown here is limited to electors who supported the Conservatives or Labour. 'Middle class' is defined as occupational grades A, B or C1.

the figure a curve which seems to fit the observed relationship well, although it is of course true that there are substantial variations about such a curve.[1]

[1] We may regard some part of the scatter about a best-fitting curve as the inevitable consequence of basing our estimates on samples. That is, if the proportion Conservative in the middle class were a strict mathematical function of the proportion middle class in the constituency as a whole, some blur would be introduced into their observed relationship in our sample data because of the error inherent in estimating these proportions from samples even as large as those used.

Figure 6.10 exhibits a similar link between the proportion that the working class constituted of each constituency and the proportion Labour among working class voters who supported one of the two main parties within each. The pattern disclosed by the figure is the mirror image of that shown by Figure 6.9, with the constituencies of higher working class concentration tending to have a higher level of Labour support within the working class. It is important to realize that the similarity of these relationships is not in any way logically necessary or foreordained. Their likeness is an empirical fact, one that shows much about how similar

6.10 Labour Proportion of Working Class Support for Two Main Parties by Proportion of Constituency That is Working Class[a]

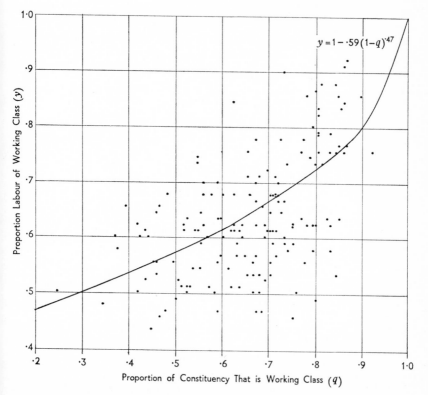

$$y = 1 - \cdot59(1-q)^{\cdot47}$$

Proportion Labour of Working Class (y)

Proportion of Constituency That is Working Class (q)

[a] This figure is based on data from 184 constituencies in which the National Opinion Polls interviewed more than 120,000 respondents from 1963 to 1966. The analysis shown here is limited to electors who supported the Conservatives or Labour. 'Working class' is defined as occupational grades C2, D and E.

are the processes of opinion formation that go on within local areas in which the relative proportions of working and middle class differ. These patterns together give impressive evidence of the tendency towards the further dominance of a party view where it is already held by a substantial majority.

Influence of this sort helps to account for the variations of class voting that are found across the regions of the country, since these regional variations may reflect the summing up of numberless face to face contacts across the local areas that comprise the different regions. If this is true, the role of class composition in regional variations may be larger than is at first apparent. We have seen that if the chances of a middle or working class elector supporting a given party were the same in all regions, differences between regions in the relative proportions of middle and working class could explain only a small part of regional variation of party strength. But differences of class composition may have a subtler and less direct influence on party strength via the processes of opinion formation in the local environment. Evidence consistent with such a view is given by Figure 6.11.

6.11 Conservative Proportion of Middle Class Vote by Proportion of Region Middle Class in Nine Regions of England[a]

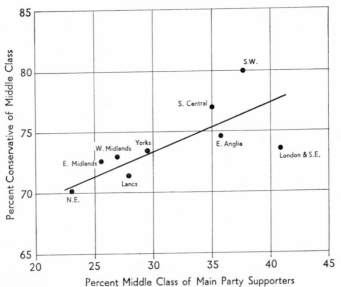

[a] This figure is based on the massed N.O.P. samples of 1963–6. The analysis shown here is limited to electors who support the Conservatives or Labour. 'Middle class' is defined as occupational grades A, B or C1.

We have plotted on this figure's horizontal dimension the proportion that middle class electors comprise of those who support one of the two main parties in each of the nine regions of England for which we have detailed data from the National Opinion Polls. And we have plotted on the vertical dimension the proportion of these middle class electors in each region who are Conservative. The chart shows a clear tendency for the Conservatives' share of the middle class vote to be greater where the concentration of the middle class is on average greater. A similar tendency is found for Labour's share of the working class vote to be higher in regions where the average concentration of the working class is greater.[1]

But no one would suggest that all regional differences have their roots, directly or indirectly, in class. The degree of scatter to the plotted points of Figure 6.10 must reflect the limits of class as a sole explanation of enduring regional differences of party strength. Part of the remaining variation is a legacy of the religious alignment; there is also a tendency for Conservative strength to be less in regions where the concentration of non-conformists is greater. If we had included a point for Wales in Figure 6.11 it would have exaggerated the trend found in the regions of England. Wales had a lower proportion of middle class electors than any other region save the North East. But the Conservatives' share of middle class support in Wales was 15 percentage points lower than in any other region of Britain.[2]

Liberals and Nationalists

An added exception to national uniformity is to be seen in the regional pattern of the successes of third and fourth parties. The Liberals have survived as a parliamentary and an electoral force and staged notable rallies in the 1960s and 1970s. The Welsh and Scottish Nationalists also made a major impact.

The Liberals, as we shall show in the next chapter, still enjoyed a residue of goodwill throughout the country that dated back to their days of power. Nationally and within each region their appeal in terms of class was very evenly spread, as Table 6.4 indicated, but although a Liberal candidate could muster significant support almost anywhere, the party's most enduring electoral strength had been highly localized. The six constituencies in

---

[1] The product moment correlation associated with the regional plot given by Figure 6.11 is +0·74.

[2] For another line of approach to these problems see I. Crewe and C. Payne, 'Analysing the Census Data', in *The British General Election of 1970*, pp. 416–36.

which they had never failed to get first or second place, like the six constituencies which they won in 1970, were all in the remoter parts of Scotland,
Wales or South West England; the party had also drawn substantial support in resorts and comfortable suburban areas where, as we saw, the Labour Party finds it harder to muster its 'natural' working class support.[1]

It is clear that in the 1960s at least the Liberals drew support relatively
evenly from the other two parties, as Table 6.12 shows. It is also clear that

6.12 Preference of Liberals between Conservative and Labour, 1964–70[a]

	1964		1966		1970	
	Con.	Lab.	Con.	Lab.	Con.	Lab.
Liberals without a Liberal candidate voted	54	46	43	57	44	56
Liberals, if deprived of a Liberal candidate, would have voted	59	41	40	60	56	44

[a] This table is confined to those Liberals who expressed a preference between Conservative and Labour.

there was a class difference in these Liberal second preferences. As Table
6.13 shows, in default of a candidate of their own, Liberals had a tendency
to side with the party of their class.

6.13 Preference of Liberals between Conservative and
Labour by Class

		1964		1966		1970	
		Con.	Lab.	Con.	Lab.	Con.	Lab.
Social Grade	I–IV	65	35	47	53	64	36
Social Grade	V–VI	50	50	40	60	48	52

The Welsh and Scottish Nationalist parties, although long established,
had on the whole attracted negligible support before the mid-1960s. But
the success of Plaid Cymru in the Carmarthen by-election in 1966 and of
the Scottish National Party in Hamilton in 1967 heralded a brief phase
when the Nationalists in both countries could count on up to a third of the
vote in by-elections and opinion polls. This sudden upsurge of support, like
that experienced by the Liberals in 1962 after the Orpington by-election,

[1] However, in 1972–3 the Liberals began to achieve some notable by-election and local
election successes in quite new areas; and in the February 1974 election made heavy in-
roads in a much more geographically dispersed set of Conservative seats, although the
fourteen constituencies in which they elected a Liberal member were almost all traditional strongholds.

showed that the monopoly of the two major parties was less absolute than had been supposed. The February 1974 elections showed a major Scottish Nationalist advance. Their vote doubled, and they won seven seats. Although most of the seats were at the expense of the Conservatives, the Nationalists plainly drew votes from each of the main parties. But of course the Nationalist parties sprang from a more limited base than the Liberals. Of the 630 constituencies returning members to the House of Commons, only 71 are in Scotland and only 36 are in Wales.

One suggested explanation for the Nationalist upsurge lies in the growing remoteness of, and alienation from, centralized London government in an increasingly complex and bureaucratic world. In 1969 and 1970 we tried to test this by putting to our sample the question: 'Some people think that government is too much centralized in London. Others are quite content with things as they are. What do you think?' In both years 36 per cent said that government was too centralized. But as might be expected the proportion varied substantially between different parts of the country. It is, however, noteworthy that, as Table 6.14 shows, alienation

6.14 Regional Views on Centralization of Government

	London and S.E.	Midlands	South West	Wales	North	Scotland
Content	72%	65%	57%	55%	52%	26%
Too centralized	21	29	37	38	43	65
Don't know	7	6	6	7	5	9
	100%	100%	100%	100%	100%	100%

from London was stronger in the North of England (where there was no Nationalist issue) than in Wales. It is also noteworthy that even in Scotland, on the heels of a great wave of nationalism, 26 per cent of people were content with the extent to which they were governed from London, although the table also demonstrates the degree of Scottish estrangement from London. Those who felt that government was too centralized were drawn fairly proportionately from each class and from those who were very interested in politics and those who were not.

Therefore regional differences in Liberal and Nationalist support accompany the marked and durable variations in the strength of the two main parties. Because these variations in Conservative and Labour support have survived in the face of substantial swings of party strength, the hold of a party that is dominant within a local area must be visible in *changes* of preference as well as in the static relationships we have examined thus far. The stronger party cannot enjoy a bonus of support in each of the class groupings without this bonus having been built up and renewed through shifts of individual preference over time. Such shifts are plainly evident in our data. We found that someone who supported one of the two leading parties at one election was far more likely to shift towards the other party at the next election if this shift moved him towards the dominant opinion within his local constituency rather than away from it.

These shifts need not alter the local strength of the parties once the stronger party has built up its net bonus. If a seat were, for example, two to one Labour and the chance of a Conservative defecting to Labour between two elections were twice as great as the chance of a Labour partisan defecting to the Conservatives, Labour would lose as many votes to the Conservatives as it gained from the Conservatives because it had twice as many votes 'at risk'. The effect of the unequal *rates* of conversion in a case of this sort would be to produce equal flows of votes between the parties and to maintain Labour's ascendancy at its prior level.

Apparently differential conversions have maintained marked imbalances of party support in local areas over long periods of time and have done so in the presence of substantial ebbs and flows of party strength. There is indeed evidence that these differentials have lent the tides of politics one of their most pronounced characteristics – the tendency for the net fraction of the electorate changing hands between the parties to be the same everywhere. This is a far from obvious result, and we should explore the paradoxical manner in which unequal conversion in local areas can contribute to uniform change across the country as a whole.

The Sources of Uniform Swing

No electoral phenomenon in Britain has been more widely remarked on than that of 'uniform national swing'. In election after election since the Second World War, the net shift of strength between the parties has amounted to a remarkably similar fraction of the electorate in the great bulk of constituencies across the country.[1] The degree of this uniformity has encouraged the view that national political issues and events are of

[1] See p. 121 above.

paramount importance for the voter and that his chances of moving from one party to another are virtually identical everywhere.[1]

Yet such a view leads to a contradiction. If the electors in each constituency were to respond to national political influences in an identical way we would *not* see the same fraction of the electorate, or total vote, change hands between the parties in each constituency. The simplest calculations will show why this is so. Let us suppose that it were everywhere true that someone who had voted Conservative at the last election had one chance in five of voting Labour at the next and that everyone else kept the same preference. A fifth of the support which the Conservatives had enjoyed in each constituency would then be transferred to Labour. But this would represent very different fractions of the total electorate in different constituencies. In a seat where the Conservatives had had 80 per cent of the vote the drop would be to 64 per cent; but in a seat where the Conservatives had had 30 per cent of the vote the drop would be only to 24 per cent. The fraction of the total vote changing hands in the safe seat would be 16 per cent; in the hopeless one, a mere 6 per cent.

In fact, if national influences were completely paramount, we should expect swings to involve not identical fractions of the total vote or electorate in each constituency but a fraction proportional to the prior strength of the party that was losing ground. This fact has indeed led Berrington to propose that swing should be calculated in proportional terms, advancing an argument that has not been adequately answered.[2] At a simple empirical level the answer is of course that observed swings do not fit this alternative formula. Instead of being proportional in each constituency to the prior strength held by the party losing ground nationally, the fraction of the total vote changing hands has been remarkably similar in Conservative and Labour seats, whether safe or marginal. This uniformity in four successive pairs of General Elections is shown by Table 6.15 on the next page, which gives the mean percentage of the total vote changing hands in safe Labour, marginal and safe Conservative seats which had only straight fights between the two main parties. The uniformity is not complete, but there is no sign of any marked tendency for swings to be proportional to the prior strength of the party that is losing ground.

[1] We may state this proposition more formally by saying that the transition probabilities governing the shifts between successive elections would be virtually identical in all constituencies; that is, that turnover tables of the kind shown in Chapter 12, if they were percentaged to add to one hundred in each row, would look virtually the same everywhere.

[2] See H. Berrington, 'The General Election of 1964', *Journal of the Royal Statistical Society*, Series A, **128** (1965), 17 ff.

6.15 Deviation from Overall Mean Swing[a] by Prior Strength
of Parties in Seats Involving Straight Fights[b]

	Conservative vote in prior election		
	Less than 40%	40–60%	More than 60%
1951–55	−0·5	+0·1	−0·1
1955–59	−0·2	+0·1	−0·3
1959–64	−0·4	+0·1	+1·4[c]
1964–66	+0·1	0·0	+0·9[c]
1966–70	+0·2	−0·1	−0·2[c]

[a] In the case of straight fights swing may be defined as simply the increase of the gaining party's percentage of the total vote between successive elections; a negative entry means a less than average swing, a positive entry a more than average one.
[b] Entries are the mean percentage deviation in the category from the overall mean percentage swing.
[c] These entries are averaged from the swings for only ten, three and three seats respectively.

But such an answer does not adequately deal with the questions that are raised by the failure of swing to be proportional. The real significance of this failure is that it implies the presence of influences which modify the effect of uniform national forces. When the tide is running against his party, why should an elector in a hopeless seat be three or four times as likely to change his vote as a fellow-partisan in a safe seat? We cannot escape from this mystery by denying that national forces are of immense importance and seeking to explain swing entirely in other terms. The evidence for the existence of national forces, including the homogeneity of change, is far too persuasive. What is needed is additional insight into the processes which modify the influence of national forces so that the fraction of the total vote changing hands is roughly the same in all constituencies instead of being proportional to the parties' prior strength.

Let us restate this puzzle in terms of a simple diagram in which we place constituencies along a 0–100 scale showing the Conservatives' percentage of the two-party vote at a given election. And let us put three specimen constituencies along the scale; in Constituency A the Conservatives received 25 per cent of the major party vote, in Constituency B 50 per cent, and in Constituency C 75 per cent. It follows from the argument we have given that, if the electorates in these three constituencies were to respond in an identical fashion to common national forces, the net transfers of strength would be very unequal. If, as in our earlier example, one Conservative in five transferred his support to Labour and no one else shifted, there would be a change of 5 per cent of the total vote in Constituency A, of 10 per cent in Constituency B and of 15 per cent in Constituency C. The relative size of these swings is suggested by the arrows we have drawn above the

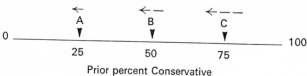

Prior percent Conservative

constituencies. Yet the empirical reality is very different. Broadly speaking, the experience of recent years would lead one to expect the arrows to be of equal length.

What is the explanation for this conflict between what is actually observed and what might reasonably be expected? It is here that we return to the clue offered by our earlier findings regarding the tendency of a party to draw additional strength to itself in areas where it is already dominant. The evidence of this chapter as to the relationship of class to party in one-party seats and the evidence we shall give as to the stronger homing tendency among those who are returning to a party that is dominant in their local area imply the presence of processes that modify the impact of more national forces. We may illustrate our hypothesis concerning the effect of these local processes by drawing a new set of arrows over our scale of prior party strength. Any such local processes would tend to move the strongly Labour seat, Constituency A, farther in Labour's direction. They would have no net effect in the marginal seat, Constituency B, where neither party

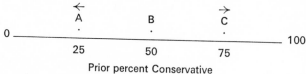

Prior percent Conservative

is ascendant. And they would tend to move the strongly Conservative seat, Constituency C, farther in the Conservatives' direction.

The relevance of such a hypothesis to the phenomenon of uniform swing is plain. The local processes of opinion change which are postulated would retard swings against the losing party in seats where the party had been strong and amplify swings against the party in seats where it had been weak.[1] If we return to our hypothetical case in which the tide is running

[1] This possibility seems first to have been hinted at by H. Berrington during the discussion of his paper on the 1964 election. See *Journal of the Royal Statistical Society*, Series A, **128** (1965), 62. But see also I. Maclean, 'The Problem of Proportionate Swing', *Political Studies*, **21** (1973), 57–63, for a development of the argument.

against the Conservatives we may suggest how the overlay of local on national forces may change proportional swings into swings that are more nearly blind to prior party strength:

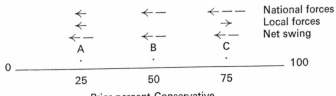

The intricacy of any such interplay of forces is not to be disposed of by a simple diagram, and before turning to the question of empirical support for such a hypothesis we should consider the nature of the influences involved. Other research would suggest that these consist mainly of the persuasive nature of personal conversation, a conjecture that is supported by findings that we shall set out in a moment.[1] If this is the case the tendency towards homogeneity of political opinion in seats where one of the parties is already dominant would reflect the fact that the persuasive contacts in such an area are mainly in one direction. The persuasive influence of personal contact may be felt in every area, including those as evenly balanced as our hypothetical Constituency B. But when such influences are summed across a constituency they are likely to have worked in mutually cancelling directions in a mixed area, and to have benefited the dominant party in a more homogeneous area.[2]

The voter's social ambience need not of course lie within his constituency. Often the constituency does provide his social environment; and even in some cases where it does not, such as the stockbroker who commutes from a comfortable suburb but talks politics mainly with his associates in the City, the partisanship of his constituency may be a serviceable guide to the political hue of his contacts elsewhere (in this case it would indeed be a far better guide than the partisanship of some wider area such as all of Greater London). Nonetheless there will be mismatches for some electors between

[1] See especially R. D. Putnam, 'Political Attitudes and the Local Community', *American Political Science Review*, **60** (1966), 640–54.

[2] The relationship between the persuasive events which we posit at an individual level and the tendency towards homogeneity of opinion at an aggregate level would of course involve a number of additional complexities, as, for example, the limit to further change when complete homogeneity is approached. Nevertheless, a variety of models of opinion change at the individual level will produce, in aggregate, something like the tendency towards homogeneity that we have postulated.

the partisanship of their constituency and the partisanship of their real social ambience, and this is one of the reasons why we would not expect the adjustment towards uniformity of swing to be everywhere equal.

There is a further complexity about the relationship between swing and the relative strength of the parties that must be taken into account. Our contrived example of the influence of national forces assumes that change will be in one direction only and that voters will move only from the party that is losing ground to the party that is gaining. But this simplification, as we shall show in Chapter 12, is quite false to reality. National politics at any moment will present a mixture of forces, and individual voters move in many contrary directions, even when the national party tide is fairly strong.

If the proportional swings attributable to national forces involved partially offsetting flows in each direction, these swings would be more variable across the scale of prior party strength than our contrived example has made them. We may illustrate this by supposing that the net transfer of 10 per cent of the electorate in our evenly matched constituency B is really the result of two opposite flows, one carrying two-fifths of previously Conservative voters (or 20 per cent of the total vote) over to Labour and the other carrying one-fifth of previously Labour voters (or 10 per cent of the total vote) over to the Conservatives. The net result of these opposite flows in constituency B would be a 10 per cent swing from the Conservatives to Labour as before.

But the effect of these opposite flows in our hypothetical safe seats would be very different. In constituency C, where the Conservatives have a very large prior vote 'at risk', the movement from Conservatives to Labour would be 30 per cent of the total vote (two-fifths of the 75 per cent previously won by the party) and the movement in the opposite direction would be only 5 per cent (one-fifth of the 25 per cent previously held by Labour). The net result would be a net movement of 25 per cent – appreciably larger than the 15 per cent which we obtained when the flow was only in one direction.

The more interesting result, however, would be obtained in constituency A, where Labour rather than the Conservatives have a large prior vote at risk. In this case the identical application of our mixed national forces would move 10 per cent of the total vote (two-fifths of the 25 per cent previously held by the Conservatives) from the Conservatives to Labour. But it would also move 15 per cent of the electorate (one-fifth of the 75 per cent previously held by Labour) from Labour to the Conservatives. Since the second of these flows is the larger the application of the hypothesized national forces has in this case produced the remarkable result of a swing *against* the national tide:

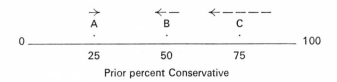

This example involves flows of individual electors which are very large by modern British standards. But the possibility of swings against the national tide, especially in seats still more one-sidedly Labour or Conservative than these, underlines the challenge of explaining the processes which modify the effect of uniform national forces so that such negative swings – or even swings much below the national average – in seats where the winning party is already strong occur very seldom. In recent elections the pattern of swings has not looked remotely like the one that we have sketched here.

We must now present our evidence for our hypothesis that observed swings are the sum, first, of the more proportional swings due to national forces, and, second, of the tendency towards homogeneity in the local constituency which retards such swings where they are strong and amplifies them where they are weak. If this sort of interplay of forces in fact took place we would expect national influences to be more apparent when they are relatively stronger. It is therefore of interest that the strongest tide of British politics in the past generation – that from 1935 to 1945 – also produced swings which were most nearly proportional to prior party strength. Indeed in seats with straight fights or with triangular contests involving the Liberals both in 1935 and 1945 the correlation of the Conservatives' strength in 1935 with their loss between 1935 and 1945 was not less than 0·55. But the analogous correlation has been very much lower in subsequent pairs of elections when the tide of change has run less strongly. When these forces have been weakest the relationship has essentially vanished.

There is, however, a more direct way of examining the adequacy of such a model. Electors differ in their sources of information about politics. Most people feel they get their information mainly from television and the national press and are therefore primarily exposed to political stimuli that are broadly similar in all parts of the country. But some apparently get their information mainly from personal conversation and are therefore exposed to political stimuli that depend more on their local social milieu. Some, of course, receive their information in both of these ways.

This rough classification of electors by sources of information can be connected to our model by dividing each group again into those living in safe Labour, marginal and safe Conservative seats and inspecting the pattern of swing found within each. Let us consider first those who seemed to follow politics through the national media. If we divide these respondents into three groups, according to the past Conservative strength in their constituencies, we find in each group the swings between 1964 and 1966 shown in Figure 6.16.[1]

6.16 Swings among Nationally-Oriented Respondents 1964–1966 by Partisanship of Constituency

In view of the almost uniform swing to Labour across the constituencies of the country between 1964 and 1966 the pattern found here is a remarkable one. The swing to Labour among nationally-oriented respondents was very much stronger in the constituencies where the Conservatives had the larger vote at risk than it was in the relatively marginal constituencies. But what catches the eye most of all in these figures is the swing *away* from Labour among nationally-oriented respondents in seats where Labour had been traditionally strong. Without our having some theoretical grounds for expecting such a result, it would seem very odd indeed.

Let us now turn to the swings in these same groups of constituencies among respondents whose sources of information about politics seemed more locally based. The pattern is equally remarkable, as Figure 6.17 on the next page shows.

In each of the traditional party areas, the swings among locally-oriented respondents were the reverse of those found among respondents whose information came from the national media. In both the strong Labour and strong Conservative areas we find a tendency towards even greater solidarity

[1] We have here based swing on the full electorate, subtracting Labour's positive or negative lead over the Conservatives in 1964 (expressed as a per cent of the full electorate) from its lead in 1966. A negative swing therefore indicates a net movement of support to the Conservatives rather than to Labour between the two years.

6.17 Swings among Locally-Oriented Respondents 1964–1966
by Partisanship of Constituency

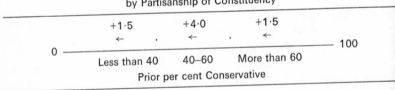

with the local majority. And on the Conservative side this required a swing *against* the prevailing national tide, a result which might also seem strange if we had no basis for interpreting it. Indeed, Figures 6.16 and 6.17 show a complete reversal of the direction of the arrows drawn for respondents in safe Labour and safe Conservative seats, a pattern that would seem very odd except in the light of our theory. The phenomenon observed here is of trivial importance in comparison with the bending of the sun's light as it passes the planet Mercury, but it is just as much an example of a puzzling empirical observation becoming comprehensible only with the aid of an adequate framework of interpretation.

We may compare these sharply contrasting patterns of swing with the swings found among respondents whose sources of political information appeared more mixed. Figure 6.18 shows the changes of preference

6.18 Swings among Respondents of Mixed Orientation 1964–1966
by Partisanship of Constituency

among those who said they followed politics both in the national media and through local conversation. Unlike the patterns for those whose orienta tions seem more purely national or local, the pattern here is of a mild swing to Labour in each group of constituencies. Sampling fluctuations can easily have produced the difference in the magnitude of the three figures. The uniform direction of swing suggests, however, the overlay of local and national forces which can produce swings that are more nearly uniform. Of course this summation of forces need not occur within the psyches of individual electors; the adding together of the votes of electors whose orientations are primarily national and of electors whose orientations are primarily local can produce a uniform aggregate swing out of fundamentally contrasting individual patterns of change.

In reporting these data we feel obliged to a quite exceptional degree to make clear the slenderness of the empirical foundations of our findings. The difficulties of measuring the elector's sources of information cut away part of our sample. When we further divide those who seem to have national, local and mixed orientations into sub-groups on the basis of the relative party strengths in their constituencies we are left with very few cases on which to base a measure of swing. We have no doubt whatsoever that the detailed patterns in Figures 6.16, 6.17 and 6.18 are partly the work of sampling accident. We are also aware of the additional blur that would be introduced into these findings by using somewhat different definitions of swing or other periods of time. Our findings are set out simply in the spirit of arguing the empirical plausibility of a hypothesis which seems to us capable of resolving what has remained a substantial, if only partially recognized, paradox of electoral change in Britain.

One other hypothesis can give additional insight into the sources of uniform swing, even if its explanatory value for Britain is somewhat limited. Let us for the moment entertain the idea that the country is divided into two groups of partisans on the basis of fixed party loyalties from which voters may occasionally stray in making their choices at the polling station. Let us, in other words, suppose that the electorate is divided by its loyalties into two fixed camps and that the likelihood of a voter's supporting a given party at a particular election depends only on which of the camps he is in and not at all on what he did at the last election. Such a model is more faithful to the realities of party support in America than in Britain, as we have seen in Chapter 2. But it is nonetheless worth noting that this model would lead to uniform swings of party support so familiar in Britain if we make certain additional assumptions.[1]

The key further assumption is that the rate of support given to a party by its own loyalists will increase for the party that is gaining ground between two elections by the same amount that it decreases for the party that is losing ground.[2] In other words, the short-term issues and events that

---

[1] This model is developed in a seminal paper by Ole Borre, 'Ecological Models for Short-Term Electoral Behaviour' (mimeo.), 1972, from a variety of earlier investigations. Borre gives the proofs of the implications of the model cited here.

[2] If P denotes the probability of a Labour loyalist voting Labour at a given election and Q the probability of a Conservative loyalist voting Conservative, the assumption required for uniform swing under such a model is that $\Delta P = -\Delta Q$, where ΔP is the

have set the national political pendulum to swinging are reflected in equal and opposite shifts in the solidarity of the two fixed camps of party loyalists.

Such an assumption is by no means an unreasonable one in view of the fact that both sets of partisans are exposed to short-term forces more favourable to one party than the other. In politics too the rain falls equally upon the just and the unjust. The real difficulty with such a model as an explanation of uniform swing is its assumption that the electorate remains divided into two fixed camps of loyalists. We have seen that established partisan self-images tend to change with electoral choices in Britain. There is, to be sure, a 'homing' tendency which draws voters back to parties they have supported before. But this tendency is almost as evident in party self-images as it is in votes. Since there is a brisk traffic between the parties in terms of loyalties as well as votes, any satisfactory account of the sources of uniform swing cannot start from the assumption of fixed party allegiance.

Nor can we suppose that some other attribute, such as class, divides the British electorate into the fixed camps required by this model of uniform change. Suspicion is cast on the idea that class in particular might play this role by the fact that the partisan solidarity of the classes varies markedly with the social character of local areas. We have seen in the findings for resorts and mining seats set out in Table 6.7 and for a much larger number of constituencies set out in Figures 6.9 and 6.10 that the level of support given to the parties within each class differs drastically according to the social and political composition of constituencies. We have argued that these differences are rooted in the persuasive influence of social interaction within local environments. But such influences may be kept from producing full local homogeneity of political outlook by the fact that locally dominant parties have more supporters to lose under the influence of national issues that benefit the opposite party. Indeed, our hypothesis is that a rough balance of these forces has maintained the long-lasting area differences of British politics as well as being at the bottom of the uniform swings that are so marked an aspect of political change.

These swings are a 'conservative' aspect of political change, since they disturb so little the prevailing pattern of party differences by region or locality. We have treated the paradox of uniform swing at the end of a series of chapters on continuities of political alignment. We now turn to

---

change in P between elections and ΔQ is the change in Q. A more complex formulation would of course be needed if voters were free to abstain or vote for still other parties rather than simply to vote for their own or for the opposite party.

the much more 'radical' or fundamental changes which have been associated with major realignments of British politics, changes which have greatly altered the geography of party support. In Chapter 7 we examine the decline of an older religious alignment and in Chapters 8 and 9 the rise and incipient decline of the class alignment which has dominated much of British politics since the First World War.

PART TWO

Realignment

7 The Decline of Past Alignments

A TWO-PARTY struggle between Conservative and Labour with party loyalty largely linked to class has dominated British politics for forty years and more. It is easy to forget that at the start of this century the basis of politics was very different. The Labour Party scarcely mattered and religion was at least as important as class in shaping partisanship. The fundamental realignments that have taken place over the last two generations have only slowly obliterated the old structure and, as we suggested in Chapter 3, it is not only in elderly survivors of a bygone era but also in their descendants that its political patterns can still be traced.

The Political Legacy of Religion

Religious issues have not been at the heart of British politics since early in this century. But they once were the principal source of party division; the battles over the position of Church Schools under the Balfour Education Act of 1902 and over Welsh Disestablishment a decade later are still remembered. Indeed, going farther back, it is hardly too strong to say that British politics, which had revolved so overwhelmingly around religion in the seventeenth century, were still largely rooted in religion in the nineteenth century. The Conservatives were accepted as the Anglican and High Church Party, while the Liberals were the spokesmen of disestablishment and dissent. The Conservatives were, moreover, the party of Ulster and the Protestant ascendancy in Ireland, and the sectarian element in the Irish struggle reinforced the imprint of religion on British politics.[1]

The legacy of past religious cleavage is still very evident in the political allegiances of today. Moreover, the patterns of present allegiances show with great clarity the way in which the impact of religion has declined.

[1] The natural way in which these religious identifications were reflected in party allegiance is suggested by the explanations given by two of our respondents of the reasons for their father's partisanship: a Glasgow chargehand said 'He was an Orangeman and a Freemason, so of course he was a royalist and voted Tory'; a London butcher's wife said 'Dad was an Irish Catholic, so of course he was against the Conservatives'.

These patterns must be examined with an eye to the influence of class, since religious preference and, still more, religious attendance differ between classes; failure to allow for this can lead to the political significance of the marked differences of party support evident in the several denominations being vastly exaggerated. Because of the dominant numerical position of the Church of England, satisfactory statistics about the links between religion and partisanship have seldom been offered. The numbers in our sample preclude us from speaking with any confidence about the strength of the parties within the smaller denominations.[1] Nonetheless, Table 7.1 makes it plain that the differences between denominations are very marked. Methodists, and Roman Catholics, as well as those of no religious preference, showed large Labour majorities. But those who adhered to the two

7.1 Partisan Self-Image by Religious Identification[a]

	Conserva-tive	Labour	Liberal	Other, None	
Anglican	45%	45	5	5	100% (n = 2596)
Church of Scotland	43%	44	5	8	100% (n = 367)
Methodist	30%	45	19	6	100% (n = 327)
Other non-conformist	36%	36	24	4	100% (n = 251)
Roman Catholic	25%	60	8	7	100% (n = 399)
No religious preference	24%	50	14	12	100% (n = 171)

a This table is based on all separate individuals encountered in our 1963 and in our 1969–70 samples.

established churches, especially the Church of England, were more nearly equally divided in 1963 when Labour was comfortably in the lead over the country as a whole.

The links between Anglicanism and Conservative political preference are still clearer if we take account of active religious observance. A very large fraction within all denominations, but above all within the Church of England, treats its church membership as entirely nominal.[2] Indeed, the

[1] Despite the decline in religious observance more than half the marriages in Britain take place in an Anglican church and more than half the babies are christened in an Anglican font. When our sample were asked their religious preference in 1970 the replies were almost identical with those we received in 1963. These are the 1970 percentages:

Church of England	62%	Other non-conformist	4%
Church of Scotland, Presbyterian	8	Jewish	1
Methodist	7	Other	1
Catholic	10	No preference	5
Baptist	2		

If we consider England only, the Church of England proportion rises to 69 per cent.

[2] One of our interviewers recorded a colloquy with a respondent who said 'none' in

proportion of Anglicans claiming to attend church at least once a month was not more than 16 per cent, as compared with 39 per cent of Church of Scotland, 45 per cent of non-conformists, and 73 per cent of Roman Catholics.[1] Figure 7.2 shows the link between attendance and Conservative

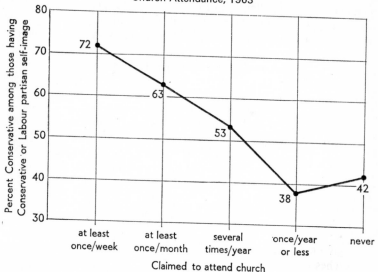

7.2 Partisan Self-Image Among Anglicans by Frequency of Church Attendance, 1963

preference among Anglicans. The Conservatives' share of allegiances to the two main parties fell from 72 per cent among Anglicans who said they

answer to her initial question about religious affiliation. She then inquired, on her own initiative, whether she ought to put him down as 'atheist' or 'agnostic'. The respondent thereupon asked to be told the difference between the two, and our interviewer, more deeply involved than she cared to be, undertook to do so. After hearing her account, the respondent said, 'You had better put me down as Church of England'.

[1] The frequency of church attendance claimed by members of the major religious groupings in 1963 were these:

	At least once a month	At least once a year	Less than once a year	
Church of England	16%	40	44	100%
Church of Scotland	39%	27	34	100%
Non-conformist	45%	32	23	100%
Roman Catholic	73%	11	16	100%

Among Anglicans the proportion claiming to attend church at least once a week was less than a tenth; among Roman Catholics, fully two-thirds.

158 The Decline of Past Alignments

go to church at least once a week to 38 per cent among those who said they attend once a year or less (and 42 per cent among those who said they never attend). The regular attender at Church of England services was overwhelmingly likely to be Conservative; the purely nominal Anglican was in most cases Labour.

Yet the patterns shown in 7.1 and 7.2 can be deceptive, since denomination and churchgoing differ between classes, as party preference itself does. Table 7.3 repeats the profile of party allegiance within each of the main church groupings separately for those in middle class and those in working

7.3 Partisan Self-Image by Religion and Social Class 1963

Occupational Grades I–III				
	Church of England	Church of Scotland	Non-Conformist[a]	Roman Catholic
Conservative	72%	74%	41%	55%
Labour	10	22	22	26
Liberal	18	4	37	19
	100%	100%	100%	100%

Occupational Grades IV–VI				
	Church of England	Church of Scotland	Non-Conformist[a]	Roman Catholic
Conservative	30%	25%	22%	18%
Labour	55	59	62	68
Liberal	15	16	16	14
	100%	100%	100%	100%

[a] Includes Methodists, Baptists and other non-conformist denominations.

class occupations. The picture that had been drawn by Table 7.1 is substantially transformed. Within all of the church groupings class is shown to be strongly linked to party. Indeed, the difference between classes within the Churches of England and Scotland is very nearly as great as in the country as a whole. But the significance of the religious groupings does not vanish altogether. There is still a discernible difference of Conservative strength between Anglicans on the one hand and non-conformists on the other in both the middle and working classes. The remarkable strength of the Liberals among middle class non-conformists is a point to which we shall return.

With allowance for class, the relationship between Conservative preference and the frequency with which Anglicans go to church is further transformed. Figure 7.4 shows this relationship separately for middle class and working class Anglicans, and makes it plain that the major political cleavage within the Church of England was by class and not by frequency of church attendance. The two slopes of Figure 7.4 are far

7.4 Partisan Self-Image of Middle Class and Working Class Anglicans
by Frequency of Church Attendance, 1967

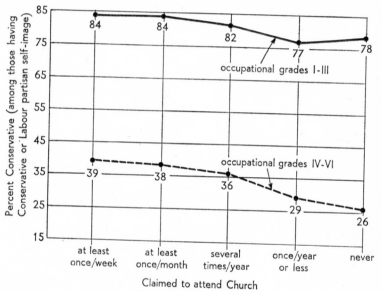

gentler than the single slope of Figure 7.2. Indeed, the tendency of Conservative support to rise much more rapidly with attendance in the earlier figure is a reflection of the fact that middle class Anglicans are more often found in church. But Conservatism did still increase with attendance, in both classes. Among middle and working class Anglicans alike, involvement in religious observance and commitment to the Conservative Party went together, although at very different overall levels of Conservative strength.

This pattern bears strongly on the questions of 'cross-voting' and working class Conservatism which we shall discuss in the next chapter. We can see that the tendency of working class Anglicans to support the party of the 'opposite' class (and the solidarity of middle class Anglicans in support of their 'own' party) was substantially greater among those who attended church. The contrast in cross-support tendencies between those who attended more than once a year and those who attended less emerges clearly from Table 7.5 which sets out four-fold arrays of party support by class for these two groups of Church of England electors. The importance of the

7.5 Cross-Support of Middle and Working Class Anglicans by Frequency of Church Attendance, 1963[a]

	Attends more than once a year				Attends once a year or less	
	Middle Class	Working Class			Middle Class	Working Class
Conservative	83%	b 37%		Conservative	77%	b 27%
Labour	c 17	63		Labour	c 23	73
	100%	100%			100%	100%
	b − c = 20%				b − c = 4%	

[a] Middle class is occupational grades I–III; working, occupational grades IV–VI.

much greater imbalance of the *b* and *c* cells of the left-hand array is enhanced by the fact that Anglican electors who attended church more than once a year comprised such a large fraction of the English electorate. We see here in fact a primary source of working class support for the Conservative Party.[1] These variations of party support within the Church of England give added significance to the differences of party strength that are observed between Anglican and non-conformist electors. If not 'the Tory party at prayer', the Church of England is nevertheless something that millions of Conservative electors identify themselves with.

Seen in this way the greater tendency of middle class electors to call

[1] We have here as well a partial explanation of the greater Conservatism of women, who tend also to be more faithful in religious observance. Twenty per cent of our women respondents but only 13 per cent of our men said they go to church once a week; 47 per cent of men but only 32 per cent of women said they go to church never or less than once a year. But this explanation is not more than a partial one: even among men and women with comparable habits of church attendance, the women are somewhat more Conservative.

themselves Church of England and, if they do, to attend church take on new meaning. Certainly the religious differences of the middle and working class ought not to be seen simply as the source of a 'spurious' correlation between party and religion. They are rather among the ties that bind the middle class more strongly to the Conservative Party. The traditional symbols of the Church of England and Conservative Party have an appeal for many working class electors too, as we have seen. But their appeal for the middle class is peculiarly strong. The British establishment has traditionally been Church of England, while non-conformity has tended to carry lower social status. The strong Anglican traditions maintained in the most prestigious parts of the educational system and the constant association of the Church with Royal ceremonies may have helped, during this period of religious decline, to preserve the social primacy of the official national religion.

Yet there is evidence that the ties of religion and party in the modern electorate are distinctly a legacy of the past. The religious differences we have found are weak compared with those which an earlier era would have yielded. Some of the most interesting evidence in the whole of our research is that describing the gradual decay of this basis of party support. The extent of this decay is at once apparent if we set out the party allegiances of Anglicans and non-conformists by class in the several age-cohorts that made up the current electorate. Table 7.6 examines the relationship of class to party within the Anglican and non-conformist groups in

7.6 Partisan Self-Image by Class and Religion Within
Pre-1918 Cohort, 1963[a]

Church of England				Non-Conformist		
	Middle Class	Working Class			Middle Class	Working Class
Conservative	82%	b 50%		Conservative	46%	b 19%
Other	c 18	50		Other	c 54	81
	100%	100%			100%	100%
	b − c = 32%				b − c = −35%	

difference of balance of cross-support in two religious groups: 67%

[a] Middle class is comprised of occupational grades I–III, working class of grades IV–VI. The definitions of age-cohorts here and in subsequent tables are those set out in Chapter 3. We have grouped Labour and Liberal partisan self-images as 'other'.

the oldest of the age groups, the pre-1918 cohort. Among those growing up before the First World War, the difference between Anglicans and non-conformists was enormous. Half the working class Anglicans and the overwhelming bulk of the middle class ones were Conservative. With the non-conformists the picture was almost exactly reversed; even among the middle class the Conservatives were in a minority. These differences are reflected in the diverging 'cross-support' tendencies in the two religious groupings. Among Anglicans cross-support in class terms (cell *b* less cell *c*) is 32 per cent in the Conservatives' favour. But among non-conformists it is 35 per cent *against* the Conservatives. The total divergence of 67 per cent between these two figures is shown at the bottom of the table.

When we turn to those who grew up during and after the Second World War these contrasts had largely disappeared. There was little difference in party support among Anglicans and non-conformists in the working class, and even in the middle class the gap was very much less than in the oldest cohort. This marked attenuation of religious differences is shown by Table 7.7. The entries of the two parts of this table make clear that the difference of the cross-support by class within the two religious groups was not nearly so large in the 1951–66 cohort as it was in the pre-1918 cohort. Indeed, the divergence of the two measures of cross-support was not more than 12 per cent (as shown at the bottom of the table), whereas in the oldest cohort it was a full 67 per cent.

We can moreover show that this change has been a continuous one,

**7.7 Partisan Self-Image by Class and Religion Within
1951–66 Cohort[a]**

Church of England			Non-Conformist		
	Middle Class	Working Class		Middle Class	Working Class
Conservative	68%	**b** 27%	Conservative	53%	**b** 30%
Other	**c** 32	73	Other	**c** 47	70
	100%	100%		100%	100%
	b − c = −5%			b − c = −17%	

difference of balance of cross-support in two religious groups: 12%

[a] See definitions in footnote to Table 7.6 above.

extending over the five cohorts comprising the present electorate. Indeed we can stretch our analysis back into generations that have passed the possibility of voting by asking our respondents about their fathers' religious and party preferences when they were growing up. On the assumption of an average gap of thirty years in the ages of father and child, such a procedure yields two additional cohorts which have passed out of the electorate: the fathers of the interwar cohort and the fathers of the pre-1918 cohort.[1]

Figure 7.8 shows, for seven cohorts, the balance of cross-support for the parties by class within the Anglican and non-conformist groups;

7.8 Balance of Cross-Support Among Anglican and Non-Conformist Electors by Cohort

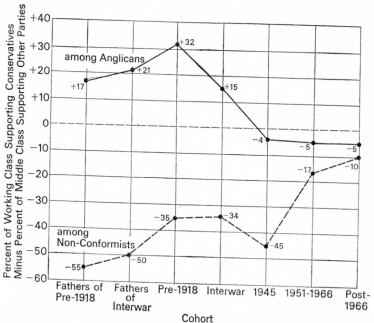

a Each of the plotted values represents the difference, within a given religious group of a given cohort, of the proportion of working class whose partisan self-image (or remembered partisanship, in the case of fathers) is Conservative and the proportion of middle class whose partisanship is Liberal or Labour.

[1] We include these figures on the fathers of our two oldest cohorts to suggest the extension into the past of the greater religious cleavage found in the pre-1918 and interwar cohorts themselves. But several considerations preclude our regarding these data as comparable to those we have from our living respondents. The data on fathers

in other words the figure plots for each religious group the difference between the proportion of working class electors supporting the Conservatives (entry *b* of Tables 7.6 or 7.7) and the proportion of middle class electors failing to support the Conservatives (entry *c*). The parallel swings of the two curves suggest the broad historical rises and falls of Conservative strength, especially the decline of Conservative support over the Second World War. But the dominant trend of the figure is the steady attenuation of the difference of the cross-support patterns in the two religious groups. The gap between church and chapel declines from 72 per cent among those who came of age in the 1880s to no more than 5 per cent among the youngest cohort.[1]

The erosion of the religious cleavage as the class alignment became more predominant has carried farthest in the working class. Figure 7.9 shows the

7.9 Conservative Strength Among Working Class Anglicans and Non-Conformists by Cohort 1963

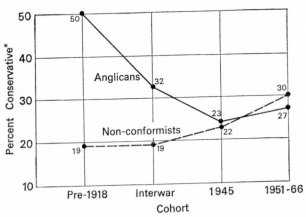

a Of partisan self-images aligned with the Conservative, Labour, and Liberal parties.

———————————

pertain to partisanship at time past, those on respondents to partisanship at the time of our studies. Our data on past cohorts pertain only to fathers, those from our living cohorts to everyone. Some fathers have reproduced themselves less than others or not at all, and therefore are under-represented in the memories of living cohorts. We shall return to the problems which these considerations pose for analysis when we examine in Chapter 10 the evolution of party strength over half a century.

[1] The religious feelings of an earlier day were captured by the remarks of a sixty-six-year-old Carmarthen painter, an elector of the pre-1918 cohort, who recalled the basis of his father's partisanship: 'If you are chapel you are Liberal. If you are church you are Conservative. My father was church.'

progressive release of working class cohorts from the religious motives which influenced party allegiance so deeply in an earlier day. In our youngest two cohorts no significant religious difference is associated with the incidence of working class Conservatism. But among our oldest respondents, religion makes a vast difference to the likelihood of a working class voter's being a Conservative.

The weakening of the religious alignment has involved a weakening of the Liberal–non-conformist axis. In much of our discussion we have grouped the Liberals and Labour as opponents of the Conservative Party. But Figure 7.10 charts Liberal strength in successive Anglican and non-conformist cohorts. Here again, we have extended our historical reach by adding two prior cohorts, the fathers of the pre-1918 and interwar cohorts. Throughout this historical period non-conformists have been more prone to Liberalism than Anglicans have. Even in the youngest of the cohorts the Liberal cause evokes a greater response among non-conformists. But the original link between Liberalism and non-conformity was so strong that its decline inevitably appears spectacular.

The displacement of the Liberals as the Conservatives' main opponent is one of the keys to the displacement of religion by class as the main

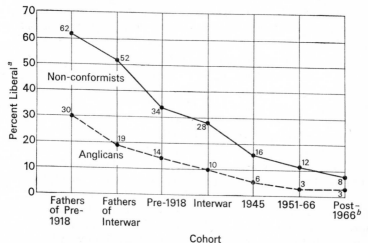

7.10 Liberal Strength Among Anglicans and Non-Conformists by Cohort

[a] Of party allegiances (or recalled allegiance, in the case of fathers) with Conservatives, Liberals and Labour.
[b] This chart is based on our 1963–4 interviews, except for the post-1966 cohort.

grounds of party support in the recent past. Once the Liberals had fallen behind an explicitly class-based party, for reasons which owed as much to the splits between Liberal leaders as to Labour's electoral appeal, it was natural that electoral support should more nearly follow class lines and that the electorate's attention should turn from the issues of church schools and disestablishment towards the class-related issues that were the basis of Labour's challenge. If Ireland had remained in the United Kingdom following a protracted struggle, a quite different religious dimension might have shaped British politics. As it was, the minority religions were left to go their own way, and the ties of religion to party steadily weakened, although they are still plainly visible in the older segments of the electorate.

The decline of the religious alignment is intimately linked with the fortunes of the Liberal Party. As new generations entered the electorate the parties arrayed against the Conservatives drew their support less from religious beliefs than from class interests. But the shifts away from the Liberals as the party of non-conformism lost out to the party of the working class were in some respects surprising, as we shall see.

The Decline of the Liberals

In 1906 the Liberals dominated the political scene. They had won the largest majority in the House of Commons since the Reform Bill; even without their parliamentary allies, the new Labour Party, they secured over 50 per cent of the popular vote. Less than two decades later, although they were still getting 30 per cent of the vote, they were struggling desperately for survival. In 1929, their last serious challenge for governmental power won them 23 per cent of the vote. Until 1974 they never again rose above 12 per cent and in 1951 and 1955, when they fought barely a sixth of the seats, they sank to a mere 2·5 per cent of the vote.

The Liberal decline is vividly sketched by the past and current preferences found in our successive electoral cohorts. Figure 7.11 shows for each cohort the trend of Liberal support in the preferences of our respondents' fathers, in their own earliest preferences, and in the partisan self-images they held at the time of our studies. The convergence of Liberalism in these five cohorts towards a common level in the 1960s is remarkable. From wide differences of Liberal support in the fathers' generation,[1] which are still

[1] There is evidence that the recall of partisanship by children somewhat understates the proportion of Liberalism in the fathers' generation. We would expect some of those

7.11 Proportion Liberal of Party Preferences of Fathers, Respondents' Earliest Preferences, and Present Partisan Self-Images, by Cohort, 1970[a]

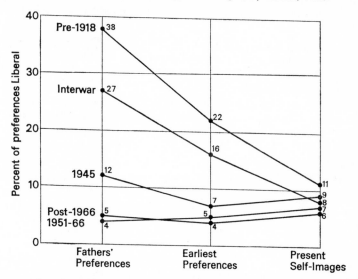

[a] Figures are in each case the per cent Liberal of those within a given group who held a preference, excluding those who had none or for whom none could be recalled.

reflected in the respondents' own earliest preferences, Liberal strength in each cohort moved towards a proportion near to 10 per cent in the present partisan self-images. In the case of the three youngest cohorts (voters who entered the electorate in the aftermath of the Second World War and those who entered in the 1950s and 1960s), this result required a net increase in Liberal strength between the respondents' earliest and present preferences; in the youngest cohort it required a net increase over the Liberalism remembered among fathers as well. But in the electorate as a whole the pattern is one of Liberal decline between father and child and across the cohorts.

Where the support released by this decline went is of course a central problem of British electoral history. Those who left the Liberalism of their fathers or of their own earliest years must have gone elsewhere, even if

---

whose fathers were in fact Liberal to have failed to recall a party preference for their fathers, who were therefore excluded from the percentage for fathers in Figure 7.11. This tendency probably has little effect on the pattern of Liberal decline shown here, but we shall be concerned at a number of points in the subsequent analysis with the effects that this frailty of recall can have on our findings.

only to non-voting or non-alignment; a law of the conservation of political matter must apply to movements of this sort.[1] Our evidence on this question is set out in Table 7.12, which shows the partisan self-images of those who

7.12 Partisan Self-Images Held by Those Whose Fathers Were Liberal or Whose Own Earliest Preferences Were Liberal, 1963

	Among those whose	
	Fathers Were Liberal	Earliest Preferences Were Liberal
Partisan Self-Image Is		
Conservative	40%	25%
Labour	34	19
Liberal	23	53
None	3	3
	100% (*n* = 300)	100% (*n* = 165)

recalled their fathers as Liberal or who gave their own earliest preferences as Liberal. The table makes clear how strong is the continuity between historic Liberalism and Liberal support in the 1960s. More than half of those whose own earliest preferences were Liberal still thought of themselves as Liberal, and nearly a quarter of those who recalled their fathers as Liberal still held such a self-image.

The outstanding feature of this table, however, is its evidence on the flows of Liberal strength into the other parties. Despite the fact that the Labour Party succeeded to the Liberals' place as the Conservatives' main opponent in the British party system, only a minority of historic Liberal support went to Labour. Indeed, the proportion that went to the Conservatives is found to be greater both among those whose fathers were remembered as Liberal and among those who gave their own earliest preferences as Liberal. This is true despite the fact that our information was gathered in an era of peak Labour strength in the early 1960s, when many of those whose partisan self-images were weakly formed might have been expected to call themselves Labour. The revelation that a greater share of Liberal

[1] Such a law must of course apply to changes over the life cycle of a given cohort, but is inexact as applied to changes between generations, since some Liberal fathers will have died without leaving progeny whose partisanship must be taken into account and others will have reproduced themselves more than once. For the moment we defer a consideration of the problems introduced by differential fertility.

strength went over to the party's historic opponents, the Conservatives, rather than to Labour as the successor party of the left, is sharply at variance with the usual assumptions both of contemporary commentators and of subsequent historians.

The growing polarization of parties on the basis of class, which we discuss in the next chapter, left its mark on Liberal support. If we disaggregate the data of Table 7.12 we find quite different flows within the middle and working classes. This separation is shown in Figure 7.13.

7.13 Proportions Conservative and Labour Among Earliest Preferences and Current Partisan Self-Images of Those Whose Fathers Were Liberal by Occupational Grade 1963[a]

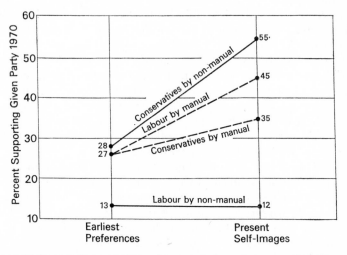

[a] Figures are the proportions supporting a given party among earliest or current preferences for all parties, including Liberals. Non-manual is defined as occupational grades I–IV, manual as occupational grades V–VI.

The two lines at the top of the figure show the dominant flows of Liberal support to the Conservatives in the middle class and to Labour in the working class. These flows are already evident in the earliest preferences reported by these children of Liberal fathers and are more pronounced in their current party self-images. Indeed, by the time of our study roughly half of those in each class group of historic Liberals had aligned themselves with the party that was dominant within their own class.

By contrast the support in each group evoked by the party of the opposite class is relatively weak. But it is not entirely missing. Indeed, the greater appeal of the Conservatives for the children of working class Liberals is part of the reason why the Conservatives have inherited more of the Liberals' former support than Labour. Among middle class children of Liberal parents support for Labour is negligible: not much more than a tenth of such respondents called themselves Labour even in the strongly Labour years of the early 1960s. But among the working class children of Liberal parents Conservative support was far from negligible: more than a quarter of such respondents called themselves Conservatives in this strongly Labour period. Although the main point of Figure 7.13 is the flow of middle and working class Liberals to the party dominant in their class, the counterpoint is the appeal of the Conservatives to the working class children of Liberal fathers.

This secondary point indeed links in an interesting way to the decline of working class Conservatism to be seen in Chapter 8. When the data set out in Figure 7.13 are further refined by cohort, we find that the tendency of working class children of Liberal fathers to become Conservative was much greater in the older cohorts than in the younger. And the experience of having a Liberal father was of course very much more common in the older age groups. As a result, the older cohorts contribute to Figure 7.13 the great bulk of manually employed children of Liberals who appear as Conservative in the 1960s. We are, in other words, speaking of a process of conversion which in most cases lay years in the past.

It would seem that most working class Conservatives who had had Liberal parents were confronted when young by a party system in which Labour was not yet a full contestant. Indeed, many would have seen Labour's challenge largely in terms of the damage it did to the Liberal Party, the party to which their families had formed an allegiance. In view of the 'intrinsic' values which Liberal success would have had for many of these children, it is possible to suppose that the Liberals' eventual displacement by Labour could have left a residue of ill-will in some, which countered Labour's appeal as a working class party and drew them to the Liberals' ancient foe. Support recruited to the Conservatives in this way would have contributed to the unequal appeal which Labour and the Conservatives had for the 'opposite' class in later years without necessarily involving factors, such as social deference, that may be cited when motives for working class Conservatism are sought in the political and social attitudes of the present.

The flows of support away from the Liberals therefore played an important role in fashioning the partisan alignment of recent decades. As we have seen, the Liberals left a larger legacy of strength to the Conservatives than to Labour, despite the fact that Labour succeeded the Liberals as the Conservatives' main opponent in the British party system. The movements into the main parties over several decades deserve closer study, and we should see what a comparison of cohorts can reveal about the background of Labour and Conservative support in the 1960s.

8 The Rise of the Class Alignment

THE decline of religion as a basis for partisanship was closely linked with the rise of the new class alignment. The emergence of Labour as a strong and explicitly class-based party was both cause and consequence of the decline of the religious alignment. In this chapter and the next we assess how and when the class alignment emerged and what the long-run implications of its emergence have been for the politics of modern Britain.

Although few party systems in the world have as long a past or as settled a character as Britain's, this century has seen profound changes in both the basis of political alignment and the identity of the leading parties. The broadest facts of the evolution of party strength are set out in Figure 8.1, which shows the share of the major-party vote won by the three parties at each General Election in this century. The Liberals after many years' alternation in government were displaced by Labour, which became the second major party after one world war and an equal contestant after another. Yet, as we showed in the last chapter, we ought not to assume too easily that Labour inherited the Liberals' mass support. The transition was accompanied by a fundamental change in the basis of party allegiance, especially the rise of the class alignment which has dominated politics for fifty years.

The Making of the New Alignment

Labour's electoral strength matured over an extended period. As recently as the onset of the First World War the party was a minor element in the party system. Labour had only a small bridgehead in Parliament and although it was a very solid one, with most members firmly entrenched in their seats, it gave little evidence of expanding. Between 1906 and 1914 the party made no headway in adding to its representation; indeed, by 1914 it had only thirty-eight M.P.s compared with an effective peak of fifty-three at the end of the 1906 Parliament, and from the by-elections of 1911 to 1914 it seemed that the party might even be declining.

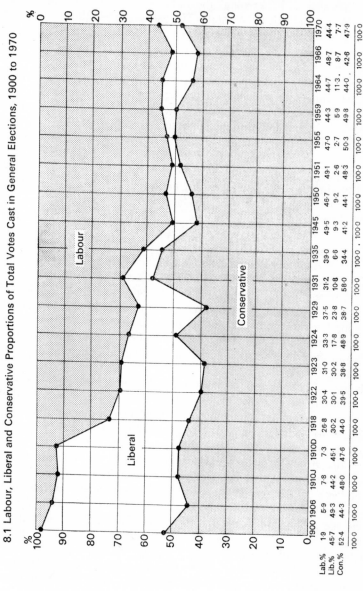

8.1 Labour, Liberal and Conservative Proportions of Total Votes Cast in General Elections, 1900 to 1970

	1900	1906	1910J	1910D	1918	1922	1923	1924	1929	1931	1935	1945	1950	1951	1955	1959	1964	1966	1970
Lab.%	1·9	5·9	7·8	7·3	26·8	30·4	31·0	33·3	37·5	31·2	39·0	49·5	46·7	49·1	47·0	44·3	44·7	48·7	44·4
Lib.%	45·7	49·3	44·2	45·1	30·2	30·1	30·2	17·8	23·8	10·8	6·6	9·3	9·2	2·6	2·7	5·9	11·3·	8·7	7·7
Con.%	52·4	44·3	48·0	47·6	44·0	39·5	38·8	48·9	38·7	58·0	34·4	41·2	44·1	48·3	50·3	49·8	44·0 .	42·6	47·9
	100·0	100·0	100·0	100·0	100·0	100·0	100·0	100·0	100·0	100·0	100·0 .	100·0	100·0	100·0	100·0	100·0	100·0	100·0	100·0

Against such a background the importance to Labour of the First World War is difficult to overstate. The war disturbed the social order in profound ways and brought a vast growth of trade unionism. In political terms it interrupted the stable competition of Conservatives and Liberals. Indeed, the split in the Liberal leadership after 1916 gave Labour the priceless opportunity of becoming the largest opposition party, even with the mere sixty-three seats won in 1918. Throughout the interwar period Labour polled at least 30 per cent of the vote at each General Election, and the results in 1924 and 1929 brought Labour Cabinets to power.

The Second World War added a fresh increment of Labour strength. Something in the experience of the war years broke the established attitudes of many people; moreover, a very large segment of new voters entered the electorate in 1945. We have seen in Chapter 3 how strongly Labour this new segment was. Fragmentary evidence suggests that some time after the Battle of Britain there was a sharp change in national political mood. Despite the wartime party truce which prevented direct confrontations between Conservative and Labour candidates, Conservatives began to fare very badly in by-elections, and when the Gallup Poll resumed questioning about voting intentions in 1943 Labour was well ahead of the Conservatives. In 1945 Labour was swept into office on a landslide with a 12 per cent swing in votes compared with 1935. In the twenty years following the war the balance of strength between Labour and the Conservatives was remarkably stable. Labour had become an equal contestant for power, and its electoral support levelled off after several decades of growth.

The rise of Labour and the new class alignment is most plainly reflected in our cohort data for the manual working class. Figure 8.2 shows the Labour proportion among the preferences which our manual respondents attributed to their fathers and gave for themselves. The trend upwards as one moves rightwards along the curves both for fathers and sons shows the strong growth of Labour support in the manual working class as the century wore on. Not more than a fourth of working class respondents in our pre-1918 cohort said their fathers were Labour, and if we were to allow for those unable to give a partisanship for their fathers the proportion would fall to less than a fifth. By contrast, two-thirds of working class respondents in the 1951–64 cohort remembered their fathers as Labour.

This profound alteration of party allegiance among manual workers did not result simply from the conversion of Liberals, as we have seen. Several streams contributed to the rising strength of the Labour Party. There were

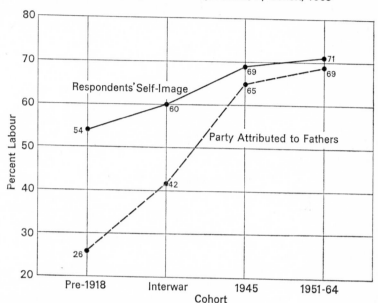

8.2 Proportion Labour of Preferences for the Three Parties Attributed to Fathers and Held by Manual Respondents, by Cohort, 1963[a]

[a] Figures are per cent Labour of Labour, Conservative and Liberal preferences attributed to their fathers and of current party self-images held by respondents in grades V and VI of the several cohorts.

some conversions to Labour among the children of Conservative parents. But our evidence suggests that Labour's new strength was achieved most of all by mobilizing the support of manual workers who grew up in relatively non-political homes.[1]

Evidence on this point is set out in Table 8.3, which shows the full turn-over between the party allegiance our manual respondents remembered for their fathers and the one they gave for themselves. The first percentage at the right-hand margin of the table shows that 37·7 per cent of fathers were remembered as having been Labour, whereas the first percentage at the bottom margin shows that 61·5 per cent of these manual workers were themselves Labour in the early 1960s, an increase of 23·8 percentage points. This increase is the result of the movements towards and away from Labour reflected by three pairs of interior entries of the table. The first of these

[1] By 'manual worker' we mean all those in our sample living in a household where the head of household was of occupational grade V or VI as defined in Chapter 4, whether or not the respondent was employed in a manual occupation.

8.3 Party Self-Image of Manual Respondents by Party of Father
Partisan Self-Image. 1963

Partisan Self-Image

		Lab	Con	Lib	Other None	
	Lab	30·5	4·1	1·7	1·4	37·7
	Con	6·5	9·4	2·2	1·2	19·3
Party of Father	Lib	6·1	3·3	2·3	0·5	12·2
	Other None	18·4	7·7	2·3	2·4	30·8
		61·5	24·5	8·5	5·5	100·0%

(n = 1229)

reflects the direct exchanges between the Conservatives and Labour: 6·5 per cent of these manual workers reported their fathers as Conservative and themselves as Labour, whereas only 4·1 per cent travelled an exactly opposite route. The result of this exchange was a small net increase of Labour strength. A rather larger gain to Labour came from movements involving the Liberal Party: 6·1 per cent of these manual workers reported their fathers as Liberal and themselves as Labour, whereas only 1·7 per cent had moved away from Labour to the Liberals by the early 1960s. But much the largest source of the increase in Labour strength reported between generations is due to the recruitment of support among manual workers who could not associate a party allegiance with their fathers. Of this working class sample 18·4 per cent did not link their fathers to a party but described themselves as Labour, whereas only 1·4 per cent remembered their fathers as Labour and gave no party allegiance for themselves. The arithmetic of these various components of change is summarized in Table 8.4.[1]

[1] We do not consider here the party preference which our respondents remembered their mothers as having, although we have seen in Chapter 3 that this could have an independent influence on the partisanship of children, when mother and father disagreed. In the great majority of cases, however, the party of the mother agreed with that of the father or was not recalled by the respondent. We have therefore simplified our analysis of change between generations by considering only the party of the father.

8.4 Source of Increase of Labour Strength Between Generations
Reported by Manual Working Class Sample[a]

	Movements towards Labour	Movements away from Labour	Net Increase
Alternative position:			
Conservative	6·5	4·1	+ 2·4
Liberal	6·1	1·7	+ 4·4
No allegiance	18·4	1·4	+17·0
	31·0	7·2	+23·8

[a] The entries of this table are taken from the turnover between the party allegiances manual working class respondents remembered for their fathers and gave for themselves, as shown by Table 8.3.

In every cohort manual workers whose fathers were not remembered as having a partisan alignment were an important source of new strength for the Labour Party. The relative importance of the several sources of additional Labour support across cohorts is shown by Figure 8.5 on the next page, which gives for each cohort the net change between generations due to exchanges with the Conservatives and the Liberals and to the recruitment of manual workers whose fathers were not remembered as having a partisan alignment. This figure shows an interesting pattern of differences across cohorts. The most important source of new Labour strength among the oldest cohort was the conversion of Liberals; the conversion of Conservatives also made an important contribution among manual workers in this age group. In the interwar cohort the conversion of Liberals and Conservatives still contributed a substantial increase in Labour strength. But in the two youngest cohorts exchanges with the other parties yielded little net change in Labour's strength among manual workers. In all cohorts, however, the inclusion of those who did not attribute a partisanship to their fathers made the balance of allegiances workers gave for themselves far more Labour than the balance they remembered for their fathers.

These data on successive cohorts help to explain the pattern of strong Labour growth earlier in the century and of more moderate growth in later years. Despite the diminishing net gains to Labour from exchanges with the Conservatives and Liberals, Labour still attracted a *proportion* of workers with Conservative or Liberal fathers that was much larger than the proportion of workers with Labour fathers that it lost to the other parties; in all four cohorts it was much more likely that workers with Conservative or Liberal fathers would become Labour than it was that those with Labour fathers would become Conservative or Liberal. But, as the century wore on, these unequal rates of conversion were applied to

8.5 Source of Increase of Labour Strength Between Generations in Manual Working Class by Cohort 1963[a]

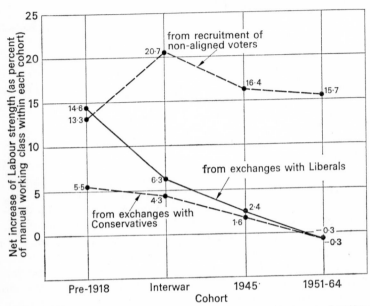

^a Figures are percentages describing net increase of Labour strength within the manual working class sample of each cohort analogous to those given for the manual working class sample as a whole by Table 8.4. The figures given here are not strictly comparable to those in Figure 8.2, where we have excluded fathers not remembered as having a party allegiance from the base on which the proportion of fathers Labour is calculated.

workers of progressively more Labour background. As a result, the loss of even a small proportion of working class sons of Labour fathers could offset the recruitment of a much larger proportion of working class sons of Conservative or Liberal fathers. In the 1951–66 cohort, for example, less than an eighth of workers with Labour fathers had become Conservative, whereas more than a third of workers with Conservative fathers had become Labour. But because so many more workers had Labour fathers, these very unequal conversion rates produced roughly equal flows of support towards and away from Labour in this cohort, as Figure 8.5 shows.

The role of recruitment to Labour of workers who did not attribute a partisanship to their fathers is more complex. In all cohorts this movement helped to make the allegiances which manual workers gave for themselves more Labour than those they remembered for their fathers, as we have seen. But we should be cautious about regarding this as indicating a net increase in Labour's strength, since a father could in fact have been Labour, even though his offspring was unable to recall his partisanship. The chance that this was the case was of course less earlier in the century, when fewer fathers were Labour, than in later years. Indeed, some non-alignment before 1918 was linked with actual disfranchisement of the working class.[1] Hence, the recruitment to Labour of workers who did not associate a partisanship with their fathers probably produced a diminishing net gain for Labour as the century wore on, just as exchanges with the Conservatives and the Liberals between generations also produced a diminishing net gain.

These trends describe the historical process by which Labour took possession of preponderant support in the working class. The way was prepared for this process by certain early formative circumstances, including the enfranchisement of workers, the identification of the new party with working class interests, and the Liberal split that gave Labour the priceless opportunity of achieving the major-party status that is so strongly rewarded by the British electoral system. Given these initial conditions, Labour came to exert a strong attraction for working class electors not aligned with it. The pull was not so strong as to break all at once the bonds to the other parties. Many working class voters remained firmly Conservative, as we have seen. Moreover, it is at least a plausible conjecture that many others were hostile towards Labour for having undercut the Liberal Party. Nonetheless, the pull of the working class party converted to Labour many younger voters whose fathers had been Conservative or Liberal or were not seen as having a clear allegiance. We shall note presently how much of the 'drift' towards Labour between parents and children in the working class was already reflected in the earliest partisan inclinations recalled by our working class respondents.

We may indeed conceive this historical process in terms of a simple model, a model which assumes there is a substantial probability that a working class child whose parents were not Labour will himself be Labour

[1] The extension of the franchise to the working class, begun by the great Reform Acts of the nineteenth century, was completed only within the lifetime of much of today's electorate. Until 1918 British franchise legislation was very complicated: only those who had a year's residence in one place could vote, and even then some categories of lodger and of sons living with their parents were not entitled to be put on the register. The registered electorate in the early years of the century constituted less than 60 per cent of the total British adult male population. But after 1918 the law and practice of registration denied very few men over 21 (and after 1928 very few women over 21) the right to vote in parliamentary elections. It is impossible to characterize very exactly the 40–45 per cent of adult males who were left off the register before 1918, but it is safe to assume that they were drawn very disproportionately from the working class.

as an adult and a much lower probability that a working class child whose parents were Labour will himself not be Labour as an adult.[1] When it is applied to the entry of successive cohorts into the electorate such a model readily generates the pattern of growth we have observed, with a rapid early increase of Labour strength tapering off as Labour takes possession of the support of a larger and larger proportion of working class parents. This pattern of growth would not be essentially different if we took account of the differences of the rates of flow between Labour and the two other parties and the circulation of electors having no party allegiance, including the differing chances that fathers of various party hues will be seen by their children as having no allegiance.

We may be sure that such a model captures an important aspect of the process by which Labour acquired dominant working class support. Yet we may also be sure that the actual process was subtle and intricate. The complexity was primarily due to the factors that conditioned the several conversion rates that we have discussed. But there are additional intricacies linked with the composition of the class groupings. We have indeed tended to treat the working class as if it remained a distinct element of the electorate throughout this period. But there was in fact substantial circulation between classes from father to son, as we saw in Chapter 5, and these movements must have affected the growth of Labour's support in the electorate.

Three differences relating to social mobility would have modified the historical process suggested by our model. The first is the greater extent of upward mobility. The evidence on the incidence of upward and downward mobility is far from conclusive, but it seems probable that there has been a long-term fall in the proportion of the electorate performing manual occupations and that this trend has been more marked since the Second World War.[2] Since those who change their social position show some

---

[1] A very simple model of this kind would be a Markov chain in which the movement between two alternative states, Labour and non-Labour, is governed by a matrix of transition probabilities that is completely specified by the two conversion rates mentioned above. If it were to govern the transmission of party allegiance between parents and children in successive cohorts such a model would lead the proportion of working class support for Labour to converge in a very few generations on an equilibrium value, which would be the same for all cohorts. For an interesting discussion of the growth of support for working class parties under alternative models of conversion see Gösta Carlsson, 'Time and Continuity in Mass Attitude Change: The Case of Voting', *Public Opinion Quarterly*, **29** (1965), 1–15.

[2] G. S. Bain has estimated that the proportion of the work force engaged in manual occupations fell 5 per cent between 1950 and 1965. See *The Growth of White Collar Unionism*, Oxford, 1970. A somewhat different assessment of the evidence of an earlier

tendency to conform to the partisan hue of their new class, this difference would have made Labour's growth in the whole electorate less rapid than would have been true with equal upward and downward mobility.

A second difference tending to the same result is the greater political impact of upward mobility. We have seen evidence in Chapter 5 that the Conservatives' share of middle class electors from Labour working class backgrounds was greater in the early 1960s than Labour's share of working class electors from Conservative middle class backgrounds, despite the strongly Labour climate of the period. This finding is consistent with evidence from a number of other studies in Britain and elsewhere.[1] Such a difference would also have made Labour's growth in the whole electorate less rapid than would have been true had upward and downward mobility been equal solvents of prior party loyalties.

The effect of these two differences was, however, partly offset by a third contrast, the greater tendency of the children of Conservative working class parents to be the ones who achieve middle class status as adults. We have commented in Chapter 5 on the evidence that aspirations of upward mobility for one's children may, together with Conservative allegiance, belong to a wider set of values held by a part of the working class, values that seem also to include the norm of smaller family size. If we see this aspect of upward mobility as limiting the proportion of the working class who lose their parents' allegiance to Labour by becoming middle class, it is a factor that must have lessened one of the constraints on Labour's growth in the modern period.

The Decline of Working Class Conservatism

The diffusion of Labour support through the working class as new cohorts have entered the electorate holds a key to understanding an aspect of party support that has been widely commented upon, the phenomenon of working class Conservatism. In recent times more than a quarter of all British electors have failed to vote in conformity with the bulk of their class.

---

period may be found in D. V. Glass, ed., *Social Mobility in Britain*, London, 1954. Further evidence of a long-term increase in the proportion of the population performing non-manual occupations is set out in Rose Knight, 'Changes in the Structure of the Working Population', *Journal of the Royal Statistical Society*, **130**, Part II (1967), 408–22.

[1] See especially S. M. Lipset and R. Bendix, *Social Mobility in Industrial Society*, Berkeley, 1959.

Social mobility can make only a partial contribution to the fact that more than a quarter of British electors fail to vote in accord with their class. Most such cross-support is to be explained in terms unrelated to class. Some of it can be traced to the survival of religious and regional differences, and of course a great deal of cross-voting is to be attributed to the multiple issues and events that at any given time hold the electorate's attention. The influences which account for Conservatism in the working class and Labour support in the middle class are very varied.

One kind of cross-voting, however, has been seen as intimately related to class. The support given the Conservatives by a section of the working class has been interpreted as a deferential response to superior elements in the social order. Unlike the working class voter who sees politics in terms of class conflict or interest, the deferential working class Tory is thought to see politics in terms of a division of labour in which a social elite quite naturally plays the leading political role. Far from being the arena of the democratic class struggle, elections are thought to be the means by which people of humble station accord the party of the ruling class the support it requires to govern the country. This hypothesis has been set out in various forms, but the idea of voting as a kind of social deference has been a recurring one.[1]

The attention paid to the working class Conservative is largely due to one grand historical paradox: the first major nation of the world to become industrialized, a nation in which 70 per cent of the people regard themselves as working class, has regularly returned Conservative governments to power. Between 1886 and 1964 the Conservative Party was defeated by decisive majorities only twice – in 1906 and 1945. Such a record could only have been achieved through heavy 'defection' to the Conservatives among the industrial working class. In recent years polling data on class and party have amply confirmed the hypothesis that the working class elector was likelier than the middle class elector to support the party of the opposite class.

[1] See R. T. McKenzie and A. Silver, *Angels in Marble*, London, 1968, for the most comprehensive discussion of this theme. See also E. A. Nordlinger, *The Working Class Tories*, London, 1967; R. Samuel, 'The Deference Voter', *New Left Review*, January–February 1960; and W. G. Runciman, *Relative Deprivation and Social Justice*, London and Berkeley, 1966. For an alternative approach see J. H. Goldthorpe and others, *The Affluent Worker*, Cambridge, 1968. See also I. Crewe, 'The Politics of "Affluent" and "Traditional" Workers in Britain', *British Journal of Political Science*, **3** (1973), 29–52. For two more argumentative views see F. Parkin, *Class Inequality and Political Order*, London, 1971, esp. pp. 84–7, and B. Hindess, *The Decline of Working Class Politics*, London, 1971. For an earlier discussion not without a modern ring, see W. Bagehot, *The English Constitution*, London, 1867.

In one respect, however, polling data have exaggerated this difference between classes. Reports of poll findings often divide a sample into its party groups, whose composition is then compared by sex, age, class and other characteristics. Such a procedure is right for describing the class origin of party support. But, because the working class so heavily out-numbers the middle class, this presentation seriously distorts the party destination of class voting. The distortion can be simply illustrated by presenting our evidence on the relationship of class and party in two contrasting ways. Table 8.6 shows the class origin of party support in 1970 by calculating the proportions of people within each party who fall

8.6 Occupational Grade by Party Self-Image, 1970

		Occupational Grade		
		I–IV	V–VI	
Party Self-Image	Conservative	**a** 55%	**b** 45	100%
	Labour	**c** 20%	**d** 80	100%

Difference, $b - c = 25\%$

in each of the two main occupation levels. The difference of 25 per cent between the cross-preference cells, b and c of this table is enormous. Even in this period of equal party strength the Conservatives drew almost half their support from the working class, whereas Labour drew only a fifth part of its support from the middle class.

It requires only a short additional step to conclude from this that the working class is vastly more disposed to support the Conservatives than the middle class to support Labour. But such a conclusion would be seriously misleading. The evidence takes on a very different appearance when we calculate the percentages within classes, instead of within parties, to show the party destination of class voting. The startling result of such a rearrangement is shown by Table 8.7 on the next page.

The difference between the cross-preference cells, b and c, is now 7 per cent instead of the 25 per cent shown by Table 8.6. This reduction by no means eliminates the problem of explaining working class Conservatism.

8.7 Party Self-Image by Occupational Grade, 1970

		Occupational Grade	
		I–IV	V–VI
Party Self-Image	Conservative	a 71%	b 36%
	Labour	c 29	d 64
		100%	100%

Difference, b − c = 7%

The working class still appears as more likely to vote Conservative than the middle class to vote Labour. Moreover, so long as any part of the working class votes for the 'opposite' party, it is of interest to know why, just as it is of interest to know why a portion of the middle class votes Labour. Nonetheless, since the imbalance of class voting between the two classes is one of the prime causes for the attention given to working class Conservatism, it is important to stress how easily this imbalance can be exaggerated.

Our view of Conservative support in the working class can also be fundamentally transformed by a further redeployment of the evidence. When we looked at the behaviour of successive cohorts, the greater cross-voting of the working class is found to occur very largely in the older age-groups. In the younger age-cohort middle class electors were no less prone to support Labour as working class electors were to support the Conservatives. Indeed, when we examined this trend separately for men and women in our sample, we found that among men of the 1945 cohort, who were peculiarly susceptible to the mood evoked by the Second World War, middle class electors were more likely to be Labour than working class electors were to be Conservative. The pattern of cross-support in successive cohorts is set out in Table 8.8.

8.8 Cross-Support by Cohort 1970

	Pre-1918	Inter-war	1945	1951–66	Post-1966
Difference between percentage of working class Conservatives and middle class Labour (b–c)	46%	16%	4%	−5%	−6%

If we look at these patterns in the light of the ideas of political inheritance and change set out in Chapter 3, we are led to adopt a fundamentally revisionist view of the phenomenon of working class Conservatism. The Labour Party is relatively very new in the evolution of British politics. It is only since the First World War that it has been a serious contender for power. By that time our oldest cohort had already come of age, and the parents of the next cohort had been socialized into a party system in which Labour had no major part.[1] Given the extent to which party loyalties are transmitted in the childhood home, time was needed for historic attachments to the 'bourgeois' parties to weaken and for 'secondary' processes to complete the realignment by class. With the collapse of their party, Liberals had of course to go elsewhere and we saw evidence in the previous chapter that substantial numbers of working class Liberals moved to the Conservatives rather than to the new Labour Party – perhaps partly in response to Labour's having undercut the position of their favoured party. And Conservative loyalties would continue to be transmitted to the working class children of Conservative parents long after the rise of a working class party.

Moreover, the Conservatives in Britain fought a brilliant delaying action in contrast to many conservative parties on the continent. The rate at which the new voters of the working class were recruited to the working class party was not a constant of nature but depended on the appeals of the parties themselves. Disraeli and Lord Randolph Churchill recognized that their party's success depended upon the wooing of the working man. On the Liberal side Joseph Chamberlain did the same and, when he changed camps in 1886, he brought over to the Conservatives a solid new body of working class support, particularly in the industrial Midlands. The receptivity of the Conservatives to new social policies after their debacle in 1945 reflected their desire not to be cut off from support in the working class.

It is only with the 1945 and post-1950 cohorts that we come to a group of electors whose partisan attachments were less strongly affected by an earlier electoral history and by Labour's late start as a national party. Among these cohorts, the Labour Party has come much closer to a full seizure of its 'natural' class base. Of course, substantial cross-voting continued to occur within each class, but the rate of such cross-voting was much more nearly equal.

This characterization of change is supported by the differing pattern of change within the two classes. When we compare over our oldest three age-cohorts the trend of the two cross-voting rates which make up our

[1] Six constituencies out of seven had never had a Labour candidate before 1918.

index of relative cross-voting, it becomes clear that the lessening of the gap between these two rates across the pre-1918, interwar and 1945 cohorts has been due more to the decline of Conservative support in the working class than to a rise in Labour strength in the middle class. As Figure 8.9 shows, the first of these rates fell by 26 percentage points

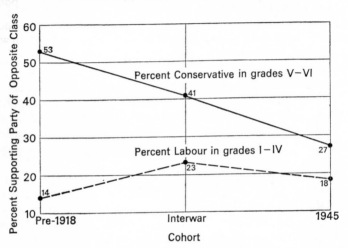

8.9 Cross-Support in Older Age-Cohorts, 1970

between the pre-1918 and 1945 cohorts, while the second rose by only 4 percentage points. This pattern for the cohorts in which Labour successively occupied its 'natural' class ground lends credence to a more historical explanation of the presence in the electorate of substantial numbers of working class Conservatives.[1] Despite the insights of Birch,[2] commentaries on Tory voting in the working class have tended to look for factors which might *de novo* deflect a working class voter to the opposite party and not to see the unequal strength of the two parties in the opposite classes as at least partially due to an evolutionary process by which the bars to Labour strength in its own class have been successively removed.

The progressive conversion of the working class to the Labour Party is confirmed by our data on the changes of party from parent to child. The attenuation of family traditions that held sway before the emergence of

[1] These figures from our 1970 sample are quite consistent with the pattern for the pre-1918, interwar and 1945 cohorts found in our samples from the 1963–6 period.
[2] See A. H. Birch, *Small Town Politics*, Oxford, 1959, pp. 110–11.

8.10 Labour and Conservative Earliest Preferences among Working Class Children of Labour and Conservative Working Class Parents 1963[a]

Respondent's Earliest Party Preference was:	Parents were:[b] Labour	Conservative
Labour	94%	19%
Conservative	6	81
	100%	100%

[a] This table is confined to children of Labour or Conservative working class parents who are themselves working class and whose own earliest political preferences were Labour or Conservative. It, together with Tables 8.11, 8.12 and 8.13, is based on data collected in our first surveys.
[b] Parents are classified as Labour or Conservative if both supported one of these parties or if one did and the other was not partisan.

Labour can be shown first by examining Labour and Conservative preferences among children of Labour and Conservative working class parents at the beginning of their political life cycle. These preferences, as shown in Table 8.10, indicate once again the profound influence of the family. But the difference of 13 per cent between Labour's share of children of Conservative parents and the Conservatives' share of children of Labour parents suggests that at the beginning of political awareness there already has been some drift of preference towards the working class party.

This drift is even more evident in the main parties' share of the current adult preferences of the same group, as Table 8.11 shows. The difference between Labour's share of children of Conservative parents and the Conservatives' share of children of Labour parents has now risen to 23 per cent, although the influence of early background is impressive among the 68 per

8.11 Labour and Conservative Current Preferences among Working Class Children of Labour and Conservative Working Class Parents 1963[a]

Respondent's Current Party Preference was:	Parents were: Labour	Conservative
Labour	91%	32%
Conservative	9	68
	100%	100%

[a] The definitions of this table conform to those of Table 8.10 except that current party preference replaces earliest preference.

8.12 Labour and Conservative Preferences among Working Class Children of Liberal or Mixed Working Class Parents 1963[a]

	First Preferences	Current Preferences
Labour	61%	61%
	↕	↕
Conservative	39	39
	100%	100%

[a] This table is confined to children of Liberal or divided working class parents who are themselves working class and whose earliest or current preferences are Labour or Conservative.

cent of children from the Tory working class who still support the Conservatives.

The drift of working class children towards the Labour Party is also seen in the first preferences and in the present partisanship of working class people from Liberal or from politically divided homes. This evidence is given in Table 8.12, which measures the tendency to move towards the working class party by the extent to which the upper proportion of either column exceeds the lower. On this basis there was a drift of 22 per cent towards the Labour Party in the earliest and current preferences of this group.

We would, however, expect the earliest and the strongest drift towards the working class party among the children of families in which no contrary partisan commitment had to be swept away. Evidence that this is the case is given in Table 8.13, where the drift may be gauged once again in terms of how much the upper entry in each column exceeds the lower. The table shows that Labour has captured nearly three-quarters of the major party preferences of this group and that this mobilization of support among children of uncommitted working class families occurred quite early in the child's political experience. Indeed, the proportion of our working class sample who could not attribute a party allegiance to their parents was sufficiently large for the crystallization of Labour preferences in this group to account for somewhat more than half the net increment of Labour strength between generations.

An evolutionary view of Conservative strength in the working class gives further insight into its sources. If these ties are partly a legacy of the past, the Conservative allegiances of many working class electors will have

8.13 Labour and Conservative Preferences among Children of Working Class Parents of No Clear Partisanship 1963[a]

	First Preferences	Current Preferences
Labour	71%	73%
Conservative	29	27
	100%	100%

[a] This table is confined to children whose working class parents are not remembered as having had a clear partisanship, who are themselves working class and whose earliest or current preferences are Labour or Conservative.

been formed long ago; indeed, in some cases they will have come down in family or local tradition from a time well before the intrusion of class into British politics in the twentieth-century sense. The intrinsic values of party ties are quite enough to have sustained the voter in his traditional allegiance for many years.

We would expect the political norms or interests of the working class to have dissolved conflicting political allegiances more fully among working class electors to whom class is relatively salient. Evidence for this emerges when we divide our sample into those who associated themselves spontaneously with a class and those who did not. At each interview we began our questions about class with one asking whether or not the respondent thought of himself as belonging to a class. The replies allowed us to separate respondents into those for whom the salience of class was relatively strong and those for whom its salience was less.

The relationship of class to party in the two groups shows an interesting contrast, which is set out in Table 8.14 on the next page. It is clear that cross-support in the middle and working classes is much more nearly equal among those for whom class is more salient. But substantial defections in the working class make it quite unequal among those for whom class is less salient; among the working class in this latter group, the proportion supporting the Conservative Party is fully 42 per cent. Working class electors who are strongly aware of class are more likely to see politics in terms of the norms and interests of their class and to accord Labour their support. Those to whom class is less evident are more likely to see politics in terms of other values, including those received from the past.

8.14 Relationship of Class to Party by Salience of Class, 1970[a]

	Salience of Class High			Salience of Class Low	
	Grades I–IV	Grades V–VI		Grades I–IV	Grades V–VI
Conservative	69%	**b** 32%	Conservative	78%	**b** 42%
Labour	**c** 31	68	Labour	**c** 22	58
	100%	100%		100%	100%
	Difference, b − c = 1%			Difference, b − c = 20%	

[a] The salience of class was measured by the question numbered 44a in the Appendix.

In this sense, it is the failure of Labour's distinctive class appeal to make an impact on a particular segment of the working class that is the key to Conservative support there. Without the restraint of this appeal, many working class electors are able to give their support to the Conservatives – and to the Liberals too – for reasons that need not be distinctive to the working class. It certainly needs no especial deference by the socially humble to the party of the ruling class to account for the Conservatives' success in drawing support. We had in our sample a number of respondents who could be described as pure specimens of the socially deferential. But we were much more impressed by the fact that the Conservatives attracted working class support for many of the same reasons they attracted support generally in the country.

The difficulties in limiting one's view to the working class may be illustrated in terms of attitudes towards one of the main traditional symbols of British society, the monarchy. When our working class respondents were asked how important they felt that the Queen and Royal Family were to Britain, a clear difference emerged between Conservative and Labour supporters. As Table 8.15 shows, almost three-quarters of the Conservative working class felt that the monarchy was very important, whereas the comparable proportion among the Labour working class was not much more than half.

This cleavage helps us to understand the value patterns which separate Conservatives and supporters of Labour in the working class. Indeed, this difference has not escaped the eye of those who have argued the importance

8.15 Belief in Importance of Monarchy by Party within the Working Class 1963[a]

	Conservative working class	Labour working class
Proportion feeling Queen and Royal Family are very important to Britain	72%	54%

[a] See question 27a.

of the deference motive. It is not difficult to suppose that attitudes towards the monarchy fit into a much more general structure of beliefs, one that includes the obligation on those of inferior social status to accord their betters the support they need to rule. Yet a note of caution is introduced into such an interpretation by extending this comparison to the middle class as well, as we do in Table 8.16.

8.16 Belief in Importance of Monarchy by Party and Class 1963[a]

		Partisan Self-Image	
		Conservative	Labour
Class Self-Image	Working Class	72%	54%
	Middle Class	70%	32%

[a] Entries of table are proportions believing that the Queen and Royal Family are very important to Britain in response to question 27a.

This table makes clear that the stronger association of the Conservatives with this traditional symbol is a general one and is by no means confined to the working class. Indeed, it turns out that the difference is rather muted in the working class. The party groups among working class electors are much more agreed on the monarchy than are those in the middle class; Labour's working class supporters are positively royalist by contrast with those of the middle class. The same point can be extended to other grounds of the Conservatives' appeal. If our view is confined to the working class it is, for example, easy to interpret support for the Conservatives because they are educated men as evidence of the deference motive. But when we see that this aspect of the party's image also reaps an advantage among middle class electors, many of whom have completed university or secondary education, we may wonder whether support on this ground need be seen as a mark of social deference.

It is clear that a great deal turns on the meaning given to the concept of deference. It is possible to see much of the Conservatives' support in the middle class as well as the working class in terms of social deference. Such a formulation would presumably be consistent with the argument advanced by Parkin and others that the Conservatives are the beneficiaries throughout British society of their alignment with the dominant religious, educational and economic institutions and that only where residential or occupational concentration allows the working class to build defences against a 'dominant' value pattern will it be able to assert its own 'deviant' values, including support of the working class party.[1] Such an argument draws attention to the importance of the structure of industry and the pattern of residential concentration for the maintenance of party allegiance, although it can too easily assume a dominant national value pattern as a first explanatory principle; we have seen in Chapter 6 that persuasion within local residential areas erodes middle class Conservative support in areas of low middle class concentration as well as builds Conservative support in the working class in areas of low working class concentration. But if the Conservatives' appeal as a 'national' party aligned with national institutions is to be styled in terms of deference, it is at least clear that this is not a deference that is peculiarly likely to be evoked among people within the lower social strata by reason of their humble station. The whole deference argument has proved to be something of a cul-de-sac in British electoral analysis.

A more evolutionary view of the relationship between class and party would also draw our attention to the rise of Labour support in the middle class. Indeed, the changing pattern of cross-support for the parties in both main classes suggests that the class alignment may have weakened somewhat even in the period in which Labour has most fully occupied its working class constituency. The possibility that these opposite currents were both present in British politics is one to which we now turn.

[1] F. Parkin, 'Working-Class Conservatives: a Theory of Political Deviance', *British Journal of Sociology*, **18** (1967), 278–90.

9 The Aging of the Class Alignment

THE class alignment has, as we have seen, supplied British politics its dominant motif for half a century. Much of the electoral history of this period can be presented in terms of a process of realignment on class lines that is in some respects still under way. It may therefore seem paradoxical to suggest that the class basis of party allegiance was becoming weaker in the 1960s. After all, the working class was at least as heavily Labour in the youngest age-group as in the older cohorts. Indeed, the 1960s continued a long process of evolution.

The key to this puzzle is a generational one. The newer cohorts entered a politics that was dominated by the class alignment and divided their loyalties along class lines more completely than did their elders, those who entered politics half a century before. But the newer cohorts felt much less keenly the social conditions from which the class alignment arose in the first place. Moreover, the social evolution of Britain, as well as certain political factors, tended to weaken the class alignment in the electorate as a whole and not only in the young. We examine in this chapter evidence of the weakening of this alignment both in recent cohorts and in the full electorate over the past decade.

Factors Weakening the Class Alignment

There are good reasons for believing that the electorate has become progressively less inclined to respond to politics in terms of class and that the class appeals of the parties themselves have become much more muted. By far the most important of the social trends which have weakened the inclination to see politics in terms of class is the betterment of the electorate's economic condition. The affluence of the postwar world is much more than an illusion of the party propagandists. Real incomes have risen steadily to levels far above those of the prewar world. Although British economic growth has not kept pace with that of some other advanced countries, it has still sufficed to bring within the reach of the mass market entirely new categories of goods and services. Even those pockets of poverty untouched by a high-wage and high-employment economy have been substantially reduced by a diversity of state welfare services. The concentration of wealth in the hands of a few may have continued to be as great as ever, but the great bulk of wage-earners are far above the poverty standards of the 1930s.

This revolution in economic conditions may not have brought about the embourgeoisement of the British worker in the sense of social identification with the middle class. Nonetheless it is very apparent that the gap in living standards and social habits between the bulk of the middle class and the bulk of the working class has diminished with the rise of disposable income and the levelling influence of the educational system and the mass media, notably television. In Britain, as in other countries, growing affluence tended to undermine the idea of politics as a zero-sum game in which the gains for one class are seen as losses for the other. It was harder to sustain embattled class attitudes when the national wealth was visibly increasing to the benefit of the great mass of the people. The bitter recital of incidents or events with which a number of our respondents expressed their feeling about party or class were related almost without exception to pre-war conditions. No one who culls the references of this sort from a sample of several thousand could miss the force of the remembrance of things past.[1]

The spread of affluence and the decline in some of the cruder contrasts in life style between a large body of slum dwellers and an upper class with large establishments and many servants must have eroded the sense of class distance. Such a trend is reflected in the electorate's own account. In 1970 more than half of our respondents said that class differences had decreased, whereas only slightly more than a tenth thought that they had increased. Indeed, 44 per cent described such differences as 'not very wide' or non-existent. Unquestionably social mobility has added to the bridges over the class divide.

Other aspects of the transformation of British society must have helped dissipate the sense of cleavage between the classes. Over the last generation there has been a revolution in life styles. Slum clearance and the development of suburban owner-occupancy has broken up many long-established

---

[1] The content of such responses is illustrated by the reasons for hating the Conservatives given by a woman of seventy-seven, who had herself been widowed at seventeen: 'I always remember when my father was killed down the pit. And later, when my mother tried to get some assistance, they threatened her with the workhouse. That's all they cared for us.'

local communities. Pop-culture and permissive attitudes have loosened traditional social frameworks and weakened loyalty to many family or class values. The widened horizons of a working class that has grown familiar with foreign travel and of a middle class that has become self-conscious about the explicit assertion of class superiority make it much harder to see the parties in class terms and accept class as a permanent basis for judging which party is to be preferred.

If the electorate's disposition to respond to politics in class terms has been weakened, the parties have also presented the electorate with a class stimulus that is very much weaker both in terms of personnel and policy. Labour's transformation has been especially striking. The party was conceived out of a belief in the 'social composition' theory of represen-tation and its early efforts were focused on increasing the representation – indeed the physical presence – of working class people in the House of Commons. In the interwar years 72 per cent and in 1945 50 per cent of all Labour M.P.s had working class occupational backgrounds. In 1970 only one-quarter did and, for the first time, a comfortable majority of Labour candidates were university graduates. In 1945, 12 out of 24 Labour Cabinet members came originally from manual jobs. In 1970 that could be said of only one out of 23. Figure 9.1 on the next page shows the way in which graduates have taken over Labour Cabinets. Of course, many leading Labour figures are of working class background, but the profile of the Labour politician has become increasingly middle class as local selection committees have preferred more educated candidates and as party leaders have sought out the administrative aptitudes demanded by ministerial office.[1]

On the Conservative side changes of social composition were less striking. But although the party remained overwhelmingly middle class, the upper middle class element became perhaps less preponderant. The percentage of Etonians on the Conservative benches fell from 24 per cent in 1951 to 18 per cent in 1970 and in the Cabinet from 40 per cent to 20 per cent.[2] A party led by the grammar school educated Mr Heath looked very

[1] It is noteworthy that despite our sample's stronger sense that the working class is united in support of Labour (62 per cent thought it was) than the middle class is in sup-port of the Conservatives (only 37 per cent thought it was), the sample placed Labour farther from the working class end of a scale running from working to middle class than it placed the Conservatives from the middle class end (see question 8a). Our interpreta-tion of this at first puzzling finding is that the terms 'Labour Party' and 'Conservative Party' evoked an image more of party leadership than of the mass following and that in these terms Labour's image was more mixed than the Conservatives'.

[2] See A. H. Halsey, ed., *Trends in British Society*, London, 1972, pp. 245–7, for details of the social composition of Cabinets and Parliaments since 1900.

9.1 University Educated Proportion of Labour Cabinet Ministers, 1924–70[a]

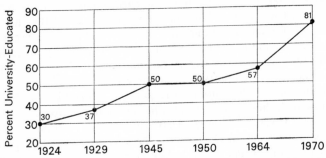

[a] This figure is based on a table in R. Rose, *Class and Party Divisions*, University of Strathclyde, 1968, p. 28.

different from one led by Sir Anthony Eden, Mr Macmillan or Sir Alec Douglas-Home. The distinction that the ordinary voter saw between Mr Heath and Mr Wilson must have been in terms of personality rather than of class.

But any social transformation of the parties or their public spokesmen has been more than matched by changes in policy. Much of postwar history has been for the British voter an education in 'Butskellism' – a phrase invented by the *Economist* in the early 1950s for the convergence in policy between successive Labour and Conservative Chancellors. The education continued apace after the changes of government in 1964 and in 1970. In searching for remedies to the perennial problems of economic growth, of national solvency, of inflation and of industrial unrest, ministers, whatever their party and whatever they may have said in opposition, have turned in succession to similar answers. In such circumstances it is not surprising that there has been a secular decline in the sense of party difference.

The Conservatives have always been sensitive to the need for appealing fairly broadly across the class spectrum. The approaches invoked by Lord Randolph Churchill and Joseph Chamberlain have had their postwar adherents in Lord Woolton and R. A. Butler. Labour has faced more fundamental dilemmas of policy. The party's historic justification for existence was the improvement of the lot of the working class, and this motive has been at the bottom of Labour's social policies, especially the successive extensions of the welfare state. But Labour in power, or near it, has also had to face problems and formulate policies touching national goals and not simply the more sectional or parochial interests of class. It is indeed arguable that only by doing so could Labour have established its qualifications to govern in the eyes of a majority of the electorate, including a substantial part of the working class itself. Yet the conflict between national and sectional interests is sufficiently real for Labour to be drawn away by the tenure of power from a primary identification with class goals and to make the difference between the parties in these terms seem less sharp. One most notable example was the adoption by Labour Chancellors in the 1960s of economic policies that would heighten unemployment and lower the real incomes of working people in order to right the country's international balance of payments and defend the pound. The dominant emphasis in Mr Wilson's 1970 campaign was indeed on having 'got the country out of the red' – by means which often dealt fairly harshly with the interests of Labour's traditional class and trade union constituency.

The difficulties the Labour Government experienced in dealing with the trade unions must have further weakened the class alignment by forcing the party to stand somewhat aloof from its trade union connections. Indeed, recognizing a need to do something about unofficial stoppages, Mr Wilson's Government in 1969 committed itself to an Industrial Relations Bill that included among other things penal sanctions against strikers. Trade union leaders bitterly attacked the proposal and after a celebrated confrontation it was withdrawn. The fact that a Labour Government could contemplate thus defying the movement that had given birth to the party must have had a powerful impact on those who still saw Labour as a clearly differentiated party of the working man. It is true that Mr Wilson did draw back – unlike Mr Heath's Government, which pushed through a similar measure a year later. But the point was surely clear for the electorate: all governments are under some very similar pressures in dealing with the industrial situation.

Opinions within the party differed but there were powerful electoral motives which drew Labour towards a collision with the union leaders. Wide portions of the electorate were unsympathetic to the trade unions and concerned about strikes. Indeed, our interviews showed that few reference objects were more salient to the mass of the people than the trade unions. In our very long schedule of subjects to be raised with respondents, only coloured immigration was more likely to provoke additional, impromptu remarks. Anxiety about strikes, always high, grew steadily throughout the period. The proportion thinking them a 'very serious' problem rose from 78 per cent in 1964 to 84 per cent in 1970.

It would also be impossible to miss the unfavourable opinion of the unions manifest in our interviews. The trade unions do of course find strong support in a large minority of electors, including many in their own ranks, and the attitude of the rest of the electorate is by no means one of unrelieved opposition. A number of our respondents distinguished official from unofficial strikes and showed in other ways as well a mixture of feelings towards the unions and their actions. There are indeed times when the opinion polls have recorded strong sympathy for striking workers. But in all our surveys a four-to-one majority said that, when they heard of a strike, their sympathies were generally against the strikers. Even among union families there were more who said 'against' than 'for'.[1]

By the end of the decade the fraction of the electorate which felt that trade unions had too much power had grown from one-half to two-thirds. In contrast, the period from 1963 to 1970 saw a drop in the percentage of respondents thinking that big business had too much power.[2]

The political consequences of the negative feeling towards the trade unions in much of the electorate depended on the way the public associates the unions and their actions with the political parties. In particular, these attitudes would have had a very different significance according to the strength of the link between the unions and the Labour Party in the public's mind. It is therefore noteworthy how weak a connection the public appeared to see between the unions and Labour in the period of our study. Despite their historical and organizational ties it was rare for respondents to project hostility to the unions on to the Labour Party; indeed, only a little more than a score of respondents mentioned the unions as a reason for disliking Labour at any of our interviews.

Moreover, the separation of the trade unions and Labour Party seemed to the great bulk of electors a desirable state of affairs. Asked whether the

---

[1] The intensity of many of the remarks offered in the generally cordial atmosphere of the survey interview was noteworthy. The Bromley clerk who declared that 'anyone stirring up strikes should be made an example of' and the Folkestone publican who said that 'the unions should be put on crime sheets for unofficial strikes – it's holding up exports' are illustrative of a much wider segment of electors.

[2] The trend in popular feeling about the power of the trade unions and big business was as follows:

	1963	1964	1966	1969	1970
Trade unions have too much power[a]	53%	54%	64%	64%	66%
Do not have too much power	31	32	25	25	24
Difference	22	22	39	39	42
Big business has too much power[b]	59	54	55	48	48
Does not have too much power	25	29	32	37	38
Difference	34	25	23	11	10

[a] See question 17a.   [b] See question 16a.

trade unions should maintain close ties to the Labour Party or stay out of politics, the overwhelming majority chose the latter alternative.[1] This was indeed true even of trade union members. Only the distinct minority of unionists who seemed to view politics as an arena of conflict between opposed class interests gave appreciably more support to the idea of close ties between the unions and the Labour Party.

The incentives to Labour, when in power, to establish its independence from the unions in the eyes of the electorate bear strongly on the discussion of Labour's loosening identification with the working class. The trade unions are of course not synonymous with the working class, nor are the interests of union members those of all working people. Nonetheless, the unions are still predominantly working class organizations, and the fact that a Labour Government sometimes had to take actions that were in sharp conflict with the demands and interests of the unions cannot fail to have blurred Labour's image as a class party. This set of relationships may indeed hold an additional key to the weakening of the class alignment. The negative attitude towards the unions and their strike weapon in much of the electorate gave the Labour Government strong inducement to assert a more general or national interest against that of the unions. This sort of motive is much less important when the party is out of office. But the risks to Labour in power of failing to stand up to a special class-based interest that evoked such wide hostility in the electorate were by no means negligible. Therefore, it might have been to a Labour Government's own self-interest to protect its standing in the country in the short run by dealing firmly with the unions' demands. But in the longer run the consequence could well be to narrow the perceived differences of the parties in terms of class and to weaken the class alignment which had been the pre-eminent basis of electoral choice in the past generation.

It is difficult to believe that the changing ways in which the media have linked political leaders and the electorate have not also played a role in the convergence of the parties in the public's eyes. In an age when television

---

[1] The firming of the public's belief that Labour should be dissociated from the trade unions is shown by these figures:

	1963	1964	1966	1969	1970
Trade unions should have close ties to the Labour Party[a]	25%	19%	16%	16%	17%
Should stay out of politics	60	69	74	72	72
Difference	35	50	58	56	55

[a] See question 17b. Note also question 17c put to a half sample in 1970 to see whether an alternative wording would elicit a different response.

has become the major source of entertainment as well as of political information, rich and poor alike have been more and more exposed to a common set of values. Even the press, although clearly divided between quality and popular papers, has become less differentiated. When party spokesmen debate together on television, it becomes clear how much they have in common both in background and in policy. This is due not only to similarities of style and attitude inculcated by a shared experience of Parliament and ministerial office. It is also due to common assumptions about how to use television, with producers giving similar professional advice to all politicians. When leaders were projecting themselves mainly in Parliament or before public meetings with partisan audiences, they naturally adopted a much more strident note than now when they are wooing moderate and relatively non-political voters, sitting at their own firesides. On television M.P.s learn to appear as reasonable, tolerant, dedicated, intelligent, friendly people whom ordinary voters could trust to act sensibly on their behalf; there is less place for the vehement differentiation of parties along a saint–devil spectrum that may be appropriate on the hustings. Television has done much to shape the party images into a common mould.

Generations and the Class Alignment

Several of the factors tending to erode the class difference of the parties were especially prominent in the 1960s. But the evolution of Britain in a social sense, especially the betterment of the conditions of life, has marked the whole period since the Second World War. We therefore looked for evidence earlier in the decade that the generation which had entered the electorate since the early postwar years would see the tie between class and politics in different terms. In particular, we examined the beliefs about class and party held by the 1951–66 cohort and each of the older cohorts present in the electorate in the early 1960s according to the typology of beliefs set out in Chapter 4.

When this classification was applied to working class Labour voters who entered the electorate in successive periods, we found that the image of politics as the representation of opposing class interests was increasingly accepted as we moved from the pre-1918 to the interwar cohort and reached a peak in the cohort which entered the electorate during the Second World War and its aftermath. But such an image was accepted less frequently among Labour's working class supporters who entered the electorate more recently. This profile is shown by Figure 9.2, which also gives the proportions of working class Labour electors in each cohort who said, in response to a more general question about the extent of difference between the parties, that there was a 'good deal' of difference between them. This

9.2 Frequency of Belief in Politics as Conflict of Opposed Class Interests and Belief in Wide Differences Between Parties Among Working Class Labour Electors in Successive Age-Cohorts[a]

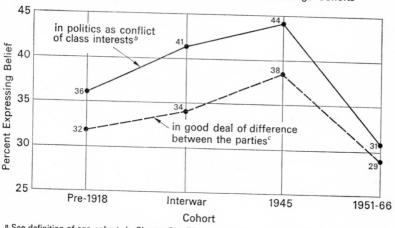

[a] See definition of age-cohorts in Chapter 3, p 59.
[b] Proportion of consistently working class Labour element of each age-cohort of three-interview panel which was coded as seeing politics in terms of a conflict of opposing class interests. See classification of beliefs, Chapter 4, pp. 81–94.
[c] Proportion of working class Labour respondents in each cohort who said in 1963 that they saw a 'good deal' of difference between the parties. See question 5a.

evidence suggests that the 1945 cohort entered the electorate at a time when party support was most clearly connected with perceived class differences and that this connection has been attenuated in the years that followed.[1]

A similar, though not identical, picture is given by the corresponding profiles of belief among middle class Conservatives in successive age-cohorts. As Figure 9.3 on the next page shows, the parties were more likely to be seen as widely differing by middle class Conservatives in the interwar and 1945 cohorts. More important, a relatively strong peaking of belief in politics as a conflict of opposing class interests is seen in the cohort which

[1] Indeed, if we consider the relative proportions of each cohort who held stable and consistent class and partisan self-image over three interviews and held a conflict view of the relation of class and party, the decline of the strength of the beliefs underlying the class alignment was still more striking.

9.3 Frequency of Belief in Politics as Conflict of Opposed Class Interests
and Belief in Wide Differences Between Parties
Among Middle Class Conservative Electors in Successive Cohorts[a]

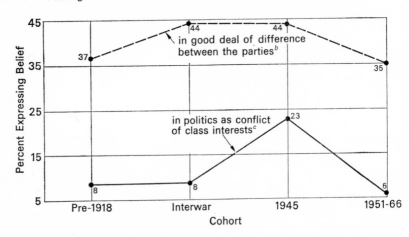

[a] See definition of cohorts in Chapter 3, p. 59.
[b] Proportion of middle class Conservative respondents in each cohort who said in 1963 that they saw a 'good deal' of difference between the parties. See question 5a.
[c] Proportion of consistently middle class Conservative element of each age-cohort of three-interview panel 1963–6 which was coded as seeing politics in terms of a conflict of opposing class interests. See classification of beliefs, Chapter 4, pp. 81–94.

entered the electorate with Labour's accession to power in the aftermath of the Second World War. In accord with the generally lower incidence of such beliefs among middle class electors, the proportion holding this view did not approach the corresponding proportion in the working class. But the hold of a conflict image on the minds of middle class voters had declined between the 1945 and the 1951–66 cohorts.

But the social trends that diminished the strength of the tie between class and party in those who entered the electorate in the 1950s and early 1960s continued to be felt throughout the later decade and must to some degree have influenced the whole electorate. We have moreover noted several specifically political factors tending to weaken the tie between class and party in the 1960s which must also have acted on the electorate as a whole. Writing several years ago we said that the changing pattern of belief about class and party was not as yet matched by a decline in the statistical association of class and partisan self-image. We should now turn to the new evidence about this association during the decade of the 1960s.

The Class Alignment in the 1960s

The evidence of a trend is remarkably clear. Indeed, the declining strength of association between class and party is one of the most important aspects of political change during this decade. Table 9.4 contrasts the strength of

9.4 Partisan Self-Image by Occupational Grade and Class Self-Image, 1963 and 1970

Occupational Grade

	1963			1970	
	I–IV	V–VI		I–IV	V–VI
	a	**b**		**a**	**b**
Conservative	75%	28%	Conservative	70%	36%
Labour	25	72	Labour	30	64
	100%	100%		100%	100%
	a − b = 47%			a − b = 34%	

Class Self-Image

	1963			1970	
	Middle	Working		Middle	Working
	a	**b**		**a**	**b**
Conservative	79%	28%	Conservative	68%	37%
Labour	21	72	Labour	32	63
	100%	100%		100%	100%
	a − b = 51%			a − b = 31%	

this tie in 1963 and 1970 both in terms of the cleavage between non-manual and manual respondents and of the cleavage between those of middle and working class self-images. The data for 1963 show how strong was the relationship between occupation and partisan allegiance in the early 1960s. There is a difference of almost 50 per cent between the proportion of Conservatives among manual and non-manual respondents. But by 1970 this relationship had become attenuated. The difference then between the proportion of Conservatives among non-manual and manual respondents had dropped to 34 per cent. This contrast is still sharper when it is drawn in terms of class self-images. The difference in the proportion of Conservatives between middle and working class respondents was just over 50 per cent in 1963 but only just over 30 per cent seven years later; people were much more ready to depart from the party usually associated with the class to which they felt they belonged.

A more detailed account of the weakening of the class alignment during the 1960s is given by Figure 9.5, which charts for five points in time the

9.5 Strength of Class Alignment with Parties, 1963–70[a]

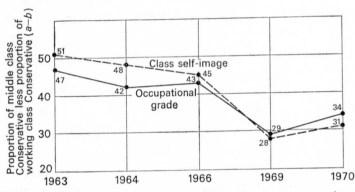

[a] This figure is limited to those having middle or working class self-images or non-manual or manual occupations whose partisan self-images were Conservative or Labour.

contrast in party support between the middle and working class (that is, the difference between the proportions denoted a and b in Table 9.4). The pattern of change over the 1960s that is shown by the figure is one of slight decline in the class alignment between 1963 and 1966, a marked fall-off by 1969, and a slight recovery by the time of the 1970 election. It can also be seen that the decline was more marked in terms of subjective class self-images than in terms of objective occupational groupings, although each showed a marked attenuation by the end of the decade.

A weakening of the class alignment could be observed in each age-cohort of the electorate during the 1960s, but this decline is linked to the generational effects disclosed by Figures 9.2 and 9.3 by the remarkable fact that the alignment was most clearly preserved in the 1945 cohort. The strength of the alignment of the non-manual and manual occupational grades with the parties within each age-cohort in 1969 and 1970 is set out

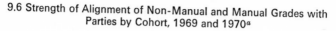

9.6 Strength of Alignment of Non-Manual and Manual Grades with Parties by Cohort, 1969 and 1970[a]

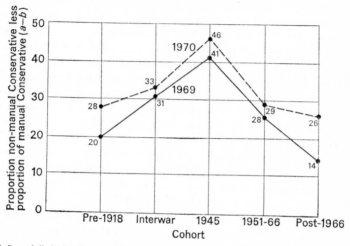

[a] This figure is limited to those in the non-manual and manual occupational grades whose partisan self-image was Conservative or Labour.

in Figure 9.6. It is clear that in the latter part of the decade the alignment of class with party was strongest among voters comprising the 1945 cohort. It was weakest in the pre-1918 cohort, the oldest segment of the electorate, and in the post-1966 cohort, the youngest part of the electorate.

The latter point suggests that the decline in the relationship of class to party across the whole electorate was partly due to the entry of a new half-cohort of voters among whom the alignment by class was quite weak. This entering cohort supplied almost a sixth of those eligible to vote in 1970. One in two of the entering cohort simply replaced dying electors, who were largely drawn from the pre-1918 cohort, in which the alignment of class to party was also fairly weak, as we have seen. Hence our evidence indicates that the weakening of the class alignment was partly due to the coming of age of new voters, whose ranks were swelled by the lowering of the voting age, as well as to a decay in the class–party relationship among those who were present in the electorate throughout the decade.[1]

[1] In 1964, when, as we have seen, our $a - b$ index of class voting had a value of 42 per cent for the electorate as a whole with class defined in occupational terms, this index had a value of only 32 per cent among those of our respondents who would be dead by 1970. Similarly, in 1970 this index had a value of 27 per cent for respondents who had entered the electorate since the 1964 election.

Volatility and the Weakened Alignment

The convergence of the parties in class terms and the weakening of the class alignment is consistent with several of the most notable recent characteristics of electoral support in Britain. The first of these is the fall in voting turnout from 84 per cent in 1950 to 72 per cent in 1970. Evidence for the ebbing of a class vision of politics is especially to be found in the fact that this fall in turnout was heavily concentrated in traditional working class areas, above all in mining seats. Participation also dropped to exceedingly low levels in urban working class areas, notably London's East End. But the fall in mining seats is the more remarkable because participation there had been so high since the rise of the Labour Party and the realignment of support on a class basis. For voters deeply imbued with a belief in working class interests, a movement by Labour away from these goals did not increase the reasons for supporting the opposite party so much as it removed the motive for voting at all.

A second characteristic of recent electoral behaviour that is consistent with a weakening of the dominant class alignment is the far greater volatility of party support. The 1960s saw a remarkable change in the regularity of voting patterns. After the cataclysm of 1945 there had been a period of great stability. The General Election swings of the 1950s were low and few by-elections showed much movement. The Rochdale and Torrington contests in 1958 gave warning that the electorate was unsuspectedly susceptible to change. And from 1962 onwards swings outside all precedent began to appear regularly. If we take as a simple measure the proportion of by-elections in which the Government's share of the vote fell by 20 per cent or more, the trend is very striking, as Table 9.7 shows. In a more

9.7 Proportion of By-Elections Showing Falls in the Government Vote Amounting to over 20% of the Total Poll

1945–51	3%
1951–5	2%
1955–9	10%
1959–64	18%
1964–6	—
1966–70	34%

modest way, General elections showed the same trend. As Table 9.8 shows, the swings in the 1960s were more than twice those in the 1950s.

If we turn to opinion polls, the electorate's greater volatility emerges even more strongly. Over the last thirty years the Gallup Poll's monthly

9.8 General Election Swings, 1951–70

1950s		1960s	
1950–1	1·4	1959–64	3·2
1951–5	2·1	1964–6	2·7
1955–9	1·2	1966–70	4·7
Average	1·6	Average	3·5

questioning on voting intention has provided an invaluable political barometer but it has recorded increasingly unsettled weather, both in the extremes of opinion reached and in the violence of the short-term fluctuation. Figure 9.9, which uses as an index the simple percentage lead of one of the two main parties over the other, shows the remarkable change that came over British politics in the mid-1960s. After 1965 the party lead fluctuated within each twelve months three times as much as it had in the 1950s, and the opposition was at times 15 per cent to 25 per cent ahead. To some extent Figure 9.9 fails to do justice to the increased volatility,

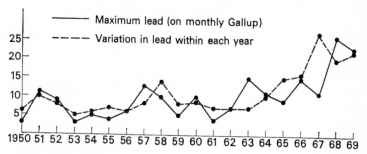

9.9 Volatility of the Electorate in the Gallup Polls, 1950–70

——— Maximum lead (on monthly Gallup)

– – – Variation in lead within each year

Source: Gallup Political Index.

for the voters often deserted Conservative and Labour almost equally to vote for a third party, leaving the major parties' lead over each other unaffected.

The sudden if erratic turning away from the established pattern that so benefited the Liberals in 1962, 1973 and 1974 and the Nationalists in 1967–8 and 1974 was certainly another manifestation of the weakening hold of orthodox party loyalty. Those who have written of the primacy of class have argued that the class alignment has been sufficiently strong to overwhelm other cleavages, especially religious or sectional ones. The direction of influence may actually have been partly the reverse, with the removal of the Irish question after 1920 preparing the way for the pre-eminent role that class was to play. But a weakening of the class alignment might lead us to expect alternative grounds of cleavage to become more evident. This may indeed have provided the background to the spectacular weakening of traditional ties in two traditionally partisan areas, Scotland and Wales. Nationalist candidates in these areas had never made much headway until the middle 1960s; the great bulk of them had lost their deposits. But a Welsh Nationalist won a by-election in 1966 and a Scottish Nationalist in 1967 and, though that tide ebbed, in the February 1974 election there were seven Scottish and two Welsh Nationalists elected.

The greater fluidity made possible by the weakening of the class alignment was still more evident in the great surges of Liberal strength in the early 60s and 70s. An electorate as polarized by class as Britain's in the aftermath of the Second World War could not countenance the appeals of a party that was not class-based. With the weakening of the class alignment in the 1960s it could increasingly do so. The actual and potential gains of the Liberals were a foremost aspect of British political change during the period of our work.

The weakening of the class alignment has, as we have seen, depended in part on the entry into the electorate of a new generation of voters less imbued with the class attitudes of those who were acculturated to politics in an earlier era. This aspect of realignment calls our attention once again to the importance of the physical replacement of the electorate for political change. In succeeding chapters we shall examine the phenomenon of replacement in detail, noting a variety of ways in which this little-understood source of change has altered the shape of British politics over several decades.

PART THREE

Replacement

10 The Study of Political Generations

THE electorate is by no means a constant, unchanging mass. Individual voters die and are replaced by new ones, perhaps fifty years younger, whose ideas and preferences may be quite unlike those their elders carried to the grave. There are also voters who leave the country, and others who come into it from the Commonwealth or other parts of the world. The scale of these demographic changes is sufficient to yield a 10 per cent turnover of the electorate within a five-year Parliament.

We therefore turn from our discussion of the political realignments in which replacement plays a role to explore how the physical turnover of the enfranchised population affects the party balance more generally. The new voters are not replicas of the old. The electorate of 1970 was not made up simply of the children of the electors of 1940. In each generation some people have more children than others, some live longer, some emigrate, and some move to Britain. The political consequences of these demographic facts repay close study.

A Generational Model of Electoral Change

Let us begin our analysis by setting out a grossly simplified model of what would be required to produce permanent political equilibrium with the party balance remaining absolutely constant as successive generations moved through the electorate. It can be stated in a single sentence: equilibrium would be preserved by a society closed to migration in which parents of all partisan persuasions have at the same age of life equal numbers of children who unfailingly inherit from their parents a party allegiance to which they actively adhere throughout lifetimes of uniform length. No society has ever come near to fulfilling the conditions set out in that sentence and such a model is certainly false to British experience in each of its particulars. But an examination of the differences between the model and the real world will direct our attention to important demographic sources of electoral change.

We may draw from such a simplified model six demographic assumptions which, together with three other conditions, would assure political equilibrium:

1. No immigration: no external addition to the electorate.
2. No emigration: no external subtraction from the electorate.
3. Uniform fertility: no difference in family size between the supporters of different parties.
4. Uniform generation length: no difference in the age at which the supporters of different parties have their children.
5. Uniform life-span: no difference in expectation of life between the supporters of different parties.
6. Uniform franchise: no variations in the franchise laws that affect the parties differently.

These six conditions, on which we shall concentrate in this chapter and the next, would be sufficient to assure political equilibrium if we could make three other assumptions as well:

that there is unfailing inheritance by children of the political allegiances of their parents;
that there are no conversions between parties during the elector's life-time; and
that the rate of participation at the polls does not vary between the supporters of each party.

These additional assumptions are useful in allowing us to remove from consideration other sources of electoral change as we focus on the effect of the demographic processes which are for the moment our chief concern. We do not of course accept the truth of these further assumptions. Indeed, the evidence of their falsehood is spread upon many of the pages of this book, and it is worthwhile saying a word about each before returning to the six demographic conditions that are mainly of interest to us here.

The assumption of 'unfailing inheritance' is false to the empirical evidence we have already examined in Chapter 3. Much can be learned, however, by studying the nature of the influences that intervene between parent and child. Not all displacements of the parents' allegiance will alter the party balance in the offspring's generation. Failures of political inheritance can be mutually offsetting and disturb neither the partisanship of generations nor the party balance as a whole; the model of unfailing inheritance is only one of a number of possible equilibrium models. But the likelihood that changes of this sort will shift the party balance is of course high.

They may do so even if these changes are largely random or idiosyncratic. Let us suppose, for example, that one of the parties has twice the adherents of another in the parents' generation and that there is a one-third chance that the child will support the opposite party, whichever that is. These assumptions imply that the ratio of support will be reduced from 67:33 in the parents' generation to only about 56:44 in the children's and to only about 52:48 in the grandchildren's.[1]

The assumption of 'no conversion' flies in the face of the familiar swings of political fortune, the response to political forces which move large parts of the electorate in a common way. It would be impossible to explain either the magnitude or the cyclical character of these swings if we were limited to demographic factors. Much of our analysis is designed to show how the relative strength of the parties has shifted with the changes of preference of voters who remain in the electorate.

The assumption of 'uniform participation' is falsified by the evidence of differences in turnout between the parties. Electors who vote on one occasion but not another provide an element of political change which at times may play a major role in swings of party strength. The importance of this flow to and from abstention will be clear at a number of points when we turn to the analysis of short-term change.

Each of the six demographic conditions incorporated in our equilibrium model is, as we have said, false to the recent experience of Britain. But the errors of each draw attention to an important demographic source of electoral change. The condition of 'no immigration' has never been completely fulfilled. In 1951, 97 per cent of the population were born in the British Isles. But this figure of course included those born in Southern Ireland and has in any case been reduced by immigration in the years since. In 1971 the figure was 95 per cent. The situation has never approached that of Australia, where immigrants or the children of immigrants provide a significant segment of the electorate, let alone Israel, where they constitute

---

[1] The original strength of the larger party would be reduced by the equation

$$67 + \tfrac{1}{3}(33) - \tfrac{1}{3}(67) = 55\tfrac{2}{3}$$

to its level in the children's generation and by the further equation

$$55\tfrac{2}{3} + \tfrac{1}{3}(44\tfrac{1}{3}) - \tfrac{1}{3}(55\tfrac{2}{3}) = 51\tfrac{5}{9}$$

to its level in the grandchildren's generation

a large majority. But we will see that immigration has had a measurable impact on the relative strength of the parties in the recent past.

The condition of 'no emigration' is falsified by the fact that emigrants continue to go to Canada, Australia, South Africa, the United States and other countries. The annual rate of emigration has never exceeded ½ per cent of the whole population, but the (net) loss through emigration during the 1960s still amounted to over a million people. The effect of this flow on the party balance has probably been slight in the recent past, but emigration must be included among the potential sources of electoral change.

The condition of 'uniform fertility' is contradicted by the fact that birth rates and party preferences both differ between classes. The census estimates that seven children were born to wives of manual workers for every five children born to wives of non-manual workers during most of the period in which the present electorate was born (although the effect of this was partially offset by greater infant mortality in the working class). Moreover, there is evidence from several interview studies, including our own, that there are differences of fertility between Conservative and Labour families *within* the working class. Indeed, as we shall show later in the chapter, our evidence suggests that beliefs as to family size tend to be tied to a wider pattern of values and beliefs, of which political allegiance and aspirations of social mobility are also part. If fertility is correlated to partisanship the long-term political consequences of such variations can be very great.

The condition of 'uniform generation length' calls attention to the fact that human beings may reproduce themselves at 17 or at 70. If supporters of one party on average had children at 25 and of the other party at 33, the former would get four generations into a century and the latter only three, so that, to maintain equilibrium, the faster breeders would need to have only three-quarters of the number of children of the slower breeders. The differences in generation-length by class and party are much less dramatic than this,[1] but age of reproduction, as distinct from fertility, can be a source of electoral change.

The condition of 'uniform life-span' is patently false to British experience. The political importance of selective death is implied by the fact that the Conservatives in the modern period have held a greater share of the

[1] We asked our 1970 respondents how old their father was when they were born. The average of the answers was:

Middle class Conservatives	32·5 years
Middle class Labour	31·4 years
Working class Conservative	32·1 years
Working class Labour	32·1 years

political allegiances of women and of the middle class, groups which are marked by longer life. Indeed, the differences of survival between men and women and between the middle and working class offer additional reasons why the oldest electors are the most Conservative: Conservatives have tended to live longer.[1]

But the inferences to be drawn from the facts of differential mortality are both subtle and mixed. The likelihood of dying varies more by age than by, for instance, class or sex; if, for reasons unconnected with selective mortality, the oldest age-cohorts disproportionately favoured one of the parties, then that party would stand to suffer unequal losses due to current deaths. We shall give evidence that this was the situation of the Conservative Party at the end of the 1950s; since it enjoyed an advantage among the oldest electors quite apart from that which the difference in death rates by sex and class would have built up over time, it stood to lose as this age-cohort moved out of the electorate.

Our final demographic condition of 'uniform franchise' has been freshly contradicted in the recent past. Until 1918 the franchise was confined to men; moreover, at the beginning of the century less than 60 per cent of adult males were on the register, with those left off being predominantly working class. Women were not fully enfranchised until 1928, and in 1970 the age of voting for everyone was lowered to 18. The party preferences of the working class, of women and of young voters plainly have never been those of the population as a whole, and changes in franchise rules have helped to alter the party balance.

These factors suggest the variety and importance of demographic sources of electoral change. When reality contradicts any of our null assumptions, substantial shifts of party strength can result. In the pages that follow we review the evidence about emigration and immigration. We also examine more closely the factors of mortality and of fertility and discuss the changes in the franchise which have determined the additions to the electorate. And we assess the evidence on selective removals from the electorate by death. At the end of the chapter we offer a retrospective account of how the present electorate has been built up as successive cohorts of electors have moved through the population. In the next chapter we offer estimates

---

[1] Let us suppose on purely hypothetical grounds that the difference in life expectancy favoured the Conservatives by four years (i.e. the life of a normal Parliament). On present life expectancies the average Conservative would have the chance to vote in thirteen elections before he died and the average Labour elector in only twelve. Thus, for a party equilibrium to be maintained, all other things being equal, the Conservatives would need to recruit only 92 per cent of the number of new voters required by Labour.

of the role of physical replacement in the changes of party strength observed in the years from 1959 to 1970.

Emigration and Immigration

The composition of the British population is constantly changing. The successive Roman, Saxon and Norman invasions probably made smaller proportional differences to the racial composition of the country than have the migrations of the twentieth century. Millions of Britons have gone to English-speaking countries overseas. Hundreds of thousands of Europeans fled to Britain from Eastern Europe before the First World War and from Western Europe before and after the Second – and a still larger number came from the West Indies and then from the Indian sub-continent in the 1950s and 1960s. Moreover, those who left bore children overseas who never reached the British electorate. Those who came added in due course, through their progeny, more than themselves to the registers of voters. The migration statistics tell less than the full story.[1]

Any attempt to measure the electoral impact of external migration is beset with pitfalls. The official statistics on emigration and immigration are incomplete and open to challenge: the estimates of the sending and the receiving countries seldom agree. Let us consider first those who have emigrated from Britain. The published data reveal nothing about the age or life expectancy, let alone the partisanship, of those who have left. To estimate what emigration has cost each party, we have to turn to the figures provided by the host countries. Since over 90 per cent of British emigrants have gone to five countries, it is reasonable to confine attention to the statistics for Australia, Canada, New Zealand, South Africa and the United States. Table 10.1 offers a summary. On the assumption that 85 per cent of these migrants were of voting age,[2] emigration could be said

---

[1] Although internal migration is not the theme of this chapter, the political effects of external migration must be seen in conjunction with it. The overseas immigrants did not come to the same areas the emigrants had left. On the whole they added to the flow towards the metropolitan areas – a long-term trend. Even without external migration, the political map of Britain had been changing continuously as people in search of jobs or wealth moved southwards and citywards from Scotland and Wales and from much of rural England. The political impact of internal migration is one of many fields where our data offer a challenge to further exploration.

[2] This proportion can vary appreciably. In Australia it ranged between 95 per cent in 1947 and 83 per cent in 1961.

10.1 British-Born Residents of Main Receiving Countries

	1930s	1960–1
Australia[a]	712,000[33]	755,000[61]
Canada[a]	1,185,000[31]	970,000[61]
New Zealand[a]	202,000[36]	219,000[61]
South Africa[b]	128,000[30]	137,000[60]
U.S.A.[b]	1,402,000[30]	831,000[60]
	3,629,000	2,912,000

[a] British Isles.   [b] British Isles *less* Eire.
Source: *Australian Year Book; N.Z. Year Book; Canadian Year Book; S.A. Year Book; U.S. Statistical Abstract.*

to have cost the electorate about 3 million members (i.e. approximately 10 per cent of 29 million) in 1930 and 2½ million (i.e. approximately 7 per cent of 35 million) in 1960, if we make no allowance for the children of emigrants.

The solidest evidence on their partisanship comes from Australia where detailed survey studies in 1967–9 showed that British-born Australian voters, when asked to recall their party preferences in Britain, divided 44 per cent Conservative, 30 per cent Labour and 9 per cent Liberal, with 17 per cent unable to say.[1] In our own survey in 1970 we found that respondents who had an emigrant brother or sister (11 per cent of the sample) were currently divided 46 per cent Conservative, 43 per cent Labour and 7 per cent Liberal – almost exactly the same proportions as the rest of the population. In answer to another question no fewer than 35 per cent of our sample admitted to having considered emigrating themselves – but they, too, were politically much like their fellow citizens (42 per cent Conservative, 43 per cent Labour and 8 per cent Liberal). An added fragment of evidence comes from our respondents who were found to have emigrated. In the course of our panel surveys in the 1960s we found that 29 of our 1963 respondents had emigrated when we sought them out for a further interview at some later stage. Although little can be said from so small a sample, 12 of the emigrants were Conservative and 14 Labour.

Hence, we are left without positive reason to suppose that emigration, despite the hundreds of thousands of people involved, has had a very significant net effect on the party balance.

A very different conclusion is, however, to be drawn from the evidence on immigrants. The only immigrants entitled to vote are those who have

[1] Michael James Kahan, unpublished Ph.D. dissertation, Ann Arbor, Michigan, 1972.

already got Commonwealth or Irish citizenship or those who have taken out naturalization papers. Naturalization has not had a major effect on the electorate. Since 1900 only 192,000 naturalization certificates have been issued, three-quarters of them since the outbreak of the Second World War, as shown by Table 10.2. Of course, aliens, whether naturalized or not,

10.2 Naturalization Certificates

1901–40	46,000
1941–50	51,000
1951–60	45,000
1961–70	50,000
	192,000

may contribute children born in Britain to the electorate and, at a guess, there may be 500,000 voters who have foreign roots, either themselves or through their parents.[1] In 1961, of the 804,000 residents in Britain who were born overseas in countries outside the Commonwealth, 312,000 were now British citizens and so entitled to vote. Of these 77,000 were from Germany, 35,000 from Poland, 20,000 from Austria and 18,000 from the territories of the U.S.S.R. The evidence on how these foreign-born electors divided their votes is limited. If we combine our 1964 and 1970 samples we find 19 people born in Europe and a further 51 with European fathers. Of these 70 respondents 47 per cent were Conservative, 37 per cent Labour and 16 per cent Liberal. However, they were very disproportionately middle class – 55 per cent were non-manual in contrast to 35 per cent in the population as a whole. Therefore their net contribution to Conservative strength seems to have been appreciably less than might have been expected. Because of the numbers involved, voters of alien origin could hardly have had a significant effect on the net party balance.

Ireland has provided much the most substantial external source of immigrants entitled to vote. Until 1922 the 26 counties of Eire were an integral part of the United Kingdom and until 1949 Eire was in the Commonwealth. In the 1960s there was still virtually free movement of population between Eire and the United Kingdom, and Eire citizens resident in Britain were entitled to vote in British elections. The 1971 census showed 1·3 per cent of the population of Great Britain as born in Eire. We ourselves found that 2 per cent of our respondents (who, of course, were confined

---

[1] 108,000 alien women and children were registered as citizens in the period 1949–70. Before 1949 children were normally included in their parents' certificate of naturalization.

to those who were of voting age and on the electoral register) were born in Eire.

When one remembers that the Conservative Party was long known as the Unionist Party and that, at least from 1886, it was seen as the barrier to Irish aspirations for Home Rule, it is not surprising that voters with a Southern Irish background proved to be disproportionately anti-Conservative, even when due allowance is made for the fact that they were disproportionately concentrated in the unskilled working class: fully 80 per cent of the Irish-born and 77 per cent of those with Irish-born fathers were in occupational grades V and VI, compared to 60 per cent of those who were British-born. If we confine our attention to those with manual occupations, we find that Labour had a 39 per cent lead over the Conservatives among the Irish-born compared to a 24 per cent lead among the British-born.

The immigration of Commonwealth citizens only reached significant proportions in the late 1950s, although throughout the century there were always some citizens from overseas territories among the electorate (and there had indeed been three Indian M.P.s). Since the British census has never taken cognizance of race, we must depend upon birthplace statistics for any estimates of the coloured proportion of the electorate. A majority of the 218,000 New Commonwealth-born residents recorded in the 1951 census appear to have been the children of British parents serving overseas.[1] But by 1961 there were 541,000 New Commonwealth-born residents and most of these had come in the previous ten years from the West Indies or the Indian sub-continent. The inflow was checked by the Commonwealth Immigrants Act of 1962 and by increasingly restrictive government policies thereafter. However, the number of non-white voters continued to grow sharply, in part through children coming of age, in part through greater efficiency in electoral registration, and in part through continued immigration, especially of the dependants of earlier arrivals. The 1966 census reported that the New Commonwealth-born population of Great Britain was 853,000[2] and the 1971 census 1,160,000.[3]

[1] In 1966 it was estimated that 130,000 of those born in the New Commonwealth were of U.K. ethnic origin. The figure is unlikely to have been any less in 1951.

[2] An amended estimate for 1966 suggested that the population of New Commonwealth ethnic origin was 970,000. See *Registrar-General's Quarterly Return*, no. 488 (no. 4 of 1970).

[3] After allowing for the children of British parents born in the New Commonwealth and for the children of New Commonwealth parents born in Britain, the 1971 census estimates that about 1 million British residents were of New Commonwealth ethnic origin.

Intense controversy has surrounded these statistics and their implications for the future. Mr Enoch Powell attracted great publicity in the 1970 election by his assault on what he claimed to be gross underestimations in the Registrar-General's projections for the future coloured population. Those who flatly refuted Mr Powell still admitted that a substantial margin of error must attach to any such calculations. Some immigrants may have been missed by the census-takers and some may have misreported their place of birth.

Moreover, assumptions about the future are bound to be uncertain. The future pattern of immigration, the extent to which immigrants will return to their native countries and their fertility in the years ahead cannot be clearly established. However, the Runnymede Trust, after painstaking research, suggested that the non-white residents of Britain would almost double in number between 1970 and 1985, as Table 10.3 shows. By 1985

10.3 Estimates of Future Coloured Population in the U.K.[a]

1970	1,679,000
1975	2,088,000
1980	2,518,000
1985	2,980,000

[a] *Race Relations Bulletin, 20,* April 1971 (Runnymede Trust).

at least two-fifths of the projected non-white population would be British-born.

There are difficulties about establishing how many immigrants were of voting age. The 1966 census showed that of the 853,000 New Commonwealth-born residents, 218,000 were under 20, but the subsequent arrival of dependants and the ordinary process of natural increase must mean that, as far as the projections in Table 10.3 are concerned, the proportion of the coloured population under voting age may reach 30 per cent to 40 per cent. On that basis the potential non-white proportion of the electorate would rise from 2 to 3 per cent in 1970 to 4 to 5 per cent in 1985. The word 'potential' should be stressed not only because of the uncertainty of the demographic estimates but also because of the gross under-registration of immigrants in the 1960s. There were some indications, however, that by 1970 immigrants were obtaining and using their vote in rather greater numbers.

How they have divided their support and, still more, how they will divide it are matters of speculation.[1] The indications are that their votes have gone heavily to the Labour Party – partly because Labour was seen as the working class party by immigrants who were quite disproportionately working class, partly because the Conservatives were regarded by many coloured citizens as the imperialist party (just as they were by many Irishmen), and partly because the Conservatives were the party of Enoch Powell. It is possible that leaders of the coloured community might try to deliver a bloc of voters to a new non-white party or to offer their support to the highest bidder among the established parties. But the traditions of the British parties and the harsh logic of the British electoral system make it doubtful that such endeavours could readily succeed. It is reasonable to suppose that for some time to come Labour stands a good chance of securing three-quarters of the coloured vote. By the time in the 1980s that the coloured vote amounts to 4 per cent of the total, this would mean a net gain of almost a million votes to Labour. It is conceivable that, if such a process occurred, and Labour came to be seen as the party of the coloured voter, there could be a 'backlash' with consequent loss of support among the white section of the population. But this is a matter of speculation and depends upon a number of assumptions about the electoral salience of issues which are set out in Chapter 13.

Mortality and Fertility

However, emigration and immigration amount to little compared to the circulation of the electorate due to death and coming of age. Of every hundred electors qualified to vote in 1959, twenty were dead by 1970. Of every hundred qualified to vote in 1970, thirty had come of age since 1959. Indeed, the electors who could have voted both in Macmillan's triumph in 1959 and in Heath's in 1970 were approached in number by those who left the electorate through death or came of age between these Conservative victories.

The transformation which death and coming of age brings to the electorate need not involve party differences in mortality and fertility. If the

[1] For studies of the immigrant vote see A. Singham, in *The British General Election of 1964*, pp. 360–8; N. Deakin, ed., *Colour and the British Electorates, 1964*, London, 1965; N. Deakin and J. Bourne, 'Powell, the Minorities and the 1970 Election', *Political Quarterly*, Oct–Dec 1970, pp. 399–415.

politics of the time leave a lasting mark on successive cohorts entering the electorate, the death of one cohort and the entry of another can alter the party balance without the supporters of different parties having unequal numbers of children or unequally long lives.

But differences both in mortality and fertility may condition the effects of physical replacement of the electorate. In the case of mortality we have noted the difference in life expectancy between men and women, whose political inclinations have been measurably divergent in recent decades, and between the middle and working classes, whose party preferences have been even more sharply divergent. Moreover, there is no evidence that the difference of life expectancy by class has lessened with the introduction of the National Health Service and other welfare measures which might be expected to have ameliorated the conditions of life for the working class. On the contrary, the age-specific death rates for the lowest of the Registrar-General's categories of social class (Class V) actually *rose* between the 1951 and 1961 Census of Population in the older age groups, whereas the death rates for the higher social classes were falling.[1]

What these differences may imply for party support can be seen by charting the contrasting survival-rates among the several political elements comprising a cohort. Let us suppose a cohort to be composed in partisan terms of only two elements, electors who would give undeviating support to the Conservatives and to Labour throughout life. In the context of British society and politics the second of these elements would be more heavily working class and male and therefore of shorter average life. This discrepancy may be represented by a hypothetical graph showing the cumulative proportions of these two elements that will have survived as the cohort moves through the electorate:

[1] For example, the age-specific annual rates of death per 100,000 of population in England and Wales given by the 1951 and 1961 censuses for men within the Registrar-General's social classes I and V, as defined in the 1951 census, were these:

	Class I		Class V	
Age group	1951	1961	1951	1961
25–34	162	76	214	179
35–44	230	165	386	381
45–54	756	528	1,027	1,010
55–64	2,347	1,765	2,567	2,716
65–69	4,839	4,004	4,868	5,142
70–74	7,614	6,278	7,631	8,390

See *The Registrar-General's Decennial Supplement for England and Wales, Occupational Mortality, 1951, Part II, Vol. 2*, pp. 23–7; *1961*, unpublished figures from the Registrar-General.

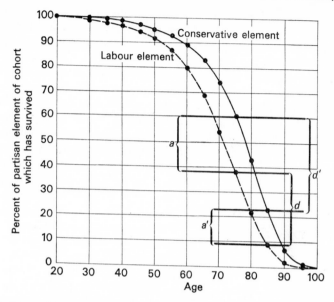

The Labour element within the cohort has the greater number of deaths early in the life cycle and therefore a lower proportion surviving throughout. In an election when the cohort was aged 75 or 85, this difference would cost Labour a real group of votes (a and a').[1] But the graph makes also the important companion point that the party that loses a greater fraction of its initial support through death early in the cohort's life cycle will lose a smaller fraction of its initial support later in the cycle. In the long run everyone in both partisan elements will be dead. Therefore, if more of the Labour element die early, more of the Conservative element must die later and move the party balance within the cohort back towards Labour. In our hypothetical example, the support lost to the Conservatives through death between ages 75 and 85 (d') is substantially greater than the support lost to Labour in the same interval (d), despite the fact that the Conservatives are in an absolute sense benefited by average life expectancy throughout this interval. If the two parties were even when the cohort entered the electorate the pattern of mortality shown by the figure would increase the Conservatives' strength until the cohort was fairly elderly and reduce the Conservatives' strength thereafter.

[1] To translate the divergence of the two curves at a given point in time into an actual difference of votes we would of course need to know the relative initial size of the two partisan elements.

The shifts of relative party strength that differential mortality has produced within each of the cohorts that have moved through the electorate in modern times may be quite substantial in a system where the main parties are evenly matched. We shall not offer precise estimates on this point, but we are impressed by the magnitude of the differentials in mortality by class. Figure 10.4 sets out the survival rates among men which we would expect in the highest and lowest of the Registrar General's social classes if mortality between the ages of 20 and 75 were governed by the age-specific death rates reported by the 1961 census for social classes I and V, as defined by the 1951 census (see note to page 222). The curves shown by Figure 10.4 diverge almost as widely as those drawn in our hypothetical sketch on

10.4 Specimen Survival Rates Among Men in Registrar-General's Highest and Lowest Social Classes[a]

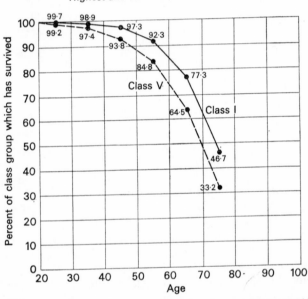

[a] These distributions are based on the age-specific mean annual rates of death reported by the 1961 census for England and Wales among males within social classes I and V, as these classes were defined by the 1951 census.

the preceding page. We would need to know the partisanship of the two classes to translate this illustrative divergence into party advantage. But if we assume that social class I will be generally Conservative and social class V generally Labour, this difference in life expectancy would plainly work substantially to the Conservatives' advantage. It seems probable that the greater life expectancy of the middle class (and to a lesser extent of women) has made each cohort that has moved through the modern electorate increasingly Conservative. Indeed, if we took account of class differentials in infant mortality as well, the relative benefit that selective death gave to the Conservatives would be found to have been even more marked.

An additional aspect of the effect of differential mortality on political change emerges only when we extend our view beyond a single cohort and take account of deaths in several cohorts at once. Death rates differ by age more than they do by any other factor, including class and sex. Hence the cohorts at the top of the age structure in a given period will move out of the electorate much more rapidly than those below. The political significance of this becomes evident when we note that the older and younger cohorts can have very different partisan composition, owing to the influence of earlier experiences, especially the issues and events that dominated the political scene when each entered the electorate. As a consequence, a party whose strength is more heavily concentrated in the older cohorts may lose far more support than its rival from selective death even in a fairly brief span of years. We shall see in Chapter 11 that this happened during the Parliaments of the 1960s, when deaths in the older age-cohorts, which were more strongly Conservative, produced a net shift towards Labour.

It is a fairly straightforward extension of this logic to use our knowledge of death rates to project future changes of party strength as the cohorts comprising the present population move out of the electorate. Such projections must be understood to be *ceteris paribus*: we may say what effect differential mortality would have under certain assumptions as to other conditions that will hold in the future, although these assumptions are certain to be wrong in detail. Indeed, the death rates that will actually govern the future mortality of the cohorts in the present electorate will themselves change in ways that cannot be entirely foreseen.

Such projections demonstrate that the movement of cohorts out of the electorate can have measurable consequences for the strength of the parties. On the assumption of constant death rates we would expect a swing to Labour as the century progressed and death claimed a heavier toll from the older cohorts, in which the Conservatives were disproportionately strong. Indeed, if we were to confine our attention to the electorate surviving from the 1960s and ignore electors who would have come of age after that, the swing to Labour due to selective death would reach 4 per cent by the end of the century. With allowance for the fact that as the century advanced the proportion of electors surviving from the 1960s would be a progressively smaller element of the total electorate, that figure would be smaller. And, it must be reiterated, all this is on an 'other things being equal' basis; it is in fact clear that there will be net changes of party support among the survivors from the 1960s – indeed, on an increasing scale, if the recent past is any guide. We may also wonder whether the main parties or the two-party system will in fact survive the century.

Movements across the threshold leading out of the electorate are likely to change the party balance less rapidly than movements across the threshold leading into the electorate. Since death claims electors in several cohorts at once, the party views of those who die are in some degree an average of several cohorts, whereas those coming of age belong to only a single cohort which may be quite distinctive in party outlook as, for example, the 1945 cohort plainly was. The distinctiveness of the young can be the result of their greater responsiveness to the forces that dominate politics when they come of age. But the party composition of those in a new cohort may diverge from that of their parents' simply because of the differing extent to which different parts of the electorate reproduce themselves. If all children were to inherit their fathers' party allegiance, the party balance in the new generation would still swing towards the party of those who had most children.

Fertility would be a factor in political change even if it did not differ by party in the parents' generation. Unless this generation were precisely representative of the whole electorate, its average fertility would affect the party balance in the electorate. If the downward trend of births in the inter-war period had continued through the Second World War and beyond the age distribution and politics of Britain in the middle 1960s – and 1970s and 1980s – would have been measurably different.

But the importance of fertility is added to by the fact that supporters of one of the parties may reproduce themselves more than supporters of the other. Several types of evidence suggest that this sort of differential has been present during much of the period in which the modern electorate was born. Glass and Grebenik's analysis of live births to wives of manual and non-manual husbands who were married during four successive intervals earlier in the century shows that the ratio of seven births in the manual group to five in the non-manual group was remarkably stable, despite the fall of the birth rate in both groups.[1] Such a ratio implies a gain in Labour's

---

[1] See D. V. Glass and E. Grebenik, *The Trend and Pattern of Fertility in Great Britain: a Report on the Family Census of 1946*, Part I, p. 106. Their figures on the average number

relative strength between generations. This implication is consistent with the evidence of several interview surveys that attest the difference of fertility between the supporters of different parties. Of Conservative respondents in the 1965 Gallup sample analyzed by Kelvin only 47 per cent said they grew up with three or more brothers and sisters, whereas 60 per cent of Labour respondents grew up in a family of this size.[1] Our own studies found the average number of minor children in the homes of Conservative parents aged 20 to 39 to be 1·57, whereas the average number in the homes of Labour parents within this age group was 1·77. Moreover, survey evidence suggests that a gradient in fertility by party may be found *within* the class groupings. Kelvin reported that the proportion of respondents who grew up with three or more siblings was 36 per cent among Conservative non-manual respondents, 49 per cent among Labour non-manual respondents, 56 per cent among Conservative manual respondents, and 69 per cent among Labour manual respondents.[2] Our own studies found a marked difference in fertility by party within the working class. Working class parents aged 20 to 39 who identified with the Conservatives had an average of 1·35 minor children in the home, whereas Labour working class parents in this age group had an average of 1·76 children in the home.

---

of live births to manual and non-manual women married below the age of 45 according to the period of marriage are these (when weighted to compensate for the bias caused 'by the selection of earlier ages at marriage to which all fertility censuses are subject'):

Date of marriage	Status group I (non-manual)	Status group II (manual)	ratio of II to I
1900–9	2·75	3·88	1·41
1910–14	2·32	3·24	1·41
1915–19	2·05	2·86	1·40
1920–4	1·89	2·67	1·41

In view of the technical difficulty and conceptual ambiguity of identifying the occupation of the father in the case of illegitimate births, it is natural that most fertility data by class refer to legitimate births. But we may suppose that the rates of illegitimate births differ even more sharply by class. However, Myra Wolf in *Family Intentions*, H.M.S.O., 1971, argues from recent survey data that expected family size is now declining among people with manual occupations while staying stable in the non-manual classes.

[1] See R. P. Kelvin, 'The Non-Conforming Voter', *New Society*, November 25, 1965, pp. 8–12.

[2] Ibid., p. 9. These differences do not strictly speaking measure fertility differentials by class in the parents' generation, since some respondents will have moved above or below their parents' social location. Yet it is most improbable that these differentials within class in the children's generation are purely a consequence of social mobility.

Changes in the Franchise

The question of who gets into the electorate depends on both legislation and administration. The proportion of the total population on the electoral register rose from 15 per cent in 1900 to 73 per cent in 1970. The proportion of the adult population rose from 27 per cent in 1900 to 98 per cent in 1969, before the definition of an adult changed.

In 1900 the only people entitled to vote were men over 21 who were ratepayers or independent lodgers and who had resided in one place for twelve months. It was also possible to be placed on the register in a second constituency as the occupier of private or business premises, and university graduates, too, had an extra chance to vote in the 12 university seats. The number in the electorate was equal to 58 per cent of the adult male population but, because of plural voting, the actual proportion of British men with the franchise cannot have been much more than 53 per cent. Registration procedures were cumbersome and in some cases whether a man got on to the register depended upon claims or objections made by the local party organizations.

In 1918 women over 30 were enfranchised and virtually all men who had a six months' residence qualification became entitled to vote. In 1928 women over 21 were also enfranchised and by 1939 the number on the register was equal to 97 per cent of the adult population. Allowing for plural qualifications (which survived until 1949), 94 per cent of adults were probably in a position to vote.

Since 1950 the numbers on the register have been virtually conterminous with the adult population. However, there seems to have been an error rate of about 4 per cent, with obsolete names roughly balancing omissions. In the early 1960s there was concern that the register was particularly inefficient in recording New Commonwealth immigrants. The last major change in the franchise came with the 1969 Act, which gave everyone the vote at their eighteenth birthday. As we show in the next chapter, only 70 per cent of 18- to 21-year-olds actually got on to the register.

When we cite the trend of election results in this century, it is easy to forget this transformation of the electorate. Those men who did not have the vote before 1918 were mainly working class. The new politics of the 1920s must have owed as much to their enfranchisement as to the after-effects of the war or the enfranchisement of women. The giving of the vote to women over 30 must, indeed, have worked in some ways in the opposite direction. The abolition of plural voting in due course offered a mild bonus to the Labour Party and so, as we shall show in the next chapter, did the enfranchisement of 18-year-olds in 1970.

Generations and Political Change

We are now ready to gather together the long-term consequences of all these factors in the replacement of the electorate, and to see what insights may be derived from a model of political change which follows the movements of successive cohorts through the electorate

The period from the beginning of the century to 1970 is roughly spanned by two thirty-year generations or four half-generations of fifteen years each, with an additional half-cohort of seven years that joined the electorate in 1967–70 (boosted by the lowering of the franchise age). Our four and a half cohorts entered the electorate approximately during these four successive half-generations of time, and an idealized sketch of their movement upwards through the age structure is shown below. This idealization halts at four points in time – 1918, 1935, 1950 and 1966 – the continuously-moving process by which individual electors come of age, advance through the life cycle, and pass out of the electorate through death. The electorate of 1970 was comprised of the four and a half cohorts for which we have direct evidence. In 1950, a half-generation before, the 1951–66 and 1966

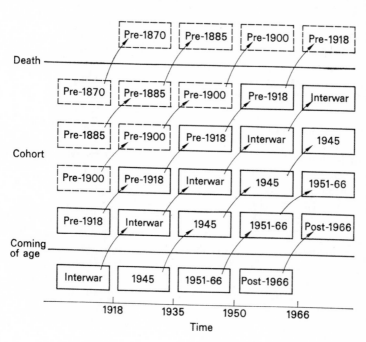

cohorts had yet to enter the electorate, all other cohorts were less old, and a 'pre-1900' cohort had yet to pass out of the electorate. In 1935, a half-generation still farther back, the 1945 cohort had yet to enter the electorate, and a cohort which came of age before 1885 had still to leave the electorate through death. The cohorts for which we do not have direct evidence are drawn more faintly in the sketch.

The two thresholds suggested by the sketch offer a simplification of reality. In the case of the threshold of entering the electorate there is the additional complication of restrictions on the franchise of women under 30 before 1928 and of all women and various categories of men before 1918. But the greater simplification is the threshold of departing the electorate, since death does not remove a cohort during a single span of half a generation. From the moment a cohort comes of age (indeed even before), death begins to take its toll, although in Britain these losses only become at all heavy after a cohort passes middle age. We may therefore see the pre-1918 cohort in the middle 1960s, for example, as the surviving element of a larger cohort which entered the electorate between 1900 and 1918 and was steadily diminished by death over the next four decades.

A series of analytical steps are required if we are to reconstruct the evolution of the strength of the parties according to the generational model set out above. Our estimates of the effects of various of these factors are too imprecise for our reconstruction to be sharply accurate. But we can still suggest how such a reconstruction would proceed, and we can set out some very tentative estimates from the evidence that we do have.

We begin with the distribution of party support in the cohorts for which we have direct evidence and from our knowledge of the relative size of each cohort within the electorate as a whole. The party division of the total electorate in the 1963–70 period can be regarded as a weighted average of the division within each of our four and a half cohorts, where the weights are given by the relative magnitude of each cohort in the whole adult population. As we carry the reconstruction back one half-generation in time, we must unravel the effects of several types of changes. First of all, the cohorts that comprised the electorate in 1950 will have been diminished by death by 1970. These losses will be relatively light in the 1945 cohort, heavier in the interwar cohort and still heavier in the pre-1918 cohort. They will have been heaviest of all in the pre-1900 cohort, which our sketch represents figuratively as having crossed the threshold leading out of the electorate during this period. Estimates of the partisan division of the 1945, interwar and pre-1918 cohorts before death took its toll can be built up from what we know of class and sex differences in party preference and mortality and of shifts of party preference among those in these cohorts who did not die between 1950 and 1970.

Reconstructing the party division of the pre-1900 cohort as it might have been in 1950 requires other means, since virtually no one from this cohort survived to the 1960s to give us direct evidence of their party preferences. We have done this by relying on the reports of parents' partisanship given by those who may be regarded as the children of the pre-1900 cohort. Such reports offer indeed a more general opportunity of pushing our inquiry back in time to encompass cohorts which have passed out of the electorate. Each of our cohorts, as we have defined them, is comprised of those entering the electorate during the same half-generation of time; hence, each is comprised of those born during the child-bearing years of the second cohort preceding them in the age structure, since the average difference in age between father and child is about 30 years. We may therefore establish a parent–child relationship between alternate cohorts in our sample and beyond it and identify the interwar cohort as the children of the pre-1900 cohort, collectively speaking.[1]

To resurrect such a missing cohort we must allow, first, for the fact that those who comprised the pre-1900 cohort were not equally present in the memories of the interwar cohort. There was no one to tell us the votes of those now dead who never married or who remained childless.[2] The true cohort was transformed into the remembered one by differentials both of fertility in the parents' generation and of mortality in the children's generation, which had already been diminished by death. We must therefore use our evidence on how fertility and mortality have differed across the social and political elements of these cohorts to remove the partisan distortion inherent in this transformation. And we must of course also allow for the net shifts of party support among those in the pre-1900 cohort who survived to 1950 from their child-rearing years earlier in the century.

With these estimates of the partisan division and the relative size of the cohorts comprising the electorate in 1950 we could form a weighted mean that will give the partisan division in the whole electorate at that time.

[1] Since a parent–child relationship can be identified between two of the pairs of cohorts for which we have direct data (the 1945 cohort are the children, collectively, of the pre-1918 cohort and the 1951–66 cohort are the children of the interwar cohort), we may use this fact to gain some insight into errors involved in the recall of parents' party allegiance, when due allowances are made for the effect of differential fertility and mortality and changes of party support in the parents' generation between its child-rearing period and the middle 1960s.

[2] We have noted the importance of differential fertility in distorting the memory of a historical cohort when we reconstructed the religious cleavage in the pre-1900 and pre-1885 cohorts in Chapter 7.

And by successive application of these procedures to earlier periods we might reconstruct the party composition of the cohorts comprising the electorate at intervals of half a generation back to the earliest decades of the century. Other factors might be taken into account in a full reconstruction of the past. The class differentials in fertility and mortality suggest the importance of taking rates of upwards and downwards mobility into account. And we might well relax the assumption that the British electorate has been closed to migration and study the effects of emigration and immigration on the social and political composition of the population.

Our own reconstruction is still quite preliminary, and we offer here much less than the estimates which might issue from an exhaustive modelling of these processes of change. We set out in Table 10.5 a tentative

10.5 Party Composition of Successive Cohorts Comprising the Electorate[a]

	Pre-1885	Pre-1900	Pre-1918	Interwar	1945	1951–66	1966–
Conservative	43%	46%	45%	43%	34%	33%	35%
Labour	12	20	39	40	49	50	50
Liberal	38	27	11	11	11	10	6
None	7	7	5	6	6	7	9
	100%	100%	100%	100%	100%	100%	100%

[a] Estimates of the party composition of the four and a half cohorts comprising the electorate in the 1963–70 period are based on the preferences given by our samples during this period. Estimates of the party composition of cohorts which have passed out of the electorate are based on the recollection of parents' preferences held by members of the cohorts which are comprised, collectively speaking, of their children. These estimates were adjusted for the greater fertility of the working class and for the mean bias of recall observed in estimating the party composition of the pre-1918 cohort from the recollection of parents' preferences held by the 1945 cohort and the party composition of the interwar cohort from the recollection of parents' preferences held by the 1951–66 cohort. In the case of the pre-1885 cohort an adjustment was also made for selective death in the pre-1918 cohort (the cohort of children of the pre-1885 cohort) over the years since it formed its impressions of parents' party allegiance.

sketch of the party composition of the cohorts which have comprised the electorate in this century. These estimates of the proportions Conservative, Labour, Liberal, and unattached in successive cohorts are especially frail where they depend on the memories within a living cohort of the political allegiances of parents who have died, corrected for the distortions we are able to observe in the memories of fathers' allegiances held by cohorts whose parents, collectively speaking, were still represented in our samples from the 1963–70 period.

Nonetheless, the estimates given by Table 10.5 offer additional insight into the electoral past, especially into the decline of the Liberals and the rise and diffusion of Labour support as the century wore on. The full array can indeed be seen as underlining the importance that the physical turnover of the electorate has for the broadest and most lasting electoral changes. Some of the change recorded in these estimates reflects transient shifts of support among those who remained in the electorate between successive periods, and these shifts would be of greater importance if we sought to account for fluctuations of party support within such periods, as we do in Chapter 12. But our estimates here show most of all the role which the replenishment of the electorate has played in the great changes of alignment that have characterized British politics in this century.

11 Replacement and Political Change 1959–70

THE parallel processes of emigration and immigration and of death and coming of age can have far-reaching political effects over the long term. In the short run their consequences must be smaller but may still be substantial. In this chapter we shall consider the role of replacement in political change in the years from 1959 to 1970. Inspection of the recent past has the advantage of limiting our view to a period for which our information is more ample. When we examine the 1960s we have less need of the speculative assumptions that must go into any judgment on the effects of replacement in decades longer past or in decades yet to come.

Replacement and Short-Term Change

The study of replacement casts further light on the processes that underlie net shifts of party support from one election to the next. It is increasingly common in Britain to reduce such shifts to a single measure of swing. This practice has undoubted virtues. But it can easily conceal two aspects of the more complex realities which underlie net change. On the one hand, it may suggest that change is the result of straight switches from the losing to the winning party rather than of an extraordinarily intricate pattern of partially offsetting changes among the several parties and of moves between voting and abstention. Much of our next chapter is a documentation of this point. On the other hand, a measure of swing may suggest that the electorate is a constant entity rather than the changing entity it actually is. The electorate is indeed like a residential hotel, with guests always arriving and departing.

It is clear that a very simple relationship obtains between the composition of the electorate at a particular point in time and its composition at some prior time. The new electorate is comprised of the old electorate diminished by emigration and death and augmented by immigration and comings of age. We may express this in terms of a simple identity or accounting equation of the following form:

$$\text{New electorate} = \text{Old electorate} - \text{Emigrants} + \text{Immigrants} \qquad (1)$$
$$- \text{Deaths} + \text{Comings of age.}$$

Since the party preferences of the departing or entering groups at the right of this equation explain part of the shift in the overall strength of the parties, we must build up an account of the influence of replacement by examining the size and party allegiance of the groups which entered or left.

This equation ignores one element of change which has been an important factor in the recent past – the inclusiveness of the electoral register. Part of what is involved here is the administrative efficiency of the registration process. But what is also involved is the question of who is legally entitled to be placed on the register. There is not much harm in our ignoring the persistent small inefficiency of the electoral register. It is reasonable to suppose that a substantial proportion of those who are unregistered in one year continue to be unregistered in the next and that the number moving on and off the register for accidental reasons between years is small enough to be of negligible political significance.[1] But much more serious inefficiencies have been detected in the registration of two groups of great importance for replacement in the recent past, Commonwealth immigrants and the newly enfranchised voters between the ages of 18 and 21. In these cases it is natural to treat inclusion in the register as a special aspect of immigration and maturation.

Electors, it should also be stressed, are not necessarily voters. The largest element of change between one contest and the next lies not in those who in the natural course of events join or leave the electorate but in those who use their franchise one time but not the other. However, we shall in the main reserve the problem of shifts between voting and non-voting for our discussion of changes between voting for one party and voting for another in the next chapter. Our present purpose is to assess the size of the groups in our accounting equation and to gauge the party preferences of these groups so that we may enter figures for the 1960s in a table of this form:

	Con.	Lab.	Lib.	Other
Emigrants	− ?%	− ?%	− ?%	− ?%
Immigrants	+ ?%	+ ?%	+ ?%	+ ?%
Deaths	− ?%	− ?%	− ?%	− ?%
Comings of age and changes in the franchise	+ ?%	+ ?%	+ ?%	+ ?%
Net party change	± ?%	± ?%	± ?%	± ?%

[1] This is confirmed by the tendency of those whom we found in our own surveys in 1963 and 1969 to be unregistered at a sample address to be still unregistered even if they lived at the same address a year later.

Emigration 1959–70

Well over 2 million citizens left the United Kingdom for more than a year during the 1960s. When allowance is made for those who were only on an overseas posting or a prolonged period of holiday or study, and for those who became disillusioned with emigration and returned home, the net loss of United Kingdom citizens was over a million. In the peak years of 1965–8 the net annual loss varied between 128,000 and 175,000.[1] In addition a significant number of Irish and perhaps of New Commonwealth immigrants went back to their own countries.

Our evidence does not enable us to discriminate between the party balance among emigrants at different points of time (it is possible that the post-pay-freeze emigrants of 1962–3 were exceptionally Labour and the post-devaluation emigrants of 1968 were exceptionally Conservative). In Chapter 10 we argued that in recent decades emigrants seem to have been drawn almost equally from the two main parties. In the 1960s, too, despite the appreciable numbers involved it would be hard to conclude that emigration had any net effect on the party balance. In Table 11.1 we draw on

11.1 Percentage Loss to the Electorate through Emigration, 1959–70

Con.	Lab.	Lib.	Non-Voters	Post-1959 Emigrants as Percent of Total Electorate
−1·1	−1·1	−0·2	−0·4	2·8

the data set out in the previous chapter to suggest the orders of magnitude of the changes in the electorate that were due to emigration in the 1960s.

Immigration 1959–70

Immigration is another matter. The number of Eire-born residents in Britain was 726,000 in 1961, 738,000 in 1966 and 721,000 in 1971. These figures go against the Government's international travel survey which reported a net gain (of residents entering for more than a year) of about 30,000 a year throughout the 1960s.[2]

[1] See 'External Migration', pp. 36–49, *Registrar-General's Statistical Review* for 1967 (vol. III).

[2] On the other hand, if the international travel survey were right and if 90 per cent of a net gain of 30,000 Irish a year were adults, this would mean that 1959–70 saw an increase of 300,000 in Eire-born electors and of, say, 200,000 in the number of Eire-born

The number of New Commonwealth-born rose from 541,000 in 1961 to 853,000 in 1966 and 1,160,000 in 1971. The number who were registered as electors and used their votes increased much more than proportionately. In a painstaking nationwide sample of qualified electors in 1964 our interviewers encountered only 8 coloured voters in a total sample of 1769. In 1970 a new sample of 1845 respondents yielded 36 who were coloured. Fourteen of these said they had voted in 1966 (and 24 said they had done so in 1970). Deakin and Bourne argued that the number of coloured people on the electoral register rose sharply and that, in contrast to 1966, they voted in as large numbers as the rest of the electorate.[1] All the evidence suggests that the votes of those born in the New Commonwealth were more overwhelmingly Labour even than those of the Eire-born. If there were 500,000 of them and if they divided 75:25 between Labour and Conservative, the net gain to Labour would amount to 250,000 votes (or almost 1 per cent of the national total). In Table 11.2 we offer a very tentative summary of the effect of Irish and Commonwealth immigration.

11·2 Percentage Gain to the 1970 Electorate through Immigration, 1959–70

Con.	Lab.	Lib.	Non-Voters	Post-1959 Immigrants as Percent of Total Electorate
+0·3	+1·0	+0·1	+0·5	1·9

Deaths 1959–70

Between 1959 and 1970, 7 million people of voting age died in Britain. Most were above the age of 60 and had acquired their politics before the Labour Party had entered fully into its political inheritance. Their departure from the electorate had a measurable impact on the party balance. Our problem of assessing this impact divided into two. To measure the change wrought by selective death between 1959 and the first of our interviews in 1963 we combined census estimates of the death rate in each of a set of

who actually cast votes. If they divided in the ratio 60:23 between Labour and Conservative (the figure we found for all our Eire-born respondents), this immigration would have added over 100,000 more votes to Labour than to the Conservatives (the equivalent of a 0·2 per cent swing). If we accept the census there is no reason to suppose that Irish immigration affected the party balance, except in so far as it offset Irish re-emigration.

[1] N. Deakin and J. Bourne, 'Powell, the Minorities and the 1970 Election', *Political Quarterly*, Oct–Dec 1970, pp. 399–415.

population categories jointly defined by age, occupational grade, sex and (for women) marital status with our knowledge of how the surviving electors in each of these categories had voted in 1959. In other words, we assumed that those who died had had the same politics as those of the same age and class and sex who survived, and worked out the partisan composition of the group that had died between 1959 and 1963 from our knowledge of the toll death would have taken from each population category.

A simpler procedure could be followed to measure the change wrought by death after the first of our interviews, since in this case we did not need to reconstruct the partisanship of people we had never reached. To assess the impact of death in each of several periods between 1963 and 1970 we have used as a benchmark the party preferences in 1963 of all members of our sample who had died by 1970,[1] corrected these to take account of the swings of party fortune between 1963 and the beginning of the period in which we wished to estimate the effect of death, and applied these corrected preferences to the fraction of the electorate we estimated from census information to have died in the period. For example, in estimating the political effects of removals by death between the elections of 1964 and 1966 we adjusted the 1963 preferences of those who died in the course of our studies to take account of the shift of party fortune towards the Conservatives between 1963 and 1964 and then assigned these corrected preferences to the fraction of the electorate that, according to census estimates, had died in the seventeen months between October of 1964 and March of 1966.

The conclusions about the effects of death reached by these methods are set out in Table 11.3. The first and last rows of the table indicate that selec-

11.3 The effect of Death, 1959–70

	Conservative	Labour	Liberal	None	Percent of electorate at beginning of period
1959–64	−3·8	−2·6	−0·2	(0·7)	6·7
1964–6	−0·8	−0·8	−0·1	(0·4)	2·1
1966–70	−2·6	−2·7	−0·3	(0·9)	7·5
1959–70[a]	−7·5	−6·4	−0·8	(1·9)	19·0

[a] Since the figures for each interval are based on the electorate at the start of the interval, the entries for 1959–64, 1964–6 and 1966–70 do not sum to those for 1959–70.

[1] We have in each case used our information about the preferences of those who died over the full period from 1963 to 1970 to increase the stability of our sample estimates.

tive death hurt the Conservatives more than Labour between 1959 and 1964. Indeed, the unequal losses of the parties due to death over the 1959 Parliament were enough to supply Mr Wilson with his final margin of victory in 1964. Because Labour was stronger at the beginning of the 1964 and 1966 Parliaments, the effects of death were much more evenly divided between the parties in these later periods.

Comings of Age 1959–70

Between 1959 and 1970 nine million people reached the traditional voting age of 21, and only a minuscule fraction of these subsequently disappeared from the electorate through death or emigration. Moreover, in 1970 the legal age of enfranchisement was dropped to 18, and an additional 2,800,000 people between the ages of 18 and 21 acquired the right to vote. Although these newly enfranchised voters were more likely than others to have been left off the register or, even if they were placed on the register, to have failed to vote, their presence gave the entry of new voters additional significance at the end of the 1960s.

Let us first of all assess the importance in the period from 1959 to 1970 of the entry of those who had reached the voting age in effect at the time. The results of our analysis of the effects of their entry, set out in Table 11.4,

11.4 The Effect of Enfranchisement, 1959–70

	Conservative	Labour	Liberal	None	Percent of electorate at end of period
1959–64	+2·7	+3·3	+0·5	(2·7)	8·6
1964–6	+0·4	+0·8	+0·1	(1·4)	2·7
1966–70	+4·0	+6·4	+0·9	(5·4)	17·7
1959–70[a]	+8·8	+11·8	+1·9	(7·8)	32·2

[a] Since the figures for each interval are based on the electorate at the end of the interval, the entries for 1959–64, 1964–6 and 1966–70 do not sum to those for 1959–70.

make clear how important they were to the fortunes of the Labour Party in this period. Of the total swing to Labour between the elections of 1959 and 1964, a seventh could be attributed solely to the unequal impact of the entry of new voters. Hence, this type of demographic change could also be said to have given Labour its final margin of victory in 1964. The shortness of the period between the 1964 and 1966 elections diminished the importance of the entry of new voters in 1966. But the table makes clear how unequal was Labour's benefit from the support in 1970 of those who had crossed the threshold of age 21 during the 1966 Parliament. Those who crossed this threshold over the entire period from 1959 to 1970 accounted for a swing to Labour of fully 1½ per cent. If the 1970 election had been decided only by the electorate surviving from 1959, Mr Heath would on this evidence have won a handsome victory and entered office with a majority around 80 instead of 30.

The lowering of the minimum voting age from about 21½ to exactly 18 on February 15, 1970, provided the first substantial increase in the franchise since the Representation of the People Act of 1928 made the voting qualifications for women virtually the same as for men.[1] It should have increased the number of people entitled to vote by about 2·8 million, or by about 8 per cent. But in practice the increase was much less. According to an unpublished Opinion Research Centre Survey, only about 70 per cent of the 18–21-year-olds were on the 1970 register.[2] Additional evidence of the extent of the omissions is supplied by the number of 18-year-olds appearing on the register. In order that an elector could vote immediately on reaching 18 the new register included the birth dates of those born between February 16, 1952, and February 15, 1953. The census indicates that about 800,000 electors from this age group ought to have appeared on the register. In fact only 464,000, or 58 per cent, did. In subsequent years the register has become more efficient, but there is no doubt that in 1970 the impact of the law extending the franchise was much less because of the failure to implement it fully.

The extension of the franchise also had less impact than some expected simply because the young were less politicized. Even those who were on the register voted in smaller numbers than any other age group apart from

[1] From 1951 to 1970 people born between June 2 and October 10 could first vote on the February 15 following their twenty-first birthday. People born between October 11 and June 1 could first vote on the October 2 following their birthday. Under the new Act passed in 1969 the date of birth of 17-year-olds was recorded in the electoral register and they could vote as soon as their eighteenth birthday was reached.

[2] The register is compiled by addition and subtraction from the previous year. Those newly qualified by age or in-moving are always the most likely to be omitted. When the age of voting was changed four new age groups were added to one register – and many householders, filling in the registration forms, were unaware of the changed qualifications. By 1972 there were indications that the number of unregistered 18–21-year-olds had been reduced to less than half the 1970 level.

the very old. This was partly due to their being exceptionally mobile and therefore likely by June 1970 to have moved from where they lived when the register was compiled in October 1969. But it was also a reflection of what every election study in western democracies has shown: electoral participation is a type of behaviour that is acquired and reinforced with the passing of the years. For most people who are just moving into adulthood, politics looms very small among the many claims on their time and interests. It is not possible to give a precise estimate of the 1970 turnout among 18–21-year-olds. But surveys after the election found non-voting higher than average among the youngest age group.[1]

It does seem clear, however, that those who voted were disproportionately Labour. Respondents less than 20 years of age in our own survey divided 53 per cent Labour to 28 per cent Conservative, which is quite consistent with the findings of other surveys. If we assume that 5 per cent of the votes cast in Britain in 1970 came from people who would have been too young to vote but for the 1969 Act and that these votes divided in the same ratio as the preferences given by the youngest respondents in our survey, they would have contributed 2·7 per cent of Labour's 43·8 per cent of the vote but only 1·4 per cent to the Conservatives' 46·2 per cent. And if these votes were uniformly spread across the country, Labour owed to the under-21 vote the seven seats they won at the 1970 election by less than 1·3 per cent. If we assume a ratio of Labour to Conservative support in this youngest age group that is only half as favourable to Labour, the party would still have owed to this group the five seats won by 0·6 per cent or less.

We can emphasize the impact of those who came of age at the 1970 election by giving four alternative readings of the relative strength of the parties. The first and most Conservative reading is the vote that would have been cast by an electorate without those who had come of age since the 1966 election. The second is the vote that would have been cast by an electorate without those who had yet to reach the age of 21: in other words, the vote that would have been cast under the old electoral law. The third is the vote that was actually cast, with the participation of part of those who had reached the age of 18. The fourth and most Labour reading is the vote that would have been cast if the 18–21 year-olds had been fully enfranchised and had participated as fully as older age groups, dividing their preferences in the same ratio as the 18–21 year-olds who actually voted.

These alternative figures are set out in Table 11.5 on the next page. The difference between the second and third lines indicates the actual difference

[1] See R. Rose, ed., *The Polls and the 1970 Election*, University of Strathclyde Survey Research Centre, Occasional Paper No. 7, 1970.

11.5 Effect of Incoming Electors, 1970

| | Expected Party Support | | | |
	Con.	Lab.	Lib.	Other
If 1970 vote had been cast by:					
Electorate 26 and above	47·4%	43·0	7·3	2·3	100%
Electorate 21 and above	46·3%	44·0	7·3	2·4	100%
Actual electorate 18 and above	45·8%	44·4	7·4	2·4	100%
Potential electorate 18 and above[a]	45·5%	44·7	7·4	2·4	100%

[a] Includes the approximately one-third of 18–21-year-olds who were excluded from the electoral register in 1970.

made in 1970 by the extension of the franchise – a 0·5 per cent swing – but the difference between the first and fourth lines – a 1·8 per cent swing – shows the potential change to the electorate when eight years of new voters are added.

Turnover of the Electorate 1959–70

We may now summarize our analysis of the replacement of the electorate in the years from 1959 to 1970 by setting out in Table 11.6 the estimates foreshadowed earlier in the chapter. By 1970 not less than 16 per cent of the 1959 electorate had been removed by emigration or death. And not less than 24 per cent of the 1970 electorate had been added since 1959 by immigration or by the entry into the electorate of those who had reached the minimum voting age.

11.6 Replacement of the Electorate, 1959–70[a]

| | Party Supported | | |
	Con.	Lab.	Lib.
Emigration	−0·8	−0·8	−0·2
Immigration	+0·2	+0·8	+0·1
Death	−6·3	−5·4	−0·6
Coming of age	+6·7	+8·9	+1·4
Totals	−0·2	+3·5	+0·7

[a] To allow the addition of percentages entering and leaving the electorate, the figures are calculated on a common base – the total electorate qualified to vote either in 1959 or 1970. The convenience of such a calculation is explained in Chapter 12.

The political effect of these changes was considerable. If the emigration of part of the electorate did not benefit either party, Labour reaped the larger direct benefit from the immigration of new voters from Ireland and the Commonwealth. And Labour drew the greater benefit both from the death of a substantial part of the 1959 electorate and the coming of age of an even larger part of the 1970 electorate, including the new voters created by the reduction in the voting age to eighteen.

On balance the Conservatives lost 0·2 per cent and Labour gained 3·5 per cent – a net change of approximately 4 per cent in the party lead. In other words, to preserve their share of the vote in the face of these adverse demographic trends the Conservatives needed to achieve a net gain in terms of party conversions throughout the 1960s. This figure is large enough to make clear that the change in the composition of the electorate had substantial consequences for the relative strength of the parties. However, the demographic trends were far from decisive. The ebbs and flows of party strength during these years were primarily the result of changes of preference by those who remained in the electorate. We turn in the next chapter to the more intricate pathways of change that lead from one party to another or to and from abstention.

PART FOUR

Conversion

12 The Scale of Short-Term Conversion 1959–70

BOTH the scale and the cyclical nature of political change make plain that the processes of realignment and replacement can only provide a partial account of its sources. It is true that several of their effects which have tended to go almost unnoticed can be far from trifling even in the short run; moreover, realignment and replacement can magnify or limit more transient shifts of party strength, as the aging of the class alignment has increased the volatility of the electorate in the recent past. But our account of political change would be very incomplete if we did not extend our analysis to the forces which convert and reconvert those who remain within the electorate. We examine in this chapter the scale of such transient conversions in the 1960s and in subsequent chapters the nature of the forces which underlie this third main type of electoral change.

We can trace the full intricate pattern of individual changes between successive points in time only by repeated contacts with the same people. Our surveys recorded the party preferences of samples of the electorate at six points in recent years – the election of 1959 (as recalled at the next election), the summer of 1963, the election of 1964, the election of 1966, the summer of 1969 and the election of 1970. We are therefore able to examine the individual changes which underlay the net changes of party strength which marked the 1960s.

The Description of Short-Term Conversion

The dangers in reducing all the complexities of individual change to a single measure of net 'swing' have become something of a commonplace in electoral commentary.[1] There are good analytical reasons for wanting a

[1] The measure established in the Nuffield studies since 1950 (the average of the Conservative gain and the Labour loss as percentages of the total vote cast) is the one most commonly used, but it is by no means the only one possible. See M. Steed in *The British General Election of 1964*, pp. 337–8, *The British General Election of 1966*, pp. 271–2 and

summary measure of the change in the relative strengths of the two main parties in the electorate between two points in time.[1] It is plain that a summary measure of this kind is useful even when we have full information about all the individual changes of behaviour whose net effect is 'swing'. Just as we find it useful to compare the relative strength of parties in classes and other groupings within the electorate at one point in time so also we need to compare the relative strength of parties across time – in the electorate as a whole and in various of its parts. Such comparisons are indispensable in much of the analysis of later chapters.

Yet for some analytical purposes it is essential to distinguish the several patterns of individual change which together yield the net shifts of strength that we see in election results. It is indeed probable that prolonged exposure to descriptions of net change has induced in many a false sense that swing typically reflects direct, one-way transfers of the vote between the main parties. In fact many streams and counter-eddies of change flow together to make up a given movement of party strength; the interpretation of the change must differ according to their relative magnitudes.

The possible variety of individual changes is suggested by Figure 12.1, which cross-classifies people according to their positions at two points of time. The thirty-five cells of this table are of three kinds. First, there are the five shaded cells representing those whose behaviour is unvarying; the number of people who fall in these cells, especially the first three, has great significance for the outcome of each election but none for electoral *change*. Second, there are the twelve lightly shaded cells representing those whose change leaves the relative strength of the main parties unaltered; the death of a previously inactive voter, for example, has no effect on the existing party balance.

It is in the third region of the table, the eighteen unshaded cells, that the keys to change in major party strength are to be found. These cells describe the behaviour of changers who supported the Conservatives or Labour at least once. We may identify in these cells five distinct processes by which the party balance may be altered.

The British General Election of 1970, pp. 386–7. H. Berrington's report on the 1964 election in the *Journal of the Royal Statistical Society*, Series A, **128** (1965), pp. 17–66, discusses the advantages of measuring swing as a percentage of the total Conservative and Labour vote. Henry Durant and James Douglas have offered enlightening calculations of swing on the basis of the total electorate rather than total votes.

[1] Perhaps it is worth pointing out that we stretch the idea of 'changing' here to include migrating and dying, even though the migrants and the dead ought not to be charged with political infidelity, as well as coming of age, even though the new elector may express a party preference which he has held for some time.

12.1 Pathways of Change (1)^a

^{a} The diagram is not quite exhaustive. The cell in the bottom right-hand corner is omitted since we are concerned only with those who qualified to vote at the first or second point of time. In any case the number of people who die after coming of age but before voting is negligible.

1. *Replacement of the electorate.* In the last chapters we discussed the turnover due to migration and to deaths and comings of age. It amounts to something approaching 2 per cent each year.[1] The turnover is represented by the last row in Figure 12.1, 'entering' electors, and by the last column for 'leaving' electors.

The relative strength of the two major parties is, however, affected only by those electors who fall into the two left-hand cells of the 'entering' row and the two upper cells of the 'leaving' column. The relative strength of the two main parties is left unchanged by the entry into and exit from the electorate of non-voters or minor-party supporters. As we showed in the last chapter, young voters have been more Labour and older voters more Conservative; at least in the early 1960s Labour's lead in votes was increased by its larger share of incoming electors, according to the arithmetic difference:

[1] It is not quite an exact exchange. The electorate in the 1950s and 1960s grew by about 100,000 each year while in 1970 it was further swelled by the addition of 18–21-year-olds (see pp. 240–2).

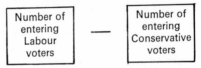

And Labour's lead in votes was increased by the Conservatives' greater share of electors who had died according to the difference:

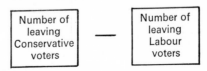

Therefore the change of Labour's lead owing to the physical replacement of the electorate was the sum of these two differences:

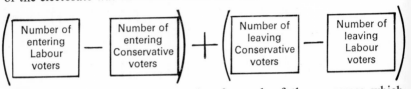

We shall offer a similar presentation for each of the processes which contribute to a net shift of party strength.

2. *Differential turnout*. Since a majority of people who go to the polls support the same party as last time, decisions on whether to vote at all may do more to decide an election outcome than decisions on how to vote. The parties strive hard to convert potential support into actual votes and their varied success in doing so is a familiar theme in electoral post-mortems. Equally familiar is the idea that electoral tides can sometimes be explained in terms of differential turnout – a fall in participation among supporters of the losing party and, perhaps, a rise in participation among their rivals. If we confine our attention to non-voters who previously supported the Conservatives or Labour and to Conservatives or Labour supporters who previously did not vote, we may represent the change of Labour's lead in votes owing to differential turnout by the sum of these differences:

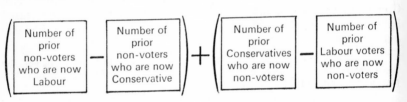

3. *The circulation of minor-party supporters.* In recent contests barely one-sixth of the electorate have been confronted by candidates from other than the three leading parties. Until 1970 only 1 per cent of all votes had been cast for such candidates and most of these have gone to Irish, Welsh or Scottish Nationalists, or to Communists in seats where these groups have fought regularly and in which they have retained some continuing support. But there do remain some voters who shift towards, and away from, such minor candidates and the significance of these shifts for the fortunes of the major parties would be greater if the level of support for the minor parties were to increase at the expense of major parties. Even in 1970 Nationalists only accounted for 1·7 per cent of the vote in Great Britain. We can once again represent the net change of Labour's lead owing to the circulation of minor party supporters as the sum of two differences:

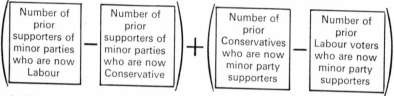

4. *The circulation of Liberals.* Over the elections from 1955 to 1970 the Liberal Party's strength varied from 2·5 per cent of the total vote to 11·2 per cent and the number of Liberal candidates from 109 to 365. Even in seats fought regularly the party's support was remarkably variable. We shall see evidence enough of what a large number of voters circulate to and from the Liberals relative to the size of the Liberal vote at any given time. The flow of former Liberals to Conservative or Labour and the flow of Conservative or Labour voters to the Liberals can have substantial influence on the relative strength of the two leading parties. The net change of Labour's lead in votes due to this circulation can be represented by the sum of these differences:

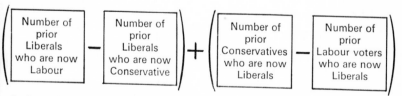

5. *Straight conversion.* Lastly, there is direct movement between the two parties of those who were Labour and have become Conservative or *vice*

versa. This is the sort of change most commonly evoked by the term 'swing' but, as we have seen, it is only one of several types of movement which can alter the relative strength of the major parties. It differs from all the others, however, in that it counts twice in calculations of the lead of one party over the other: making a Conservative of a non-voter, for example, is a gain for the Conservatives, but making a Conservative of a Labour voter is both a gain for the Conservatives and a loss for Labour. Therefore, while only one pair of terms enters the formula expressing the net change of Labour's lead in votes because of straight conversion we must count these terms twice as we calculate the net change of party strength.

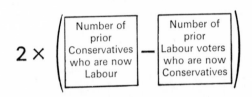

We may now complete the analytic framework by treating these several types of change together. Having written a separate statement of what each source of change contributes, we may now combine these into a single statement – one that separates the change of lead into its five components. It is convenient for this purpose to return to the earlier table and to denote each of its unshaded cells, as well as each total of Conservative or Labour strength at the margin of the table, by an explicit symbol (see Figure 12.2). We shall express each of these figures as a percentage of the total number entering all cells of the table. The total of these entries $p_{..}$ is thus equal to 100 per cent.

From these definitions it follows that the change of Labour's percentage lead over the Conservatives from time 1 to time 2 can be written as follows:

	Source
$(p_{.2} - p_{.1}) - (p_{2.} - p_{1.})$	
$= 2(p_{12} - p_{21})$	Straight conversion
$+ [(p_{13} - p_{23}) + (p_{32} - p_{31})]$	Circulation of Liberals
$+ [(p_{14} - p_{24}) + (p_{42} - p_{41})]$	Circulation of minor party supporters
$+ [(p_{15} - p_{25}) + (p_{52} - p_{51})]$	Differential turnout
$+ [(p_{16} - p_{26}) + (p_{62} - p_{61})]$	Replacement of electorate

12.2 Pathways of Change (2)

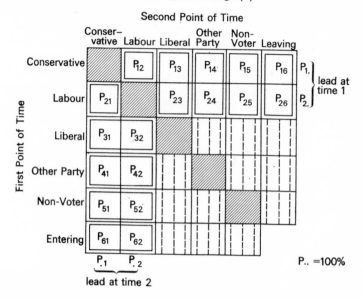

The sums on the two sides of this 'accounting' equation will be positive when Labour increases its strength from one time to another, as it did from 1959 to 1963, from 1964 to 1966 and from 1969 to 1970. But the sums will be negative when the tide moves the opposite way, as it did from 1963 to 1964 and from 1966 to 1970.

Short-Term Conversion 1959–70

The period to which we have applied this framework was one of strong electoral tides. The swings of party fortune as recorded by the Gallup Poll are charted in Figure 12.3 on the next page. This time series and the results of parliamentary by-elections and of local government elections suggest five main turning points. The first of these came in the winter of 1960–1 when a long period of Conservative decay and Labour gain began. The second came in the winter of 1963–4 when the Conservatives began the recovery which almost carried them to another victory in 1964. The third came during the 1964 Parliament when the Labour Party began the consolidation of power that was capped by the triumph of 1966. The

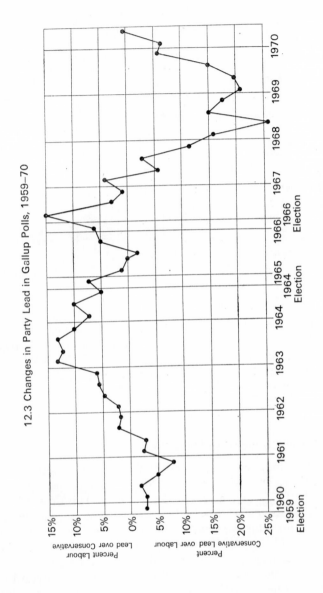

12.3 Changes in Party Lead in Gallup Polls, 1959–70

fourth came with Labour's subsequent decline into the abyss of 1967–8 and the fifth led to Labour's astonishing recovery in the months before the 1970 election. Therefore our own measurements of the public's preference in 1959, 1963, 1964, 1966, 1969 and 1970 divide the period into five natural eras: the Conservative decline from 1960 to 1963, the Conservative recovery from 1963 to 1964, the consolidation of Labour's power from 1964 to 1966, Labour's decline from 1966 to 1969 and its comeback in 1969–70. Let us now see what the framework of analysis which we have just set out can disclose about the sources of change in each era.[1]

The full variety of individual preference at the 1959 election and at the 1964 election is set out in Table 12.4.[2] The table shows a net change of

[1] In the tables that follow we have introduced one simplification of the exhaustive possibilities of change set out in Figure 12.1. We have treated the votes for minor parties as abstention. The total vote for minor parties represented only 0·4 per cent of the full electorate in 1959, 0·7 per cent in 1964, 0·9 per cent in 1966 and 2·0 per cent in 1970, and it was very unevenly spread. Our sample was insufficient to provide reliable estimates of where minor party votes (cast chiefly for Welsh and Scottish Nationalists) were drawn from. It is plain that, for our present purposes, no serious distortion will arise from this disregard of minor party support.

[2] We should say a word about the detailed steps by which we have estimated the entries of this table and of Tables 12.5 to 12.11. First of all, we have used census data on deaths and comings of age and our information on emigration and immigration to estimate the marginal totals of the row for entering voters and the column for leaving voters. Second, we have allocated the marginal total of the row for entering voters across the cells of that row by examining the party preferences at the later point of time of respondents who had been too young to be qualified electors at the earlier point of time or who had immigrated into Britain. Third, we have allocated the marginal total of the column for leaving electors across the cells of that column by applying census mortality rates to the distribution of party support found within each of a number of demographic groups defined by age, sex, social grade and marital status in a manner similar to that used in Chapter 10 and by examining the party preferences of those most 'akin' to emigrating voters, as explained above. Fourth, we have used the turnover data from our panel to estimate the entries of the main body of the table representing individuals who were qualified electors at both points of time. Fifth, we have adjusted the entries of the table, as estimated by the above steps, so that the marginal totals of the first four rows would agree with the relative proportions voting for the several parties and failing to vote in 1959 as disclosed by the election returns and by the figures for the total electorate in that year. We have similarly adjusted the marginal totals for the first four columns to agree with the election returns and figures for the total electorate in 1964. The procedure by which this adjustment was effected is described in Frederick Mosteller, 'Association and Estimation in Contingency Tables', *Journal of the American Statistical Association*, **63** (1968), 1–28. We have introduced this information so that our estimates of certain entries, especially those involving abstainers, will be less affected by non-response. It will be clear from the subsequent tables that we have also introduced the known marginal totals for 1966 and 1970 where appropriate.

The figures for the gap between the two main parties in 1959, 1964, 1966 and 1970 may surprise readers familiar with those normally presented. They are to be reconciled with

12.4 Pathways of Change, 1959–64

	1964							Percent of 1959 Electorate
	Con.	Lab.	Lib.	Didn't vote	Leaving			
Con.	22·3	2·1	2·9	4·4	3·5	35·2 ⎫		38·5
Lab.	1·8	21·4	1·4	5·2	2·4	32·2 ⎭	−3·0	35·3
1959 Lib.	1·0	0·7	1·8	0·6	0·2	4·3		4·7
Didn't vote	3·3	4·9	1·6	9·3	0·6	19·7		21·5
Entering	2·5	3·1	0·5	2·5		8·6		
	30·9	32·2	8·2	22·0	6·7	100·0		
	+1·3							

Percent of 1964 Electorate   33·1   34·6   8·8   23·5   100·0

Components of change
Straight conversion 2 × (2·1 − 1·8)   +0·6
Circulation of Liberals (2·9 − 1·4) + (0·7 − 1·0)   +1·2
Differential turnout (4·4 − 5·2) + (4·9 − 3·3)   +0·8
Replacement of electorate (3·5 − 2·4) + (3·1 − 2·5)   +1·7

Net change in Labour's lead   +4·3

---

the usual figures in three ways: (1) We are concerned with the figures for Great Britain not the United Kingdom; this reduces any Conservative lead by 1–1½ per cent. (2) We use the total electorate and not just those voting as the basis of calculation; with up to 25 per cent abstention, this may in fact cut down the percentage gap between the parties by about a quarter. (3) We bring into our calculations all those who were in the electorate at either of two points of time; this further reduces the proportion of active voters contributing to the major party percentages.

As in many places in the book we rely here on our respondents' recall of their 1959 vote several years after the fact, a procedure which is known to introduce some errors of report. The marginal totals for 1963 and 1969 in later tables are calculated from our own percentage lead between the two elections of 4·3 per cent. The contributions to this net shift made by each of the sources of change are set out below the table. Easily the largest contribution to Labour's return to power came from the physical renewal of the electorate. Indeed, either the electors who entered or those who left could be said to have supplied the last vital margin of Labour's victory. As we noted in the preceding chapter, if the 1964 vote had been cast by the 1959 electorate, the Conservatives would have been returned a fourth successive time with a quite adequate majority. The Liberals, taking votes from the Conservatives, also emerge as an important factor. Yet here we must be cautious in attributing a decisive effect to their appeal, for many of those who switched from Conservative to Liberal might have gone all the way to Labour in the absence of a Liberal candidate. The small net contribution of straight conversion to Labour serves as a salutary warning to anyone who automatically interprets 'swing' simply as a direct and uni-directional switch from one side to the other and not as the complex product of a large number of often contrary movements.

However, the picture of what happened over the full Parliament appears rather differently if we introduce the evidence from an intermediate point. When we took our first sample in mid-1963 the Labour Party had a lead of more than 11 per cent. The rise of Labour in 1959–63 and its slump in 1963–4 were largely due to elements in electoral change which were not so prominent in the net movement of the whole 1959–64 period. Table 12.5 on the next page shows the changes in 1959–63.

These detailed figures throw fresh light on the politics of the period. The most striking fact is that barely a fifth of the change in party lead was due to straight conversion between Conservative and Labour while the much publicized Liberal upsurge contributed even less to the change in major party fortunes (in part because former Liberals were still drawn more to the Conservatives than to Labour even in a period when considerably more Conservative than Labour voters were deserting to the Liberals). The physical replacement of the electorate was more important; three-

---

sample in those years, with two exceptions; we have fixed the marginal totals of the entering and leaving electors on the basis of demographic evidence, as explained above; and we have raised the total of potential abstentions to a level consistent with actual abstentions in 1959 and 1964, and in 1966 and 1970 the two pairs of 'adjacent' elections for which we have such figures.

Although, to avoid excessive rounding errors, we present our figures to one decimal point, we should warn our readers that considerations of sample size, as well as of inaccurate recall, mean that too much reliance should not be placed on the exact figures quoted here.

12.5 Pathways of Change, 1959–63

| | | 1963 | | None Don't | | | | Percent of 1959 |
	Con.	Lab.	Lib.	know	Leaving			Electorate
Con.	22·8	1·8	3·3	5·7	2·7	36·3 ⎫		38·5
						⎬ −2·9		
Lab.	0·6	26·2	1·5	3·3	1·8	33·4 ⎭		35·3
1959 Lib.	0·2	0·4	3·5	0·2	0·2	4·5		4·7
Didn't vote	2·9	4·7	1·9	10·3	0·4	20·2		21·5
Entering	1·1	2·8	0·3	1·4		5·6		
	27·6	35·9	10·5	20·9	5·1	100·0		
	+8·3							

Percent of 1963 Electorate   28·9   37·6   11·0   22·5   100·0

Components of change
Straight conversion 2 x (1·8 − 0·6)   +2·4
Circulation of Liberals (3·3 − 1·5) + (0·4 − 0·2)   +2·0
Differential turnout (5·7 − 3·3) + (4·7 − 2·9)   +4·2
Replacement of electorate (2·7 − 1·8) + (2·8 − 1·1)   +2·6
                                                                     ─────
Net change in Labour's lead   +11·2

fifths of major party supporters who died were Conservatives as compared with barely a quarter of those who came on to the electoral register. In fact, of the total swing against the Conservatives, a tenth could be attributed to the net effect of deaths and a seventh to the net effect of coming of age. In a period of strong pro-Labour movement, it was the young, with their less-established voting habits, who were most influenced. The aged were less susceptible to such short-term factors. But the aged were more likely to die, and those who died were mostly Conservative: in this period the higher rate of death among the aged, who tended to be Conservative, was only partially offset by the higher rate of death among men and the working class, groups which tended to be Labour. But the largest apparent source of change lay in differential turnout: 1959 Conservatives were much more likely than 1959 Labour supporters to say they wouldn't vote and 1959 non-voters were much more likely to prefer Labour to the Conservatives. What people said on this score must be taken with some caution, for the 1963 interview was not conducted in an election situation. Nonetheless the potential contribution of turnout to electoral tides is very manifest.

The Conservative slump after 1960 had come unexpectedly; the Conservative recovery in 1963–4 was even more unexpected. The large reduction in the Labour lead in the fifteen months before the 1964 election coincided with a period of economic expansion, but it also coincided with the Conservative leadership struggle and the row over resale price maintenance. Nonetheless, opinion polls, local elections and by-elections agreed in charting a recovery that went on until September 1964, when the party entered the election on almost level terms with Labour.

Table 12.6 on the next page sets out the changes between the voting intentions expressed by our panel in the summer of 1963 and their actual behaviour on October 15, 1964.

The Conservatives' rally was insufficient to offset their earlier decline. Even fewer voters remained in an identical position from 1963 to 1964 than from 1959 to 1963, but their changes were more mutually cancelling. Among those who were in the electorate on both occasions as many wavered between the latter two moments as between the former two; one elector in three had a different electoral stance in 1964 from his position in 1963. The replacement of the electorate contributed much less to change in this period because the time that elapsed was shorter. Even so it contributed doubly to the Conservative trend. Labour's earlier advantage in terms of differential mortality (chiefly because Conservative electors, being more elderly, died at a higher rate) was now offset by the fact that the death rates were being applied to a greater pool of Labour than of Conservative supporters – in 1963 there were a third more of the former than of the latter. New electors, too, showed their plasticity by tending to the Conservatives now that the tide was flowing in that direction. In 1963–4 straight conversion comes to the fore as, marginally, the largest contributor to the Conservatives' net gain; in some measure, as we shall show later, this represents the recovery of earlier losses. The Conservatives also gained substantially from the Liberals as well as from the fact that the Liberals

12.6 Pathways of Change, 1963–4

1964

	Con.	Lab.	Lib.	Didn't vote	Leaving			Percent of 1963 Electorate
Con.	21·2	1·3	1·1	3·9	0·6	28·1 ⎫		28·9
							+8·5	
Lab.	2·5	25·5	1·5	6·4	0·7	36·6 ⎭		37·6
1963 Lib.	3·2	1·7	3·5	2·1	0·2	10·7		11·0
None, Don't know	4·1	4·4	2·2	10·2	0·4	21·3		22·5
Entering	1·5	1·0	0·3	0·5		3·3		
	32·5	33·9	8·6	23·1	1·9	100·0		

+1·4

Percent of 1964 Electorate

33·1	34·6	8·8	23·5		100·0

Components of change
Straight conversion 2 × (1·3 − 2·5)   −2·4
Circulation of Liberals (1·1 − 1·5) + (1·7 − 3·2)   −1·9
Differential turnout (3·9 − 6·4) + (4·4 − 4·1)   −2·2
Replacement of electorate (0·6 − 0·7) + (1·0 − 1·5)   −0·6
_____
Net change in Labour's lead   −7·1

were on balance gaining from Labour. But the change in turnout was more important. Once again we must allow for the difference between hypothetical behaviour in 1963 and actual behaviour in 1964, yet it is significant that the Conservatives benefited much more than Labour from those who declared a preference in 1963 but did not vote when it came to the point in 1964. The traditional pre-election recovery of the party in power came, according to our data, almost equally from direct transfers between the main parties and changes in the turnout pattern.

The picture shown in 12.5 and 12.6 is in notable contrast to that in 12.4. Over the full Parliament the two factors that were strongest in 1963–4 – straight conversion and differential turnout – were the least important. It is particularly interesting that differential turnout made so much less contribution to the net change between the two elections than it did to the swings measured hypothetically at a point in the summer of 1963 outside the context of an actual election.

In the 1966 election Labour gained the biggest increase in majority any British party has ever won after a term in office. Table 12.7 shows the

12.7 Pathways of Change, 1964–6

		1966						Percent of 1964 Electorate
		Con.	Lab.	Lib.	Didn't vote	Leaving		
	Con.	24·6	2·3	0·8	3·9	0·8	32·4 }	33·1
	Lab.	0·7	27·6	1·1	3·2	0·8	33·4 } +1·0	34·6
1964	Lib.	1·8	1·3	3·8	1·6	0·1	8·6	8·8
Didn't vote		3·4	4·3	0·6	14·2	0·4	22·9	23·5
Entering		0·4	0·8	0·1	1·4		2·7	
		30·9	36·3	6·4	24·3	2·1	100·0	
		+5·4						

Percent of 1966 Electorate   31·5   37·0   6·6   24·9   100·0

Components of change
  Straight conversion 2 x (2·3 − 0·7)   +3·2
  Circulation of Liberals (0·8 − 1·1) + (1·3 − 1·8)   −0·8
  Differential turnout (3·9 − 3·2) + (4·3 − 3·4)   +1·6
  Replacement of electorate (0·8 − 0·8) + (0·8 − 0·4)   +0·4

    Net change in Labour's lead   +4·4

pathways by which the electorate changed in the first seventeen months of Mr Wilson's Government. The accompanying breakdown of Labour's marked increase of lead shows some interesting contrasts with the earlier surge in Labour's strength from 1960 to 1963. We saw that direct conversions accounted for little more than a quarter of the Conservative decay in the period up to 1963. But from 1964 to 1966 such conversions were of paramount importance, accounting for three-quarters of the net increase in Labour's lead. This contrast suggests that the fact of a Labour Government, established in power, made the act of voting Labour much less difficult for many former Conservatives. The size of the step involved in such changes may have appeared a good deal smaller in 1966 than it did three or four years earlier; if that were so, such half steps as voting Liberal or staying at home would have appeared less attractive. It is significant that 1964–6 provides an example of where one of our sources of change worked in the opposite direction to all the others: our data suggest that the net effect of the circulation of Liberals may have hurt Labour marginally. As in 1963–4, time was too short for the replacement of the electorate to have much net effect on party fortunes, although Labour's two to one advantage among new voters is noteworthy. Once again a national tendency may have been exaggerated among those less set in their ways; but the national tendency also had the unusual effect of encouraging Conservatives to abstain in greater numbers than their opponents.

During the 1966 Parliament there was a 4·4 per cent swing to the Conservatives, and the Conservatives regained power on 18 June 1970 on the biggest turnover of votes recorded since 1945. Table 12.8 shows the pattern of change between the 1966 and 1970 elections. In this period straight conversion emerged as the largest element in the change. The numbers moving between voting and non-voting were much greater but were mutually cancelling to a degree that gave differential turnout a secondary role, though one still large enough to have made a decisive contribution to the Conservative victory. The circulation of Liberals also contributed to the Conservative swing. But perhaps the most striking aspect of this table is the way in which the replacement of the electorate partially offset the general trend. Those leaving through death or emigration were drawn equally from the two parties. But new electors, whose ranks were swelled by the lowering of the voting age, were strongly Labour and prevented the Conservatives from achieving a far greater triumph in 1970.

Once again we can throw a different light on this picture by our evidence from mid-Parliament. As Figure 12.3 on p. 254 showed, the Labour Party

12.8 Pathways of Change, 1966–70

	1970						Percent of 1966 Electorate
	Con.	Lab.	Lib.	Didn't vote	Leaving		
Con.	19·1	0·8	0·4	3·7	2·8	26·8 ⎫	31·5
						⎬ +4·6	
Lab.	3·2	18·0	0·8	6·5	2·9	31·4 ⎭	37·0
1966 Lib.	1·5	0·7	2·0	1·1	0·3	5·6	6·6
Didn't vote	3·5	3·5	1·1	12·1	1·0	21·2	24·9
Entering	3·5	5·9	0·8	4·8		15·0	
	30·8	28·9	5·1	28·2	7·0	100·0	
	−1·9						

Percent of 1970 Electorate   33·1   31·1   5·5   30·3   100·0

Components of change:

Straight conversion 2 × (0·8 − 3·2)	−4·8
Circulation of Liberals (0·4 − 0·8) + (0·7 − 1·5)	−1·2
Differential turnout (3·7 − 6·5) + (3·5 − 3·5)	−2·8
Replacement of electorate (2·8 − 2·9) + (5·9 − 3·5)	+2·3
Net change in Labour's lead	−6·5

fell to unprecedented depths in the opinion polls in 1968 and 1969 and then recovered spectacularly to enter the 1970 election as favourite to win. Our survey in the summer of 1969 found the Labour Party near to rock bottom – there was a Conservative lead of more than 17 per cent. Table 12.9 on the next page shows our respondents' intention then compared with their report of their 1966 vote.

The table makes clear that each type of change contributed to Labour's collapse. Even electors who had come of age since 1966 were in 1969

12.9 Pathways of Change, 1966–9

		1969					Percent of 1966 Electorate
	Con.	Lab.	Lib.	Didn't vote	Leaving		
Con.	24·5	0·2	0·4	1·9	2·2	29·2 ⎫ +5·1	31·5
Lab.	4·0	16·1	1·8	10·1	2·3	34·3 ⎭	37·0
1966 **Lib.**	1·3	0·3	3·4	0·8	0·3	6·1	6·6
Didn't vote	6·2	2·6	0·9	12·4	1·1	23·2	24·9
Entering	2·5	2·1	0·5	2·1		7·2	
	38·5	21·3	7·0	27·3	5·9	100·0	
	⎰ −17·2 ⎱						
Percent of 1969 Electorate	41·0	22·6	7·4	29·0		100·0	

Components of change

Straight conversion 2 × (0·2 − 4·0)	−7·6
Circulation of Liberals (0·4 − 1·8) + (0·3 − 1·3)	−2·4
Differential turnout (1·9 − 10·1) + (2·6 − 6·2)	−11·8
Replacement of electorate (2·2 − 2·3) + (2·1 − 2·5)	−0·5
Net change in Labour's lead	−22·3

somewhat more inclined to support the Conservatives. By the standards of earlier years straight conversion made an enormous contribution to the swing. Indeed, straight switches to the Conservatives outnumbered straight switches to Labour by the astonishing margin of 20 to 1. But the largest single element in Labour's collapse was differential abstention. Almost a third of those who voted Labour in 1966 were by 1969 undecided or intending not to vote. And of those who abstained in 1966 far more had by 1969 gone over to the Conservatives than to Labour. The net effect of these movements to and from abstention and indecision was a shift of almost 12 per cent in the party lead.

In 1970 we re-interviewed our 1969 respondents, and Table 12.10 shows

12.10 Pathways of Change, 1969–70

1970

	Con.	Lab.	Lib.	Didn't vote	Leaving		Percent of 1969 Electorate
Con.	24·6	2·6	1·1	8·4	0·7	37·4 ⎫	41·0
Lab.	0·7	13·5	0·5	5·4	0·5	20·6 ⎭ −16·8	22·6
1969 Lib.	1·1	1·3	1·6	2·6	0·2	6·8	7·4
Didn't vote	4·3	10·3	1·7	9·7	0·4	26·4	29·0
Entering	1·8	2·8	0·5	3·7		8·8	
	32·5	30·5	5·4	29·8	1·8	100·0	
	−2·0						

Percent of 1970 Electorate   33·1   31·1   5·5   30·3   100·0

Components of change
Straight conversion 2 × (2·6 − 0·7)	+3·8
Circulation of Liberals (1·1 − 0·5) + (1·3 − 1·1)	+0·8
Differential turnout (8·4 − 5·4) + (10·3 − 4·3)	+9·0
Replacement of electorate (0·7 − 0·5) + (2·8 − 1·8)	+1·2
Net change in Labour's lead	+14·8

the components of Labour's spectacular recovery. The great swing to Labour from 1969 to 1970 did not repair the full damage suffered by the party between 1966 and 1969. But it was twice as great as the swing to the Conservative Government in the year before the election of 1964. In 1969–

70 Labour enjoyed a handsome margin in straight switches between the two major parties. And Labour drew a far larger share of the votes of newly qualified electors, including those enfranchised by the lowering of the voting age to 18, although two-fifths of new electors failed to vote. But differential turnout was the largest factor in Labour's recovery, as it had been in Labour's earlier collapse. In 1970 Labour lost less of its 1969 support to abstention than did the Conservatives. And Labour attracted a far larger share of those who in 1969 had been undecided or who planned not to vote. Indeed, these movements changed the net lead by fully 9 percentage points and brought Labour within sight of a third successive victory.

It remains to summarize the movements of party strength over the longest period for which we have detailed individual evidence. Table 12.11 shows the changes between 1959 and 1970 by examining the preferences of surviving panelists and of those who entered or left the electorate. The relative strength of the two main parties was remarkably similar at the beginning and end of this historical period. As calculated from the marginals of Table 12.11, the Conservatives held a 2·4 per cent lead in 1959 and a 1·7 per cent lead in 1970, a net gain of 0·7 percentage points for Labour over eleven years. As the components of change show, this near-stability was the result of the effects of two pairs of virtually offsetting factors.

To begin with, the Conservatives enjoyed a slight advantage in the straight conversions between the two main parties of voters who remained in the electorate from 1959 to 1970. There were switches in both directions, and these figures lend little credence to the idea that conversion of aging electors to the party of the right is a main engine of political change. Indeed, the Conservatives profited more handsomely from net differentials of turnout, in particular from the withdrawal into non-voting in 1970 by a substantial proportion of those who gave their support to Labour in 1959.

Against these factors were two others which worked to Labour's advantage. Labour enjoyed a small net gain from the circulation of Liberals. But the party's main advantage came from the replacement of the electorate. The flows into and out of the electorate over eleven years were enormous and amounted to more than two-fifths of all those qualified to vote at the beginning or end of this period. Labour gained almost a full percentage point from the greater losses suffered by the Conservatives through death. And the party gained nearly 3 percentage points by its greater appeal to those who entered the electorate. If those dying and those reaching voting age had been exactly representative of the rest of the electorate, the Conservatives would in 1970 have had a majority of over 100 rather than just 30. In the broad picture of the 1960s, despite the new levels of volatility,

12.11 Pathways of Change, 1959–70

1970

	Con.	Lab.	Lib.	Didn't vote	Leaving		Percent of 1959 Electorate
Con.	14·9	1·4	1·3	4·4	7·1	29·1 ⎫	38·5
						⎬ −2·4	
Lab.	2·0	11·6	0·6	6·3	6·2	26·7 ⎭	35·3
1959 Lib.	0·7	0·6	0·7	0·8	0·8	3·6	4·7
Didn't vote	3·3	2·8	0·5	7·7	1·9	16·2	21·5
Entering	6·9	9·7	1·5	6·3		24·4	
	27·8	26·1	4·6	25·5	16·0	100·0	
	−1·7						

Percent
of 1970
Electorate   33·1   31·1   5·5   30·3   100·0

Components of change:
Straight conversion 2 × (1·4 − 2·0)   −1·2
Circulation of Liberals (1·3 − 0·6) + (0·6 − 0·7)   +0·6
Differential turnout (4·4 − 6·3) + (2·8 − 3·3)   −2·4
Replacement of electorate (7·1 − 6·2) + (9·7 − 6·9) +3·7
___
Net change in Labour's lead   +0·7

the demographic turnover of the electorate produced the largest net changes from 1959 to 1970. The Conservatives survived the demographic tide that flowed against them only by their advantage in straight conversions and differential abstention.

Volatility and the Cumulation of Change

The most notable feature of the shifts in individual preference is their sheer volume. Our evidence indicates that the movements of party strength between successive elections may involve a turnover of something like a third of the electorate.[1] Indeed, in the five intervals of change that we have examined in the 1960s, there were never as much as two-thirds of the public positively supporting the same party at two successive points of time; the fraction remaining steadfast through several successive intervals of change was even smaller. Such figures indicate how widely the sources of change are dispersed through the electorate. Electoral change is due not to a limited group of 'floating' voters but to a very broad segment of British electors.

The increase in political volatility so manifest in the 1960s raises important questions about Britain's electoral system. It is natural that most observers should have stressed the virtues of electoral fluidity, arguing, for example, that the expectation of a future swing of the pendulum and a change of government is essential if the opposition is to attract and retain the parliamentary talent it needs. But all such arguments have assumed that swings will be moderate; for this reason the way in which swings in votes are exaggerated in terms of parliamentary seats has been regarded as a cardinal virtue of the single-member constituency system. But if the parties' consistent support were to be drastically reduced and turnovers of party strength were to involve a vast majority of electors, a very different verdict on the electoral system might be called for.

Table 12.12 summarizes the rates of change in the political intervals for which we have evidence. These entries are obtained by combining the much more elaborate data given for these periods earlier in the chapter, excluding only those who have entered or left the electorate. The percentage moving between voting and non-voting at times reached a quarter of the electorate and never fell below 18 per cent, while the number moving between parties varied from 8 per cent to 13 per cent. Moving to or from the Liberals was always more prevalent than direct switches between the two main parties. The proportion consistently supporting the same party at the beginning and end of these intervals never rose as high as 60 per cent. Indeed, the fluidity of behaviour disclosed by Table 12.12 leads us to ask how large a fraction of the electorate would be shown to have remained constant

---

[1] We include among changers here those who voluntarily abstained at one election. The extent of turnover would be larger still if we were to include deaths and comings of age.

12.12 Rates of Individual Constancy and Change
between Two Points in Time during the 1960s

	Time Periods							
	59–63	63–64	59–64	64–66	66–69	69–70	66–70	59–70
Remained constant *by twice* voting for same								
party	59	51	54	59	51	44	50	46
abstaining	12	11	11	15	14	11	16	13
Total constant	71	62	65	74	65	55	66	59
Changed by moving *between* Conservative and								
Labour	3	4	5	3	5	4	5	6
Conservative or Labour, and Liberal	6	9	7	5	4	4	4	5
Voting and abstention	20	25	23	18	26	37	25	30
Total changing	29	38	35	26	35	45	34	41
Grand Total	100	100	100	100	100	100	100	100

supporters of a party if we were to analyse their behaviour at three or more points in time.

In certain respects the rates of change in relatively brief intervals can give a misleading picture of the amount of change during more extended periods. If we were to impute a cumulative quality to change, assuming that at each successive interval of change every voter was equally likely to switch, the rates shown by Table 12.12 would have involved the vast majority of electors in some sort of motion across these points of time for which we have measurements – 1959, 1963, 1964, 1966 and 1970. Indeed, if the changes shown by the table had cumulated across all the intervening intervals, less than 40 per cent of the electorate would have held to a constant position, including abstention, at the five points which define these intervals.[1]

But, as might be expected, a cumulative assumption conflicts with the

[1] The meaning we give to 'cumulative' here is simply that changes in any two intervals are statistically independent; that is, that these changes conform to a first-order Markov process – although not in general to a stationary one!

evidence. Its failure is linked to two distinct and important aspects of change over longer periods of time. The first of these is that the propensity to change, not surprisingly, is far from being uniform throughout the electorate. If the image of a nation sharply divided into 'stalwarts' and 'floaters' is false to reality, so is the opposite image of an electorate in which everyone is equally likely to change. Our evidence suggests that those who change in one interval are much more likely than those who do not to shift again in a successive interval.

This aspect of our panel's behaviour is illustrated by Table 12.13, which crosses the occurrence of changes in the months prior to the election of 1964 and the months between the elections of 1964 and 1966. Plainly changes in these successive intervals were substantially interlinked. People who had moved between 1963 and 1964 were almost three times more likely to move again between 1964 and 1966. And six-sevenths of those who

12.13 Rates of Change 1964–66 by Change 1963–64

| | | Between 1963 and 1964 | |
		Constant	Changed
Between 1964 and 1966	Constant	85%	56%
	Changed	15	44
	Totals	100%	100%

remained fixed over the first period remained fixed over the second compared to four-sevenths of those who switched. The consequence of this difference is that the fraction of the electorate which keeps to a constant position over a fairly extended period of time is very much larger than it would be if all change were cumulative, with all voters always equally at risk.

The cumulation of change is limited by a second and perhaps less evident aspect of the electorate's behaviour, the tendency of change to be in the direction of a position which the elector has taken before. Any conception that change in one interval is independent of change in prior intervals is false not only because some electors are more prone than others to change at all; it is also false because the direction of change shows the marks of the voter's prior partisan history. Our evidence on this point is illustrated by Table 12.14, which compares the rates at which movers shifted towards the Conservative Party between the elections of 1964 and 1966 according to whether they had been Conservative in 1959. The table seeks to answer this question: among those voters who did not vote Conservative in 1964 but

12.14 Proportions Moving to the Conservatives between 1964 and 1966
by 1959 Preference

| | Among movers whose 1959 preference had been | |
	Conservative	Other than Conservative
Proportions moving to the Conservatives between 1964 and 1966	67%	17%

who were going to shift their position by 1966 how did the likelihood of the
shift being towards the Conservatives compare among those who had been
Conservative in 1959 and those who had not? The contrast of the two
groups is very marked. The likelihood of a mover becoming Conservative
between 1964 and 1966 was vastly greater among those who had been
Conservative at the General Election of 1959.

The influence of prior partisanship in movements to Labour over the
same period is shown by Table 12.15. The likelihood of a mover's shifting

12.15 Proportions Moving to Labour from 1964 to 1966
by 1959 Preference

| | Among movers whose 1959 preference had been | |
	Labour	Other than Labour
Proportion moving to Labour between 1964 and 1966	74%	28%

towards the Labour Party between the election of 1964 and the election of
1966 is seen to have been far greater among those who supported Labour
in 1959 than among those who did not. This pattern is indeed quite general
in our evidence. It holds for both the major parties – and for the Liberals
as well. Moreover, it holds for any three of the several points of time for
which we have evidence. The pattern is, for example, just as apparent in
changes during the seventeen months prior to the election of 1964 as it is
in changes between the elections of 1966 and 1970. But in the later 1960s
these 'homing' tendencies took on greater importance as the volatility
of the electorate increased.

The combined effect of the 'gradient' in propensity to change and the
'homing' tendency of those who do change is to prevent change from

being as widely dispersed across the electorate over an extended interval as we would expect by observing rates of change within briefer intervals. This combined effect can be summarized in two turnover tables which show the changes of party preference between the relatively remote points represented by the 1959 and 1970 General Elections calculated in two contrasting ways. The first of these tables is hypothetical and is based on the assumption that the changes observed from 1959 to 1963, 1963 to 1964, 1964 to 1966, and 1966 to 1970 were in fact independent or 'cumulative'.[1] The second table gives the actual turnover of party preference observed between the elections of 1959 and 1966.

As set out in Table 12.16, the contrast between these two arrays is very marked indeed. The entries of Table 12.16a, formed under the assumption of perfectly cumulative change, show a marked diffusion over the table, with less concentration along the ridge of the main diagonal from upper left to lower right, the cells that represent electors with unchanged positions. In the true turnover table, 12.16b, this ridge is much higher. Considerable erosion has moved electors into the 'low' regions on either side of the main diagonal, but this movement is less marked than the assumption of independent or cumulative change would lead us to expect. The contrast of expected and actual erosion is summarized by the curves drawn in Figure 12.17 on the next page.

Of particular interest in the pattern of change over several points in time is the scale of the movements between the two main parties, either by direct switches or by indirect movements through the more 'neutral' intermediate positions of Liberalism or non-voting. In our panel of electors who

---

[1] As indicated above, we have interpreted the idea of perfectly cumulative change in terms of a (non-stationary) Markov chain. Thus, for each of our four intervals of change we may calculate from the observed turnover of party preference a transition matrix whose generalized elements we may denote as

$$P_{ij1}, P_{ij2}, P_{ij3} \text{ and } P_{ij4}$$

respectively for our four intervals. If change were in fact perfectly cumulative, the probability

$$P_{ij}{}^{(4)}$$

that an elector who preferred the ith party in 1959 preferred the jth party in 1970 would be the sum of the probabilities of the occurrence of all possible paths which lead between these two positions, or

$$P_{ij}{}^{(4)} = \sum_{\eta}\sum_{\nu}\sum_{\lambda} P_{i\eta1}P_{\eta\nu2}P_{\nu\lambda3}P_{\lambda j4},$$

where the probability of the occurrence of any given path is the product of the probabilities of each of its steps, in accord with the idea of independent or 'cumulative' changes.

12.16 Turnover of Party Preference Between Elections of
1959 and 1970

a. *Assuming Cumulative Change*

		Preference in 1970				
		Con.	Lab.	Lib.	Abstained	
Preference in 1959	Con.	49%	19	5	27	100%
	Lab.	23%	42	5	30	100%
	Lib.	38%	25	8	29	100%
	Abstained	33%	30	6	31	100%

b. *Turnover Actually Observed*

		Preference in 1970				
		Con.	Lab.	Lib.	Abstained	
Preference in 1959	Con.	68%	6	6	20	100%
	Lab.	10%	56	3	31	100%
	Lib.	25%	21	25	29	100%
	Abstained	23%	20	3	54	100%

furnished information for the four elections of 1959, 1964, 1966 and 1970
we found a total of 13 per cent who had at one time or another cast their
votes both for the Conservatives and for Labour: just over an eighth
of the electorate found its way from one of the main party camps to the
other as changes accumulated over four elections. Plainly a number of
major-party supporters moved to the halfway houses of Liberal support or
non-voting without completing the journey to the other major party.

12.17 Proportions of Electors Holding the Same Position, 1959 and 1970

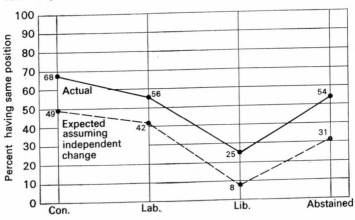

This tendency was very clear in our evidence on movements to the Liberal position. It might be argued that the presence of the Liberals would ease the journey between the two main parties, since a Conservative or Labour voter who availed himself of this halfway house would not have to make a more extreme transfer of loyalties all at once. In fact, Liberalism seemed much more of a turn-around station. Liberal support was sufficiently evanescent for our samples to include many electors who moved to the Liberals from one of the major parties only to move away again. But in almost every case this second move was back to the same party.

For example, of those in our sample who moved from Labour to the Liberals between 1963 and 1964, not a single one moved on to the Conservatives in 1966. That may not seem very surprising in view of the Labour tide then flowing. But a very similar picture is offered by those who moved from the Conservatives to the Liberals between 1963 and 1964 and then changed again: fully 94 per cent of them moved back to the Conservatives despite the Labour tide. There were many voters in our sample who moved from the Conservatives to Labour between 1963 and 1966. Almost none used the Liberals as a halfway house. The pattern of changes between 1959, 1963 and 1964, or between 1964, 1966 and 1970, was very similar. Indeed, the presence of the Liberals may well have retarded the traffic of electors between the two main parties by giving the voter who had lost faith in his own party a means of not taking the greater plunge.

The changes examined here should dispel all doubt as to the importance of short-term conversion for the net shifts of strength between the two main parties. The volume of conversion is so great that we should look deeply into its sources. In this chapter we have described the scale of conversion in the 1960s. In the chapters that follow we consider the forces to which the electorate responds in giving and withdrawing its support for the various parties.

13 The Analysis of Short-Term Conversion

In the last chapter we attempted to measure the extent to which electors change their positions. It now remains to examine why they did so. The schoolbook accounts of democracy assume that the electors act like a jury passing judgment on current policies and current leaders, responding to the merits of the issues before them. The earlier chapters of this book were devoted to showing how far votes are linked to loyalties formed deep in the past and to causes that have little to do with contemporary questions, and how far elections are decided by the changing composition of the electorate as a whole, as distinct from the conversion of individual electors. However, as the last chapter showed, many people do switch their votes, apparently in response to current events or propaganda. Which of the many stimuli to which the elector is subject are most likely to move his vote? Before we can answer this question we need to explore the ways in which the link between issues and changes of political attitude can best be analyzed.

It may help if we think in terms of the links that are formed between issue and party and between self and issue, for this determines the influence of issues on the strength of the parties. We shall have to explore in detail

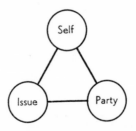

what these links involve and how widely their nature varies. But we cannot deal adequately with the role of issues in electoral change without paying due attention to how both types of bonds bear on the remarkable assortment of issues that confront the electorate over time.

The Limits of Policy-Defined Issues

A 'political issue' is a highly ambiguous concept which has misted up many windows to political reality. Perennial controversies, such as 'Do issues matter?' and 'Is the elector rational?' frequently turn on the varieties of meaning the phrase has acquired. In focusing on these different meanings, we shall not offer a single 'correct' usage but shall instead use the term even more inclusively than is common in everyday speech. But we shall at the same time enforce a number of distinctions, too easily overlooked, which reveal some important differences in the bases of electoral choice.

One of these is the distinction between issues that are defined in terms of alternative course of government action and issues that are defined more in terms of goals or values that government may achieve. It is natural that the analysis of issues should have a bias towards issues that have meaning in terms of alternative policies. The government's policy decisions constitute much of what politics is about; the interplay between public attitudes or demands, governmental decisions, and the consequences of those decisions provides one of the great challenges of political analysis, a 'feedback' loop at the heart of democratic government.

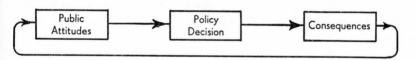

As a result, analyses of political issues often tend to cast the public in the role of an informed spectator at the game of government, one who sees policy issues much as they are seen by the political leaders who play the game. Since the political controversies of Westminster and Whitehall focus upon choices among detailed policy alternatives, why should these alternatives not be taken as defining the issues of the day? In this spirit the newspaper polls take samplings of public opinion on such assorted questions as prices and incomes policy, the merits of a particular strike, the proper level of pensions, or even on more highly detailed and specific problems of foreign affairs or defence strategy.

But the simplest evidence about the extent of popular attention to the affairs of government must challenge any image of the elector as an informed spectator. Understanding of policy issues falls away very sharply indeed as we move outwards from those at the heart of political decision-making to the public at large. The fall-off is partly a matter of how fully the alternatives are seen. For example, on the issue of Britain's entry into Europe the real insider, the politician or the civil servant involved in preparing the British application, sees a number of alternative courses, distinguished in terms of the conditions of entry, the strategy of approach, the way obligations to other Commonwealth countries are discharged and so on. Many of these are not apparent even to sophisticated observers, such as backbench M.P.s or academic onlookers, who nonetheless see the choices in complex terms. To great sections of the public, however, the question before the country comes down to the unadorned dichotomy – 'In?' or 'Out?'

The broad public also falls short of the 'informed spectator' role in terms of how well it can link means to ends. Not only is it very incompletely informed of the cards the Government can play; it seldom can understand how putting down a single card is likely to affect the course of the game. Having but a weak sense of how a particular policy line will have an influence on anything it values, the electorate may form only weak and ephemeral preferences even among the policy alternatives it does perceive.

These reservations about the image of the elector as a fully informed spectator are familiar enough. Those who practice or observe politics at an elite level are often reminded how different the political world looks to the broad public. An M.P. returning to a meeting of his constituency party must always be reminded how far, psychologically, he has travelled from Westminster. A lobby correspondent must realize from the conversations he overhears on the train how little of the framework which he has developed for the analysis of policy issues is shared by those who have no daily contact with public affairs.

Yet the true limits of the public's views on policy are likely to be missed. In part this is due to a subtle bias which affects an elite observer's contacts with the general public. The politician, the journalist and the political scientist all tend to encounter people whose interest in politics is grossly unrepresentative of their fellow citizens. Those, for example, whom an M.P. confronts at a local party meeting, innocent though they are by Westminster standards, will still have much more developed ideas about current policy issues than the average elector.

How weak the public's policy preferences really are can be most tellingly demonstrated by studying them over time. Satisfactory evidence on this has seldom been presented.[1] Newspaper opinion polls do frequently put the

[1] But see Philip Converse's seminal analysis of materials from the American panel followed by the Institute for Social Research over the four years from 1956 to 1960, 'The Nature of Belief Systems in Mass Publics', in *Ideology and Discontent*, ed. D. E. Apter, New York, 1964, pp. 206–61.

same policy questions to successive samples and show the wobbles – as well as some meaningful trends – in public sentiment for and against an issue. They also record substantial proportions who admit to being 'Don't knows'. But the ephemeral quality of many of the positive responses emerges only when the same individual's preferences are followed over a period of time.

This point can be illustrated by changes of attitude towards policy issues which have not been matters of sharp and prolonged conflict between the parties. On the issue of Britain's entry into Europe, for example, fully half of our sample conceded either at the interview in the summer of 1963 or at the interview in the autumn of 1964 that they had no opinion.[1] The views of those who did offer an opinion at both interviews proved quite unstable. Less than four-fifths of this group and therefore less than two-fifths of the whole sample voiced the *same* opinion at both points in time. A highly fluid pattern of individual replies was found beneath the surface of an over-all division of opinion that was almost unchanged between the summer of 1963 and the autumn of 1964.

It could, of course, be suggested that the switches represented large blocs of opinion moving in mutually cancelling directions – perhaps of Conservatives reverting to their earlier suspicion of Europe following the Macmillan era and of Labour voters no longer driven to disapprove of Europeanism as a key Conservative policy. The switches might then be seen as genuine changes of attitude, whose volume might be a good deal less at other times. But any such interpretation collides with the evidence: movements in both directions were found in each party, as well as in each class, and in every other category for which an hypothesis as to the direction of change suggested itself. The most reasonable interpretation of the remarkable instability of responses is that Britain's policy towards the Common Market was in 1963–4 a matter on which the mass public had formed attitudes to only a very limited degree.

The limits of popular attitude towards policy issues are even more persuasively attested to by the fluidity of opinion on questions which have been at the heart of the party battle for many years. An impressive example of this is provided by the nationalization of industry, a matter that for a generation has never been far from the centre of political controversy. At each round of interviews we asked our respondents to choose one from an

---

[1] The circulation of those giving a 'don't know' response is itself an indication of the fluidity of opinion. At the first interview 38 per cent said they had no opinion; at the second interview 34 per cent did. The turnover of those giving this response was, however, sufficient that fully half said 'don't know' at one interview or the other.

ordered set of positions on nationalization – or to say that they had no opinion. The overall responses remained quite constant over our first three rounds of interviews, as Table 13.1 shows. At each interview something like

13.1 Profile of Opinion Towards Nationalization of Industry

	1963	1964	1966	1970
A lot more industries should be nationalized	10%	8%	8%	10%
Only a few more industries, such as steel, should be nationalized	14	17	17	9
No more industries should be nationalized, but industries that are nationalized now should stay nationalized	36	45	42	40
Some industries that are nationalized should now be denationalized	22	18	19	29
No opinion	18	12	14	12
	100%	100%	100%	100%

one elector in six said that they had no opinion even on such a long-established policy issue as this. But the distribution of views among those with a declared view seemed fairly stable – and appeared to confirm the clear majority against further nationalization recorded in so many public opinion polls over the last twenty years. Indeed the steadiness of the percentages in these interviews over a period of almost seven years apparently gives support to the idea that most British electors have made up their minds on this perennial issue. Even the 1970 figures are not very far from those of 1963.

When individual responses are examined, however, the truth is found to be very different. Table 13.2 shows the full turnover of views between our first and second interviews. A glance at the squares in the main diagonal shows that only 39 per cent stuck to an identical and definite position on the broad lines of nationalization policy. There was a good deal of wavering between having and not having an opinion and even more between different opinions. By any standard statistical measure, the stability of the entries is decidedly modest.[1] The turnover of opinion carried many re-

[1] For example, Kendall's tau–b rank correlation coefficient is only $+0.4$ for this array, even when we exclude those who failed to express a definite opinion on both occasions. The magnitude of this coefficient may have been falsely inflated not only by our exclusion of the explicit 'don't knows' but also by our counting as real and stable opinion the choice of the 'no more' position at both interviews. It is not implausible to suppose that some who gave this opinion both times were expressing a species of 'don't know'.

13.2 Turnover of Opinion Towards Nationalization of Industry, 1963 to 1964

Autumn 1964

		Lot more	Few more	No more	Less	No Opinion	
	Lot more	3	3	3	1	1	11
	Few more	1	6	6	1	1	15
Summer 1963	No more	1	5	21	6	3	36
	Less	1	1	10	9	1	22
	No opinion	1	2	5	2	6	16
		7	17	45	19	12	100%

(n = 1473)

spondents across the line between those who believed in more national-ization and those who did not, the critical divide in the struggle over nationalization at the elite level.

This line is blurred still more when we lengthen our time interval and examine the movements of opinion over our four interviews. Even when we collapse our four alternatives into two and consider only whether a respondent was for more nationalization or not, an intricate pattern of change emerges, as Figure 13.3 on the next page shows. Fully 26 per cent said in one or more interviews that they had no opinion on nationalization. Only 43 per cent were consistent in supporting or opposing nationalization over the four interviews.

In the case of nationalization, as in the case of the Common Market, there is little empirical support for any hypothesis attributing these cross-currents of change to forces moving blocs of opinion in mutually cancelling directions. It seems more plausible to interpret the fluidity of the public's views as an indication of the limited degree to which attitudes are formed towards even the best-known of policy issues. For it must be stressed that the issue of nationalization is plainly one which has seeped far into the

13.3 Pathways of Opinion Towards Nationalization, 1963 to 1970

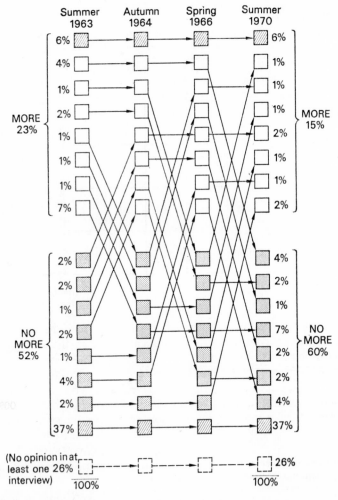

public's consciousness; among those expressing a view, there was virtually no confusion about which party was more likely to go in for further nationalization, as we shall show later. But this stable and almost universal perception contrasts sharply with the changeability of attitude towards the merits of nationalization.

The extent to which the changeability of attitude is a reflection of the sheer uncertainty that surrounds many people's beliefs emerges from another property of opinion revealed by repeated canvassing of individual views. The essence of this property is that substantial short-run reshuffling of views fails to yield the longer-run movement of individual position which we would expect from real and cumulative attitude change. This is a subtle and paradoxical empirical point. There is quite enough circulation of opinion to shatter any idea that the bulk of electors hold to fixed views, as the unchanging total proportions in successive polls might suggest. Yet, if genuine and cumulative attitude change were to occur at the rate of the circulation of opinion between one survey and the next, the correlation of opinions at more remote points of time would decay faster than it in fact does. The slower rate of decay may therefore be seen as further evidence that the circulation of opinion is substantially due to mere uncertainty of response and not to genuine attitude change.[1]

This aspect of popular response to policy issues emerges clearly from the turnover of opinion on nuclear weapons policy. At each round of interviews we asked our respondents which they favoured of the following positions on the issue:

Britain should keep her own nuclear weapons, independent of other countries

Britain should have nuclear weapons only as a part of a Western defence system

[1] The comparison of the actual decay rate and that implied by a Markov chain or other process under which change is genuinely cumulative has attracted the attention of several writers. Philip Converse has given an exceedingly interesting treatment, with American examples, of a 'black-white' model under which each of those interviewed over time gives either completely stable or completely random responses. The presence of only these two types of responses in sample data will yield a correlation of opinions over time which does not diminish as the time interval lengthens, a fact which Converse uses to test the fit of actual responses to the model. See P. E. Converse, 'The Nature of Belief Systems in Mass Publics', in *Ideology and Discontent*, ed. D. E. Apter, New York, 1964, pp. 206–61. A similar empirical property is implied by the 'mover-stayer' model which has been adumbrated by Blumen, Kogan, McCarthy, Goodman and others. See I. Blumen, M. Kogan and P. J. McCarthy, *The Industrial Mobility of Labor as a Probability Process*, Ithaca, New York, 1955, and Leo A. Goodman, 'Statistical Methods for the Mover-Stayer Model', *Journal of the American Statistical Association*, 56 (1961), 841–63. Coleman has proposed a model for the case in which response variation is due partly to response uncertainty and partly to genuine, cumulative change. Under this model the correlation of opinions over time will diminish as the time interval lengthens but not as rapidly as would be true if change were free of response uncertainty. See J. S. Coleman, *Models of Change and Response Uncertainty*, Englewood Cliffs, New Jersey, 1964. This empirical property is fairly typical of policy responses given by our British panel and is additional evidence that considerable uncertainty attaches to these responses.

Britain should have nothing to do with nuclear weapons under any circumstances

Individual attitudes towards the Bomb were as fluid as those towards nationalization and the Common Market. The correlation between opinions on nuclear weapons expressed in 1963 and 1964 was only $+0.33$ and between 1964 and 1966 only $+0.38$.

But what is significant for our present purpose is a comparison of the rate of change between two pairs of closer interviews (1963–4 and 1964–6) with the rate between the more distant pair of interviews in 1963 and 1966. Although we shall not develop the point in full detail, the essential idea is plain. If changes of response reflected only genuine attitude change and occurred at a rate fast enough to have produced the very modest correlations between the first and second, and second and third, interviews, then the correlation between the first and third interviews ought to be almost non-existent. Indeed, on these assumptions we would expect the correlation between 1963 and 1966 to be only $+0.13$.[1] In fact, however, the observed correlation was $+0.31$, not much lower than the correlation between opinions at the two closer pairs of interviews.

Perhaps no one should be surprised that policy questions such as entry into Europe or retention of nuclear weapons, whose consequences for the lives of ordinary people are uncertain and indirect, should be matters on which attitudes are formed only to a limited extent. Even the policy of nationalization, the consequences of which the elector might be expected to know a good deal about as a user of fuel and transport, is really an issue of this kind. There are, however, some issues, such as restricting coloured immigration, which do evoke a strong and well-formed response from the public, as we shall see. But such issues are exceptions and most of the policies which provide the focus of conflict at the elite level excite little reaction in the mass electorate.

From this it follows that in seeking out the issues which are genuinely involved in the public's assessment of the parties it is especially important to inquire into the public's awareness of the policies and the strength of the attitudes it has formed. In this the replies that a pollster receives to a once-only questionnaire may be of very limited help, for it is difficult to distinguish between the questions which the elector cares a good deal about and those which simply collect lightly held and transitory opinions.

---

[1] This value has been calculated from the 'expected' turnover table between the first and third interviews which can be obtained by treating change over the three interviews as a (non-stationary) Markov chain.

Some observers, sensing how little the ordinary man cares about the detailed policy choices facing government, have concluded that issues do not matter. A more useful response is to widen the conception of what issues are about and to ask *in what terms* they are likely to matter, for this may lead to a broader view of the sources of political change.

Issues and the Values Government May Achieve

The pre-eminent means by which the public simplifies the complexity of government action is by shifting its attention from policies to consequences – from government action to the values that government may achieve. We have noted in Chapter 2 that the public tends to focus on certain conditions or values of which it has more direct experience, rather than attempting the more complex assessment of means and ends which in some form must enter the Government's choice among alternative policies. The issue of the handling of the economy provides the outstanding example. How alternative policies affect income, prices and employment is a matter of exceeding complexity. But the conditions that governments seek to influence can be seen and known by ordinary people everywhere.

The connections electors form between these conditions or values and the parties are influenced by the arguments about these links among political leaders and elite observers. But under the British party system these connections are also formed by simple inferences from who is or was in power. A government is credited or blamed for many things while it is in office without the public's having undertaken any serious analysis of the role of government policy in producing the conditions of which it approves or disapproves. The economy once again provides a telling example. A government can profit handsomely from good times without having to prove that prosperity has flowed from its own policies. The Conservatives were able to benefit from the expansion of the 1950s without really having to show that their own role was decisive. In a similar way, a government can be severely damaged by bad times whatever its degree of actual responsibility. We have cited before the analogy of sport: the public may hold a government answerable just as it holds answerable the captain or manager of a losing team – and with even less understanding of what went wrong. This sort of *post hoc ergo propter hoc* reasoning is of course conditioned to some degree by the public's beliefs about what governments can actually affect; the British Cabinet is not answerable for flood damage in Italy, but it can suffer for a fuel shortage in a severe British winter. Yet simple inferences from the control of office are immensely important to the electorate's choice.

It is true that a system of alternating party control introduces an uncertainty into the public's assignment of responsibility. There is plainly some basis for the efforts of party leaders to transfer blame for what the country disapproves of onto their predecessors, or successors; we shall note in Chapter 18 Labour's remarkable success in 1966, eighteen months after taking office, in portraying the country's economic difficulties as a legacy from the Tories.

The conversion of values into electoral issues is of course not limited to values involving material well-being. There are many other values whose attainment, or lack of it, will provide issues between the parties without the public's having penetrated very far into reasons or causes. Threats to peace or to national prestige can easily yield issues of this kind. In America the Republicans' effort to depict the Democrats as the war party for having been in office during two world wars as well as the Korean and Vietnamese conflicts must be one of the purest examples of *post hoc ergo propter hoc* argument in modern politics.

The range of goals or values which can enter the public's assessment of the parties is exceedingly broad. For many people the connection between the parties and such general values as 'freedom' or 'social equality' has a good deal more meaning than the evaluations they are able to form from the calculations of means and ends about the specific policies debated at Westminster. General values of this kind may at times be invoked in particular policy controversies; for example 'freedom' is cited in relation to the issue of nationalization. But even without any clear tie to specific government action, such values can be enough to distinguish the parties in the public's mind.

Indeed some of the values which divide the supporters of the parties are unlikely to become matters of policy conflict. In Chapter 8, for example, we saw how Labour and Conservative voters, in both the middle and the working classes, tend to divide over the role of the sovereign. No one imagines that Labour is a republican party or that the Conservatives wish to restore to the Crown any of the power wrested from it in centuries of constitutional evolution. Nonetheless the higher valuation set by the Conservatives on the symbols of the monarchy is not missed by the broad public.

Thus many of the issues of electoral politics owe more to the voters' orientation towards values or goals than to their assessment of policy alternatives. They tend to start with conditions that they can know from their experience and to connect these to the parties, using whatever cues they are offered. These will at times include some understanding of the relation between means and ends, between policies and goals. But many of the ends which the public cares about will depend on means which are so complex or so conjectural that the link to the parties will be formed in other ways, including inferences from the simple possession of power.

The distinction between issues defined in terms of policies and issues defined in terms of values does much to clarify the ways of assessing the force of issues on electoral choice. The issues which have altered the party balance in a given period are not to be studied simply in terms of electors' answers to questions about the policies debated at the elite level; we must also discover the goals and values that have shaped the public's response to the parties. The 'image' of the parties – to invoke a much abused phrase – will consist partly of links to these goals or conditions which are valued by part or by all of the electorate but which are not directly reflected in current policy debates. Much of the terminology of party 'images' may be the invention of public relations men. The reality behind it is not. We return in Chapter 16 to the content of the party 'images', examining the way the public associates with the parties goals or values that are so general or diffuse that they could hardly be given meaning in direct policy terms.

Analyzing the Effect of Issues

Despite the variety of the issues acting on the electorate it is possible to lay down two conditions that will have to be met if an issue is to exert genuine force on the individual elector. The first involves the individual's orientation to the issue itself – the link, in terms of our initial diagram, between self and issue.

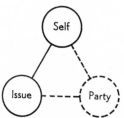

This must entail something more than simple awareness. We have seen how the great bulk of the electorate is aware of nationalization as an issue and knows the relative positions of the parties without having gone on to strongly rooted attitudes towards nationalization. If an issue is to sway the elector it must not only have crossed the threshold of his awareness; he must also have formed some genuine attitude towards it. The more an issue is salient to him and the subject of strong attitudes, the more powerful will be its influence on his party choice. Indeed, given the multiplicity of influences upon the individual elector, only issues that excite strong feeling are likely to have much impact.

The bond we have drawn between self and issue is also designed to suggest important questions about the terms in which the issue is seen. We have already argued the importance of the broad distinction between issues whose content is supplied by alternative policies or government actions and issues whose content is supplied by alternative conditions or values. But important differences also arise from the number and relationship of the alternative actions or conditions. In the simplest case the alternatives are reduced to two. 'Europe, in or out?' must be the form in which Britain's entry into the Common Market had meaning for many electors over a decade. Similarly, for some people class interests simply pose the issue of whether the government is for 'us' or for 'them'. But the alternatives associated with other issues in the public's mind cover a much wider range. Rhodesia was such a case after the Smith regime had unilaterally declared its independence during the 1964 Parliament. It was widely understood that Britain might take several alternative courses, ranging from settling on Smith's terms to sending troops to put down the rebellion.

Indeed, the range of policies or values entailed by some issues is virtually limitless. How much nationalization? or economic prosperity? The answers could be infinitely varied. In cases of this sort a powerful simplifying device, available to political leaders and the public alike, is to order other alternatives and compare the conditions or policies of the past or future with those of the present. The issue of prosperity is likely to be seen in terms of how much the economy, or the elector's welfare, has moved ahead or slipped back. Similarly, the issue of nationalization may be simplified for the voter in terms of whether there should be more or less of it than now, the elector in effect positioning himself with respect to the present state of affairs along a continuum describing degrees of nationalization:

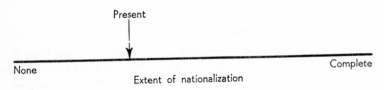

At other times a government proposal, such as the extent of takeover involved when steel is nationalized, will supply the point of reference about which a large set of ordered alternatives is divided. Whether a given issue is seen in these terms is of course an empirical question that is not to be settled by *a priori* argument. But there is no doubt that the interplay between political leaders and the mass of the electorate does frequently entail such a simplification of discourse about issues. We shall draw out some of the implications of this in a moment when we consider the circumstances under which an issue will affect the standing of the parties in the country as a whole.

The influence of an issue on the elector's choice depends on more than the presence of the bond between self and issue. It also depends on the links in his mind between the issue and the parties. However well-formed the individual's attitudes towards an issue, they will not affect his party choice unless the connection he sees between the issue and the parties gives reality to the second of the bonds in our diagram.

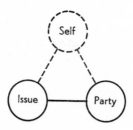

In some cases, this link need involve only one of the parties, especially when it mainly depends on judgments about the government of the day. We shall see in Chapter 18 evidence that the public tends to link economic issues mainly with the government, judging its performance as satisfactory or not, and giving less attention to the likely performance of the other party. But the link may involve a differing perception of the parties, with the elector judging the relative chance of achieving certain values if one or if the other comes to power. The voter who wishes pensions increased may indeed see one of the parties as far likelier than the other to increase them.

The bonds suggested by our diagram plot the conditions that must be fulfilled if an issue is to sway the individual elector. But we cannot say what impact an issue may have over the whole country without examining these bonds more generally, extending our framework of analysis to the electorate as a whole. Such an extension brings into view some distinctions which can easily be missed so long as our concern focuses on the individual. Let us see what conditions must be met before an issue can be said to have made a net alteration to the strength of the parties.

A first condition is a straightforward extension of the need for the individual to perceive an issue and to form some attitude towards it if it is to influence his behaviour. For an issue to have much impact in the whole electorate the bond of issue to self must be formed in the minds of a substantial body of electors. Many issues have meaning only for tiny fractions of the electorate, but some are salient to much wider portions. The greater the proportion of people to whom an issue is salient and the subject of strong attitudes, the more powerful the impact it can have on the fortunes of the parties. When we take up the issues of the 1960s we shall enforce a rough distinction between those which were of higher salience and attitude formation and those which were of lower salience and attitude formation.

A second condition that must be met for an issue to influence the relative standing of the parties has to do with the balance or skewness of attitudes towards it. What this condition entails is most easily seen in the case of an issue that poses only two clear alternatives. When, for example, the issue of Britain's entry into Europe came down to a choice between 'In' or 'Out', the issue was likely to affect the relative standing of the parties only when there was a surplus of opinion for one or other of these alternatives. The country might be strongly aroused by such an issue; but unless opinion were strongly on one side or the other, the parties would be unlikely to gain or lose much support by favouring going in or staying out.[1]

What we mean by the balance or skewness of attitudes becomes more complicated when issues involve more than two alternative policies or conditions. But when these fall into a natural order, as they do, for example, in the case of degrees of prosperity, the division of opinion may still be determined by comparing the electorate's preferences to present conditions.

---

[1] If we exclude the possibility that those on opposite sides will differ in the intensity of their views, an issue that differentiated the parties in the eyes of the electorate would not alter the prior strength of the parties if the division of opinion matched the prior division of party support. The possibility that the intensity with which views are held will differ is a standard point in treatments of the role of public opinion on political issues. See, for example, V. O. Key, Jr., *Public Opinion and American Democracy*, New York, 1961, pp. 206–33, and R. A. Dahl, *A Preface to Democratic Theory*, Chicago, 1956, pp. 90–123. Parties and governments do often pay heed to intense minorities in preference to more passive majorities. In many cases the reasons for this have more to do with money and organizational support and other 'supply' factors of politics than with calculations based on the 'demand' of those who may give or withhold their support at the polling station. But plainly there are some cases where more votes are to be won or lost from the reactions of an intense few than from the reactions of a less intense many.

Once again the issue of nationalization provides a suggestive example. Let us suppose that the electorate is spread along a continuum of support for nationalization:

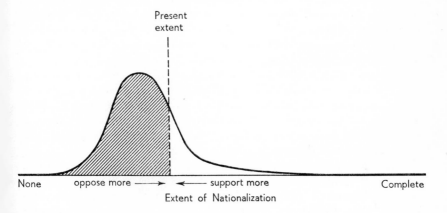

Present
extent

None   oppose more ———▶   ◀——— support more   Complete

Extent of Nationalization

By seeing how opinion is distributed along this continuum, we could see how favourable the country is to additional nationalization; and indeed the debates at Westminster might well give meaning to the issue in this way. In other cases, as we have said, a proposal put forward by a government or party, such as a new level for pensions, will provide a focal point about which the division of opinion in the country can be measured. When we examine the issues of the 1960s we shall distinguish between those which showed a strong trend of opinion and those which divided the country more evenly. It is the first of these, the issues on which the distribution of opinion was a skewed one, that are most likely to shift the balance of support between the parties.

The importance of the skewness of opinion calls attention to issues involving values that are widely shared in the electorate. Many issues present alternative policies or conditions whose value is a matter of disagreement in the country. Nationalization is one of these, but other issues, especially those which are seen in terms of the consequences of government action, involve a virtual consensus in the electorate, and indeed among the parties as well, on the values entailed by different alternatives. The issues connected with the state of the economy offer outstanding examples. There is no body of opinion in the country that favours economic distress, and thereby cancels some of the votes of those who want better times; the whole weight of opinion lies on the side of prosperity and growth.[1] Issues of this sort do not find the parties positioning themselves to appeal to those who favour alternative policies or goals. Rather the parties attempt to associate themselves in the public's mind with conditions, such as good times, which are universally favoured, and to dissociate themselves from conditions, such as economic distress, which are universally deplored. Such a distinction between *position* issues, on which the parties may appeal to rival bodies of opinion, and *valence* issues, on which there is essentially one body of opinion on values or goals, is too often neglected in political commentary. But the parties themselves are well aware of the potential of such valence issues as peace and economic prosperity and national prestige. Their potential derives from the fact that they satisfy so well the second of our conditions for an issue to have impact on the strength of the parties: that the distribution of opinion be strongly skewed.

The third condition for an issue to alter the net strength of the parties is that it be associated differently with the parties in the public's mind. Unless there is a difference of this sort, an issue will not sway the electorate towards one party or the other, however strongly formed and skewed opinion may be. In some cases a difference may arise from the fact that the public links a policy or condition to the governing party and not to its rival; this may be especially true of economic issues, as we shall see. But in other cases the electorate takes account of both parties at once and sees them as having different positions or different capacities to achieve some goal that is universally valued.

Issues do in fact vary widely in the degree to which they differentiate the parties in the public's mind. The extent of these contrasts is illustrated by the issues of nationalization and of Britain's entry into the Common Market. We saw earlier in the chapter that these issues were alike in the low degree of attitude formation towards them in much of the electorate. But these two issues differed profoundly in terms of the separation of parties they achieved in the public's mind. This contrast is set out in the entries of Table 13.4. As the gap between the first two percentages in each column shows, the consensus on the party difference was almost four times greater over nationalization than over entry into Europe.

The importance of taking explicit account of the bond the public perceives between issue and parties is illustrated by the problem of industrial conflict. There is no doubt that the British electorate is concerned about

---

[1] We shall consider in Chapter 18 the possibility that the 'trade-off' between high employment and price stability is converting the handling of the economy into a 'position' issue as this is defined below.

13.4 Perceived Party Differences on Nationalization and the Common Market, 1964

	Party more likely to extend nationalization	Party more likely to enter Common Market
Labour	90%	22%
Conservative	6	44
Not much difference	3	21
Don't know	1	13
	100% (n = 1563)	100% (n = 1161)

84% difference (between Labour and Conservative for nationalization); 22% difference (for Common Market)

strikes and very often denies its sympathy to the strikers. In 1964 some 79 per cent of our respondents said that they thought strikes were a 'very serious' problem (a further 14 per cent thought them a 'fairly serious' problem) and three times as many respondents said that their sympathies were generally against the strikers as said that their sympathies lay generally with the strikers. On this basis, the issue might seem to be excellently suited to the exploitation which it has received, at least implicitly, at the hands of the Conservatives in recent general elections. But the falseness of such a view in the mid-1960s is suggested by the evidence on the public's perceptions of which party had the better approach to strikes. Only one in ten of our 1964 respondents said the Conservatives did, while more than a quarter thought Labour's approach better. The rest saw the parties as much the same or said that they had no clear view. An issue that met all the tests of strength of attitude and surplus of opinion in one direction was effectively defused by the electorate's failure to differentiate the parties sharply in relation to it.

The conditions of an issue's influence imply the conditions under which that influence will change. The net 'force' which an issue exerts on the party balance can be altered by a change in the strength of the public's feeling, the distribution of that feeling across alternative policies or goals, and the way the parties are linked to these alternatives in the public's mind. Because each of these conditions is necessary for an issue to have effect, all three must be considered before we can say whether a change in one will alter the issue's influence.

The sharpest impact on party strength will be made by issues which simultaneously meet all our three conditions, that is to say by issues on which attitudes are widely formed, on which opinion is far from evenly divided and on which the parties are strongly differentiated in the public's mind. We may represent the confluence of these properties as one region in an eight-fold geometric figure suggested by the joint classification of how well these three conditions are satisfied.

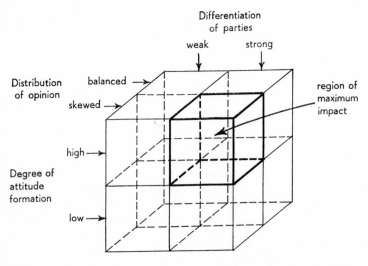

There is, of course, no reason to think of properties such as the differentiation of parties in the simple dichotomous terms suggested by the diagram: each of the ideas represented here can be regarded as a continuum, capable of many gradations. But to simplify the argument that follows we do treat them as roughly dichotomous. On this basis, only one of the cells in this eight-fold classification will include the issues that have maximum impact on the party balance. In each of the other seven the issues will lack one or more of the necessary properties.

Moreover, the appeal of the party leaders can in certain respects be brought within this framework. Britain's politics are not so dominated by the parties as collective entities that the leaders fail to enter the voters' calculations; identifying particular actions of government is in fact an important means by which the voter connects his choice to future policies or goals. For example, some who voted Labour in 1966 identified Mr Wilson with defence of the pound, Britain's presence east of Suez, firm handling of strikes and other actions which were by no means simple extensions of Labour's traditional policies. Even fairly generalized perceptions of a leader as 'able' or 'trustworthy' help the voter to say something about future actions of government on the basis of the leader's past handling of issues. These inferences may be less sure than they would be in a presidential system; the French peasant who trusted De Gaulle may have had a surer guide to the future so long as the President loomed large in it. But these inferences are by no means unknown to the British voter. We shall consider these and other aspects of the appeal of the party leaders in Chapter 17. Meanwhile we shall consider the issues of the 1960s to see how they fit into this pattern of analysis.

14 Issues and Change

OVER the years, as we have seen, large numbers of voters shifted their allegiance. What specific issues moved them to change? We have stressed the diversity of political behaviour – the numerous cancelling cross-switches, some of them often ascribable to personal events unconnected with public affairs; we cannot hope to 'explain' all the strands in the pattern of change. But we can examine the potential contribution to the aggregate movements made by a few of the most publicized issues and we can suggest how well, at different points in the decade, they satisfy the three conditions for major impact set out in the last chapter. We shall at least be able to show that the issues to which the parties gave most prominence were not always those which had the greatest potential for change. We shall, moreover, demonstrate the way in which the power of particular issues to affect the party balance could alter dramatically in a short space of time. We leave till later chapters the electors' more generalized images of the parties and the leaders that are, of course, inextricably linked with their reaction to issues. We also, because of their special character, put on one side economic issues for treatment in a separate chapter.

Issues of Strongest Impact

Outside the economic field, the issues which in the mid-sixties seemed to have the most impact were those involving social welfare. We can show how they then fully satisfied each of the three conditions of strength of feeling, skewness of opinions and differentiation of the parties. But by the end of the decade, though still important, their impact was much less.

There can be no doubt that real and strongly held attitudes were associated with welfare issues, especially housing and pensions. In our 1963 survey and again in 1970 we asked our respondents to tell us what they thought were the most important problems facing the Government. Some named several and some named none but their replies, summarized in

Table 14.1 shows vividly how prominent pensions and housing were, and continued to be, in the electorate's thinking, although their salience plainly was greater in the earlier year. By contrast the whole realm of foreign affairs and defence provided less than one in ten of the problems mentioned.

14.1 Most Important Problems Perceived as Facing the Government, 1963 and 1970

Type of Problem	% of Mentions	
	1963	1970
Social welfare, including	25	18
Pensions and old people's welfare	17	11
Health service	4	2
Give family allowances only to needy	2	2
Housing, including	24	11
Build more houses	12	7
Improve standards, clear slums	4	1
Keep house prices and mortgages down	4	2
Reduce rents	2	1
Economic problems, including	17	23
Keep down cost of living	4	12
Reduce unemployment	4	2
Bring jobs to particular areas	3	1
Education	9	5
Defence and international affairs	7	7
Transport	6	2
Taxation	5	12
Immigration	2	8
Industrial relations	2	8
All other problems	3	6
	100%	100%

The salience of issues of this kind was not, of course, peculiar to the 1960s. The values underlying them are easily understood by the mass of people; the rise and endurance of the welfare state is directly related to this fact. Variations in the impact of these issues over time must have depended principally on the other two conditions – the skewness of opinion and the differentiation of the parties in the public's mind.

Our evidence makes it very plain that in the early 1960s the public took a very one-sided position in support of further outlays on the social services. The spontaneous references summarized in Table 14.1 were overwhelmingly angled towards increased government expenditure on pensions and housing. Of those who mentioned social welfare issues fewer than one in ten sounded a restrictionist note, such as confining family allowances to the needy. Of those who mentioned housing even fewer raised themes such as the charging of economic rents for local authority housing to reduce the burdens on government. Even if all references to the need to cut taxes were regarded as implicit calls for the limitation of spending on the social services, an interpretation that could hardly be sustained, the negative view would have been very much a minority one. On the evidence of these comments the public mood, in this field at least, continued strongly interventionist.

The evidence is equally clear that in the mid-1960s the mood benefited Labour more than the Conservatives. Those who in 1963 mentioned as a problem the need for some expansion of the social services were asked which party could handle the matter best. As Table 14.2 shows, Labour was seen as very much more likely to expand the services. The point is reinforced by the tendency of those few who sought some curtailment of the social services to see the Conservatives as somewhat more likely to achieve such a result; thus, had curtailment been a dominant public desire, Labour would have benefited much less from the differentiation of parties so clearly shown by the entries of Table 14.2.

14.2 Perceived Ability of Parties to Expand or
Curtail Social Services, 1963

	Con.	Lab.	No Difference	Don't Know	
Respondent favours[a]					
Expanding social services	18%	51	20	11	100% (1537)
Curtailing social services	28%	23	28	21	100% (113)

Party Perceived as Better Able to Achieve Goal

[a] The perceptions included in this analysis are those associated with the respondent's identification in the 1963 interview of the major problems facing the Government. Responses advocating that the pension be put up, more houses be built, etc., were counted as wanting to expand the social services, while those advocating that family allowances be cut, a higher rent be charged for municipal council housing, etc., were counted as wanting to curtail the social services. After each problem mentioned the respondent was asked, 'What would you like to see the Government do about that?' and 'Which party would be the most likely to do what you want on this, the Conservatives, Labour, or the Liberals, or wouldn't it make much difference?'

In the mid-1960s the social services provided the one issue that fully satisfied the three conditions. The evidence suggests that for a time the issue's impact was substantial. Table 14.3 compares the 1959–63 swing

14.3 Swing to Labour 1959–63 by Attitudes on Social Services

	Wanted social services expanded and preferred Labour handling of issue	Did not mention social services	Wanted social services curtailed and preferred Conservative handling of issue
Swing	+9·6%	+2·0%	−1·9%

to Labour among these groups: those who wanted the social services to be expanded and saw Labour as better able to do so, those who did not mention the social services in 1963, and those who wanted the social services curtailed and saw the Conservatives as better able to do so. Since, as we have seen, the first of these groups was very much larger than the third, this issue worked strongly to Labour's advantage.

Our evidence shows that social services issues worked less strongly to Labour's advantage after its accession to office following the party's return to power in 1964, first because opinion became less skewed in favour of additional spending and later because the parties became less clearly differentiated in the public's mind. In 1964, in 1966 and again in 1969 we inquired whether our respondents thought that expenditures for the social services should be increased or should be kept at their existing level. The change is set out in Table 14.4. Apparently the action of the new Labour

14.4 Perceived Need for Increased Spending on Social Services, 1964, 1966 and 1969

Do you feel that the Government should spend more on pensions and social services or do you feel that spending for social services should stay about as it is now?	Autumn 1964	Spring 1966	Summer 1969
Should spend more	77%	54%	43%
Should stay about as it is now	20%	42%	52%
Don't know	3%	4%	5%
	100%	100%	100%

Government in putting up pensions and removing prescription charges for medicines had lessened the gap between what the average elector felt desirable and what he thought the Government was doing. Following a line of reasoning employed in Chapter 12, we can suggest the nature of this change between 1964 and 1966 in terms of a dimension showing degree of support for the social services on which we can place a distribution of voter preferences for government spending on social services together with their perception of the extent of present government spending. The situation in 1964 might be represented as follows:

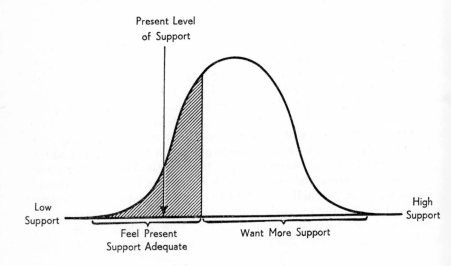

The perceived level of existing support for the social services was low enough for only a minority of electors to be satisfied, those who are shown in the interval marked 'feel present support adequate'. The majority had preferences far enough above what they perceived the existing level to be to record themselves as favouring an increase in spending. These are the people who fell in the interval marked off for those who 'want more support'.[1] By 1966, however, the actions of the Labour Government had presumably shifted the perceived level of existing support, so that opinion was much less skewed in favour of additional spending.

[1] We have prepared these sketches to convey a few main ideas for which the empirical warrant seems clear. We do not at all regard them as literal representations of reality. We do not know the shape of the electorate's distribution along such a dimension or even the extent to which it sees such a continuum of support for the social services. A fully realistic representation would have to take account of a number of further complications, especially the differing perceptions individuals would have of the existing level of support.

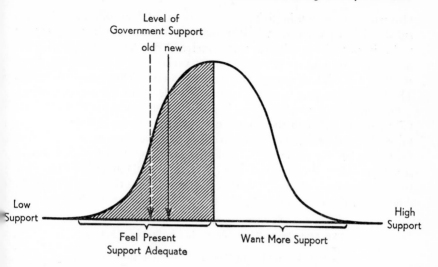

A more complex set of reasons lay beneath the still further diminished demand for increased spending on social services in 1969. As the Labour Government was obliged to adopt more stringent financial policies, spending on the social services was actually curtailed. But the nation's economic difficulties undoubtedly left wide sections of the public with the feeling that there was little or no social dividend to be distributed.

Towards the end of the 1960s Labour lost much of its advantage as the party more likely to increase social services spending. As Table 14.5 shows,

14.5 Perceived Positions of the Parties in Spending on the Social Services, 1964–70

Which party would be more likely to spend more on pensions and the social services	Con.	Lab.	Not Much Difference	Don't Know	Totals	Lab.% minus Con.%
Autumn 1964	8%	69	16	7	100%	+61
Spring 1966	7%	64	23	6	100%	+57
Summer 1970	17%	48	29	6	100%	+31

this perception continued to be overwhelmingly held in 1964 and 1966. By 1970, however, the picture was markedly different; as the last column demonstrates, the party gap had been halved. Undoubtedly the Labour

Government's action in giving first priority on taking office in 1964 to a substantial increase in pensions helped to reinforce the distinctness with which its position in this area was perceived.[1] But such impressions could not fully withstand the impact of other events over the following years. By 1970 Labour's advantage was much less conspicuous on two counts. The force of the social services issue was, at least for the moment, spent.

One other issue which declined in potential during the life of the Labour Government – though the decline may only have been temporary – was the problem of strikes. There was no doubt of its salience: in all our surveys four-fifths of our respondents said that they considered strikes a very serious problem. Opinion was clearly skewed: in all our surveys they were four times more likely to feel their sympathies against than for the strikers. And the parties were differentiated: as Table 14.6 shows, in 1964 and 1966

14.6 Attitudes to Party Approaches to Strikes, 1964–70

	Which party has the better approach to strikes?				
	Conservative	Labour	No Difference	Don't Know	
1964	10%	32	43	15	100%
1966	11%	31	51	7	100%
1969	22%	20	49	9	100%
1970	23%	20	45	12	100%

they were three times as likely to say that Labour had a better approach to the problem than the Conservatives. Yet even in 1964 and 1966 a majority of those with an opinion saw no difference between the parties and by 1969 and 1970 Labour's advantage had disappeared. Industrial relations may have provided an issue that helped Labour in the mid-1960s (though not as much as social welfare matters), but in 1970 it is hard to see that it could have had much net effect on the party balance. However, the history of subsequent years shows how the issue could grow again in importance. What would result from a general election fought on the question of industrial order became a live issue.

If in the period when we collected our evidence, social services and, to a much smaller extent, strikes may have ceased to fully satisfy our three conditions for impact, immigration moved in the opposite direction.

[1] In November 1964, despite the economic situation, the new Government announced that the election promise to raise pensions would be met as soon as possible. In March 1965 the basic rate was increased by 20 per cent.

Issues of High Potential

The explosive possibilities of the issues raised by coloured immigration were only partially recognized during the early 1960s. Yet the question was very salient to the mass of the people. As Table 14.1 showed, immigration was spontaneously mentioned in 1963 by a substantial number of our respondents, even though it was then playing a relatively small role in public debate. Moreover, a specific question about immigration elicited fewer 'don't knows' than any other issue question in our survey, except for one about the importance of the Queen and Royal Family. Indeed, a remarkable proportion of our respondents – fully a quarter – felt strongly enough to go beyond the 'closed' question and to offer spontaneous elaborations of their hostility to coloured immigration.[1] In 1964, 1966 and 1970 we found that half our sample felt 'very strongly' about immigration and a further third felt 'fairly strongly'.

The evidence for the one-sidedness of the public attitude is equally overwhelming. Table 14.7 shows the undeviating opposition to coloured

14.7 Attitudes Towards Immigration

Do you think that too many immigrants have been let into this country or not?	Summer 1963	Autumn 1964	Spring 1966	Summer 1969	Summer 1970
Too many	84%	81%	81%	87%	85%
Not too many	12	13	14	10	10
Don't know	4	6	5	3	5
	100%	100%	100%	100%	100%

immigration reflected in each of our interviews. Its entries match closely the findings of the opinion polls.

The degree of concern with this problem varied between classes and generations. Those in the higher occupational grades were less opposed to immigration and were markedly less likely to feel strongly about the issue. Indeed, the proportions feeling strongly that too many immigrants had been let in rose almost without a break across our six occupational grades,

[1] Spontaneous objections centred on competition for housing and jobs ('there's not enough work for our own as it is') and the deterioration of health and living standards the immigrants were thought to bring ('up in Birmingham they crowd twenty into a house'; 'it's the way they're let in without any medical checks, bringing tuberculosis and things like that').

from 28 per cent among higher managerial (grade I) to 48 per cent among unskilled manual (grade VI).

There was also a fairly steep gradient in opposition to immigration by age. The proportions recording themselves as strongly opposed to entry of so many immigrants were quite different across our age-cohorts. Among the pre-1918 cohort 52 per cent did so, and among the interwar cohort the proportion, 47 per cent, was only slightly less. Yet among the 1945 and post-1951 cohorts the proportions strongly in opposition were only 35 and 37 per cent.

But at the beginning of our period the immigration issue, although it lost the Labour Party three seats against the tide in 1964, and probably prevented them from winning several others, never exercised anything like its potential impact on the party balance, because the public failed to differentiate the party positions. This was partly because the parties themselves were each visibly divided. Moreover, while the Labour Party had opposed the Conservatives' Commonwealth Immigrants Act of 1962, the first restriction on immigration, it was a Conservative Government that had been in power during the period in which mass immigration had taken place. When Labour came to power in 1964, after a campaign which in Smethwick and a few other constituencies had revealed the dynamite that lay in the issue, the new Government quickly moved to a position on immigration control that was quite as tough as that of its predecessor.

Our respondents at first gave clear evidence of failure to differentiate between the parties' positions. In 1964, 26 per cent of the electorate thought the Conservatives were more likely to keep the immigrants out and 19 per cent thought Labour more likely to do so; as many as 55 per cent saw no difference between the parties or didn't know which party was the likelier to keep immigrants out. In 1966 the figures were similar (26 per cent, 13 per cent and 61 per cent). In such circumstances the issue can hardly have had great influence on the strength of the parties across the country as a whole. However, the picture was different in some localities. The electorate's perception of party difference varied appreciably with the degree of immigrant concentration. The country as a whole saw only a moderate difference between the parties, but in the areas most affected the perception of differences was much sharper. Table 14.8 shows this contrast for 1964. Where there had been negligible immigration, virtually equal numbers of respondents saw each party as the more likely to shut off the flow. But where immigration had been substantial, three times as many people thought the Conservatives would be more restrictive.

The evidence about how people formed their perceptions of party

14.8 Differentiation of Parties' Perceived Position on Immigration
by Degree of Immigrant Concentration, 1964

Which party is more likely to keep immigrants out?	Degree of Immigrant Concentration in Local Area		
	None	Low	High
Conservative	22%	31%	43%
Labour	21	14	14
No difference	42	45	31
Don't know	15	10	12
	100%	100%	100%

positions on the issue is very limited. It was only in Smethwick and one or two other places of high immigrant concentration that the local Conservative Party explicitly identified itself with an anti-immigrant position, and it was relatively rare for local Labour Parties to take well-publicized positions which would make them be seen as much more pro-immigrant. Granted the potential of the issue, the way in which local Conservative Parties forbore from exploiting it is very notable. Leaders at the national level, apart from any private moral and political convictions, had the strongest pragmatic reasons for not pursuing any line that smacked of racialism. The price in division within the party and in international relations would have been prohibitive. But local politicians living among people with very deep feelings must have been sorely tempted to develop an issue that might, as Smethwick showed, have yielded spectacular gains. In this local sense, immigration had satisfied our three tests for an issue of maximum impact. But in the country as a whole in the mid-1960s we could place immigration in the region of our schematic diagram, adjacent to the one where issues have their maximum impact, as in the diagram on the next page.

It was an issue that then involved the necessary salience and the necessary skewed opinions – but it failed to involve sufficiently widespread differentiation in the perception of the parties' positions. But it was different from other issues in this region in that there obviously was a very real possibility of its potential being realized through a further differentiation of the parties' stands in the public mind, and of its moving to the region of maximum impact that the social services then occupied.

In fact, by the end of the decade the parties had become sharply differentiated in the public's mind across the country as a whole. Table 14.9 on the next page, which summarizes the data for 1963–70, shows that by

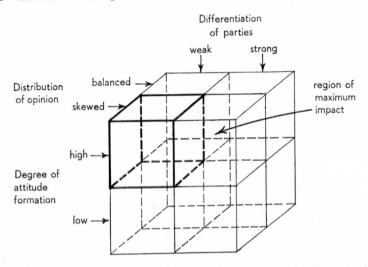

1970 the difference between the percentage thinking that the Conservatives were the more likely to keep immigrants out and the percentages thinking that Labour had increased sevenfold since 1964.

Therefore, by the end of the 1960s the immigration issue passed the three tests of maximum impact. Why then did it not in fact have a greater impact? Our view is that its true influence may well have been understated because the media, with the memory of Smethwick and other local contests of the mid-1960s so clearly in mind, searched for differential effects between areas of high and of lesser immigrant concentration. But we have seen that strong and overwhelmingly hostile attitudes towards immigration were quite general in the country. When in the later 1960s the perception that

14.9 Perceived Position of Parties on
Control of Immigration

Which party is more likely to keep immigrants out?	Autumn 1964	Spring 1966	Summer 1969	Summer 1970
Conservative	26%	26%	50%	57%
Labour	19	13	6	4
No difference	41	53	36	33
Don't know	14	8	8	6
	100%	100%	100%	100%
Con.% − Lab.%	+7	+13	+44	+53

the Conservatives were the most restrictionist party also became quite general, the issue may have had a pervasive and by no means negligible effect in the swing towards the Conservatives.

Evidence for this is offered by the shifts of party strength both between 1966 and 1969 and over the full life of the 1966 Parliament. Those who in 1969 were convinced that the Conservatives were likelier to keep immigrants out had shifted much more strongly towards the party than had those who saw no difference between the parties or thought Labour was likelier to keep immigrants out.

Table 14.10 contrasts the swing towards the Conservatives in 1970 of

14.10 1970 vote of 1966 Labour Supporters by 1970 Perception of Party More Likely to Keep Immigrants Out

| | | Party more likely to keep immigrants out | |
		Conservative	Labour or No Difference
1970 vote	Conservative	21%	11%
	Labour	76%	83%
	Liberal	3%	6%
		100%	100%

those who had supported Labour in 1966 according to perceptions of the stands of the parties on the issue of immigration. Among 1966 Labour supporters almost twice as many switched to the Conservatives among those who saw the party of Heath and Powell as more likely to keep immigrants out. Here is strong prima facie evidence of an issue affecting party strength.[1]

The change in public attitude took place at a time when there was no deep divide in official Conservative and Labour policy on immigration: both accepted that dependants must be allowed in to join their bread-winners, both agreed that the flow of new migrants must be severely restricted, and both agreed that once in the country migrants must be treated as equal citizens. In 1968 the Labour Government, with Conservative support, even passed a bill restricting the entry of Indian-origin holders of British passports living in East Africa.

But Mr Enoch Powell stepped into the void, created because neither front bench voiced the strong anti-immigrant feeling that existed so widely.

[1] The case is not conclusive. Voters who switch support are likely to see virtues in their new party even in areas which did not actually influence their change of allegiance.

In April 1968 he gave an inflammatory speech in Birmingham which, apart from leading to his dismissal from the Shadow Cabinet, provoked the most extraordinary public response. Thereafter Mr Powell repeatedly kept the issue before the country. Indeed, during the 1970 campaign he made great headlines and almost lost his official Conservative label through the vehemence of his remarks on the subject.[1] Even if Mr Powell was far from being the spokesman of his party, it is hard to doubt that he had succeeded in associating the Conservatives with opposition to immigration in the public mind.

Few, if any, issues in our period deserve to be classified in a second region which also lies adjacent to the region of maximum impact. Our schematic classification allows for issues which are highly salient and which strongly differentiate the parties but on which opinion is fairly evenly divided between competing policies or goals. When they occur these are the issues which divide a society most profoundly. In the 1880s Irish Home Rule may have been one such case. But in the 1960s, although there were issues on which opinion was fairly evenly divided, none of these was a matter both of strong feeling in the country and of sharply differentiated party positions. As for the other issues which had currency in this period, they all seem to have been of much lower salience for the mass electorate.

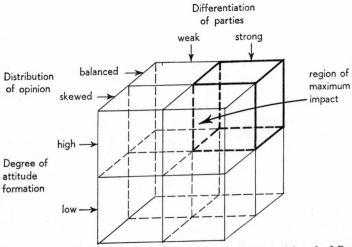

[1] In the election's aftermath, 75 per cent of the electorate had heard of Powell's proposals on immigration and almost all of these had a clear view of where Powell stood. Moreover, 78 per cent were 'glad he spoke out' while only 16 per cent were sorry and 6 per cent didn't know.

Issues of Less Potential

The vast majority of issues which gave content to political debate within the parties and at Westminster during our period plainly belong in the lower tier of our schematic diagram in one of the regions of low attitude formation. In Chapter 13 we discussed the interesting case of nationalization. Our data showed that the public differentiated the party positions on this very clearly and, furthermore, that a clear majority of the electorate expressed opposition to further nationalization. Yet our data made plain, especially in the instability of individual opinion over time, the slight extent to which the issue of nationalization was a matter of genuine attitude formation among the mass electorate.

A very similar judgment can be made about the issue of nuclear weapons. Before Labour came to power in 1964 the parties were perceived as having strongly divergent positions on the nuclear deterrent (although this perception had become much more blurred by 1969). Opinion on the issue, although less one-sided than on nationalization, leaned heavily towards the retention of British nuclear weapons. But what made the Bomb ineffective as an issue was the limited hold it had on either the attention or the strong attitudes of the electorate, even in 1964. Once again our data showing how unstable individual opinions were over time make plain the limits of attitude formation on this issue.

The issue of Britain's entry into the Common Market is of unusual interest because of the sharp fluctuations in the balance of opinion. It is one of the ironies of history that a subject which loomed so large in British politics in 1962, in 1967 and again in 1971–2 should never have been a major election issue in the period before Britain joined the European Community. In the 1964, 1966 and 1970 elections the issue was either regarded as dead or as one on which there were no clear party differences. Our own surveys tapped an ebb and flow of support for membership similar to that recorded by the public opinion polls, as indicated in Table 14.11 on the next page.[1]

There is no evidence that people felt very strongly about the issue or saw a great party difference on it. In 1966, just after Mr Wilson had accused Mr Heath of 'rolling over like a spaniel' before the French in his eagerness, our respondents, by 57 per cent to 16 per cent, did see the Conservatives as more likely than Labour to take Britain in, but by 1969 the position had been reversed to 22 per cent to 32 per cent in the other direction (with as

[1] See U. W. Kitzinger, *Diplomacy and Persuasion*, London, 1974, pp. 352–70, 411–20, for a full discussion of opinion polls on the Common Market.

14.11 Attitudes Towards Common Market Entry, 1963–70

	1963	1964	1966	1969	1970
For entry	32%	33%	54%	34%	18%
Against entry	29	32	17	41	58
Don't know	39	35	29	25	24
	100%	100%	100%	100%	100%
% For − % Against	+3	+1	+37	−7	−40

many as 46 per cent saying 'no difference' or 'don't know'). The Common Market hardly arose as an issue. In 1963 and again in 1969 less than 2 per cent mentioned it among the three most important problems facing the country and less than 1 per cent of respondents in any of our surveys mentioned a party's Common Market stance as a reason for liking or disliking it or its leader. Thus, although opinion on the Market and on party stands was unevenly divided, and although it changed quite sharply during the period of our study, intensity of feeling about it was never sufficiently widespread to have much effect on party fortunes. Indeed, even when the issue was much at the centre of the political stage in 1971–2 the fluctuations of the polls suggested that it was not stirring very deep passions.[1]

The impact of Rhodesia, which became a prominent issue with the unilateral declaration of independence by the Smith Government in November 1965, offers a different example. The issue made headlines throughout that autumn and early winter. The Prime Minister projected himself as a national leader defending the Crown and the Commonwealth. The Conservatives were deeply divided: a compromise arrangement to avoid a vote at their party conference in mid-October was presented as a capitulation to Lord Salisbury and the right wing, and in November and December when the issue was debated in Parliament the party split three ways between opposition, abstention and support on a motion approving the Government's policy.

The issue was undoubtedly given prominence by the mass media and there is no doubt that the parties were differentiated in the electorate's mind. Figure 14.12 shows the clear tendency of the public to see the Conservatives as favouring a compromise with or an outright grant of

[1] All the nationwide polls showed a three to one majority against entry in June 1971 dissolve to virtual equality in August. A substantial majority against in October 1971 had turned into a majority for by June 1972; by 1973 there was a majority against once more.

14.12 Perceived Positions of Parties on Rhodesia, 1966[a]

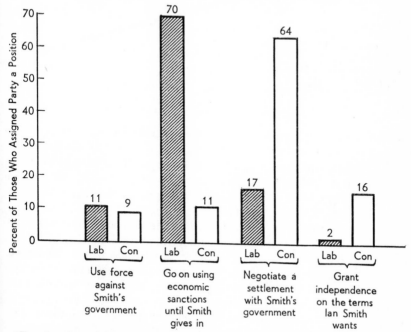

[a] The values given are the proportions of those assigning a given party to each of several alternative positions in response to question 25b of the 1966 questionnaire. Those who replied 'don't know' (9 per cent in the case of Labour, 15 per cent in the case of the Conservatives) are excluded from the analysis.

independence to the Smith Government and to see Labour as committed to going on with sanctions. A few in our sample could not associate a position with Labour, and somewhat more were unable to place the Conservatives. But of those who could, the great majority were clear that Labour stood for tougher handling of the Smith Government.

The extent to which the electorate had well-formed opinions of its own on the issue is more doubtful. Few of our respondents volunteered Rhodesia as one of the main issues of the 1966 campaign or as a ground for liking or disliking either of the main parties or their leaders. One in five of our respondents said they did not have any opinion on Rhodesia. Of those who did endorse one of the several alternative positions, a narrow majority came down on the side of a negotiated settlement rather than the continued application of sanctions, as Table 14.13 on the next page shows. It is

14.13 Opinion on Rhodesia

	1966	1970
Grant independence on the terms Ian Smith wants	5%	9%
Negotiate a settlement with Smith's Government	40	47
Go on using economic sanctions until Smith gives in	29	19
Use force against Smith's Government	8	7
Don't know	18	18
	100%	100%

doubtful whether these opinions were very strongly held. Surveys of this period repeatedly showed the public as likely to accept the Government's lead.[1] Probably the issue's main importance lay in the 1965–6 period when it supplied Mr Wilson with a vehicle for showing his leadership and the Conservatives with an occasion for displaying disunity and underlining the presence of a vocal extreme wing.

There were a number of additional issues in this period which were of limited salience, engaging the concern of individual electors or groups of electors but having little hold on the electorate as a whole. The impact of each such issue on the relative strength of the parties must have been small, although taken together they had, of course, an influence on the choices of a large number of people. For example, however faint the issue of the nuclear deterrent for the great bulk of the electorate, there is no doubt that it mattered enormously to many thousands of individuals.

If perceptions of the parties' ability to deal with a number of distinct issues are inspected closely, it becomes plain that the electorate tends to gain or lose confidence in a party in several areas at once. In 1963 and again in 1969 we invited our respondents to say not only what they thought were the major problems facing the country, but also what they thought should be done about each of the problems they named, and which party was likelier to do it. The result in 1963, when Labour had instilled a fairly general confidence, was that Labour was thought better able to handle most (though not all) of the particular issues which engaged our sample's concern. But in 1969, when Labour was in a deep trough of public dis-

[1] In October 1965, for example, National Opinion Polls recorded 82 per cent of the electorate as accepting the Government's position with the encouragement offered by this question: 'The British Government insist that independence can only be granted to Rhodesia if the conditions are acceptable to the people of Rhodesia as a whole, and not just to the whites. Do you think this is right or wrong?' The same survey showed that the ratio of whites to blacks in Rhodesia was known to only a very small fraction of the public.

favour, confidence in its ability drained away across a wide range of particular problems mentioned by our sample.

A similar parallelism could be seen in changes in the public's confidence in the parties' generalized ability to cope with foreign and home affairs. Figure 14.14 shows that in the field of foreign affairs (about which the

14.14 Perceptions of Party Ability to Handle Home and Foreign Affairs, 1964–70[a]

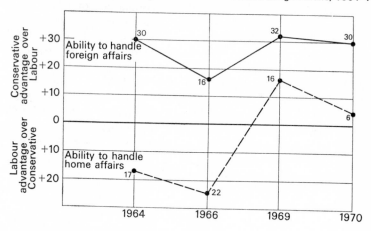

Answers to questions 11a and 11b.

electorate seemed to care relatively little) the Conservatives did better in the public eyes throughout the 1964 to 1970 period. But the figure also shows that parallel shifts occurred in the parties' relative esteem in both foreign and domestic affairs.

This phenomenon draws attention to more general aspects of popular attitudes towards the parties, in particular to elements of the parties' images that are susceptible to marked change over time. Therefore we shall now go beyond the electorate's perception of the parties' positions or abilities in relation to particular issues and explore the more generalized impressions of the parties in the public's mind.

15 Ideological Factors in Change

POLITICAL change – whether in the individual elector or in the mass electorate – will seldom be provoked by a single issue, standing on its own. Most voters have attitudes towards many issues, and these may fall into discernible patterns. Such patterns could obviously have a bearing on the sources of electoral change. Indeed, one of the most familiar frameworks for interpreting change – the schema of left and right – assumes that the public sees a number of political issues in terms of an ideological spectrum and responds to leftward and rightward movements of the parties along this spectrum. But this sort of ideological framework may not be the only source of pattern or structure in attitudes towards issues. We might, for example, suppose that many voters would simply adopt the pattern of issue positions contained in their party's policies.

Parties as Sources of Pattern

Since most electors have partisan dispositions and since the parties themselves offer a lead on most issues, it would be surprising if the parties did not assume a special status in giving structure to attitudes. When they do so, the flow of cause and effect is not from issue to party preference but the other way round, from party preference to belief on the issue. Attitudes towards issues then have only a conserving or reinforcing influence on party choice and not a formative one. How often do the parties in fact shape the beliefs of their followers into a consistent pattern?

Our empirical evidence reveals astonishingly little support for such an interpretation of British electoral attitudes. This is indeed implicit in the evidence of Chapter 13 about the instability of views on policy. If voters are bound to their party, and if they have fairly stable perceptions of party stands but unstable attitudes of their own, then their 'learning' of party stands cannot have lent much pattern to their views on issues.

It is not that the electorate is ignorant of party stands; on a number of issues there is a clear understanding of the line each party takes. The 'structure' uniting these perceptions is illustrated by the relationship between the positions which their supporters thought their parties were taking on the issues of nationalization and nuclear weapons. There was fairly high consensus that the Conservatives stood for keeping the Bomb and Labour for extending public ownership. Table 15.1 shows how closely

15.1 Party Stands on Nationalization and Nuclear Weapons as Perceived by Labour and Conservative Voters, 1964[a]

		Party most likely to extend nationalization	
		Own	Other
Party most likely to keep nuclear weapons	Other	76%	5%
	Own	24	95
		100%	100%
		($n = 461$)	($n = 496$)

[a] This table includes all supporters of Labour and the Conservatives who themselves expressed a view on the issues of nationalization and nuclear weapons.

the two perceptions were related in 1964. Indeed, any standard correlation calculated from the frequencies underlying this table would have a value approaching +0·7.

Nothing like this coherent structure is, however, found when we examine the attitudes that partisan voters expressed towards these same two issues. Table 15.2 shows a very much weaker correlation between these attitudes;

15.2 Attitudes towards Nationalization and Nuclear Weapons Held by Labour and Conservative Supporters, 1964

		Extend Nationalization	
		Should	Should Not
Give up Independent Nuclear Weapons	Should	65%	51%
	Should Not	35	49
		100%	100%
		($n = 364$)	($n = 806$)

by most standard measures it would be little more than +0·1. Plainly the degree to which voters pattern their beliefs on those of their parties, even on key issues, can be very modest.

Even party activists fail to conform. We shall not set out the evidence in detail, but it is striking that the tie between attitudes on nationalization and nuclear weapons was no stronger among those minorities who subscribed to a party or did party work than among the bulk of the electorate. There could be few more forceful comments on the limited extent to which party orientations reach down into the mass public, or on the limited role which tightly clustered policy beliefs play in the motives for party work.

Thus the fluidity of attitudes discussed in Chapter 13 finds a parallel in the limited interrelationships of such attitudes. Our findings show that, far from comprising a tightly formed cluster of beliefs, attitudes towards such policy issues as nationalization of industry, retention of nuclear weapons, entry into the Common Market and levels of spending on the social services were only weakly related at any of our three rounds of interviews.

The Structure of Stable Opinions

The fact that weakly formed attitudes will tend to change over time suggests an analytic step for us to take in searching for pattern in the attitudes of those who do hold genuine issue beliefs. If we exclude from consideration those whose views wavered between interviews and examine the interrelationships of the attitudes only of those whose views remained fixed, we will be able to clear away most responses that had a random element and allow us to detect any pattern in the beliefs of the minority whose views were more genuine and stable.[1]

Let us begin with a single policy issue, such as the nationalization of industry, dividing our respondents simply by whether they favour more nationalization or not. With the replies to two separate interviews, we can distribute the full sample into four categories.

[1] We do not suppose that all change is response instability; neither do we suppose that constancy is always evidence of genuine attitude. There is some true attitude change in response variation, and some random responses will be consistent from one time to the next for accidental reasons, as explained below. Nevertheless, if we assume that response instability is greater in some people than others, this procedure will take us closer to any true pattern of attitude in the minds of those whose beliefs are relatively well-formed and stable. A good deal of empirical evidence, including many of the later findings of this chapter, supports the assumption that there is normally a gradient in response instability across a sample of the general public. This gradient is not in general such that all respondents have either real and perfectly stable or unreal and random responses, although Converse has shown that this condition may occasionally obtain. But the evidence suggests that the gradient is fairly steep on a good many issues.

Should more industries be nationalized?

Earlier interview	Yes	Yes	No	No
Later interview	Yes	No	Yes	No

Since we are concerned only with those who have stable views, we may exclude from the analysis all those whose variable responses have placed them in one of the shaded cells. Of course, anyone who tossed a coin to decide their response at each interview would have a 50 per cent chance of landing in an unshaded cell, but we have at least eliminated about half the people with high response instability.

The process can be carried further by repeating the question. With a third interview we can divide our respondents into eight cells. The likelihood of anyone falling in an unshaded cell by giving the same reply by chance at all three interviews would by now be reduced to 25 per cent: three quarters of those with high response instability would now have been eliminated from the analysis.

Should more industries be nationalized?

First interview	Yes	Yes	Yes	Yes	No	No	No	No
Second interview	Yes	Yes	No	No	Yes	Yes	No	No
Third interview	Yes	No	Yes	No	Yes	No	Yes	No

Since we wish to explore the relationship between two or more stable attitudes we may go farther in elimination. If the eight-fold classification of responses on nationalization in three successive interviews is crossed with a similar classification of successive responses to another policy issue, such as whether Britain ought to give up the Bomb, we obtain the following sixty-four-fold array and reduce the chance of a random answerer falling into an unshaded cell to only one in sixteen.[1]

[1] Assuming a probability of 0·5 for a given response at a given interview, the likelihood of a 'pure' random answerer falling in a given unshaded cell is $(0·5)^6 = 0·0156$. Since there are four such cells, the probability of his landing in one of the four is 0·06. These

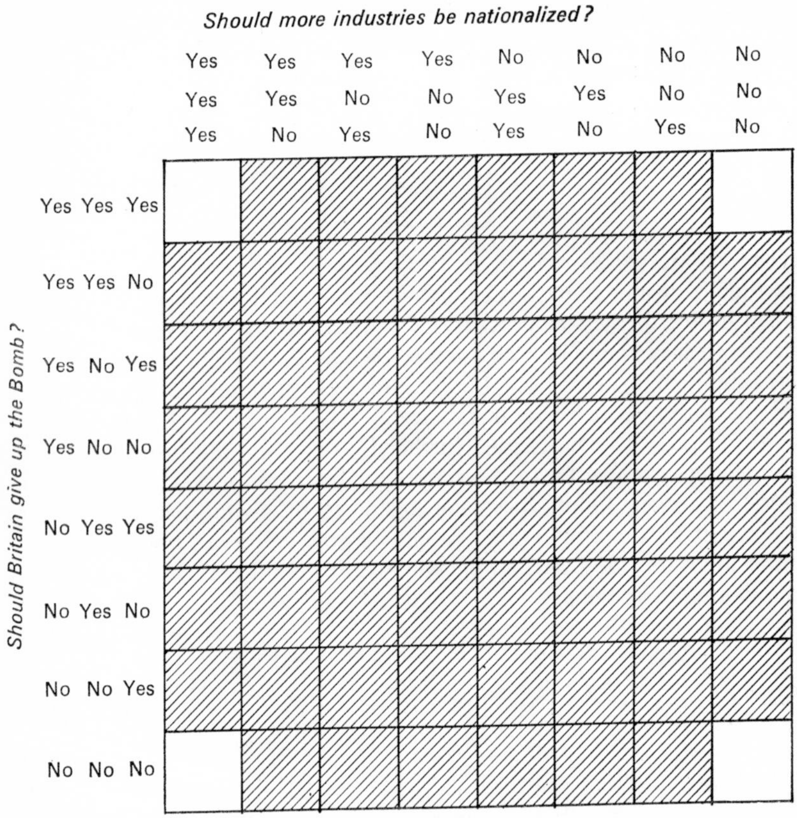
Should more industries be nationalized?
Yes Yes Yes Yes No No No No
Yes Yes No No Yes Yes No No
Yes No Yes No Yes No Yes No
Should Britain give up the Bomb?
Yes Yes Yes
Yes Yes No
Yes No Yes
Yes No No
No Yes Yes
No Yes No
No No Yes
No No No

When this procedure was applied to the pairs of issues for which we have responses at two or three of the interviews, varying proportions of the sample fell into the unshaded cells of such tables. In some cases the fraction giving constant responses on both issues in a pair was as high as half, in others as low as a tenth. The average across all pairs of issues was about three-tenths; our procedure for removing those with unformed or changing opinions has thus on average cut away seven-tenths of the total sample.

It is important to see that this procedure for removing people of changeable opinion in no way prejudges the relationship of the remaining re-

---

calculations are of course only suggestive since the probabilities governing the responses of those of high response instability will not in general be as simple as the law governing the toss of a fair coin.

spondents' attitudes on any two issues. For example, if we draw from the arrays the four unshaded corner cells (describing the joint distribution of the opinions of those who voiced a stable view both on nationalization and nuclear weapons over the three interviews) we do nothing to force a positive or a negative association between these attitudes. Rather, we can now look at the structure of attitudes without its being so heavily overlaid by the effects of random responses.

What in fact emerges from the correlations obtained in this way is that there is no strong pattern linking the attitudes even of those who do have stable attitudes. Compared with the expectation that any reader of the *Economist* or *New Statesman*, say, would have about political positions that naturally go together, the actual correlations are strikingly low.

This conclusion emerges clearly from Table 15.3 on the next page. Each of the figures in the table has been calculated from a fourfold table of constant opinions similar to that shown above. The general consensus of informed opinion, reflecting on the whole the official party lines in 1963, explains the direction we have given to the issues. Thus support for nationalization, opposition to nuclear weapons, opposition to the Common Market, tolerance of immigration, opposition to hanging, suspicion of big business, lower esteem for the monarchy and support for trade unions were all treated as if they lay in one direction and the reverse of these positions as if they lay in the opposite direction. There was one case in which such informed judgments as to the direction of items was mildly contradicted by the attitudes held by the mass public. Despite the alignment on the Common Market which the parties assumed under Mr Macmillan and Mr Gaitskell, electors who held the 'left' position on other issues were the more likely to favour *entering* Europe and those who held the 'right' position to oppose it. This reversal is indicated by the negative value of the correlation between

15.3 Correlations of Stable Attitudes Towards Issues[a]

	Nuclear Weapons	Common Market	Too many Immigrants	Death Penalty	Big Business Power	Queen and Royal Family	Trade Union Power
Nationalization of Industry	*0·14*	*0·10*	*0·06*	0·13	*0·37*	*0·26*	*0·65*
Retention of Nuclear Weapons		−0·26	*0·07*	0·20	*0·09*	*0·23*	*0·12*
Entry into Common Market			−0·07	−0·20	*0·00*	−0·01	−0·02
Whether too many Immigrants let in				0·33	−0·06	*0·10*	*0·18*
Abolition of Death Penalty					*0·09*	*0·14*	*0·18*
Whether Big Business too Powerful						*0·10*	*0·17*
Importance of Queen and Royal Family							*0·18*

[a] The entries in the matrix are Kendall's tau–b rank correlation coefficient calculated from the four-fold table describing stable opinion towards the two items in question, as explained in the text. If both items appeared in all three interviews the figures are in italics and are calculated for opinions that were stable over all three. If both items appeared together in only two of the interviews the correlation is calculated for opinions that were stable between the two waves at which the questions were asked. The detailed wording of items may be found in the Appendix. As also explained in the text, the direction in which the items were scaled conformed to the trend of 'left' and 'right' opinion at an elite level at the outset of the study.

attitudes towards the Common Market and attitudes towards nuclear weapons, immigration, the death penalty, the monarchy and trade union power.

The links found in Table 15.3 extend to matters of very dissimilar outward appearance. For example, attitudes towards nuclear weapons were systematically tied to attitudes towards nationalization, as well as to immigration, the death penalty, big business power and the trade unions. People who opposed the recent level of immigration were more likely to be for the death penalty and against the power of the trade unions. Those who discounted the importance of the monarchy were likely to accept nationalization, oppose the Bomb, accept recent immigration, condemn hanging and the power of big business and be tolerant towards the trade unions.

Yet the main impression left by Table 15.3 is of the weakness of the links between attitudes. These figures are based on the drastically reduced groups of electors who held stable opinions on each of two issues over two or three interviews. On average something like 70 per cent of our full sample has been cut away. Yet even when we go to such lengths to confine our attention to the minority of people who have well-formed and enduring views, the association of attitudes is relatively feeble. An occasional correlation, such as that between nationalization and trade union power, rises to an impressive level. But most of these figures are notable mainly for their modest size. There is a mild tendency here for opinion to organize along the left–right lines which would be recognized by political insiders. But by the standards of elite opinion the tendency is very mild indeed.

The remarkably weak structure of mass opinion was again evident when we tried a different approach to the problem in later surveys. In 1969 and 1970 we asked our respondents to rate the warmth of their feeling towards a number of politically significant people or groups on a thermometer scale that ran from 0° to 100°.[1] The average warmth ranged from 82° (the police) and 78° (the Queen) to 38° (coloured immigrants) and 22° (unofficial strikers).

How well this technique can detect relationships among highly correlated attitudes is shown by the intercorrelations of our respondents' thermometer ratings of the parties and the party leaders. Table 15.4 shows how strong are the positive correlations among attitudes towards the Conservative Party, Mr Heath and 'other Conservative leaders' (upper left-hand triangle) or among attitudes to the Labour Party, Mr Wilson

15.4 Correlations of Attitudes Towards Parties and Leaders

	Heath	Other Conservative Leaders	Labour Party	Wilson	Other Labour Leaders
Conservative Party	0·81	0·81	−0·60	−0·57	−0·52
Heath		0·85	−0·53	−0·50	−0·52
Other Conservatives			−0·58	−0·52	−0·47
Labour Party				0·86	0·79
Wilson					0·82

Average absolute value = 0·64.   Maximum = 0·86.   Minimum = 0·47.

[1] See question 9a.

and 'other Labour leaders' (lower right-hand triangle), and how plain are the negative correlations of attitudes towards any element of one of the groupings and attitudes towards any element of the other (the rectangle at the upper right).

But when this same technique was applied to a number of other groups or 'reference objects' involved in political debate the correlations were remarkably weak. These results are set out in Table 15.5. No entry in this table has an absolute value approaching the smallest entry of Table 15.4. Indeed, the mean absolute value of the correlations shown by Table 15.5

15.5 Correlations of Attitudes Towards Different Reference Objects

	Trade Unions	Commonwealth	Coloured Immigrants	Common Market	Unofficial Strikers	Queen
Comprehensive Schools	0·31	0·12	0·12	0·04	0·20	−0·11
Trade Unions		0·11	0·15	0·10	0·26	−0·13
Commonwealth			0·11	0·07	−0·11	0·28
Coloured Immigrants				0·24	0·12	0·01
Common Market					0·10	0·01
Unofficial Strikers						−0·15

Average absolute value = 0·14.   Maximum = 0·31.   Minimum = 0·01.

among attitudes towards those issue-laden groups or objects is a negligible 0·14. Certain of the correlations do command attention, such as those between trade unions and comprehensive schools or between the Common Market and coloured immigrants. But, on suppositions familiar to political leaders and political observers, we could equally imagine a number of the correlations, such as warmth towards the Queen and coldness towards trade unions, being of far higher magnitude.

We have here further and telling evidence of how loosely structured are the views held by the mass of the electorate. This leads us naturally to the question of how important the left–right framework is to the public's appraisal of politics. The looseness of the ties between issues which might be expected to evoke more coherent responses, especially from the minority of electors we have considered here, leads us to examine other evidence as to the importance of conceptions of left and right in the public's response not only to issues but also to the parties and leaders who appeal for electoral support.

The Left–Right Framework of Issues

The notion that policies and leaders can be ranked on an ideological scale running from left to right is perhaps the commonest of all political abstractions. It is not just a piece of academic conceptualization; the words 'left' and 'right' are constantly used in everyday political comment and reporting. The suggestion that matters of political controversy can be interpreted along a continuum from left to right is as old as the French Revolution. A quotation from the 1920s still sums up the widely held approach to the use of the terms.[1]

> The broad question which the two-party system asks: 'Do you incline, on the whole, towards the Right, or towards the Left?' is the most sensible question which it is possible to ask of the electorate. It is a question which corresponds far more closely to the realities of human psychology than the more complicated questions which a multiple-party system inevitably raises. The issue is one which presents itself in every department of life. Wherever men take part in collective action, and questions of policy arise, there is a fundamental cleavage between the more adventurous and the more cautious, the more open-minded and the more prejudiced, the more progressive and the more conservative. Men fluctuate, of course, pass from the one camp to the other, find themselves ranged on particular issues against those with

[1] H. D. Henderson, *The Nation*, November 5, 1927, quoted in T. Wilson, *The Decline of the Liberal Party*, London, 1966, p. 124. For a brief account of the origins of the terms and their introduction into British political parlance see S. Brittan, *Left or Right: The Bogus Dilemma*, London, 1968.

whom they are normally in sympathy; and some are not quite sure to which camp they normally belong. But the two camps are there. Who does not recognize their existence?

The meaning given to left and right has, of course, varied widely. Indeed much of the usefulness of the terms comes from the openness of possible interpretations. Left and right have been general labels under which a welter of political matters could readily be classified. But the basic picture evoked, both in normal parlance and in academic literature, is of a spectrum or scale along which electors and parties can be placed from Communist on the left to reactionary on the right or, to press the analogy, from infra-red to ultra-violet. It is an implied commonplace of contemporary British political discussion that the parties and their leaders, as they contend for mass support, manoeuvre along a line from left to right – and that the electorate too is distributed along that line. Several academic writers, fascinated by the similarities between, on the one hand, the manoeuvring of the parties along a left–right dimension and on the other, the strategic problems faced by firms competing for customers in a linear market place – such as a busy High Street or a transcontinental railway – have presented this one-dimensional aspect of the party system in terms of a formal model paralleling a well-known economic model.[1]

In this left–right model the parties take their place along the spectrum according to the stands which they adopt on issues. Voters too take their place according to their position on issues. The central assumption of the

---

[1] There is an extensive theoretical literature on spatial models of party competition, much of it inspired by location theory in economics. See in particular H. Hotelling, 'Stability in Competition', *Economic Journal*, **39** (1929), 41–57; Arthur Smithies, 'Optimum Location in Spatial Competition', *Journal of Political Economy*, **49** (1941), 423–29; Anthony Downs, *An Economic Theory of Democracy*, New York, 1957, pp. 114–41; Gerald Garvey, 'The Theory of Party Equilibrium', *American Political Science Review*, **60** (1966), 29–39; and James M. Buchanan, 'Democracy and Duopoly: A Comparison of Analytical Models', *American Economic Review*, **58** (1968), 322–40. For interesting efforts to extend such models to more dimensions than one, see Otto A. Davis and Melvin Hinich, 'A Mathematical Model of Policy Formation in a Democratic Society', in Joseph L. Bernd, ed., *Mathematical Applications in Political Science, II*, Dallas, Texas, 1966, pp. 175–208, and Gordon Tullock, *Toward a Mathematics of Politics*, Ann Arbor, 1967. For a sampling of empirical applications of these ideas, see P. E. Converse, 'The Problem of Party Distances in Models of Voting Change', in M. K. Jennings and L. H. Zeigler, eds., *The Electoral Process*, Englewood Cliffs, N.J., 1966, pp. 175–207, B. Särlvik, 'Voting Behaviour in Shifting Electoral Winds', *Scandinavian Political Studies*, **5** (1970), pp. 262–76, and M. N. Pedersen, Erik Damgaard, and P. N. Olsen, 'Party Distances in the Danish Folketing, 1945–1968, *Scandinavian Political Studies*, **6** (1971), pp. 87–106.

model when it is taken as a theory of electoral behaviour, is that voters' preference for a party depends on how far its position is from their own along the left–right dimension. Thus, they will most prefer the party that is closest to them and least prefer the party that is farthest from them; any other parties will enjoy an intermediate degree of preference. If the parties are too far away electors may of course not vote at all. But the order of their preferences among the parties will depend exclusively upon the parties' distances from their own ideological positions. Because of the central role that this idea of a left–right spectrum plays in most ideological discussion, we should explore in detail how far the left–right spectrum provides a realistic model of the relationship between parties and voters.

A natural approach to the problem is to see how far the assumption that electors judge the parties by the distance from their own positions does in fact fit the preferences felt by voters towards the Conservative, Labour and Liberal Parties. The electors' preferences depend of course not on where the parties really are, in some objective sense, along the ideological spectrum, but on where the voters think they are. However, when the number of major parties is small there is likely to be substantial consensus among that portion of the electorate which thinks in these terms on the placement of the parties from left to right. Certainly our own respondents who said that they thought of the parties as being to the left, centre or right politically were virtually unanimous in placing Labour to the left, the Conservatives to the right and the Liberals somewhere in between. Fewer than one in twenty ranked the parties in an order that differed from the conventional one.

It is, of course, quite possible to have a sophisticated view of politics and yet to say that Labour is now right-wing and that the Conservatives are the progressive party. Articles about the conservatism of Labour and assertions of the Liberals' claim to be left-wing are frequently to be found. Such paradoxes are, however, the preserve of a negligible minority. None among the few respondents who claimed to think in left–right terms, but who placed the parties in other than their conventional order, gave any evidence in the rest of their replies that they were taking an ultrasophisticated position. They were not drawn from those who were particularly interested in politics and there is little doubt that their eccentric placing of the parties reflected political innocence rather than independence of judgment.

General agreement on the ordering of the parties helps in testing the assumption that party preference is based on ideological proximity, since it limits the number of ways in which a voter can arrange his preferences among the parties. Consider a simple representation of the placing of the

British parties on a dimension divided into three regions – left, centre and right – a dimension along which the electorate too could be distributed.

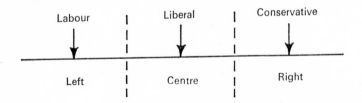

If ideological closeness were in fact the basis of preference, all voters in the left region would like Labour best, the Liberals next best and the Conservatives least. Similarly all voters in the right region would like the Conservatives best, the Liberals next best and Labour least. Voters in the centre region would like the Liberals best but their second and third choices would depend on whether they were to the left or right of a point halfway between Labour and the Conservatives. Nevertheless, voters in the centre must have one of only two orders of preference and every voter one of only four orders of preference:

1 Labour	1 Liberal	1 Liberal	1 Conservative
2 Liberal	2 Labour	2 Conservative	2 Liberal
3 Conservative	3 Conservative	3 Labour	3 Labour

There are, however, two other sequences in which a voter might order his preferences:

1 Labour	1 Conservative
2 Conservative	2 Labour
3 Liberal	3 Liberal

But to have either of these orders of preference would be to contradict the assumption that ideological closeness is the basis of party choice. If the model is true, no one who most prefers the party which is farthest to the left should have as his next choice the party which is farthest to the right – or vice versa.

Yet in fact many voters do order the parties in this way. Among Labour supporters in the summer of 1963 fully a third preferred the Conservatives to the Liberals as a second choice and among Conservatives more than a quarter preferred Labour to the Liberals despite all the talk on television and in newspapers (much of it inspired by the left–right model) about the Liberals as an alternative to the Conservatives. What is more, there was little tendency for these 'inadmissible' orderings to vanish in the heat of a campaign. After the 1964 General Election 21 per cent of Conservative voters gave Labour as their second choice. When we probed these choices, moreover, we sought to remove the problem of the 'wasted vote', the sense that voting Liberal was futile, by asking voters which of the three parties, named in turn, they would prefer to see 'form a government' if the party they preferred most did not do so.[1]

Removing considerations of tactical voting does not of course mean that the Liberals' perceived weakness as a governing party had no influence on the preference order given by our respondents; on the contrary, we have evidence that such a perception was held by many of the people who placed the Liberals last. The point to be made in the present context is that there is at least a second dimension, perceived competence in governing or something like it, cutting across the left–right dimension in shaping the orderings of preference offered by our sample of electors.[2] No one-dimensional model of party distance can account for the fact that some Conservative and Labour partisans reach right over to the other side of the spectrum and name the opposite major party as their second choice rather than the party that is ideologically closer to their own.

How are these inadmissible orderings to be explained? The failure of the preferences of so many electors to conform to the dimensional model has implications reaching far beyond the discussion of left and right. It is a finding that casts doubt on any one-dimensional model of this kind, whether content is supplied to the dimension by social class or by a psychological orientation such as tough- and tender-mindedness, or by perception

---

[1] It is significant that while in 1964 and 1966 Conservative and Labour voters agreed by about 3 to 1 in preferring a Liberal Government to one run by their larger rival, by 1970 Labour voters only preferred a Conservative to a Liberal Government by 5 to 3. This underlines the danger of assuming that preference orderings between the parties are static. Interesting light is thrown on this by William Miller in 'Cross-Voting and the Dimensionality of Party Conflict in Britain during the Period of Realignment, 1918–31', *Political Studies*, **19** (1971), 454–61. In an examination of the details of vote splitting in the two-member seats that then existed, he shows that Liberals choosing between Labour and Conservatives had different preferences at different points of time. (The number of Labour voters preferring Conservative to Liberal or of Conservative voters preferring Labour to Liberal was, however, small throughout the period.)

[2] But perceptions of Liberal strength held nothing like a full explanation of the discrepant preference orderings. Even among those who rated the Liberals as a 'strong' party the frequency of preference orderings inconsistent with the traditional left–right ordering of the parties was high.

of issues and parties in terms of left and right.[1] We focus attention here on the concepts of left and right because they seem to offer the only possibility within the contemporary British political culture of organizing a wide range of political issues in terms of a single dimension. But the more general implications that must be drawn from the presence of inadmissible preference orderings should be kept in mind.

One possibility is to imagine that preference is related to ideological distance in some much more complicated way. It could be suggested that ideological closeness, in some circumstances, breeds hostility or contempt, as it occasionally does between some rival parties of the left within European multi-party systems. The Communist who hates Social Democrats more than he hates adherents of right-wing parties might have his analogue in the Conservative who is furious with the Liberals for letting the Socialists in. There is no evidence, however, that this sort of response was involved in the preferences of those who gave the inadmissible orderings. The feelings that these electors expressed in answer to questions about the Liberal Party were in fact remarkably neutral.

A much simpler explanation is that many electors do not in fact see politics in terms of a single ideological dimension. There is no point in devising complex reasons why the left–right model fails to account for popular preferences if in fact a substantial proportion of the public is quite innocent of the left–right distinctions that are so constantly employed by insiders. Let us therefore try to measure more directly the extent to which the notions of left and right are comprehended by British electors.

Recognition of the Concept of Left and Right

Because our findings are at variance with widely held preconceptions we should begin by recording that in 1964 and 1965 we put to a number of leading politicians and political journalists the question, 'To what proportion of the electorate would you say the terms "left" and "right" are meaningful, even in the shadowiest of ways?' The replies ranged widely,

[1] Moreover, our demonstration that a single-dimensional model does not account for preferences for the three parties at once in no way depends on our having *a priori* knowledge of what the likely order of the parties is. For convenience of exposition we have availed ourselves of the consensus among the few who think in left–right terms that Labour is to the left, the Liberals in the middle and the Conservatives to the right. But the method of unfolding analysis would have disclosed the presence of inadmissible preference orders without our having such advance knowledge.

but the great majority put the figure as high as 60 per cent and some went up to 90 per cent. Among political insiders, it would appear, the words were so universally employed that they found it difficult to conceive that anyone for whom contemporary politics had the slightest meaning could fail to recognize them. The sophisticated are of course aware of the ambiguities of the concepts and of the confused and confusing way in which they are employed, but almost none escapes from using them – and from assuming that they are generally intelligible.

A first indication of the limited extent of ideological thinking at the mass level comes from the electors' answers to the question 'Do you ever think of the parties as being to the left, the centre or the right in politics or don't you think of them in that way?' Not many of them did – only 21 per cent of our respondents answered 'Yes'. Given the opportunity to confess the remoteness of such terms most people took it.

In a widely separated place in our interview we asked our respondents if they ever thought of themselves personally as being to the left, centre or the right in politics. Only 25 per cent said that they did so; three-quarters of our sample indicated that these concepts were not among their working stock of ideas when they thought about politics. These figures contrast sharply with the fact that 96 per cent of our respondents conceded readily enough to some degree of party commitment. Allegiance to party is one of the central facts of the British elector's political awareness. Identification with the ideological symbols of left and right is clearly one of the more peripheral facts of such awareness. We shall return later to the intriguing difference between the 25 per cent who thought of themselves as being to the left or right and the 21 per cent who thought of the parties in this way.

These sobering proportions do not of course show the full extent to which these ideological symbols are recognized. There is a clear difference between associating the symbols of left and right with a party or with one's own attitudes and merely having some minimal recognition of the words. In order to see how many among that vast majority of electors who did not think in these terms nonetheless had some awareness of them, we included in our interviews an alternative approach to the question. Our respondents were asked to rate the parties along a series of scales involving such polar extremes as United/Split, Expert/Clumsy, Middle Class/Working Class and, among a number of other qualities, Left-wing/Right-wing.[1]

---

[1] We followed a modified version of the semantic differential technique, which proved in this instance an admirable means of drawing replies from reluctant subjects. The standard work on the semantic differential technique is C. E. Osgood, G. J. Suci and P. H. Tannenbaum, *The Measurement of Meaning*, Urbana, Illinois, 1957.

Our respondents found these questions quite comprehensible. On eleven scales almost everyone was able to give a rating to the parties: only about one in twenty said 'Don't know'. But on the Left-wing/Right-wing scale more than one elector in five was too baffled to give any reply at all, a proportion which suggests the difficulty the public had in using these terms.

Let us look more closely at the places given to the Labour Party along this Left-wing/Right-wing scale for evidence of the limits of ideological awareness. To begin with, among the 78 per cent of our respondents who would place Labour at all, a further 17 per cent of the total sample placed Labour in the middle position on the scale, as Table 15.6 shows.

15.6 Ideological Perceptions of the Labour Party ,1963

	Very	Fairly	Slightly	Neither	Slightly	Fairly	Very	
Left wing	30%	13%	7%	17%	2%	4%	5%	Right wing

In view of the almost complete consensus among the ideologically aware section of the electorate that Labour is to the left, it is reasonable to think that the 'neither' position was chosen as a way of evading a genuine answer by respondents seeking to conceal their bafflement. Hence we are left with 61 per cent who gave Labour a position other than 'neither'. But a further 11 per cent chose a point on the right side of the scale. Once again on the basis of the consensus that Labour is to the left, we may label these replies as no more than guesses. And if we assume that a guesser was as likely to say left as right we may add to the 11 per cent who guessed 'wrong' by putting Labour on the right a further 11 per cent who presumably guessed 'correctly' by putting it on the left. Deducting, therefore, a further 22 per cent from 61 per cent we end up with 39 per cent who could be presumed to connect the left and right symbols correctly with Labour. The arithmetic by which we would identify the proportion correctly placing the Conservatives gives very similar results.

That only about two electors in five had any real recognition of the terms left and right is confirmed by examining the consistency of answers between the summer of 1963 and the autumn of 1964. Of respondents who were asked at both interviews to place Labour along the left–right scale, we found 29 per cent who confessed at one interview or the other that they were unable to do so. We found another 28 per cent who at one interview or the other placed Labour at the middle or to the right. Moreover, since 3 per cent put Labour on the right both times, we can assume that a further 3 per cent were guessing when they put Labour on the left both times.[1] Thus we end up with approximately two-fifths of the electorate who can be presumed to connect the left and right symbols with the Labour Party in a meaningful way.

Total sample asked to place Labour at both interviews		100%
Said 'don't know' at one interview or other	29	
Placed Labour in middle or on the right in at least one interview	28	
Placed Labour on the left both times by guessing	3	60
Genuinely perceived Labour as on the left		40%

In other words, in addition to the 20–25 per cent who said that they thought in terms of left and right, there was a further stratum of 15–20 per cent who showed some ability to link these ideological symbols with the parties. But we are still left with a substantial majority of the British people unfamiliar with these concepts.

In some respects, however, the most impressive evidence of the lack of ideological thinking in the British public came from the fifth of the public who claimed that they did think of the parties in terms of left and right. It would be wrong to imagine that all of them interpreted the words anything like as fully as most political activists do. Some did, but most had a much less elaborated understanding of the terms. In some cases the understanding was very nominal indeed.

Levels of Ideological Interpretation

To probe what meaning the words left and right imparted we asked those of our respondents who said they thought of the parties in such terms what they had in mind when they said a party was to the left, centre or right politically. Their replies could be sorted into three levels of ideological sophistication. The highest involved a well-elaborated interpretation, one

---

[1] The advantage of longitudinal data is of course that it makes unnecessary our assuming that all those who placed Labour in the middle or right (and an equal number who placed Labour to the left) at a given interview were offering insubstantial responses. Their insubstantial nature is plain enough in the way those who gave them wobbled between interviews, by contrast with those who genuinely saw Labour as being to the left.

in which the concepts of left and right seemed to organize the respondent's attitudes to several issues at once. Such interpretations seemed also relatively 'dynamic', in the sense of providing the grounds on which electors might decide that the parties, or they themselves, had moved to the left or the right. An interpretation of this sort is reflected in the remarks of a London Transport supervisor:

> To the left means increased social and welfare benefits, the elimination of private wealth, and nationalization. To the right means the preservation of private wealth and the reduction of expenditure on social benefits.

By a fairly generous classification not more than one in ten of those who associated the words with the parties (which means only two in a hundred of the entire electorate) gave answers at this level.

A second level involved a less developed interpretation in which the concepts were given meaning in terms of only one kind of content, usually identifications with a social class. Interpretations at this level seemed not only less capable of organizing attitudes towards various issues at once but also more static in the sense that the parties' behaviour in relation to contemporary issues, or changes of the voters' own issue beliefs, would be unlikely to change their placement of the parties or themselves on the left–right spectrum. Such an interpretation in terms of a single attribute is illustrated by the remarks of an Edinburgh man:

> The Conservatives are to the right, the Liberals are in the middle, and Labour is left. The Conservatives favour the middle and upper classes and Labour only the working class.

Just under three out of four of those who associated the terms with the parties gave answers at this level (or about 14 out of 100 of the entire electorate). Remarks such as the ones just quoted illustrate a tendency among those who gave less developed interpretations to understand the terms nominally, to maintain that the Conservatives *are* the right and Labour *is* the left.

A third level of interpretation was provided by respondents who seemed unable to give any meaning to the concepts other than such a purely nominal one. They had learned to know which term was linked with which party – but nothing more. Consider, for example, the remarks of this Sheffield lubricating engineer:

> Well, when I was in the Army you had to put your right foot forward, but in fighting you lead with your left. So I always think that the

> Tories are the right party for me and that the Labour Party are fighters.
> I know that this isn't right really, but I can't explain it properly, and
> it does for me.

Plainly the meaning given the words here is nothing more than a memory
device for attaching ideological names to the parties. This 'meaning' is
unrelated to any left–right spectrum along which individual or party
positions could move. Similarly a number of our respondents clung to the
fact that the Conservatives were the 'right' party because their policies
were 'correct' or 'upright'. In all, nearly one in four of our respondents
who said they thought of the parties as being to the left or to the right could
offer only an empty, nominal interpretation of this sort.[1]

This evidence of how often the interpretation is purely nominal suggests
a key to the puzzle about why some respondents said they thought of themselves as being left or right but denied thinking of the parties in these terms.
An explanation now emerges. Some of those who have learned a set of
ideological labels for the parties have also come to think of themselves, in a
wholly nominal way, as being left or right according to their party persuasion. To such people, being asked whether they think of *themselves* as
left or right means nothing more than being asked whether they have a
preference for one of the leading parties. But the question whether they
think of the *parties* as being to the left or to the right is more likely to be
seen as asking whether they have any concept of the meaning of the terms
as applied to the parties. Some whose use of the terms is purely nominal
will say 'no' even though they have reported thinking of themselves as left
or right. Electors who 'know' their own ideological locations simply because they know which party they support stand in flat contradiction to our
ideological model; they have stood on its head the basis of political choice
which it assumes – their 'ideology' follows their partisanship, not their partisanship their ideology. But our evidence leaves little doubt that this is a
very common phenomenon: voters come to think of themselves as right
or left very much as Conservatives in Birmingham or Scotland used to
think of themselves as 'Unionist' because that is what their party was called
locally.

[1] As suggested above, one of the criteria used in classifying people into these several
levels was the ease with which their interpretations of left and right could provide a basis
for perceptions of changes of position along the left–right spectrum. It is therefore interesting to note the frequency with which those at the three levels reported perceiving
changes of party positions when we probed for such perceptions in a separate question.
Of those we coded at the highest level of interpretation, 72 per cent said they thought one
of the parties had moved; at the second level the figure was only 36 per cent; and at the
third level only 12 per cent.

By adding to these three levels of ideological sophistication the two remaining categories into which the electorate can be placed – those who can at least connect the terms left and right correctly with the parties when obliged to do so and those who cannot – we summarize in Table 15.7 the ideological awareness of the mass public. Even with full allowance for the approximate nature of the methods leading to this distribution, we must regard it as a remarkable profile of popular acceptance – or rather non-acceptance – of the left–right framework.[1]

15.7 Levels of Interpretation of Left–Right Concepts

Fully elaborated dynamic interpretation	2%
Partially elaborated static interpretation	14
Nominal interpretation	4
Minimal recognition	20
No recognition	60
	100%

Ideological Awareness and the Organization of Issues

We may now return to our findings on the small degree to which individual political attitudes are organized. The low awareness of the left–right concept helps to explain why 'left' and 'right' positions on issues are so little reflected in popular thought. But our classification of ideological awareness now offers a way of identifying parts of the electorate in which there should be a relatively greater consistency in the organization of attitudes. Let us see how the degree of voters' ideological awareness is related to the structure of their political attitudes and to the link between their beliefs on issues and self-identification in left-right terms.

Nationalization, so long at the heart of the struggle over socialism in Britain, provides an excellent example of the relevance of ideological symbols to the electors' positions on an issue. Figure 15.8 shows the

[1] The extent of this sort of cognitive organization in different political cultures is an interesting problem for comparative study. Repeated surveys in France have found that 85 to 90 per cent of French electors are prepared to place themselves along a five-point scale extreme left/moderate left/centre/moderate right/extreme right, and other evidence from these surveys suggests that the terms were in fact meaningful to a much larger fraction of French than of our British respondents. See E. Deutsch, D. Lindon and P. Weill, *Les Familles Politiques*, Paris, 1966. See also the references given at p. 324 above.

relationship of our respondents' positions on this issue to their place-ment of themselves in left–right terms, at each level of ideological aware-ness (except the lowest). The decline of this association as we move down the hierarchy of awareness suggests the declining importance of the ideas of left and right in shaping responses to issues once we leave the tiny fraction of the electorate which thinks in ideological terms in a fully developed way.

15.8 Relationship between Attitude towards Nationalization and Own Left–Right Placement, by Ideological Level[a]

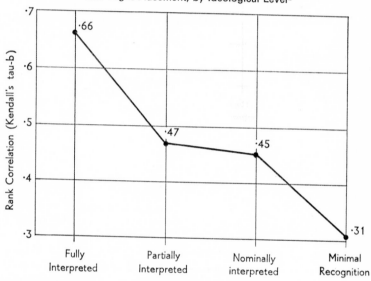

Level of Ideological Awareness

[a] The minimum recognition group are the few people, discussed above, who said that they thought of themselves as being to the left, centre or right politically but went on to say later in the interview that they did not think of the parties in those terms. We may therefore expect that this sub-group of the full set of respondents with 'minimal recognition' will, if anything, be relatively more familiar with the terms.

But ideological interpretation can scarcely be tested in terms of a single issue; what really distinguishes those who think ideologically is the extent to which their attitudes towards several issues are part of a larger structure. Left and right positions can be identified by the ideologue on issues as dissimilar in subject matter as colonialism and the handling of sex offenders. Indeed the reduction of a multiplicity of issues to a single ideological dimension is, as we have seen, necessary for the ideological model to work.

The greater coherence of attitudes towards issues among those at the highest ideological level is illustrated by Figure 15.9, which shows the declining correlation of attitudes towards nationalization and expenditure on the social services as we move down the hierarchy. Among the most sophisticated the correlation is fairly high, but it falls away sharply even at the next highest ideological level and decreases almost to vanishing point among those who are not able even to recognize the symbols of left and right. A similar pattern of relationships obtains between attitudes towards a number of other political issues.

15.9 The Correlation of Issue Attitudes by Level of Ideological Interpretation

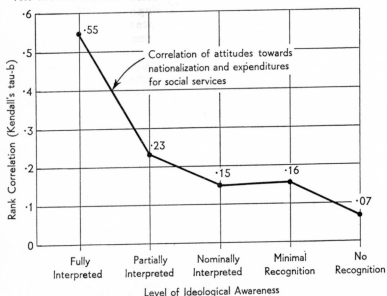

From all that has been said, it is clear that the theory that voters choose among parties on the basis of distances from their own positions along a left–right spectrum is very far from describing how the great bulk of British electors make their choice. The assumption that people order their preferences for the parties according to the parties' distance from their own position on the spectrum is contradicted by the preferences expressed by many of our respondents. The assumption that voters see themselves or the parties on a left–right dimension at all is contradicted by our evidence on the slightness of the role that the words left and right played in the political thought of the British mass public. A thin layer of the most ideologically aware did seem to use left and right to organize their views about where they and the parties stood on current issues. But such people were vastly outnumbered by those who had more impoverished and static interpretations of the concepts. And a large majority of the electorate apparently gave left and right no political meaning at all.

It follows from this that the classical model of ideological distance offers little towards the explanation of British electoral trends. For a tiny minority, the model may render a useful account of partisan change. But when we looked in our sample for electors who associated themselves and the parties with the left–right symbols and who perceived the parties as having recently moved to the left or right – a group which might reveal the impact of changing ideological distance on party preference – the numbers with which we might work simply melted away. Electors who obeyed the assumptions of the basic left–right model, applied as a theory of electoral change, seemed virtually non-existent.

However, the fact that attitudes on issues are so little organized into an embracing ideological structure does not mean that voters do not have some fairly stable generalized images of the qualities of the parties, which can have a dominant influence on their reaction to day-to-day political events.

16 Images of the Parties

IN the 1960s, as for a century past, the behaviour of the electorate was shaped by generalized attitudes and beliefs about the parties far more than by any specific policy issues. People respond to the parties to a large extent in terms of images they form from the characteristics and style of party leaders and from the party's association, intended or not, with the things governments may achieve. The importance of such images has been recognized since Graham Wallas' day, and the terminology of party images moved from academic to popular discussion in Britain in the later 1950s.[1]

Some of the most general and salient beliefs about the parties are very slow to change. The outstanding examples in Britain are of course the links of the Conservatives with the middle and upper classes and of Labour with the working class. We have argued that there has been a profound change in the beliefs about the relation of class and politics over the past generation. But the pace of this change, depending as it has on the entry of new cohorts into the electorate, must be a very long-term affair.

Other elements of the parties' images, however, are much more plastic. The electorate may in a fairly short span come to associate qualities with the parties which have a substantial influence on its choices at the polling station. Indeed, the presumption that this is so underlies the very considerable efforts by the parties themselves to help form the images that the public holds. Towards the end of the 1950s the Conservative Party sought with considerable skill to heighten the public's sense that it was the party of good times; the 'life's better with the Conservatives – don't let Labour ruin it' campaign is still a model of its kind. At the start of our studies, in the years 1963–4, the public was subjected to an unprecedented amount of advertising by both parties, each trying to associate itself with the symbols of modernization, optimism and strong leadership.[2] We examine here the

[1] See G. Wallas, *Human Nature in Politics*, London, 1908; R. S. Milne and H. C. Mackenzie, *Marginal Seat*, London, 1958; J. Blondel, *Voters, Parties and Leaders*, London, 1965, pp. 81–4; P. Pulzer, *Political Representation and Elections*, London, 1968, pp. 113–14; and D. E. Butler and R. Rose, *The British General Election of 1959*, London, 1960, pp. 17–34.

[2] See R. Rose, *Influencing Voters*, London, 1967, and Lord Windlesham, *Communication and Political Power*, London, 1966.

nature of the images of the parties formed by the public, giving particular attention to evidence of how these may have helped to account for fluctuations of party strength in the 1960s.

The Nature of Party Images

Much in the discussion of issues in preceding chapters anticipates our treatment of party images here, and we shall not draw any sharp distinction between the two. Indeed, once issues are conceived more broadly than in terms solely of competing policies we move into realms of attitude and belief that are frequently associated with the concept of image, as our reference to the class images of the parties suggests. If a distinction is to be enforced it seems to us most natural that it should be drawn in terms of whether at least a vaguely defined class of potential outputs of government is involved. The 'issue' of class benefit evokes some set of possible effects of government action, however diffuse and general the set may be. But some qualities of party image, such as strength or modernity or reliability, are so broad that they could be linked to almost any set out of government outputs. A party may be seen as trustworthy or as bound to make a mess of things without any necessary reference to the area in which it can be trusted or in which it is bound to make a mess. Indeed, some image qualities have much more to do with 'intrinsic' values of party, which are not related to the outputs of government at all. The value of a party to the voter who finds it 'exciting' rather than 'dull' may be the psychic gratification of breaking the dullness of most political news.

The intimate link between issues, broadly conceived, and party images argues the utility of applying a common framework to the effects of each on party strength. The framework for the analysis of issues set out in Chapter 13 can also give insight into the impact which image properties may have on the electorate's choice. To begin with, we may inquire which properties are genuinely salient to the electorate. What are the qualities which the public tends to see in the parties? The salience of different properties may of course be influenced by political leaders, either through explicit propaganda or through the subtler processes by which the conceptions developed by those near the centre of politics radiate outwards, via the mass media, to those who are more peripheral. There is a parallel here with the importance that political leadership has in shaping the bond between issue and self in the voter's mind.

But we may in some cases be sceptical about the insider's idea of the terms in which the parties are viewed by the mass electorate. Those on the stage of politics often see in the reaction of their audience perceptions that are in fact held only by the actors themselves. To what extent, for example, does the public weigh up the parties in terms of how united they are? Those immersed in the affairs of Westminster frequently express the view that the public cares a good deal about party unity, and this argument enters discussions of the need for cohesion in the division lobbies or in statements to press and television. But the salience of this and other image qualities to the electorate is really an empirical question on which little evidence is available.

In a similar way, we may ask how 'skewed' are the electorate's preferences among alternative properties the parties may exhibit. The example of cohesiveness is again instructive. Not only is it unclear how much the public sees the parties in terms of whether they are united or split. It is also unclear which of these the public likes its parties to be. This is again an empirical question that is not to be settled by *a priori* argument. The standard assumption at Westminster, as we have noted, is that the public approves of unity and abhors disunity: a party must after all, in the conventional phrase 'show that it knows how to govern'. But there is really very little evidence that the public may not at times love a party better if it exhibits a little disorder, which may help to lessen the ennui of the evening paper and to show that its leaders are independent and care.

The question of the skewness of opinion about image qualities is one that can be brought within the distinction between 'valence' and 'position' dimensions that we set out in Chapter 13. Probably it is true that most image qualities belong to dimensions on which there is high consensus about where a party should be. A party should be 'wise' rather than 'foolish', 'strong' rather than 'weak', 'expert' rather than 'clumsy', perhaps even 'united' rather than 'split'. The presumption that this is true explains why the party managers invest so much effort in projecting image properties to the mass electorate: the votes gained by persuading the country that a party is 'forward-looking' are not partially offset by the lost votes of those who want a party to be 'backward-looking'. But we shall apply at least a limited test to the possibility that some of the dimensions of party image are ones on which there are differences of opinion about where a party should be. Plainly there are some qualities that are central to the parties' images about which tastes differ. The electorate lacks a united view about whether a party should be 'middle class' or 'working class'. It is not altogether unreasonable to think that tastes may also differ about whether a party should be 'traditional' or 'modern'.

Finally, we have to take account of the extent to which the parties are differentiated in terms of the various properties which define their images in the public's mind. This question is closely linked with our first point in that the qualities which are likely to be most salient are precisely those on which the parties are most sharply set apart. But it is also of interest to see how well the public differentiates the parties in terms of various generalized qualities; clearly the relative standing of the parties in the country can be affected only by qualities which set them apart in the electorate's eyes.

Our assessment of the images of the parties in the 1960s relies chiefly on three types of data. First, we asked our sample to say freely in their own words what they liked and disliked about each of the parties. From these unprompted responses there emerged a remarkable portrait of the parties as the British electorate saw them at successive moments over a seven-year period. The advantage of such an approach was that it allowed a represent-ative group of electors to choose the concepts they spontaneously associ-ated with the parties, favourably or unfavourably; the answers that were volunteered give above all an indication of the relative salience of various properties of the party images. But they also reveal a good deal about how the electorate valued these properties and about the extent to which it distinguished the parties in terms of them.

Our second approach was to ask our sample to place the parties on each of a dozen scales designed to assess how they were seen in terms of simple image properties such as good/bad, or honest/dishonest. The properties we measured were chosen in the light of some extensive exploratory inter-views.[1] The majority of these scales were 'valence' dimensions of the sort that we have cited, on which the electorate's valuation could be presumed to be heavily skewed towards one end of the scale.

Our third approach, which was only adopted in our 1969 and 1970 surveys, was to ask our sample to express their views of warmth or coldness towards a number of people, institutions and concepts in terms of a thermometer reading from 0° to 100°.[2]

---

[1] In its main outlines the empirical technique we have followed here is that of the 'semantic differential' due to Charles Osgood and his colleagues. See C. E. Osgood, G. J. Suci and P. H. Tannenbaum, *The Measurement of Meaning*, Urbana, 1957. For the preliminary work on the selection of scales appropriate to the British parties we are grateful to John Clemens of Marplan Ltd. who conducted research in this field for the *Sunday Times* early in 1963.

[2] See pp. 321–2 above.

Themes Associated with the Parties

We have already explored several of the ideas that are most central to the electorate's images of the parties. In Chapters 4 and 5 we showed how enormously class and other group associations entered into the image of the Labour Party and, to a lesser extent, of the Conservative Party. In each of our rounds of interviews references to group and class associations accounted for between 10 per cent and 20 per cent of all the spontaneous comments offered about the parties.

In the mid-1960s those who made remarks used class in a way that was on balance overwhelmingly favourable to the Labour Party ('above all, it's for the working class'). But, as Figure 16.1 shows, by 1970 the picture was very different.

16.1 Attitude Expressed in Class- and Group-Related References to Parties[a]

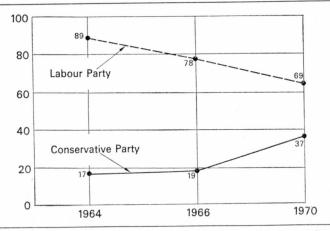

[a] Each entry is the proportion favourable of all class- and group-related references to a given party in reply to questions 4a to 4d.

In Chapter 14 we also discussed how the parties were seen in relation to various themes of domestic and foreign affairs. Very few of our respondents' comments were focused in any precise way on the policy debates of Westminster, but quite a number touched more generally on policy-defined or goal-defined issues; indeed between 20 and 30 per cent of all these spontaneous references to the parties dealt with issues in this very loose sense. At each round, references to domestic issues far outnumbered those to foreign and defence affairs, with the Labour Party, as we have seen, always enjoying a strong advantage.

In our present context, however, two additional types of references are of particular interest. The first were references to the leadership of the parties. Some of these, which we shall reserve to the next chapter, dealt with the Prime Minster and the Leader of the Opposition. But some concerned the leadership of the parties in a more general or collective sense. A Bridgwater nurseryman, for example, liked the Conservatives because of 'their type of men – higher education gives them a better grasp of things', while a Birmingham fitter liked Labour because of 'the level-headedness of their top men'. A clerk in Blackpool said that 'the atmosphere with the Conservatives is sober and there's a common sense approach, with a decent amount of breeding and well-mannered behaviour towards opponents'.

It is notable how much the balance of favourable and unfavourable feeling in such references shifted away from the Conservatives and towards Labour. These trends are shown by Figure 16.2. Whereas positive and

16.2 Attitude Expressed in Spontaneous References to Leadership of the Parties[a]

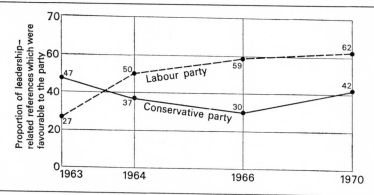

[a] Each figure is the proportion favourable of all spontaneous references to the leaders of a given party, other than the party leader himself, in reply to questions 4a to 4d.

negative references to the Conservative leaders were fairly evenly balanced in 1963, the proportion which were favourable fell to 37 per cent in 1964 and to 30 per cent in 1966 and only recovered to 42 per cent in the aftermath of the 1970 victory. The shift of the balance of feeling in spontaneous references to Labour's leader was even more striking. In 1963 little more than a quarter of such references were positive, suggesting the deep reservations held by many electors about a party that had then spent twelve years in Opposition. But by 1964 the proportion of references which were favourable rose to half and by 1966 it stood at almost three-fifths. In 1970

Labour drew a more favourable balance of comment in terms of leadership than it had in 1966.

The image of the parties' general ability to govern the country moved along more expected lines. The trend of favourable and unfavourable feeling in this closely related category of spontaneous references to the parties is set out in Figure 16.3. At our first round of interviews in 1963 the balance of such references was in the Conservatives' favour, and this balance had become even more favourable over the period of Conservative recovery from 1963 to 1964. But with the Conservatives out of power from 1964 to 1966 the reduction of positive feeling towards the party in these terms was fairly marked while the trend of such references to Labour became increasingly favourable. In 1963 there were still on balance more negative than positive references to Labour in these terms. But feeling was evenly balanced by the time of Labour's accession to power, and over

16.3 Attitude Expressed in Spontaneous References to the Parties' Ability to Govern[a]

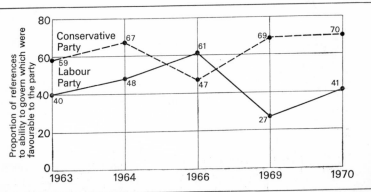

[a] Each entry is the proportion favourable for all spontaneous references to a given party's ability to govern in reply to questions 4a to 4d.

the period of the 1964 Parliament there was a further increase in the proportion of favourable references to Labour's ability to govern.

But the bad times after 1966 dispelled all that. Although in the run-up to the 1970 election Labour regained a little ground, it was plain that the events of 1967 to 1969 had seriously eroded the sense of Labour competence and, by contrast, restored faith in the Conservatives' ability to govern.

The growing acceptance of Labour's capacity to govern in the 1963–6 period is consistent with the changing appraisals mirrored through our 'semantic differential' scales. At each interview we asked half our respondents to say where they would put each of the parties on a seven-point scale ranging from weak to powerful. In 1963 the electorate perceived little difference in the average placement of the two main parties although the Liberals were seen as relatively weak, as Figure 16.4 shows. In 1964 the

16.4 Perceptions of the Strength of the Parties, 1963

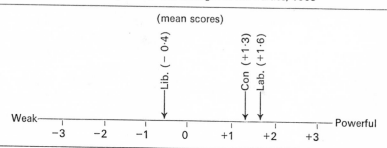

position of the parties was much the same, but when we come to 1966 we find a great increase in belief in Labour strength – and a corresponding decline for the Conservatives as 16.5 shows.[1]

16.5 Perceptions of the Strength of the Parties, 1966

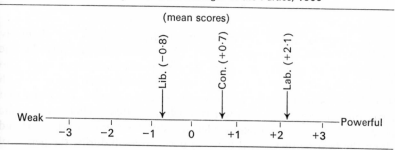

[1] The average positions shown in these figures do not reveal the reservations about Labour that were evident in the spontaneous comments on the parties' capacity to govern. No doubt this was due partly to the fact that our two devices were tapping slightly different aspects of the parties' imagery and partly to the fact that the scale approach involves the average of the answers of *all* respondents. When we examine how the subgroup of respondents who spontaneously referred to the parties' qualities of strength of leadership placed the parties on the strong/weak scale, a rather different picture emerges. This part of our sample, to whom the question of party competence seemed salient, did have a view of the relative forcefulness of the parties which was on balance appreciably less favourable to Labour than the image held by the electorate as a whole.

The images changed more dramatically during the 1966 Parliament, as Figure 16.6 shows. In the trough of 1969 the Conservative and Labour positions were reversed but Labour made a notable recovery by 1970.

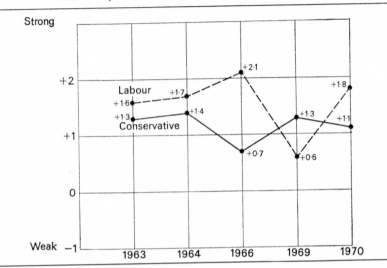

16.6 Perceptions of the Strength of the Parties, 1963–70

Other aspects of the parties' images include qualities less obviously related to the business of government. The explorations that preceded the construction of our image scales suggested that the parties were also differentiated in the public's mind in terms of qualities that had to do with their freshness and interest and responsiveness to change. The belief that governments grow tired in power is much more than a cliché of the elite observer. We therefore sought evidence about perceptions of this sort and about the bearing they might have on party strength during the period of our studies.

The Image of Newness

We included in our questionnaire three related scales that sought to tap this aspect of the electorate's image of the parties. Our respondents were asked to place the parties in terms of scales ranging from 'out of date' to 'modern', from 'old' to 'young' and from 'dull' to 'exciting'. In 1963, as Figure 16.7 shows, Labour was seen as more modern, younger and more exciting.

16.7 Images of Party Newness, 1963

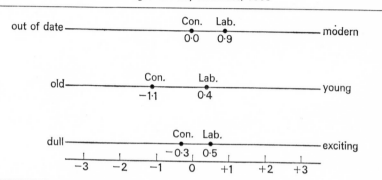

Over our next four surveys responses on all three scales followed a similar pattern, with one significant exception: the only way in which the Conservative image improved (if movement towards newness is improvement) during 1964–6 was that it became more youthful: it is impossible not to attribute this to the 49-year-old Mr Heath succeeding the 63-year-old Sir Alec Douglas Home. As Figure 16.8 on the next page shows, the Labour image slumped very sharply in 1969 and then recovered; the Conservatives rose steadily from 1966 on.

As we gauge the impact which these differences of image may have had on the party balance, we can assume that we are largely dealing with 'valence' properties and that the electorate's 'ideal' would lie overwhelmingly on the side of a party's being modern, youthful and exciting. Such an assumption finds clear justification in the party preferences of our respondents; for example, among Conservative and Labour supporters who in 1963 saw one of the parties as 'modern' and the other as 'out of date' 89 per cent supported the party which they saw as the more modern. We do not from this suppose that these aspects of the party images are preeminent in determining party choice; the extent of agreement between the two is largely due to electors' making their images of the parties fit their pre-existing preferences. But in either case, the close relationship between party choice and perceptions of the modernness of the parties shows the

16.8 Images of Party Newness, 1963–70[a]

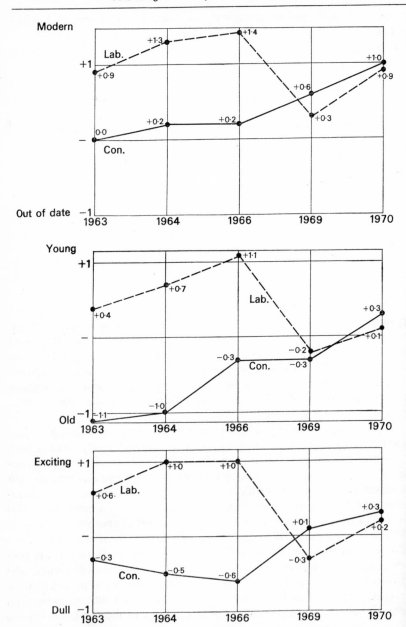

[a] The scores charted here are the mean placements of a given party on a seven-point scale extending from −3 at one pole to +3 at the other pole. Although the Liberal scores are not presented here, at each wave of interviews the Liberals were given an average position between the larger parties.

high valuation placed on the 'modern' position by the vast majority of electors.

We did, however, probe further to see whether a fraction of the electorate might actually have preferred a party whose image was the less modern. In 1963 we asked our respondents directly whether they preferred things that were 'traditional and well-tried' or 'modern and up-to-date' and a heavy majority came down on the modern side. We could test whether tradition-ally inclined respondents preferred the less modern party by investigating whether those who perceived one of the parties as modern and the other as not were more likely to support the less modern party. In fact there proved to be no difference of this kind; traditionally inclined respondents were just as prone as the rest of our sample to prefer the party they saw as the more modern. We have therefore felt more confidence in the inference that the difference of party image disclosed in Figure 16.8 is one which carried a genuine, if small, advantage for Labour, especially in 1964 and 1966, that was dissipated in the years that followed.

Our confidence that we are here touching upon an aspect of the parties' image which influenced their standing in the country in the middle 1960s is strengthened by the very null results obtained from our measures of other image qualities. At each round of interviews we also probed the public's view of the parties as honest or dishonest, united or split, foolish or wise, and other dimensions along which perceptions might differ. For the period of this work, the results were outstandingly negative. Many voters did tend to associate their own party with the more approved of two con-cepts defining such a scale. However, across the electorate as a whole these tendencies were mutually cancelling. But this was not true, as we have seen, of perceptions of the interestingness and modernness and youthfulness of the parties. In each case Labour apparently enjoyed for a while a modest advantage in the eyes of the typical elector, an advantage that it lost by the end of the decade.

There are reasons why the Conservative Party might be seen as 'older' throughout the period since the Second World War; indeed the distribu-tion of party support between successive age-cohorts might help to create such an image. But there are other reasons why such a difference could be especially strong in the early 1960s; the Conservatives had been long in power, longer than any government in this century, and they were led by an aging Prime Minister whose Edwardian style was underlined by its contrast with the new Kennedy era. Mr Macmillan was succeeded by another man in his sixties with old-world associations. Furthermore, the cadre of Conservative leaders which had seemed fresh in the 1950s could not appear so novel or interesting in the 1960s. By contrast the Labour Party had in 1963 acquired a leader who was of the Kennedy generation and who showed unrivalled skill in associating himself with the ideas of youth and modernization. When Labour took office in 1964 it was bound for a while to have a novelty and appeal that its predecessors could scarcely match. But the ratings of 1969 and 1970 show that the party of the right could be seen as just as modern, young and exciting as the party of the left. If our ratings had been taken only in a time of Labour ascendancy we would not have known whether the relative position of the two parties was due to a permanent differentiation in their images or merely reflected a particular period in the political cycle. The sharp ups and downs of the readings in 1969 and 1970 make clear that we are dealing here more with images that change with the cycle of power than with enduring aspects of party image. In all likelihood such changes are an important feature of the popular attitudes on which the alternation of governments rests.

Several of the qualities of the party images emphasize the importance of the party leader. The parties do plainly owe some of their personification in the public's mind to their identification with those who lead them, and a great leader, a Disraeli or a Roosevelt, may impart something of themselves to images of their parties that are held long after they have gone. But the leaders may make a more direct contribution to their parties' strength. The visibility of the men at the head of the parties is sufficient for them to affect more immediately their parties' standing in the country. We should therefore inquire further into the role of the leaders in electoral change.

17 The Pull of the Leaders

POLITICS in Britain, to a remarkable degree, are based on the competition between cohesive parties which act together in the national legislature and offer unified appeals for the support of the mass electorate. A member almost never goes against the party whips in the division lobbies, and very few candidates diverge from the party line in their election appeals.[1] The familiar American phenomenon of the candidate who plays down his party affiliation and emphasizes local rather than national issues is much less common in Britain.

In the light of the evidence about the limited influence of personalities at the constituency level, which we discuss in a moment, it is sometimes assumed that those standing for the premiership, the party leaders, have negligible impact too. Elections can be portrayed as plebiscites between alternative governments, each with their own policies, the choice being made in terms of the parties as a whole, not their leading spokesmen. But the opposite view has at least equal currency. A large part of modern British electioneering displays the personalities of the two main leaders. The Prime Minister and, to a lesser extent, the alternative Prime Minister are now seen as very much more than the 'first among equals' of the traditional text-books. The increasing complexity of government and the extension of the system of Cabinet committees have made the Premier appear more and more presidential. His share in the moulding of his party's image is much enhanced by the coming of new styles in journalism and even more by the advent of television. It is understandable that pre-eminent electoral importance should often be attributed to the rival leaders.

Yet it would be wrong to present the dominance of the leaders as a wholly new development. It is true that the mass media focus a sharper spotlight on the leaders than before. Perhaps Mr Attlee could not have survived at the head of his party for twenty years in a television age. But the hero-leader, made the vehicle for all sorts of issues and emotions, is hardly a new phenomenon. The qualities of Gladstone and Disraeli – and even Baldwin – were projected as central issues in election campaigns.

In fact, little has been known about how a leader's image intertwines

[1] See, e.g., *The British General Election of 1970*, pp. 437–42.

with his party's image or with the other issues of politics in the voter's mind. We may, however, apply to the effect of the leaders the same analytical tests that we have applied to issues and the parties' images. The impact of the leaders too may be assessed in terms of their salience to the public, the skewness of opinion towards them and their differentiation by party in the public's eyes, although the last of these tests can hardly fail to be met. Let us see what such a framework would suggest about the pull of the leaders on the electoral tides.

The Salience of the Leaders

There can be no doubt that the Prime Minister and the Leader of the Opposition are highly visible figures who excite a great deal of feeling, both positive and negative. But their salience may vary widely. For example, we found that in the summer of 1963 a series of free-answer questions about the party leaders elicited nearly 40 per cent more comment about Harold Macmillan, then near the end of his premiership, than about Harold Wilson, who had led the Labour Party for only four months. In turn, however, the latter elicited 40 per cent more comment than the Liberal leader, Jo Grimond.

The relative salience of Mr Wilson and the Conservative leader altered dramatically over the next three years. By the autumn of 1964 Mr Wilson attracted as much comment from our respondents as the retiring Conservative Prime Minister, Sir Alec Douglas-Home, and by the spring of 1966 he had achieved a greater level of visibility than any other leader in the period of our studies. Figure 17.1 shows the number of remarks offered about the leaders and the parties. The comments volunteered about Mr Wilson were a third greater than about Mr Heath, the new Conservative leader. In the less electoral atmosphere of 1969 both leaders had declined in salience, but the 1970 election seems to have resensitized the voters about their qualities. Mr Heath excited more comments than any Conservative leader during our surveys and Mr Wilson recovered to his 1964 level, though not to that of 1966. Figure 17.1 also shows how the trends in the volume of comments in answer to our quite separate questions about the parties, matched very closely to those about the leaders, although in the latter part of the decade Mr Heath moved ahead of his party while Mr Wilson dropped behind. It should be stressed that we are dealing here simply with the volume of comment. We shall return later to the balance that was struck between favourable and adverse remarks.

17.1 Salience of the Parties and Leaders, 1963-70

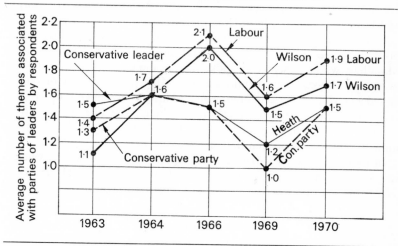

Secondary Leaders

It does seem clear, however, that the party leader in Britain is vastly more salient than his colleagues; the only possible exceptions in recent times, apart from ex-Prime Ministers, have been Mr Bevan and Mr Powell. Survey evidence suggests an absence of public awareness of the secondary leaders of the parties that many insiders find hard to credit. We cited earlier the example of a *Sunday Times* survey in 1962 which showed that, in spite of all the coverage given to front benchers by the mass media, a majority of the electorate was unable to give the name of any front bencher in either party aside from the party leaders themselves.

Our own findings are in the same vein. In 1963 we asked our respondents to express their feelings about any other party leaders after we had inquired about Mr Macmillan and Mr Wilson. Remarkably few names were volunteered either favourably or unfavourably. George Brown attracted the strongest positive and negative responses (slightly more positive than negative) but fewer than 3 per cent of people spontaneously referred to him and scarcely any other Labour figure attracted mention. On the Conservative side, R. A. Butler, Edward Heath, Ernest Marples and

Reginald Maudling were each mentioned by just under 1 per cent of our respondents in a positive way; similar numbers mentioned Mr Marples and Lord Hailsham (Quintin Hogg) negatively.

In 1964 the situation was similar. On the Conservative side Mr Butler, presumably because of sympathy over his leadership defeat, and Mr Maudling, who had served as spokesman at the Conservatives' campaign press conferences, were mentioned favourably by 4 per cent of our respondents, while 5 per cent commented unfavourably on Quintin Hogg in the wake of his campaign explosions. On the Labour side George Brown leapt to new prominence, with no less than 12 per cent mentioning him unfavourably and 2 per cent favourably.

In 1969 and 1970 we also asked our respondents quite neutrally whether they could name any leaders other than Mr Wilson and Mr Heath. Table 17.2 shows all who received as much as 5 per cent mention.

17.2 Secondary Leaders, 1969–70

Conservative leaders	1969	1970	Labour leaders	1969	1970
Douglas-Home	17%	22%	Castle	23%	20%
Maudling	13	20	Brown	17	22
Hogg	11	12	Callaghan	17	18
Macleod	7	13	Jenkins	12	15
Powell	24	16			
All others	27	17	All others	31	25
None mentioned	36	22	None mentioned	32	25

It is perhaps surprising that Mr Powell was not even more mentioned, especially in 1970. Nonetheless, because of his support from voters of all parties, Mr Powell achieved the highest rating of any politician in our feeling thermometer, both in 1969 and 1970.[1]

Table 17.3 shows our sample's feelings towards the secondary leaders in 1963, 1964 and 1970. Once again they had stronger feelings when interviewed in an election season. It is notable that there was less indifference in 1970 than 1964 and that, despite the political trend, Labour leaders shared to some degree in the increase in liking. These figures and the contrast of Table 17.2 with the *Sunday Times'* figures for the early 1960s suggest that the secondary leaders may have become more visible to the electorate over

[1] See pp. 321–2 above.

17.3 Attitudes towards Secondary Leaders[a]

	Towards Conservative leaders			Towards Labour leaders		
	1963	1964	1970	1963	1964	1970
Likes	21%	28%	36%	23%	27%	30%
Neutral, mixed, don't know	68	62	57	64	57	53
Dislikes	11	10	7	13	16	17

[a] Answer to question 7b.

the course of a much-televised decade. But they remained much less salient than the primary leaders.

Constituency Candidates

Electors may decide their allegiance in terms of national parties and leaders and issues. But they can record their allegiance only by marking a cross against the name of their party's local candidate. It has long been suggested that, at least in general elections, the personality of the local candidate makes very little difference to voters. But the campaign does make them better known. In the summer of 1969 only 75 per cent of our sample knew (or guessed) their Member's party and only 49 per cent the Member's name. Immediately after the 1970 election the proportions had risen to 86 per cent and 73 per cent. But the education was short-lived. In 1964 we found that while 94 per cent of our respondents interviewed one week after the election could name the successful candidate, by three weeks after the election the proportion fell to 81 per cent. The 1969 change in the law which allowed party labels on the ballot paper may account for the fall from 79 per cent in 1966 to 73 per cent in 1970 in the number of respondents correctly naming their M.P. Since there was no decline in the proportion (37 per cent) who recalled having seen or met their member, it is not unreasonable to see the fall as due to the lower need for the parties to teach the voters their candidate's name.

The name is all that most voters know about their candidates. Despite all the efforts that some M.P.s make to communicate their personal stand on issues, very little seems to reach down to their constituents. After the 1966 General Election the proportions of our respondents who had heard anything about their M.P.'s stand on four leading issues was very small, as Table 17.4 on the next page shows.

17.4 Awareness of M.P.'s Stand on Issues, 1966

		Proportion Aware of M.P.'s Stand
Issues	Nationalization of Industry	26%
	Common Market	16%
	Capital Punishment	16%
	Nuclear Weapons	12%

It would certainly seem that any special appeal exercised by M.P.s was through their general personal qualities rather than their stand on issues. Michael Steed, after examining the 1970 results, found no link between the success of candidates and their declared positions on two of the most emotive issues of the day – Powellism and entry into Europe.[1] Nor is there much indication that more local matters are important. Despite the lengths that many M.P.s go to in identifying themselves with constituency problems and interests, only one elector in seven could think of anything the M.P. had done for the people of the constituency.

The fact that the public's impression of the M.P.s' stands is so faint does not of course prevent electors from connecting their votes with policy choices. Knowledge of the candidate's party is close to universal, and we have seen in Chapters 13 and 14 that the public has a sharp image of party positions on various issues. Hence the elector's support of a candidate may involve a calculus of policy choices. But it is a calculus to which the parliamentary candidate adds little beyond adherence to party.

It would also be a mistake to suppose that, because the public's knowledge of the candidates is so limited, it must necessarily have little effect. In the vastly different constitutional setting of the United States, Congressmen are on an average even less known to their constituents than are British M.P.s, but the limited information that does reach American constituents can have very marked influence on their voting, allowing entrenched Congressmen to build up a formidable incumbent's advantage over a period of years.[2]

[1] *The British General Election of 1970*, pp. 405–6.
[2] Evidence on this point is presented in D. E. Stokes and W. E. Miller, 'Party Government and the Saliency of Congress', *Public Opinion Quarterly*, **26** (1962) 531–46; reprinted in *Elections and the Political Order*, pp. 194–211. See also M. Cummings, *Congressmen and the Electorate*, New York, 1966. For a revisionist British view see P. M. Williams, 'Two Notes on the British Electoral System', *Parliamentary Affairs*, **17** (1966), 13–30.

The Content of Leader Images

In what terms is a party leader seen? There is an obvious distinction to be drawn between perceptions that have to do with his personal characteristics and perceptions that have to do with policies or outputs of government. It is quite imaginable that a leader might be seen largely in instrumental terms, with his image formed out of his perceived association with government actions or goals or class interests; in short, the leader's image might repeat many of the themes that are found in the images of the parties.

Our evidence suggests, however, that the image of the leader is a much more personal one. Table 17.5 shows that at each round of interviews the vast majority of the positive and negative themes spontaneously associated with the Conservative and Labour leaders were personal rather than ones whose content was supplied by the goals which the leaders were seen as the

17.5 Content of Likes and Dislikes About Leaders, 1963–70

	1963	1964	1966	1969	1970
References to Wilson[a]					
Personal characteristics	79%	84%	84%	81%	85%
Philosophy and goals, issues, class or group interests	14	14	13	17	13
Other	7	2	3	2	2
	100%	100%	100%	100%	100%
References to Conservative Leader[a]					
Personal characteristics	86%	85%	87%	89%	92%
Philosophy and goals, issues, class or group interests	10	10	11	8	7
Other	4	5	2	3	1
	100%	100%	100%	100%	100%

[a] References tabulated here are the distinct themes volunteered by our samples in response to the questions: 'Is there anything in particular that you like [or dislike] about Harold Wilson [or Harold Macmillan, Sir Alec Douglas-Home, or Edward Heath]?' Up to five likes and dislikes about each leader were coded for each respondent at each round of interviews.

instrument for achieving. This does not necessarily represent a triumph of the cult of personality in British politics or the pre-eminence in these reactions of non-rational factors deep in the psyche of the individual elector. Plainly images of a leader do give scope to such psychological factors. But many of the references to the leader's personal characteristics can also be seen as 'instrumental' in a broader sense. The leader's experience, his intelligence, his sincerity, his calmness, his eloquence, his likeability – or his shortcomings by these standards – can be regarded as qualities which will affect the likelihood of his achieving goals which electors value.

Tables 17.6 to 17.9, which set out the positive and negative themes mentioned in each round of interviews, give an interesting collective portrait

17.6 Favourable References to Personal Characteristics of Wilson, 1963–70[a]

Nature of reference	1963	1964	1966	1969	1970
Good man, well qualified, good leader	261	256	415	139	265
Experienced, informed, knows job	17	47	87	29	44
Intelligent, able, shrewd, wise, astute	92	137	137	85	133
Honest, sincere, fair, straightforward, keeps promises	270	462	590	216	284
Strong, decisive, courageous	58	138	133	97	133
Hard working, dedicated, efficient, gets things done	99	126	175	151	126
Steady nerve, calm under fire (esp. from hecklers)	13	54	91	32	56
Age: not too old, young	35	51	7	4	0
Physical appearance – handsome, homely	34	67	55	18	32
Manner – dignified, gracious, humble	34	67	55	58	77
Personally likeable, 'I just like him'	64	138	199	85	157
Education well educated, university background	23	43	16	0	10
Good speaker. Like his TV appearances	115	319	385	146	187
Other personal references	72	204	145	111	480
Total references to personal characteristics	1187	2109	2490	1171	1984

[a] In this and Tables 17.7 to 17.9 we report the actual frequency with which each theme was mentioned at each round of interviews, after adjusting the frequencies for the second and third rounds so that their sample size is in effect set equal to the sample of 2000 electors interviewed at the first round.

17.7 Unfavourable References to Personal Characteristics of Wilson

Nature of reference	1963	1964	1966	1969	1970
Not a good man, not qualified, poor leader, poor PM	65	28	29	101	34
Inexperienced	11	13	2	7	4
Unintelligent, stupid, foolish	5	3	7	9	1
Dishonest, insincere, arbitrary, breaks promises, too clever by half	94	116	216	441	369
Weak, indecisive, hasn't courage to make hard decisions	33	12	14	92	35
Inefficient, lax, doesn't get things done	4	0	8	29	16
Could not stand up under fire	2	4	7	7	2
Too young	1	1	0	0	1
Physically unattractive	22	23	24	45	57
Manner undignified, ungracious, aggressive, big-headed, smug	140	178	212	169	190
Don't like him as a person, colourless	24	58	73	79	61
Too ambitious, just out for himself, wants office	22	36	70	43	114
Mudslinging in campaign	0	89	66	7	37
Other personal references	46	63	122	154	124
Total references to personal characteristics	469	624	850	1183	1045

of the images of the leaders from 1963 to 1970. In one respect the most notable feature is the stability of the picture. Despite a changing situation, the same characteristics are seen as pre-eminent in each leader. Mr Wilson, the one most exposed to public scrutiny, does suffer one major decline.

17.8 Favourable References to Personal Characteristics of the Conservative Leaders

Nature of reference	Macmillan 1963	Home 1964	Heath 1966	Heath 1969	Heath 1970
Good man, well qualified, good leader, good PM	311	190	196	115	144
Experienced, informed, knows job	46	44	36	13	18
Intelligent, able, shrewd, wise, astute	77	59	46	40	39
Honest, sincere, fair, straightforward, keeps promises	248	298	272	306	445
Strong, decisive, courageous	58	28	32	38	36
Hard-working, dedicated, efficient, gets things done	99	51	53	50	91
Steady nerve, calm under fire	124	49	16	11	13
Age; not too old, young	8	0	19	4	5
Physical appearance – handsome, attractive	13	5	30	29	23
Manner dignified gracious	47	77	72	59	69
Personally likeable 'I like him'	116	139	148	144	155
Education: well educated, university educated	20	21	16	9	132
Class background – upper class	82	111	16	14	16
Good speaker	77	80	145	124	121
Other personal references	54	47	63	50	78
Total references to personal characteristics	1380	1199	1160	1006	1385

17.9 Unfavourable References to Personal Characteristics of the Conservative Leaders

Nature of reference	Macmillan 1963	Home 1964	Heath 1966	Heath 1969	Heath 1970
Not a good man, not qualified, poor leader, poor PM	123	286	245	221	157
Inexperienced	37	15	62	5	7
Unintelligent, stupid, foolish	18	11	24	11	12
Dishonest, insincere, arbitrary, breaks promises, too clever by half	108	67	99	59	101
Weak, indecisive, hasn't courage to make hard decisions	179	260	129	214	121
Inefficient, lax, too many holidays, doesn't get things done	90	37	37	25	15
Can't stand up under fire	7	16	11	5	4
Too old	205	11	9	0	0
Physically unattractive. Dislike face, clothes	58	116	52	59	79
Manner undignified, ungracious, cold, smug conceited, condescending	95	155	290	189	208
Don't like him as a person	57	113	174	104	147
Educational background, snobbish	29	25	25	14	267
Family and wife	22	1	0	0	0
Being a bachelor, not a family man	0	0	109	59	126
Poor speaker	56	253	146	79	95
All other personal references	68	119	88	110	107
Total references to personal characteristics	1152	1485	1500	1154	1446

In 1963 to 1966 the outstanding element in his picture was the growing sense of his straightforwardness: the view of him as tricky or too clever by half, so widely held among insiders, was not at that time so widely held by the mass public. By 1969 and 1970, although his honesty was still his most mentioned good characteristic, the number of mentions of his deviousness had vastly increased. Nonetheless, the general portrait of him in 1970 (though not in the abyss of 1969) was on balance very favourable.

The three Conservative leaders in our period evoked a more mixed reaction. All were commended for sincerity, all appealed to people who just 'liked' them, and all attracted some general commendation as good leaders. Although Mr Macmillan was much more appreciated than his successors for leadership, industry and steady nerve ('he's a strong man let down by his party'), it was the negative comments on the three men that varied most. Mr Macmillan was especially condemned for his age, Sir Alec for his looks, his weakness, and his poor speaking, and Mr Heath for his manner and for his unmarried state ('he wouldn't understand family problems').[1]

What is most striking is how little Mr Heath's image was affected by his very personal triumph in 1970. Our interviews were conducted in the immediate aftermath of the victory when he was enjoying all the publicity honeymoon of an incoming Premier, yet the balance of comment was still unfavourable. The improvement in his image through more people seeing him as straightforward and fewer people seeing him as weak was offset by an increase in the expression of personal dislike, above all in a sense of his snobbishness.

Since the party leader undoubtedly is extraordinarily salient in British politics, he meets the first test for a force that can generally deflect the party balance. A second test is plainly met as well; the party leaders are, in the nature of things, differentiated on a party basis. A third test, then, is the crucial one: the electoral effect of the leader will depend primarily on how unevenly balanced are the favourable and unfavourable elements in his image.

[1] But the idea that Mr Heath, as a bachelor, was especially disowned by women finds scant support in our data. In 1966 57 per cent, and in 1970 52 per cent, of the hostile references to his marital status came from women, percentages that differed little from the 53 to 47 ratio of women to men in the sample. Moreover, the ratio of favourable to unfavourable comment about Mr Heath in the whole sample was by a small margin *higher* among women.

The Net Direction of Attitudes Towards Leaders

Over the period of our studies the balance of positive and negative comments on the leaders varied even more than their relative salience. In the summer of 1963 the themes volunteered about Mr Macmillan were as frequently sympathetic as hostile. Despite the Profumo affair, then at its height, and all the other troubles that had beset Mr Macmillan's leadership, he attracted as many favourable as unfavourable mentions; his image was indeed a good deal more positive than either of his Conservative successors' was to be. References to Mr Wilson in 1963, although fewer in number, were solidly favourable by a margin of roughly two to one. But Mr Grimond, though less noticed, had the most sympathetic image of all; three comments mentioned reasons for liking him to every one containing a reason for disliking him.[1]

By the autumn of 1964, as Figure 17.10 shows, the balance of comments on Mr Wilson had become still more favourable – and the volume of comment even greater. Sir Alec Douglas-Home, who had just lost office after a year as Prime Minister, attracted rather more negative than positive mentions.[2]

17.10 Direction of Attitudes Towards the Leaders, 1963–70

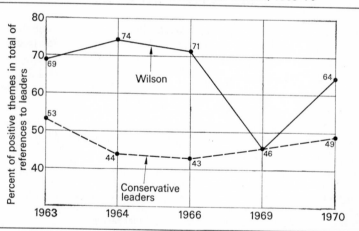

[1] We were unfortunately not able to ask the same question about Mr Grimond in 1964 or 1966, or about Mr Thorpe in 1970.

[2] We cannot rule out the possibility that the outcome of the election and the formation of a new government influenced the perceptions of the leaders which our respondents expressed in 1964 or 1970. But the readings of public opinion polls on the standings of

In the spring of 1966 attitudes towards the Labour and Conservative leaders were just as widely divergent. Mr Wilson, at a record level of salience, attracted almost two and a half times as many favourable as unfavourable references. Mr Heath, on the other hand, in addition to being far less salient to the electorate, drew more negative than positive references not only in 1966 after his shattering defeat but also in 1969, when his party was handsomely ahead in the polls, and in 1970 after his remarkable victory. Mr Wilson's standing slumped catastrophically in 1969 but recovered to a notable degree in 1970.[1]

The Electoral Impact of the Leaders

What effect did the substantial gap between the Conservative and Labour leaders shown in Figure 17.10 have on the electorate's decision in 1964, 1966 and 1970? The answer to such a question is complicated by the fact that attitudes towards the leaders are only a limited part of the influences on the electorate. Since an elector's party preferences can bias his perceptions of leaders we need evidence that the effect of attitudes towards the leaders is independent of the influence of attitudes towards the parties themselves.

We can help to distinguish between these effects by comparing our respondents' reactions to the leaders and to the parties. Our free-answer responses offer an index of whether the elector's attitudes were favourable or unfavourable, or were neutral or mixed, towards the Labour and Conservative parties; they also offer a similar index of attitudes towards

---

the leaders showed no sharp discontinuities in the autumn of 1964 or the summer of 1970. Moreover, in 1964, 1966 and 1970 the report of the vote elicited from our sample never showed any significant 'bandwagon' – or for that matter 'underdog' – effect when compared to the actual election returns.

[1] It is worth recording that during the 1960s the public opinion polls revealed a notable decline in the ratings of the leaders. At the beginning of the decade well over half the Gallup Poll's respondents would say that each of the two party leaders was doing a good job. By 1969 the figure was under one-third. If we add the ratings of the two men to form an index of leader popularity we can see a spectacular falling-off.

1960	1961	1962	1963	1964	1965	1966	1967	1968	1969
114	103	97	98	105	98	94	78	62	67

This decline may be attributed in part to the personal failure of Mr Heath to get himself across and to the disasters that befell Mr Wilson's Government, but it may well reflect a more fundamental disillusion.

the Labour and Conservative leaders. We can compare these indices to see how strongly each is related to the way in which the elector voted.[1]

The results of such a comparison are given for 1964 in Table 17.11, which shows the percentage voting Conservative among people with each potential combination of attitudes towards the leaders and parties.

17.11 Conservative Voting by Attitudes towards Parties and Attitudes towards Leaders, 1964[a]

		Attitudes towards leaders		
		Pro-Conservative	Balanced, Neutral	Pro-Labour
Attitudes towards parties	Pro-Conservative	97%	91%	76%
	Balanced, Neutral	86%	48%	28%
	Pro-Labour	35%	19%	6%

[a] This analysis is limited to electors who voted Conservative or Labour in 1964.

Several aspects of this table invite comment. First, it is clear that attitudes towards the parties were a better guide to voting behaviour than were attitudes towards the leaders. Such a conclusion may be drawn from the fact that the gradient of Conservative voting is much steeper within columns than within rows, that is to say, from the fact that voting varies more strongly by attitudes towards parties among those having a common attitude towards leaders than it does by attitudes towards leaders among those having a common view of the parties.[2] Indeed, those who were

[1] In fact we have formed distinct indices of attitudes towards each of the major parties and towards each of the leaders; but in our presentation of results here we combine the two party indices and the two leader indices.

[2] This aspect of the conditional distributions shown here coincides well with the partial regression slopes obtained by regressing voting choice on separate measures of attitude towards the two parties and the two leaders. For this purpose we have scored a Labour vote 1 and a Conservative vote 0 and have formed indices of attitude towards Labour (L), the Conservatives (C), Wilson (W) and Home (H) by taking the arithmetic difference of the number of favourable and unfavourable references to each given spontaneously in 1964 as responses to questions 4 and 6 in Appendix B. We then expressed the probability of voting Labour as a linear function of these four indexes of attitude, choosing the values of the coefficients by the ordinary least-squares criterion:

pro-Conservative in terms of parties but pro-Labour in terms of leaders voted Conservative by three to one, while those who were pro-Labour in terms of parties but pro-Conservative in terms of leaders voted Labour by two to one. It is interesting to note that those who were of neutral or mixed view both towards parties and leaders divided their votes almost evenly, as if they decided by tossing a coin. But the table makes it equally clear that substantial effects on voting can be traced to attitudes towards the leaders. Although these effects were less than those of attitudes towards the parties they were nonetheless visible.

Table 17.12 shows the results of similar analysis of our findings for 1966.

17.12 Conservative Voting by Attitudes towards Parties and Attitudes towards Leaders, 1966[a]

| | | Attitudes towards Leaders | | |
		Pro-Conservative	Balanced, Neutral	Pro-Labour
Attitudes towards parties	Pro-Conservative	99%	89%	72%
	Balanced, Neutral	76%	54%	26%
	Pro-Labour	49%	16%	6%

[a] This analysis is limited to electors who voted Conservative or Labour in 1966.

The correspondence with the 1964 table is remarkable. Once again attitudes towards the parties emerge as the stronger influence on voting, but attitudes towards the leaders did make a distinct contribution. Those who expressed neutral or mixed views towards the parties once more divided their votes almost evenly.

Table 17.13 shows the picture yielded by a similar approach in 1970.

$$P(Lab) = -0.0022 + 0.139L - 0.071C + 0.069W - 0.046H$$
$$ (0.033) \quad (0.033) \quad (0.032) \quad (0.030)$$

The values of these coefficients suggest that in each case choice was more strongly related to the elector's attitudes towards the party than towards its leader, but that attitudes towards each made a distinct contribution to choice in an immediate sense.

The Electoral Impact of the Leaders 365

17.13 Conservative Voting by Attitudes Towards Parties and Attitudes Towards Leaders, 1970[a]

		Attitudes towards Leaders		
		Pro-Conservative	Balanced, Neutral	Pro-Labour
Attitudes towards parties	Pro-Conservative	95%	83%	57%
	Balanced, Neutral	75%	43%	21%
	Pro-Labour	43%	19%	4%

[a] This analysis is limited to those who voted Conservative or Labour in 1970.

While the pattern resembles the previous years, Mr Wilson's role in influencing people who had pro-Conservative but pro-Wilson attitudes seems stronger: only 57 per cent of these voted Conservative compared to 76 per cent in 1964 and 72 per cent in 1966.

Although Tables 17.11 to 17.13 show that the chances of voting Conservative under each of these combinations of attitude did not alter very greatly, what did change were the proportions of people holding each of these combinations of attitude. As Table 17.14 shows, there was a strong

17.14 Attitudes Towards Parties by Attitudes Towards Leaders, 1964–70[a]

		1964			
		Attitudes Towards Leaders			
		Pro-Conservative	Balanced, Neutral	Pro-Labour	
Attitudes Towards Parties	Pro-Conservative	19	9	12	40
	Balanced, Neutral	3	5	10	18
	Pro-Labour	2	4	36	42
		24	18	58	100%

17.14—continued

1966

Attitudes Towards Leaders

		Pro-Conservative	Balanced, Neutral	Pro-Labour	
Attitudes Towards Parties	Pro-Conservative	20	6	9	35
	Balanced, Neutral	2	4	8	14
	Pro-Labour	3	4	44	51
		25	14	61	100%

1970

Attitudes Towards Leaders

		Pro-Conservative	Balanced, Neutral	Pro-Labour	
Attitudes Towards Parties	Pro-Conservative	30	7	9	46
	Balanced, Neutral	5	4	8	17
	Pro-Labour	3	4	30	37
		38	15	47	100%

[a] This analysis is limited to electors who voted Conservative or Labour.

shift towards Labour between 1964 and 1966 in terms of attitudes towards the parties and a moderate shift in terms of attitudes towards the leaders as well. Between 1966 and 1970 both trends were reversed and there was a corresponding improvement in attitudes towards the Conservative Party and towards its leader.

That attitudes towards the leaders were in fact involved in shifts of votes between the parties is confirmed by our panel data on individual electors. We saw in Chapter 12 how much of the swing to Labour between 1964 and 1966 was due to the straight conversion of Conservatives. If we now divide

1964 Conservatives into those whose view of the party leaders in that year was consistent with their party stand and those whose view of the leaders was inconsistent with it, we find a stronger movement towards Labour between the two years among those who had valued Mr Wilson more highly than the Conservative leader, as Table 17.15 shows.

17.15 Conversion from Conservative to Labour Voting, 1964–6, by Attitude Towards Leaders in 1964[a]

| | Attitudes towards leaders in 1964 | |
	Pro-Labour	Pro-Conservative
Shifted vote towards Labour	14%	5%
Did not shift vote	86	95
	100% (n = 131)	100% (n = 206)

[a] This analysis is limited to electors who voted Conservative in 1964 and Conservative or Labour in 1966.

Complementary findings emerge when we divide 1964 Conservatives according to whether their attitudes towards the party leaders became more favourable to Labour between 1964 and 1966. Table 17.16 shows that among those whose attitudes did shift in this way the stronger movement to Labour occurred. Indeed, one in five of those who adopted a view of the party leaders more favourable to Labour transferred their allegiance from the Conservatives to Labour.

We conclude therefore that the party leaders have enough hold on the public's consciousness and are, by the nature of their office, sharply enough set apart by party for popular feeling towards them to have demonstrable

17.16 Conversion from Conservative to Labour Voting, 1964–6, by Shifts of Attitude Towards Leaders[a]

| | Attitudes towards leaders | |
	Shifted towards Labour	Did not shift
Shifted vote towards Labour	20%	10%
Did not shift vote	80	90
	100% (n = 94)	100% (n = 224)

[a] This analysis is limited to electors who voted Conservative in 1964 and Conservative or Labour in 1966.

effects on the party balance when it becomes preponderantly positive or negative. If these effects are less marked than in America they are nonetheless clear. In the period of our work they benefited Labour; in another period, such as Mr Macmillan's heyday at the end of the 1950s, the advantage would have been otherwise. Indeed, the difficulties that beset Mr Wilson later in the decade plainly diminished his party's advantage along these lines, although the polls do suggest that changing estimates of Mr Heath had little to do with the Conservative recovery. The fact that the Conservative upsurge in 1967–8 was not linked to any increase in their leader's standing should remind us that the pull of the leaders remains but one among the factors that determine transient shifts of party strength; it is easily outweighed by other issues and events of concern to the public, including the movements of the economy which do so much to set the climate of the party battle.

18 The Economic Context

'A GOVERNMENT is not supported a hundredth part so much by the constant, uniform, quiet prosperity of the country as by those damned spurts which Pitt used to have just in the nick of time.' So wrote Brougham to Thomas Creevey in 1814. The fact that he could attribute the Tory hegemony in the 1790s to the same cause that was commonly given as the reason for the party's success in the 1950s shows how deeply rooted in British politics is the idea that the Government is accountable for good and bad times. Popular acceptance of this idea means that the state of the economy has loomed large in the minds of all modern Prime Ministers as they pondered on the timing of a dissolution. And in the post-Keynesian era more than one government has been tempted to seek a favourable context for an election by expanding the economy, although dissolutions are more easily timed to coincide with expansion than the other way round.

The Government's responsibility for the economy is a fundamental assumption of the contemporary dialogue between the parties and the electorate. In the 1959 Parliament economic conditions provided the dominant theme, from the 'never had it so good' euphoria of the 1959 election, through the pay pause of 1961 and the 1962 recession, to the recovery of 1963–4. From 1964 to 1970 the attempts to stave off devaluation and then the protracted wait for it to take effect, together with mounting problems of inflation and unemployment, ensured that economic questions stayed in the forefront of politics.

On fairly uncertain evidence many observers have assumed that the state of the economy was the main cause for the Conservatives' decline in 1961–2 and for their recovery in 1963–4 as well as for Labour's decline in 1966–9 and for their recovery in 1969–70. In this chapter we explore the extent to which support can be found for such a view. The way in which the economy shapes the electorate's behaviour is complex, and the conclusions to be drawn about the effect of the economy on party advantage in the 1960s are sometimes surprising.

The Economy as an Issue

Of all the outputs of government, good times and bad must be among those most strongly valued by the mass of the people. The material and psychic deprivations of being out of work are vivid to those who experience them – as well as to many who only observe them in others. Similarly, the consequences of having a fatter pay packet or of being on short time or of having to contend with higher prices in the market are directly felt by those whose lives are touched. Changes of personal economic condition are overwhelmingly salient to the mass of electors and evoke in them strong and definite attitudes.

This does not, of course, mean that voters respond only to those aspects of the state of the economy that they can themselves see. Many will be responsive to the more generalized information about economic conditions that reaches them through the mass media. A rise in the unemployment figures has a clear meaning for the ordinary citizen because he can picture its consequences in personal terms and news of such a rise may create a sense of unease in millions of people who themselves are for the moment quite unaffected by it. In a similar way, news of a general price increase can give point to price changes that the voter can recall from recent shopping. Even a national deficit in the balance of payments has some meaning for ordinary people who could not trace the effects that the deficit will have on their own well-being but who know from everyday experience the unpleasant consequences of a deficit in their personal or household accounts.

We may also note that the issues of economic well-being probably come as close as any in modern politics to being pure 'valence' issues, as we have defined these.[1] If we conceive of economic issues in dimensional terms, the electorate is not spread along a continuum of preference extending between good times and bad; its beliefs are overwhelmingly concentrated at the good times end of such a continuum. This is, of course, an empirical observation and not a logical necessity. There are in British society isolated individuals who see genuine moral values for others, or even for themselves, in a degree of severity to economic life. This view was expressed to us by an aging widow in Poole, who said, 'It's awfully good for one to have to get along on less, isn't it?' Indeed, at an elite level one can find some very conservative observers as well as some doctrinaire Socialists who view with ambivalence the rising affluence of recent years. But such views are the perquisite of a tiny minority. The goal of economic betterment enjoys

[1] See Chapter 13.

overwhelming mass support and any values that may lie in economic adversity are not visible to most people.

It is of course true that the relationship between rival economic goals does offer possible dimensions of political conflict. The classic example of this in most western economies lies in the 'trade-off' between economic expansion and price stability; all too often governments can buy economic expansion only by allowing inflation, or stable prices only by limiting expansion. For a nation as dependent on international trade as Britain, there are further trade-offs between domestic expansion on the one hand, and the balance of international payments on the other. The dilemma of choosing an appropriate position on such a continuum has faced Conservative and Labour Governments alike.[1] Moreover, if an understanding of the relationships between these goals were to reach more deeply into the public's consciousness, the dialogue between parties and the electorate on economic issues might involve genuine position dimensions, with the parties manoeuvring for the support of electors who had very different preferences between, let us say, economic expansion and stable prices. Although little is known about the reality of such dimensions to most voters, the dominant mode of popular response to economic goals seems to be one that approves at the same time of full employment, larger pay packets, stable prices, and, to the extent that they are salient for the public, a strong currency and balanced international payments – and that disapproves of the opposite of these conditions.

We may assume therefore that the economic outputs of government are very salient to the electorate, although there are some short-run variations as between different economic goals, and that opinion is overwhelmingly skewed in favour of the achievement of rising prosperity and related economic goals. It follows that the political consequences of economic issues depend almost entirely on the way in which the parties come to be linked

[1] Economists on both sides of the Atlantic have discussed the electoral implications of the relationship between unemployment and price inflation for those in power. See in particular the excellent papers by C. A. E. Goodhart and R. J. Bhansali, 'Political Economy', *Political Studies*, **17** (1970), 43–106, and by Susan J. Lepper, 'Voting Behavior and Aggregative Policy Targets', New Haven, 1968 (mimeo.). If, as is generally supposed, the structure of the economy imposes an inverse correlation between unemployment and inflation, those who take economic decisions are likely to be very aware of the trade-off between the two, and their choice of an optimal combination may be deeply influenced by their judgments of the electorate's sensitivities. But this by no means implies that the structural relationship between the two is understood by the electorate itself. For a more negative view of the electoral effect of economic trends see W. L. Miller and N. Mackie, 'The Electoral Cycle and the Asymmetry of Government and Opposition Popularity', *Political Studies*, **21** (1973), pp. 263–79.

in the public's mind with the achievement of these goals, or the failure to achieve them.

The type of connection that has dominated both academic and more popular views of the electorate's response to the economy is one under which voters reward the Government for the conditions they welcome and punish the Government for the conditions they dislike. In the simplest of all such models the electorate pays attention only to the party in power and only to conditions during its current tenure of office.[1] Such a model might be extended in either of two directions. On the one hand, we might suppose that the electorate judges the performance of the governing party to some extent against what the Opposition party might do if it were in charge of affairs. In a country where politics is in the main a regularized competition between two major parties, it is unlikely that a comparison of this kind would be entirely absent from the electorate's mind, although public reactions to economic conditions may focus much more on the Government than on the Opposition.[2] This is a question to which we shall return later.

On the other hand, the links between economic conditions and the parties might be built up in the electorate's mind over much longer periods of time. A good deal of evidence from electoral surveys suggests that this is the case. For example, Milne and Mackenzie's studies early in the postwar period suggest that the British electorate held strongly negative feelings towards the Conservatives on the basis of what it remembered of the depressed economic conditions between the wars. Despite the other dislocations of life, the Second World War had brought rapid economic expansion and increases of real incomes for millions of people. This transformation could well have put a different face on the long decades of economic hardship that had gone before.[3] But the austerity of Labour's policies in the late forties followed by the new expansion that became visible in the 1950s

[1] Borrowing a term from Herbert Simon, Gerald Kramer has characterized models of this kind as ones entailing 'satisficing' behaviour, since the electorate judges only whether economic conditions are satisfactory, not whether they are optimal. See his penetrating analysis of the relationship of economic to electoral series over more than half a century of American experience, 'An Empirical Analysis of Some Aggregate Hypotheses About U.S. Voting Behavior, 1896–1964', *American Political Science Review*, **65** (1971), 131–43.

[2] This possibility is not really excluded from the class of 'satisficing' models proposed by Kramer; nor is it excluded by the results of the empirical tests he applies to the economic and electoral data of the American past.

[3] See R. S. Milne and H. C. Mackenzie, *Straight Fight*, London, 1954, p. 136, which records that in 1951, a dozen years after the end of mass unemployment, over half their Labour respondents in N.E. Bristol gave full employment or the fear of unemployment as a reason for voting Labour.

after the Conservatives had taken office may well have left the electorate with a somewhat different view on how the parties are associated with good and bad times. One important factor in any such transformation over the years lies, of course, in the extent to which the electorate had been physically replaced.

In a similar way the American electorate may have drawn from the Republican prosperity under McKinley ('the full dinner pail'), following the severe depression under the Democrats in the early 1890s, an image of better times under the Republicans which carried over well into the twentieth century and was reinforced by the general prosperity of the Republican twenties. But any such image was drastically transformed by the Great Depression of the 1930s, and survey evidence from twenty years later showed how strongly the Democrats were linked with good times in the public's mind, and the Republicans with economic distress.[1] The links that survive in popular consciousness over longer periods are of course modified by new experience and will occasionally be entirely overthrown, as our account suggests. The absence of a serious depression under the Republicans in the 1950s attenuated the party's association with bad times. But this change was overlaid on a substratum of belief in better times under the Democrats which probably continued to work to the Republicans' disadvantage throughout the Eisenhower years.[2]

Any tendency of the electorate to reward the parties for achieving conditions that are universally approved and to punish them for failing to achieve these conditions is consistent with our view of economic issues as 'valence' issues. Such a model of the economy's political effects can, however, be distinguished broadly from a quite different class of models under which the parties are in some way thought to hold differentiated 'positions' with respect to the economy. A possibility discussed by Kramer is that one of the parties would in general be seen as expansionist and the other not.[3] The consequence of a downturn might in such a case not necessarily be the lessening of the voters' esteem for the governing party but rather a

[1] See in particular *The American Voter*, pp. 45–6.

[2] Since longer-surviving beliefs about the performance of the parties in relation to the economy can be modified by new experience, their presence is not at all inconsistent with the relationships that have been found between short-term economic changes and changes of party strength. It would be a mistake, however, to conclude from the relationships found between short-term economic and political changes that the electorate's horizons are limited to the very recent past in the connections that it forms between parties and economic conditions. This is a point on which survey and aggregative evidence needs to be interpreted together.

[3] Gerald Kramer, 'An Empirical Analysis of Some Aggregative Hypotheses About U.S. Voting Behavior, 1896–1964', *American Political Science Review*, **65** (1971), 131–43.

strengthening of their desire to have the more expansionsist party in power.

Such a view of the bearing that the economy has on the strength of the parties may be much less applicable in an era when all governments are committed to using their powers, subject to the other constraints upon them, to assure high employment and economic expansion. But it may have been more plausible in an earlier day. Indeed, the American experience during the 1930s might be seen partly in these terms. The Democrats under Roosevelt were far more expansionist than their Republican predecessors under Hoover, and the contrast was vividly imprinted on the electorate's mind. As a result, the continued economic distress did not diminish support for Roosevelt, although his administration made little headway in reducing unemployment before the Second World War came at the end of the decade. It would seem that economic distress persuaded the country that it ought to keep the more expansionist party in power.

Another 'position' model of the links of economic conditions to party support is one under which the strength of the class alignment increases with economic distress. According to such a view, the consequence of hard times is not the lessening of support for the governing party generally in the country but rather an increase of support for each party in the class whose interests it represents and a decline of support for each party in the opposite class. We have already suggested in Chapter 9 that a rising level of affluence in Britain may gradually have reduced the strength of the alignment by class. It is quite possible to conceive that such a pattern would apply to shorter-term changes of the economy with the 'polarization' of party support by class rising in hard times and falling in good.[1] We shall return later in this chapter to the evidence that can be found to support such a model of the response of the British electorate to the economic conditions of the 1960s.

The State of the Economy 1959–70

The health of an economy is too complex to be charted by any single index. Several aspects of national prosperity can each have their own political effect and we can identify in the period from 1959 to 1970 economic changes which must have worked upon the electorate in different

[1] For a systematic statement of such a model see P. E. Converse, 'The Shifting Role of Class in Political Attitudes and Behavior', E. E. Maccoby and others, eds., *Readings in Social Psychology*, London and New York, 3rd edition, 1966.

ways. One extra complication in describing the economic context of politics is that the absolute level of the various economic indices may be less important than a comparison of their present levels against past or anticipated levels. The number of unemployed may be less significant than whether the number is rising or falling – or is expected to rise or fall. In all this we must consider the electorate's perceptions as well as the objective economic realities.

In Figure 18.1 we summarize a number of economic indicators. They make plain that the fluctuation of the period must not be exaggerated. The national product went on rising although in 1962 there was a brief

18.1 The British Economy 1959–70

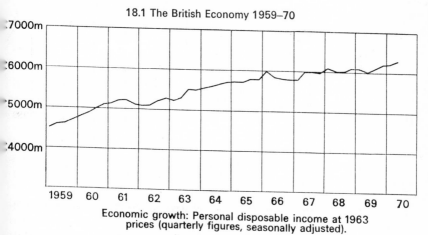

Economic growth: Personal disposable income at 1963 prices (quarterly figures, seasonally adjusted).

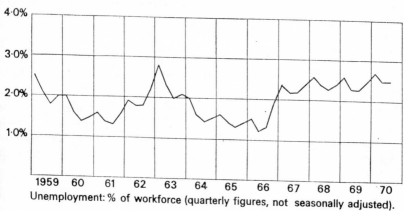

Unemployment: % of workforce (quarterly figures, not seasonally adjusted).

18.1—continued

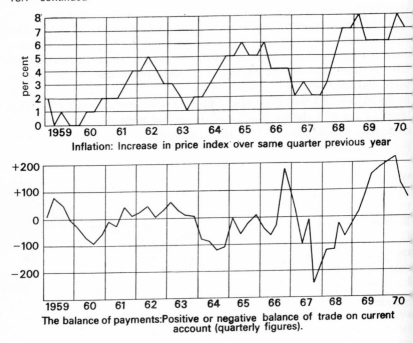

Inflation: Increase in price index over same quarter previous year

The balance of payments:Positive or negative balance of trade on current
account (quarterly figures).

plateau and in 1967–9 a wider one. But over the whole period wages and
salaries increased faster than prices.

Unemployment fluctuated between 1 per cent and 3 per cent. The proportion of the work-force unemployed fell markedly in the six months
before the Conservative victory in 1959 and continued low until mid-1961.
But with the policies associated with the pay pause, as well as an unusually
severe winter, unemployment climbed upwards to a high peak in early
1963 and then fell just before the Conservative recovery of 1964. Unemployment continued low for the first two years of the Labour Government until
the July 1966 measures took effect. Thereafter it rose to a higher sustained
level than at any time since 1940, staying close to 2½ per cent for the rest of
our period. If we had deployed the figures for workers on short time, the
improvement in employment in the run-up to the 1959 and 1964 elections
would have appeared even more sharply.

The upward movement of prices that is so familiar an aspect of modern
economies became more evident as the 1960s advanced, though it still fell

ar short of what was to happen in the mid-1970s. The rate of increase varied substantially. There were those periods of particular acceleration. The first sharp advance took place in 1961–2 when the Ministry of Labour's index of retail prices recorded increases of 5 per cent over the corresponding quarter of the preceding year. The second period was in Labour's first year of power when slightly greater increases occurred. The wage and price standstill of 1966 produced a let-up for eighteen months. But then the effects of devaluation and wages awards produced new record levels of increase, notably in the quarter before the 1970 election. (By contrast, the months before the 1959 and 1964 elections had seen relative price stability.)

Somewhat more removed from the lives of ordinary people but the subject of extensive discussion in the mass media were the vicissitudes of Britain's trading position. The last chart in Figure 18.1 shows the quarterly trends in the balance of visible trade. How these external constraints on Britain's economic position affected popular attitudes and behaviour is far from clear. They must of course have had great indirect influence by inducing the Government to take deflationary measures and, in the extreme case, the devaluation of the pound. But the extent to which Britain's balance of trade or of international payments was of direct concern to the electorate remains problematic. The very distance of these questions from ordinary people's experience may help to explain the parties' brisk skirmishing over their responsibility for Britain's position. But Mr Wilson by the emphasis he placed during 1968–70 on getting Britain out of the red may have given the monthly balance of payments figures a new electoral significance. The switch from deficit to surplus in the autumn of 1969 heralded the Labour recovery and there are those who argue that the deficit for May 1970 announced on June 15, three days before the election, may have caused the Labour defeat. The first deficit for nine months gave dramatic support to the Conservative claim that, despite Mr Wilson's boasts, the economy was in a shaky state.[1]

Lying behind the movement of these various indicators are several of the relationships which gave structure to Britain's economic affairs. In particular, the characteristically inverse relationship between unemployment and inflation was very evident.[2] So too was the relationship between domestic expansion and the deterioration of Britain's trading position

[1] See *The British General Election of 1970*, pp. 166–7, 347.
[2] The (product moment) correlation between the unemployment figures in Figure 18.1 and the average rate of price increases over the preceding and following six months is –0·66 over the period 1959–66.

which dogged Chancellors of both parties. As we use these indicators to describe the changing state of the economy we would do well to distinguish changes which can alter the electorate's mood by directly affecting individual well-being from changes whose effects are less direct. We shall see ample evidence later in this chapter that the influence of the economy on the electorate's mood can depend as much upon impressions of the state of the economy derived from the media as upon direct changes of individual well being that result from changes of employment or income or prices.

Perceptions of Individual Well-Being

At each of our interviews we sought to measure our respondents' sense of whether they and their families were better or worse off than at some previous time, or had remained about the same. We also probed the detailed reasons why our respondents felt that their economic condition had changed. The results suggest that the effects of broad changes of the economy were overlaid on differences linked to the individual's life cycle. In general, those who were younger were more likely to feel that their well being had improved, those who were older that their well-being had remained the same or worsened. In 1963, for example, those in the post-1951 cohort who felt better off were in a 33 per cent majority over those who felt worse off; in the 1945 cohort this majority was only 21 per cent; in the inter-war cohort there was no majority either way; in the pre-1918 cohort it was those feeling worse off who were 12 per cent more numerous.[1] Moreover, variations in the reasons for changes of economic circumstances make quite clear how often changes associated with the life cycle – marriage, child-bearing, the movement of grown children out of the home, retirement and the like – are seen as the source of changes of well-being.

Yet it is plain that our sample as a whole saw the Government as being of great significance for their economic condition. Even among those who gave personal reasons for their circumstances having improved or worsened

[1] The detailed definitions of cohorts are set out in Chapter 3. The full figures for perceptions of changes of economic well-being by cohort in 1963 are these:

	Pre-1918	Interwar	1945	Post-1951
Better off	19%	26%	38%	47%
About the same	50	49	45	39
Worse off	31	25	17	14
	100%	100%	100%	100%

almost two-thirds were prepared to say that the actions of government could affect how well off they were. Among the rest of the sample this proportion stood at more than 70 per cent. Some (7 per cent) actually cited the Government's fiscal or monetary policies as the direct reason for their change in prosperity.

The electorate's sense of economic well-being differed measurably between the five periods in which we took interviews. Table 18.2 sets out the reports of recent changes given by our sample in each of these periods. The figures suggest that the electorate's judgments in the summer of 1963 were not starkly negative, although a fifth of our sample said that their condition had worsened: whatever the degree of economic difficulty in the prior winter and the years before, almost half had noticed no change.

18.2 Perceived Changes of Economic Well-Being, 1963–70

Compared with a year ago (three or four years ago; two or three years ago) are you and your family[a]	Summer 1963	Autumn 1964	Spring 1966	Summer 1969	Summer 1970
Better off now	33%	21%	22%	28%	29%
Worse off now	21	17	23	32	27
About the same	46	62	55	40	44
	100%	100%	100%	100%	100%

[a] See question 14a. In 1963 the question referred to 'three or four years', in 1964 and 1966 to 'a year ago' and in 1969 and 1970 to 'two or three years ago'.

The reports given at the four later points of time were distinctly mixed. In the autumn of 1964 a little more than a fifth thought that their condition had improved over the prior year and a few less than a fifth thought that their condition had worsened. In the spring of 1966 the two proportions were roughly equal. Surprisingly they continued to be so in 1969 and 1970, although the proportion who felt their situation had changed, one way or the other, had increased.

Expectations of future changes of well-being also fluctuated over the period of our studies. As Table 18.3 on the next page shows, our interviews in 1963 revealed that among those who expected their economic conditions to change over the next year, a clear majority expected them to improve. By the time of our second interview, in the autumn of 1964, this majority was somewhat greater. But in 1966 the mixed assessment of economic conditions was clearly reflected in the fact that those who expected their circumstances to improve were not much more numerous than those who

18.3 Perceived Economic Prospects, 1963–70

Now looking ahead over the next three or four years (year or two) do you think that you will be[a]	Summer 1963	Autumn 1964	Spring 1966	Summer 1969	Summer 1970
Better off then	24%	30%	26%	21%	31%
Worse off then	9	11	19	24	14
About the same then	48	40	45	44	45
Don't know	19	19	10	11	10
	100%	100%	100%	100%	100%

[a] See question 14b. In 1969 and 1970 the period was 'year or two' not 'three or four years'.

expected them to worsen. 1969 produced more pessimists than optimists and 1970 saw a sharp recovery. What is surprising, perhaps, is that even in 1969 the figures did not fluctuate more and that so many continued to expect little change.

In 1963 and again after the elections of 1966 and 1970 we probed directly into the connections that had formed in the voter's mind between the parties and economic well-being. We did so only among those respondents, about 70 per cent of the total, who told us that they believed that the Government could affect how well off they were. The results of this assessment in the summer of 1963 are set out in Table 18.4. It is immediately apparent that the individual elector did tend to form a contrasting view of the actual performance of the Conservatives in power and the putative performance of Labour were it to be brought to power. The largest number of respondents fell in the cell for those who said their well-being would remain unchanged under either party. But among those who felt that their well-being would change, there was a marked tendency to see one party or the other as more likely to improve their economic condition, a tendency that is shown by the greater number of respondents who fell in the cells at the lower left and upper right.

But what is mainly of interest in judging the impact of economic perceptions for party support is the way the sample was distributed in this table above and below the main diagonal running from the upper left to the lower right. Respondents below this diagonal felt that they had done relatively better under the Conservatives, while those above it felt that they would do relatively better under Labour. Opinion at this moment was not strongly skewed upon either side of this question. But it certainly could not be said that the Conservatives were at a deep disadvantage in the summer

18.4 Perceived Bearing of Parties on Economic Well-Being, 1963

Conservative government
has made respondent

Better off About same Worse off

	Better off	3	14	12
Labour government would make respondent	About same	11	32	5
	Worse off	15	7	1

100%

of 1963. It is difficult to know whether this reflects the degree of recovery between the prior winter and the middle of 1963 or whether it shows that the Conservatives carried over from the 1950s a fairly clear image as the party better able to handle the economy and assure prosperity. If the latter were true the electoral cost of the Conservative Government's economic difficulties in 1961–2, while real, would merely have been somewhat to reduce a strong advantage over Labour in the economic sphere which had been built up during the 1950s.[1]

[1] Evidence of the sort presented in Table 18.4 is of course subject to the biasing effects of party allegiance, and when we compare the perceptions of the economic performance of the parties held by those who have always been Conservative and Labour we do in fact see a marked contrast, as this table shows. But this table also shows that traditional

		Traditional Allegiance[a]	
		Conservative	Labour
Conservative government had made respondent	Better off	42%	16%
	About same	50	54
	Worse off	8	30
		100% ($n = 310$)	100% ($n = 346$)

[a] Traditional Conservative and traditional Labour supporters are those who replied to questions 37a, b and c of the 1963 questionnaire by saying that they had never supported another party. Perceptions of changes of well-being under the Conservative Government were assessed in terms of replies to question 14d of the 1963 questionnaire.

Conservatives were far readier in the summer of 1963 to say that they had prospered under the Conservatives than traditional Labour supporters were to say that their well-being had declined under Conservative rule. A reasonable conclusion to be drawn from these data is that the Conservatives were disadvantaged little by the links between the

A comparable assessment of perceptions of the parties with Labour in power is set out in Table 18.5 for the election of 1966. These figures again show a marked inverse correlation of perceptions of the two parties; the mass of the table tends to run from the lower left to the upper right. But once again neither party seemed strongly advantaged by perceptions of this sort; this is shown by the relatively equal numbers of our respondents who fell in the cells above and below the main diagonal of the table from upper left to lower right. This pattern is quite consistent with the distinctly mixed perceptions of individual well-being in the spring of 1966 which we examined before in Tables 18.2 and 18.3.

18.5 Perceived Bearing of Parties on Economic Well-Being, 1966

		Labour government has made respondent		
		Better off	About same	Worse off
Conservative government would make respondent	Better off	1	8	11
	About same	9	39	12
	Worse off	9	9	2

100%

The most one-sided perceptions of the relevance of the parties to individual well-being were those recorded by the electorate in 1970. These are set out in Table 18.6. In the Conservative trough of 1963 the entries above and below the main diagonal of Table 18.4 were fairly evenly balanced, indicating that about equal parts of the electorate thought they would prosper better under Conservative or Labour governments. Likewise, in the Labour zenith of 1966 the entries above and below the main diagonal of Table 18.5 were fairly well balanced, indicating that about equal parts of the electorate thought they would do better under Conservative or Labour management. But in the Conservatives' narrow victory of 1970 very much more of the electorate was found above than below the main

parties and personal well-being that were evident to the electorate at this time, although the Conservatives may well have dissipated a far greater advantage with which they had begun the 1959 Parliament.

18.6 Perceived Bearing of Parties on Economic Well-Being, 1970

Labour Government
has made respondent

	Better off	About same	Worse off
Better off	2	12	29
About same	11	26	12
Worse off	4	3	1

Conservative Government would make respondent

100%

diagonal of Table 18.6; whereas 53 per cent of our respondents in that year felt they would do better under the Conservatives, only 18 per cent felt they would have done better under Labour. In this case perceptions of the bearing of the parties on economic well-being can hardly have failed to influence the electoral outcome.

The extent to which such perceptions do in fact affect support for the party in power emerges plainly from our findings. Let us consider, to begin with, how support for the Conservative Government changed between the elections of 1959 and 1964 according to whether the individual saw his economic well-being as having improved or not. We shall for this purpose consider only those who had the same perception in both the first and second of our interviews; that is to say those who, both in 1963 and 1964, thought that their economic well-being had improved, had worsened, or had stayed about the same. The remarkable contrast of the movements of support towards and away from the Conservatives in these three groups is set out in Table 18.7 on the next page. Those who consistently saw their condition as worsening exhibited a much stronger than average trend away from the Conservatives, while those who found their condition unchanged moved fairly much with the national party tide. But those who consistently felt their position had improved showed a strong trend *towards* the Conservatives and *against* the general movement of the party tide between these elections.[1]

[1] An interesting aspect of these findings is that the trends that were above and the trends that were below the average for the electorate as a whole were disproportionately

18.7 Change of Conservative Support, 1959–64 by Perceived Change
of Own Economic Condition, 1963 and 1964

Among those whose report of change of their condition was consistently	Change of Conservative support 1959–64[a]
Better off now	+7%
About the same	−3%
Worse off now	−8%

[a] Each entry is the change of the Conservatives' support from 1959 to 1964 expressed as a percentage of the total number of respondents in a given group. A positive value means a swing towards the Conservatives, a negative value a swing away from the Conservatives.

Figures such as those in Table 18.7 naturally suggest that reactions to changes of economic condition follow the lines of a 'valence' model, with the Government of the day, whichever party is in power, being rewarded for good times and being disapproved of for bad times. Additional evidence that this is a realistic image is supplied by changes of party support over a period when there was a turnover of party control. For this purpose we may examine the movements of support between the two main parties according to three patterns of perceived well-being that the individual could have had in 1964 and 1966. We shall consider, first, those who thought that their economic well-being had improved over the last year of the 1959 Parliament but had deteriorated over the 1964 Parliament; second, those who thought that their well-being had remained roughly the same during both these periods; and third, those who thought their well-being had worsened over the final year of Conservative rule but had improved during the first year of Labour rule.

The contrast of movements of support in these three groups is very sharp, as Table 18.8 shows. Among those who thought their position was improved at the end of the Conservatives' years in power but worsened under Labour, there was almost no movement of opinion during a period when the country as a whole swung markedly towards Labour. Among those who thought their position had remained unchanged under both parties the swing to Labour was about average. But among those who thought their well-being had changed from one of decline to one of improvement, the swing towards Labour was fully 13 per cent, far beyond that recorded in the electorate as a whole.

the result of younger electors' responding to their perceived economic conditions. Not only were younger electors more likely than older ones to see their condition as having improved, as we have noted; they were also more likely to be *moved* by such perceptions, whether they were of an improvement or worsening of their condition, as we would expect from the argument of Chapter 3.

18.8 Increases of Support for Labour, 1964–6 by Perceived Changes
of Economic Well-Being 1963–4 and 1965–6

Perceived Changes of Economic Well-Being, 1963–4 and 1965–6	Change of Support for Labour, 1964–6[a]
Thought well-being improved in 1963–4 and worsened in 1965–6	0%
Thought well-being remained unchanged in both 1963–4 and 1965–6	+3%
Thought well-being worsened in 1963–4 and improved in 1965–6	+13%

[a] Entries are increases in percentage Labour between the elections of 1964 and 1966.

A very similar pattern could be noted in changes of party support later
in the decade. When we divide our 1969–70 panel according to perceived
changes in economic well-being, as is done in Table 18.9, we find that
Labour enjoyed a strong swing among those who felt their well-being had
improved after a period of decline and actually lost ground among those
who felt their well-being had worsened after a period of improvement. The
latter figure is especially notable in view of the strength of Labour's general
recovery between 1969 and 1970.

18.9 Increases of Support for Labour, 1969–70 by Perceived Changes
of Economic Well-Being 1966–9 and 1969–70

Perceived Changes of Economic Well-Being, 1966–9 and 1969–70	Change of Support for Labour, 1969–70[a]
Thought well-being improved 1966–9 and worsened in 1969–70	–3%
Thought well-being remained unchanged in both 1966–9 and 1969–70	+7%
Though well-being worsened in 1966–69 and improved in 1969–70	+10%

[a] Entries are increases in percentage Labour between the 1969 and 1970 interviews.

We find added support for a valence model of economic effects when
we disaggregate our evidence for the electorate as a whole and examine
the support for the governing party within the middle and working class.
Let us make such a comparison for the summer of 1963, when the Conservatives held power. Figure 18.10 on the next page shows the proportion
supporting the Conservatives by class according to whether the respondents
felt their well-being had improved or worsened or stayed the same over
the preceding three or four years. The slope of the curve downward to the

18.10 Conservative Support Within Middle and Working Class by Perceived Change of Economic Well-Being, 1963[a]

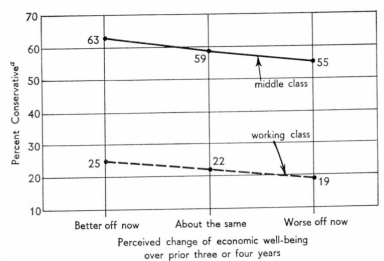

ª Per cent Conservative of support for three main parties. Middle and working class groups are defined in terms of class self-images.

right within each class shows the lessening of support for the Conservative Government among those who felt their economic well-being had not improved over the previous three or four years, although the figure also makes clear once again the dominant political alignment of the two main classes.

A very similar portrait of support within classes for the outgoing Conservative Government emerges from the 1964 figures for those who felt that their well-being had improved or worsened or stayed about the same over the year prior to the elections. The slope downward to the right within each class shows the lessening of support for the Conservative Government among those who felt they had stood still or gone downhill economically. This suggests that support for the Conservatives was noticeably stronger among working class electors who thought their well-being had improved over the prior year.

Further support for a valence model of economic effects, under which the ruling party, whichever party it is, gets the credit or the blame, comes when we compare these figures with the pattern for 1966. Figure 18.11 shows the proportion supporting the Conservatives within the two main

18.11 Conservative Support Within Middle and Working Class by Perceived Change of Economic Well-Being, 1966[a]

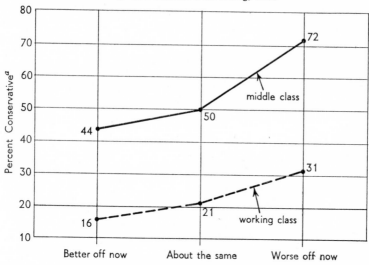

Perceived change of economic well-being
over year preceding 1964 election

[a] Per cent Conservative of support for three main parties. Middle and working class groups are defined in terms of class self-images.

classes according to whether the respondents felt that their well-being had improved or worsened or stayed about the same over the year before the 1966 election. With the Conservatives now in opposition the slope of the curves in the figure is dramatically reversed. Support for the governing party still is higher among those who felt they were better off than before. But the identity of the Government had changed. The Conservatives in their new role as the opposition party received greater support from those who experienced economic stagnation or decline and this now lends the curves a slope *upward* to the right.

Although these results mainly confirm a valence model of political effects, they do also faintly suggest that economic deprivation may lead to greater polarization of class support. The figures for 1966 show that the difference in Conservative support between the middle and working class was least among those who experienced economic improvement and greatest among those who experienced decline. Moreover, the general alignment between class and party was somewhat stronger in the summer of 1963, in the immediate aftermath of the economic distress of the winter of 1962–3, than it was at the General Elections either of 1964 or 1966.

But this faint support for a link between the level of individual prosperity and polarization of classes is not more than a trace finding by comparison with the stronger tendency of both classes to reward a governing party for economic benefit and punish a governing party for economic deprivation. The evidence of such a tendency draws us back to the question of how the public in fact assessed the Government's handling of the economy during this period – and how perhaps it assessed the potential handling of the economy by the opposition party.

The Parties and the Economy

In view of the very real effects which changes in the economy have on the lives of ordinary people, many observers have naturally assumed that economic change is translated into party support by the shifts of those whose economic lot has been worsened or improved. On this view, the political impact of changes in the economy is simply aggregated out of the individual decisions of those whose well-being has been affected. But there are reasons to be sceptical about such a view. For one thing, the shifts of party support that have been associated with economic changes have been larger than could be explained by summing together such individual effects. The ebbs and flows of the party tide have, for example, been far greater than the numbers of people who have entered or left the ranks of the unemployed.[1]

It would indeed be surprising if the state of the economy did not colour the view of the Government taken by many people who do not see their own well-being as directly involved. There is of course a shading between actual and potential effects, and considerations of economic self-interest can still influence those who themselves are relatively unaffected by recent or prospective changes in the economy. But the economic health of the country as a whole is given the widest coverage in Westminster and in the mass media. It would be astonishing if this great national issue, or cluster of issues, altered the standing of the parties only in the segment of the electorate on which the penalties or blessings of economic change fell most

---

[1] This point is carefully documented by the estimates of the relationship of changes of unemployment and party strength set out by C. A. E. Goodhart and R. J. Bhansali in 'Political Economy', *Political Studies*, **17** (1970), 43–106.

directly. This segment will be peculiarly responsive to economic change, as was indicated by our evidence of the shifts among those who felt their well-being had changed. But a Government's successes or failures in handling the country's economic affairs can alter the attitudes of many other people as well.

This point can be very sharply made by comparing the shifts over the 1966 Parliament in the proportions of our respondents who thought Labour had affected their own economic well-being and the proportions who felt satisfied with Labour's handling of the country's economic affairs. This contrast is shown in Figure 18.12. Two of the curves in the

18.12 Economic Perceptions over the 1966 Parliament[a]

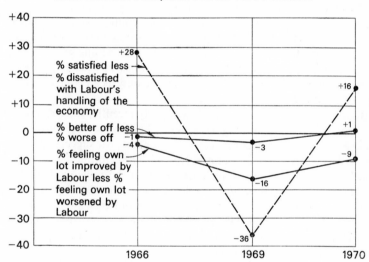

[a] The wording of the questions defining the three series is given by section 14 of the summary of the questionnaires in the appendix. The proportions saying that Labour had made them better or worse off are adjusted to reflect the percentage they comprise of the electorate as a whole.

figure touch upon individual economic well-being and are remarkably flat: the series describing the balance between perceptions of being better or worse off economically shows almost no change from 1966 to 1969 and from 1969 to 1970, and the series describing net feeling on whether Labour had made the respondent better or worse off swung only a little more widely across a period that included moments both of hope and despair for Labour's economic policies. But the third curve, which shows instead the balance between those who were satisfied and those who were dissatisfied with Labour's performance in handling the economic problems of the country as a whole, is in marked contrast to the other two series: this measure of feeling about the economy as a national issue recorded a balance of satisfaction with Labour in 1966, a heavy balance of dissatisfaction in 1969, and again a balance of approval in 1970.

Two lessons are to be drawn from this remarkable contrast between the electorate's response to Labour's stewardship of the economy as a whole and to Labour's perceived responsibility for changes in individual well-being. The first is that we should pay the closest heed to the links the electorate draws between the parties and the economic health of the country as a whole. Since the goals of economic policy are so largely agreed upon between the parties and enjoy overwhelming approval in the electorate, the economy is a valence issue in which everything is likely to depend on the way the electorate holds the parties responsible for failure or success in reaching these goals. Here Labour's success in unloading responsibility for economic difficulties on to its predecessors must be seen as an important factor in the electorate's response to the economy as an issue in the middle and later 1960s.

Because Labour had come to power fairly recently, their responsibility for Britain's economic difficulties was in 1966 a somewhat open matter in the eyes of the electorate. Our evidence from that year suggests that Labour had in fact persuaded a substantial part of the electorate that the Government's economic travails were inherited from the previous Conservative administration. Asked in 1966 whether Britain's economic problems were mainly the fault of the Labour Government or of their predecessors, fully 43 per cent of our sample laid the blame on the Conservatives, 44 per cent thought both parties equally to blame or didn't know, and only 13 per cent laid the blame at Labour's door.

By 1969 these figures were markedly different, although they were by no means fully reversed. As Table 18.13 shows, more of the electorate by 1969 was prepared to say that Britain's economic difficulties were the fault of Labour than of the Conservatives. But even in 1970, in the wake of Mr Heath's conquest of office, fully a third of the electorate was prepared to say that Britain's economic problems could be traced back to the Conservative Government of the early 1960s.[1]

[1] Apparently this sort of allowance was extended to Labour in 1966 on a much broader front. We asked our sample the question: 'Did you feel before the election that the Labour Government had been in office long enough to have had a fair trial?' Only 26 per cent said that they did, whereas fully 71 per cent said that they did not. The remaining 3 per cent, a remarkably small percentage, were unable to answer.

18.13 Perceived Responsibility of the Parties for Britain's Economic Difficulties, 1966–70

Do you think that Britain's economic difficulties are mainly the fault of the Labour Government or of the last Conservative Government?

	1966	1969	1970
Labour Government	13%	29%	25%
Last Conservative Government	43	21	33
Both equally	30	38	29
Don't know	14	12	13
	100%	100%	100%

The second lesson to be drawn from the notable disparity between perceptions of the Labour Government's impact on individual and national economic well-being is that what the economy means as a national issue depends on the economic debate between the parties and is capable of changing over time. During the 1960s attention was given to a series of economic problems – unemployment, sluggish economic growth, the balance of payments, rising prices. Among these, unemployment probably provided the leading test of a Government's handling of the economy from the end of the Second World War until the middle 1960s. The economic experience of the war had convinced the electorate that the unemployment of the interwar period could be avoided. The mass of the people, as well as the political and economic elite, came to accept a more Keynesian view and to expect governments to take effective action against unemployment.

The rise of the opinion polls with their frequent readings of party strength greatly extended the opportunities for analyzing the political impact of changing employment levels and other changes in the economy. The importance of the parties' perceived ability to deal with economic affairs is plainly evident in the polling results for the early years of our own research. This is seen by superimposing, as is done in Figure 18.14, two statistical series that may be calculated from the Gallup Poll during these years. The first of these is the positive or negative lead which Labour enjoyed over the Conservatives in voting intentions as recorded by Gallup's monthly index. The second is the positive or negative 'lead' of Labour over the Conservatives in terms of the proportions in successive Gallup samples that said they approved or disapproved of each party's handling of economic affairs.[1]

[1] From December of 1959 till August of 1964 Gallup asked each sample these questions: 'How strongly do you approve or disapprove of the way the Government is handling the

There is in fact a remarkable agreement of these two series over a period of nearly five years. Some divergence is evident towards the beginning and end of this span; the Conservatives did less well in terms of voting intentions than in terms of their perceived ability to handle the economy in the prosperous year of 1960 and in the period of economic recovery from mid-1963 to late 1964. But the agreement between the two series is very marked.

The difficulties in the way of placing too clear a causal interpretation upon such an agreement are familiar enough. Party preference may colour the voter's perception of the parties' ability to handle the economy. Some of the agreement shown by Figure 18.14 must therefore be due to the tendency of voters, having attached themselves to a given party, to see its performance on economic matters in a more favourable light. Indeed, the match of the two series is partly the result of nothing more than the accidents of sampling which have drawn into different samples different proportions of these who incline towards the same party both in voting intention and in perceptions of the parties' ability to cope with economic affairs.

These qualifications are genuine ones. Yet their force is somewhat lessened by two additional observations. The first of these is that the strength of the parties in successive samples shows much less tendency to vary with perceptions of the Government's and the opposition's ability to handle other types of problems or issues. If party bias and sampling error were mainly responsible for the agreement of the two series shown in Figure 18.14 they ought to produce equal agreement between the party lead in terms of votes and in terms of the handling of international affairs and health and housing and other areas about which Gallup questioned their samples. But if the agreement shown by Figure 18.14 is partly the result of the genuine impact of changing economic perceptions and if the impact of perceptions in other areas, for example pensions and housing, varied much less in the short run (as is almost certainly the case) then there ought to be a closer agreement between short-term variations of party strength and variations of the parties' perceived success in handling the economy. And this, indeed, is what we found.[1]

---

problem of economic affairs?' and 'How do you rate the way the Labour Party Opposition is handling the problem of economic affairs in the House of Commons debates and elsewhere?' To form the index of Labour's 'lead' in these perceptions we have subtracted the proportion approving of the Government's handling of the economy from the proportion approving of Labour's handling of the economy.

[1] We have measured the greater tendency of the party lead in votes to match the 'lead' in the parties' perceived ability to handle the economy by utilizing the coefficient of

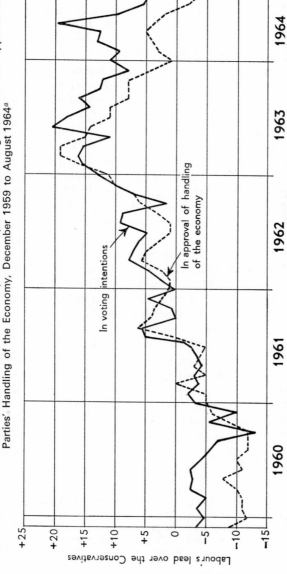

18.14 Labour's Lead Over the Conservatives in Gallup's Monthly Series on Voting Intentions and Approval of Parties' Handling of the Economy, December 1959 to August 1964[a]

[a] These series are derived from the Gallup Poll's published figures for December 1959 to August 1964. Labour's lead in voting intentions is the arithmetic difference of the proportions giving their voting intentions as Labour and Conservative. Labour's lead in approval of parties' handling of the economy is the arithmetic difference of the proportions approving the Labour Opposition's and the Conservative Government's handling of economic affairs.

It should be emphasized that the fact that the party lead in votes matches best with the series showing judgments on the economic performance of the parties does not call into question the importance that the electorate's response to other problems or issues had for the division of party strength at a given moment. The closeness of the match does suggest that fluctuations in the parties' perceived ability to handle the economy had more to do with short-run fluctuations of party support. But motives of much longer duration may enter the electorate's choice of party throughout such a period. This would obviously be true, for example, of perceptions of class interest. If we were to be furnished with a monthly index of perceptions of the Government's link with the interests of a given class it is unlikely that such an index would exhibit a variation that closely matched short-run fluctuations of party support. Yet perceptions of class interest would in every month be of immense importance for the strength of British parties.

A causal interpretation of the agreement over the 1959–64 period of the two series in Figure 18.14 is strengthened when we disaggregate the electorate's comparative judgment of the two parties and examine separately its evaluation of government and opposition. This separation is accomplished by Figure 18.15. It is at once apparent from the contrast of Figures 18.14 and 18.15 that perceptions of the Government's economic performance were much more variable and matched more closely the movements of party strength. If party bias and the accidents of sampling accounted for the agreement of the series in the earlier figure (18.14), the party lead in votes ought to provide an equally good match with each of the two series showing the changing approval of the economic performance of government and opposition. The fact that the agreement with approval of the Government was much the closer of the two is evidence that we were tapping changes which had genuine influence on party strength in these years and is at the same time evidence that it was the Government's performance that was of greater salience for the electorate.

The most important analytical opportunity that these polling series provides is the possibility of measuring the relationship between fluctuations of party strength and fluctuations of the economy itself. Indeed,

---

agreement proposed by W. S. Robinson. See 'The Statistical Measurement of Agreement', *American Sociological Review*, **22** (February 1957), pp. 17–25. This coefficient achieved a value of $+0\cdot56$ when applied to the movements over time of the lead in votes and the lead in the parties' perceived handling of the economy; but a value in no case higher than $+0\cdot04$ when applied to the movements of the lead in votes and the party 'lead' in terms of each of a number of other issues, including international affairs, housing, pensions, health and education.

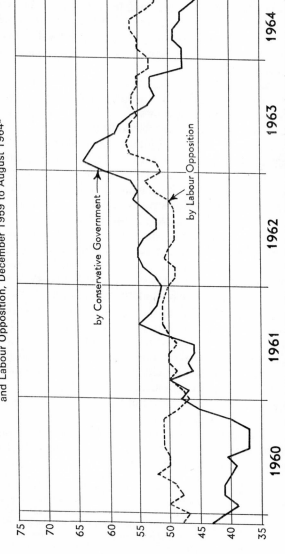

18.15 Gallup's Monthly Series on Approval of Handling of Economic Affairs by Conservative Government and Labour Opposition, December 1959 to August 1964[a]

[a] These series are derived from the Gallup Poll's published figures for December 1959 to August 1964 and show the per cent approving a given party's handling of economic affairs.

analyses of this sort are becoming a standard part of the repertory of those who wish to account for electoral change.[1] A number of factors, including the time a party has been in office, will intervene between changes of party support and changes of the economic realities that are experienced by millions of electors. But it would be very surprising if approval of the Government's economic record were not systematically tied to the performance of the economy itself.

A strong presumption of unemployment's impact on party support in the early period of our research is raised if we plot together the time series for unemployment and the Gallup series for the party lead during the years from 1959 to 1964. A marked relationship between the two is evident in Figure 18.16. Closer inspection makes it plausible that changes in the level of unemployment precede changes of party support; Goodhart and Bhansali estimated that an average lag of four to six months separated a change of unemployment from its maximum political effect in this period. In particular, the decline of Conservative support between 1959 and 1963 and the partial Conservative recovery between 1963 and 1966 seem to have owed a good deal to changes of unemployment levels in 1961–2 and 1963–4.

But changes in unemployment were much less able to explain the variations in party support over the later years of the 1960s. If the unemployment and party support series for the years from 1966 to 1970 were superimposed, the fit between the two would be much less close than in Figure 18.16. Such a divergence is plainly damaging to the unemployment thesis. Labour won its 1966 victory at a time of low levels of unemployment, as we have seen in Figure 18.1. The rapid rise in unemployment after the severely restrictionist measures adopted by the Labour Government in July 1966 to defend the pound and the continued high unemployment throughout the 1966 Parliament must have been major factors in eroding Labour's support to very low levels. But the later variations in party support were not matched by large fluctuations in employment. In particular, Labour's remarkable recovery in the first six months of 1970 was not accompanied by a marked reduction in unemployment from the levels that had prevailed for three and a half years.[2]

---

[1] Pathbreaking analyses of this sort in Britain are reported by C. A. E. Goodhart and R. J. Bhansali in their paper 'Political Economy', *passim*, and W. L. Miller and N. Mackie, 'The Electoral Cycle and the Asymmetry of Government and Opposition Popularity: An Alternative Model of the Relationship between Socio-economic Conditions and Political Popularity', *Political Studies*, **21** (1973), pp. 263–79. For a similar analysis of American polling data see J. E. Mueller, 'Presidential Popularity from Truman to Johnson', *American Political Science Review*, **64** (1970), pp. 18–34.

[2] It was widely suggested that, as the 1960s advanced, unemployment came to be

18.16 Gallup's Poll's Monthly Series on Labour's Lead Over Conservatives and Monthly Series on Thousands of Unemployed, Seasonally Adjusted, 1959–64

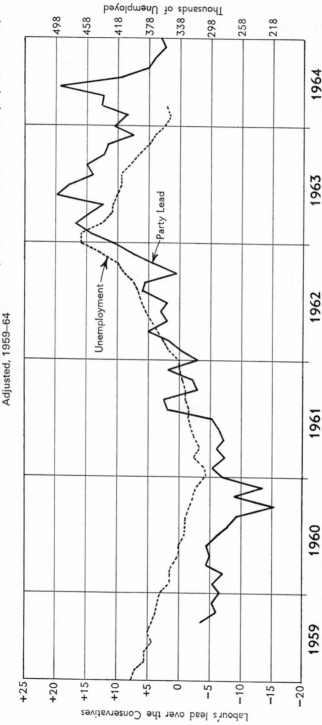

[a] The series for Labour's lead over the Conservatives is taken from the Gallup Poll's published figures for 1959 to 1964. The series for wholly unemployed, seasonally adjusted, is taken from the *Ministry of Labour Gazette*. That source gives a seasonally adjusted series only from June 1963. For the earlier period the figures given for actual number of wholly unemployed, excluding school leavers, were adjusted for seasonal variation by applying a constant seasonal adjustment factor computed as the mean of the adjustment factors used by the Ministry of Labour for the years 1964–7.

These facts led some observers to wonder whether there might not be a natural cycle of party support, not mainly dependent on economic conditions, under which a Government loses support in the middle of a Parliament and regains support as a new election approaches.[1] The view was put forward that the earlier parallelism of changes of unemployment and party support was merely coincidental, since unemployment had happened to rise towards the middle of Parliaments and fall as the next election approached. It was further said that governments, believing their strength depended on reducing unemployment, tended to expand the economy and bring unemployment down before going to the country, thereby strengthening a correlation which did not describe a true causal link since they would have regained support in the absence of such measures.

We might in any case be uneasy about a theory which gave so formal an interpretation of large shifts of party support. Those who have propounded such a theory do, of course, offer reasons why such a cycle should obtain.[2] Nonetheless, there is a good deal about the size and timing of the shifts of party support that would remain unexplained if we were to see a rhythmic cycle of electoral support for the Government as the explanation. The shifts have, after all, varied greatly in magnitude and in detailed timing during the several post-war Parliaments.

An alternative view is that the electorate's judgment of the Government's economic performance has continued to shape the movements of

---

much less feared and therefore to have much less political impact, partly because memories of the 1930s were growing dimmer, but more because the adoption of statutory redundancy payments and of markedly more generous unemployment benefits made the loss of a job, in the short run at least, much less unpleasant than it used to be.

[1] See in particular A. King, 'Why All Governments Lose By-elections', *New Society*, 21 March 1968, pp. 413–15; Nigel Lawson, 'A New Theory of By-elections', *Spectator*, 8 November 1968, pp. 650–2; and W. L. Miller and N. Mackie, 'The Electoral Cycle and the Asymmetry of Government and Opposition Popularity: An Alternative Model of the Relationship between Socio-economic Conditions and Political Popularity', *Political Studies*, **21** (1973), pp. 263–79. Of course the propounders of such a theory were aware of the causal ambiguity surrounding the generalization that a Government's strength returned as a new election approached, since a return of strength could bring on an election.

[2] One species of the theory comes very close to saying that the reduction in a Government's strength both in the opinion polls and by-elections during the course of a Parliament is more apparent than actual. With an election far off, a poll respondent is free to withdraw support from the Government without any thought of bringing it down. In this sense the question 'If there were a General Election tomorrow which party would you support?' has a different meaning from what it would on the eve of an actual General Election. A similar point could of course be made about by-elections – or even about local elections if these are seen by the voters, as Chapter 2 suggests they are, as popularity contests among the national parties.

party support, but that the test of economic success can change – and indeed, that it did change in the later 1960s and again in the early 1970s. The circumstances surrounding Labour's accession to power in 1964 and the substance of the economic debate between the parties in the 1966 Parliament promoted Britain's balance of payments to a more central place in the electorate's judgment of the economic performance of the Government. Labour found a large international payments deficit when it took over from the Conservatives in 1964 and Mr Wilson missed no opportunity to remind the country of the fact in later years. When Labour encountered its own difficulties in righting the balance of payments, adopting the July measures of 1966 and a series of further policies including eventual devaluation, Mr Wilson virtually invited the country to judge his government by whether it could overcome Britain's trade deficit. The Conservatives, believing that Labour could not do so, to a remarkable extent agreed upon this test. When Labour did eventually produce a payments surplus its standing in the country rose rapidly, and the Conservatives seemed to have fallen into a trap they had partly set for themselves (although the unfavourable trade figures published three days before polling day in 1970 may have supplied the final margin needed for a Conservative victory).

There is at the very least a suggestive fit between Britain's payments deficit (or surplus) and party strength over the latter years of the 1966 Parliament. This relationship is charted by Figure 18.17 on the next page.[1] The one interval in which the two series diverge widely is in the aftermath of the July measures of 1966. These policies brought a transient payments surplus but cost Labour dearly in public support, dispelling the goodwill left over from the party's victory in March. Thereafter the deterioration in Britain's trading position, which even the devaluation of November 1967 did not seem to check, was accompanied by further drops in Labour strength, until the appearance of a payments surplus in September 1969 set the stage for Labour's revival in the first six months of 1970.

---

[1] We have pursued the relationship between Labour's (positive or negative) lead over the Conservatives to the (positive or negative) balance of payments by regression methods. Since the party lead is highly autocorrelated in succeeding months, and since we had evidence from our exploratory analysis that changes in the party lead were sensitive to the balance of payments in the preceding month, we expressed the party lead in the ith month, Y_i, as a linear function of the preceding month's party lead, Y_{i-1}, and balance of payments, X_{i-1}, as follows:

$$Y_i = a + bY_{i-1} + cX_{i-1} + e_i$$

and estimated the coefficients a, b and c by least squares methods. The coefficient of determination, R^2, expressing the closeness of fit of such an equation, was equal to 0·72; the value of the Durbin–Watson statistic was equal to 2·28.

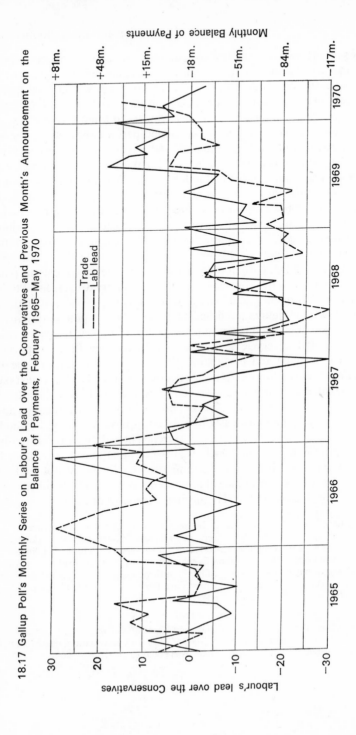

18.17 Gallup Poll's Monthly Series on Labour's Lead over the Conservatives and Previous Month's Announcement on the Balance of Payments, February 1965–May 1970

The hypothesis that the country came in these years to judge Labour's economic performance mainly in terms of the balance of payments is consistent with the evidence, which we gave earlier in Figure 18.12, that in 1970 more of the electorate approved than disapproved of Labour's handling of the economy. It would be hard to reconcile this judgment with the state of other indicators of the country's economic health. Indeed, unemployment then stood at its highest level since the war, and prices were rising more rapidly than they had for a generation. The hypothesis is also consistent with Labour's success over its whole period in office from 1964 to 1970 in keeping alive the idea that it had inherited its main economic difficulties from the Conservatives, a success reflected in the entries of Table 18.13 above. It is hard to imagine such a result apart from the hostage the Conservatives gave to Labour in leaving a payments deficit of £400 million for 1964.

We do not regard this alternative account of the role of the economy in the 1966 Parliament as more than a hypothesis. But it can explain much of the gross variation of party strength in these years without jettisoning the view that the electorate will judge a Government partly in economic terms. Indeed, such an account also helps explain Labour's final shortfall in its quest for a third successive victory. There will always be some uncertainty as to whether the pre-election polls consistently overstated Labour's strength in late May and early June or whether they were right until they failed to take adequate account of a last-minute trend to the Conservatives.[1] Such a trend would be more natural if the electorate were prepared to judge the Labour Government in terms of Britain's trading position. The trade figures released in the final days of the campaign showed a fresh deficit. The Conservatives and their allies in the media gave these figures extraordinary prominence, and Mr Wilson probably further increased their visibility by his efforts to explain the deficit away. A Government that subordinated almost everything else to meeting a single test of its competence to manage the country's economic affairs was in the end denied a victory to which it thought this test would show that it was entitled.

There is no reason to believe that the balance of payments has permanently displaced other aspects of the economy as the major test of a Government's economic performance. On the contrary, the way changes in the economy are translated into shifts of party strength is itself subject to

---

[1] For the evidence that there was a late trend see *The British General Election of 1970*, pp. 185–6. See also F. Teer and J. Spence, *Political Opinion Polling*, London, 1973, pp. 183–202, and the Report of the Market Research Society inquiry 'Opinion Polling and the 1970 Election', published by the Market Research Society in 1972.

change and will depend on the way economic issues are defined by the parties and the media as well as on the economic experiences of ordinary electors. Rising prices may, for example, at times dominate the economic resposes of the electorate, and in the early 1970s they seemed to have usurped the position that the balance of payments had recently held. In many countries besides Britain, inflation came to have pre-eminent importance. The argument over the role of wage inflation and whether an incomes policy should be voluntary or compulsory dominated the economic debate in Britain even before the energy crisis and the miner's strike led to the February 1974 election. In a crisis contest, fought on economic issues, neither unemployment nor the balance of payments loomed very large, even though there was talk about an impending slump and even though the country was experiencing a record trade deficit. Indeed, when disastrous balances of payments figures emerged near the end of the campaign, the Conservatives could even present them as an argument for rallying to the government!

Such changes in the terms of the electoral argument, in so far as it centres on political economy will add to the difficulties both of interview studies and of studies which relate economic to electoral series. These changes will oblige the survey analyst to probe more deeply into the expectations and beliefs which give to the economy its political translation. And they will shorten the periods in which it is safe to fit a single aggregative model of economic and political change. They will also raise the importance of anchoring both types of studies in a better description of what the parties and the media say about the economy in a given period. But if we take account of these things we will hear more clearly one of the drums to which the electorate marches.

Conclusion

19 Continuity and Change

THE sheer complexity of the processes which change the parties' strength is underlined again and again throughout this book. Indeed, the variety of the factors at work has dominated our discussion of the physical replacement of the electorate, of fundamental shifts of party alignment, and of more transient variations of electoral strength. Any catalogue of the factors involved in these processes must include some that are to be found in the voter's mind, some in the circumstances that govern his chances of being born and of surviving to any given age, some in his interaction with his family and with his neighbours and workmates, some in the structure and operations of the communications media, some in the behaviour of political leaders and party organizations, and some in the trends of the economy or in world events – and even this list is far from exhaustive.

Approaches to Change

The complexity of change naturally inspires a diversity of approach. We have brought to these manifold problems a wide variety of analytic frameworks rather than any one approach. Only by cutting away huge segments of political reality would it be possible to apply a single, elegant model of change that was parsimonious in its terms. It may sometimes be desirable to attempt this and to treat change as a property of a very simple 'closed' system. For example, we might follow some theorists in supposing that voters respond to governments in terms of movements of prices and employment and that governments seek support by choosing a position along the melancholy continuum of modern economics that lies between full employment and inflation on the one hand and unemployment and price stability on the other. Or we might suppose that electoral change results from movement of voters along a dimension between left and right on which the parties seek maximum support and voters choose the party closest to themselves. When each of these quite widely held conceptions of the sources of political change is captured in a suitable model, it is found to imply patterns of change that provide new insights into the behaviour of actual party systems. But the value of such models lies partly in showing that the systems they represent are too closed to be real. The party systems in which change actually occurs need to be seen in more complex and open terms.

We have shunned the adoption of any single model of change, trying instead to distinguish in the system we are studying some persistent processes that give partial clues to change. An understanding of these processes can be of considerable explanatory or predictive value. Yet the explanations and predictions are conditional ones. The parts of the system represented by our analytic frameworks are open in the sense that although the frameworks connect consequence with cause they do not account for the occurrence of the cause itself.

This simple point is well illustrated by our analysis of the rise of Labour support in this century. Accepting as given certain basic conditions involving the institutional framework of the electoral system, the split of the Liberals, and the presence of a new party specifically aligned with working class interests, we have examined how the processes of the socialization of new electoral cohorts can account both for the form of Labour's growth – rapid in earlier decades, levelling off in later ones – and for the pattern that is found in today's electorate of greater Conservative support among manual workers in the older cohorts. But such explanations are only conditional and accept as given the conditions that set the stage for Labour's growth.

The conditional nature of what we can say about change means that it will often be more profitable to explain the changes of the past than to predict those of the future. The conditions from which past changes sprang tend to be known, while those of the future tend to be unknown. Since we know of the Liberal split in the days of Asquith and Lloyd George together with much else about the conditions of the time, we can use this knowledge to work out the electoral consequences of the split. But we do not know whether another of the major parties will split in the years ahead, and we do not know many of the other conditions that would influence the electoral consequences of such an event. In view of this, it may be quite unrewarding to set forth propositions about what would happen if certain future conditions were met.

The tendency to focus more on explaining the past than predicting the future is a familiar one in the social sciences. But the social sciences are not alone in experiencing a gap between explanation and prediction. A similar disjunction tends to manifest itself in every field of study which must treat complex and uncontrolled natural systems rather than controlled experimental ones. Evolutionary biology offers a particular instructive example. The Darwinian framework gives fundamental insights into the processes by which species evolve, offering an explanation that is quite different from Lamarck's. But the natural systems in which species actually evolve are so complex that this framework offers very little by way of prediction. Not only is it unable to foretell the random mutations that underlie genetic 'drift'; these random events occur in systems which are so complex that it is very difficult to foretell which mutations will better adapt a species to survive – and so predict the course of evolution. But this does not prevent the natural scientist from using the framework after the fact to help work out why evolution followed the course it did. In other words, the Darwinian framework brings us closer to explanation of past changes even if it is seldom of help in foretelling changes yet to come.

Much the same could be said about the analytic frameworks we have offered in this book (although we draw such a parallel with due diffidence). For example, the framework we have offered for gauging the impact of political issues helps to explain observed shifts in the relative strength of the parties without extending very far our ability to foretell such shifts. Once we know for a given period whether popular attitudes towards an issue were strongly or weakly formed, whether they were balanced or skewed, and whether the positions of the parties were sharply differentiated in the public's mind, we can explain the extent and direction of the issue's impact on party strength. But the framework itself will not tell us whether opinion will become stronger or weaker, more balanced or skewed, and the parties more or less sharply distinguished in the public's mind – and thereby help us predict the issue's future impact on party strength. Like the seismologist, the student of electoral politics is better able to account for past tremors than to predict future ones.

It will be clear from what we have said of the 'openness' of the system of which the electorate is part that we certainly do not see electoral behaviour or change in any narrowly deterministic way. No one who undertakes a study of this kind can suppose he has penetrated the dynamics of electoral politics very far. If by a wild fancy we imagine our frameworks having been refined and extended to the point where the system they describe was 'closed' (a fancy that seems to us philosophically untenable in any case), it is plain how very much more open are the systems we have treated here. This is a realm in which the understanding of human behaviour is so incomplete that it would be grotesque to portray the electorate as playing out any fully determined role.

This point seems to us a partial antidote for exaggerated fears that politics may be nearing a day when the findings and methods of research such as ours will allow party leaders to manipulate the public at will. The role of public relations consultants and advertising agencies in promoting the electoral fortunes of parties and individuals has attracted wide attention in the United States and is increasingly discussed in Britain. There is no escaping the fact that governments and leaders do at times have immense impact on mass opinion: this is presupposed by the very concept of leadership in a democracy. In any case, this influence was there long before the rise of opinion polls and is certainly not their creation. Studies of mass opinion may give party leaders information that helps them in winning office. This information is accessible in principle to all parties and leaders, although those in power may be more able to obtain it and to act upon it. The leading example is the additional information on the mood of the country that is now available to a prime minister contemplating an election. It is indeed arguable that contemporary prime ministers are less likely to repeat the mistakes occasionally made by their predecessors who had to rely on by-election returns or any other more primitive omens. But this does not guarantee that a prime minister will always be able to choose a time when his party will win, as Mr Wilson demonstrated in 1970 and Mr Heath in 1974. All this indeed is a far cry from the view that governments now have a guaranteed power to manipulate consent and that political surveys are eroding the sovereignty of the people.

On the contrary, a lengthening series of electoral studies might simply give repeated evidence of how very limited is the influence which political leaders are able to exercise over the mass electorate. Certainly it would be quite wrong to assume that the extension of this knowledge of electoral behaviour must also extend the manipulative power of the leaders who might want to exploit it. Observation of economic affairs suggests how finite are the limits of a government's power. Recent studies, as we suggested in Chapter 18, have done something to clarify the role played by economic trends in changing the parties' standing in the country. It is possible that these findings will convey to party leaders some information they did not have before, such as the electorate's relative dislike of unemployment and inflation. But a government seeking to win support on economic grounds does not need surer information about the public's response to economic stimuli so much as surer information about how to provide the right economic stimuli. Any suggestion that the management of the economy offers governments an infallible tool for the engineering of electoral consent is likely to win only wry smiles from prime ministers or chancellors of the exchequer until economic change becomes far more predictable and economic science far more exact.

So diverse are the sources of change that a study such as this may leave the reader with a sense of limitless variety. There is in one sense no end to the things that impinge on the electorate's choice, determining the movements of party support. But all things are not of equal importance. As we gain a clearer view of the sources of political change, we also gain a clearer sense of the importance of each. From this we can build up a coherent analysis of the changes which have occurred in a given period. We therefore offer in the pages that follow an account of changes in Britain in the 1960s while we were conducting our research.

A Decade of Change

We have given structure to this book by distinguishing at the outset between three broad types of change – those involving lasting changes of party alignment, those involving the replacement of the electorate through the processes of birth and death and migration, and those involving the conversion and reconversion of people remaining in the electorate. Even these are linked in important ways. Replacement plays an important role in the great realignments, and the aging of such alignments influences the scale of short-term conversions. But these three basic types of change supply a framework within which to develop an account of change in a given period.

The effects of realignment, replacement and conversion could be seen both in the patterns we found early in the 1960s and in the changes observed later in the decade. The initial patterns presented, as it were, a single frame from a motion picture. The arrested action shown by this frame told a great deal about what had gone before and what would come after. But our inferences about each main type of change were greatly strengthened by being able to see as well the frames from later in the decade, to watch the motion picture of change during the years of our work.

Any period of change must open up fascinating vistas to the student of politics. The 1960s in British politics offer a richly varied span of contemporary history. The extent and pace of change in this period broke through some of the barriers to understanding that would confront the analyst in a stabler era.[1] The evidence of the 1960s showed the marks of two

[1] When our first edition was published in 1969, some critics objected that our picture

great realignments of electoral strength. On the one hand, the cleavage of Conservative support between Anglicans and non-conformists in the oldest age cohorts (and the even greater cleavage of support they remembered in their parents' generation) still preserved the traces of a religious alignment which had been of great importance in British politics before the First World War. At the start of our studies, only the cohort that had entered the electorate after 1950 showed little sign of the difference between Anglican and non-conformist. As we continued our research, this cohort was joined by a second, the group of voters entering the electorate after 1966 (including those enfranchised by the lowering of the voting age in 1970), in which this religious cleavage had left no trace.

On the other hand, the electorate of the 1960s had been deeply marked by the rise of the class alignment that had dominated British politics since the First World War. The patterns of party support by age that we found early in the decade described the historical process by which Labour took possession of its 'natural' support, its working class constituency. The way was prepared for this process, as we have seen, by the enfranchisement of the working class, by Labour's espousal of working class interests, and by the split of the Liberals that made Labour one of the two main parties. But the appeal which these conditions allowed Labour to exert on working class electors did not at once dissolve all working class loyalties to the established parties. We have seen that many working class electors re-mained firmly Conservative and many others may have become Conserva-tive when the Liberal Party, with which they identified, was undercut by the upstart party. As a result, the realignment took decades to complete and was in some respects still unfinished by the 1960s.

The emergence of the class alignment in successive generations had left two notable legacies of the past. The first was the role of former Liberals in adding to the strength with which the Conservatives confronted their new adversary. Despite the historical truth that Labour succeeded to the Liberals' position as the Conservatives' opponent, it was the Conservatives and not Labour which held the support of a majority of those whose parents and earliest allegiance had been Liberal and who yet remained in the electorate in the 1960s. These hidden flows into the parties that dominated politics for half a century helped explain how the Conservatives

---

was distorted by drawing evidence solely from 1963–6, a plateau of Labour strength. Ironically, we were at that moment analyzing findings from the Conservative zenith of three years later. We welcomed the increased understanding that such a reversal of party fortune could bring, but, in fact, it increased our understanding by giving us more change to work with and not by removing a party 'bias' from our earlier findings.

could so effectively contain the challenge of a party that had a far larger class base.

The second, closely related, legacy of the emergence of the class alignment was an age profile of party support in the 1960s which gave the Conservatives substantial support among older working class voters. This profile was the unrecognized source of much of the comment about the phenomenon of working class Conservatism. Despite the popularity of the idea of deference voting by the working class, the greater share of 'cross-support' which the Conservatives drew from the working class was concentrated in the aging cohorts which had come into the electorate before Labour's time and often as the children of Liberal parents. Indeed, this pattern gave a very different perspective on the success of the Conservatives in appealing for the working class support which had kept them in power or near it.

Paradoxically, the realignment which was still incomplete in the 1960s was already becoming obsolete. The working class segment of the younger cohorts might give their support to Labour in greater proportions. But the young were less disposed to see politics as an arena of class conflict. Such beliefs were most strongly developed in the cohort that had become conscious of politics during the Second World War and Labour's conquest of power in its aftermath. These beliefs were weaker in the cohorts that had entered the electorate before the new alignment had fully emerged. And they were weaker in the cohort that had emerged in the growing prosperity of the Conservative 1950s as the leadership of the Labour Party became less and less working class and the policies of the two main parties seemed in many respects to converge.

The aging of the class alignment continued through the 1960s, speeded up perhaps by the dilemmas which Labour faced when it took office and had to serve national rather than sectional goals despite its working class origins. When a Labour Government enforced a wages freeze and proposed penal sanctions against strikes, it was not so easy to see its policies as fundamentally opposed to those of the Conservative class enemy. By the end of the decade the support for the parties differed less between classes than it had in the early 1960s, and a new cohort had entered the electorate in which the polarization of party support by class was very weak. The decline in the relationship between class and party was seen in every cohort, but it affected least the cohort which had fixed its beliefs about class and party in the period which brought Labour to power after the war.

The aging of the class alignment gave the electoral politics of the 1960s two of its most pervasive qualities. One of these was the continued decline of participation. It is noteworthy that the years in which the class alignment came strongly to the fore after the Second World War also saw electoral turnout at its highest level. Participation in the elections of 1950 and 1951 was by a wide margin the highest recorded in any general elections since 1910 and therefore the highest since the enfranchisement of the electorate has been complete. During the 1950s and 1960s turnout fell, with only a brief upturn in 1959, to a level a full 12 per cent below its high point of 1950. In the crisis contest of February 1974, fought in good weather on a new register and with the additional enticement many more Liberal and Nationalist candidates offered part of the electorate, turnout was restored only to the level of 1959.

Of even greater importance was the role of the aging of the class alignment in the volatility of electoral support that became so marked in the 1960s. Just as participation had been highest when the class realignment was at its peak following the war, so the stability of voting strength had been most marked, as reflected in by-elections and the opinion polls. But as allegiances based on class weakened in subsequent years, other influences affected the electorate. By the 1960s the way had been prepared for the fires of nationalism to burn fiercely in Wales and Scotland for part of the decade. A Liberal revival burst upon the country in the early 1960s, much stronger than an earlier revival in the 1950s, but to be exceeded by a still later revival in the 1970s. Moreover, the electorate's volatility was plainly expressed in the increasing ease with which support moved between the two major parties. An electorate less strongly committed to class parties proved that it could be converted and reconverted in a few short years by particular issues, leaders and events which cut across the aging class alignment.

These broad patterns of change depended in many ways on the process by which generation succeeds generation through an electorate that is constantly renewed by replacement. During the 1960s death carried off a part of the electorate in which the influence of religion on party choice could still be seen, replacing it with a cohort from which this influence was almost completely absent. The cohort in which the class alignment was strongest had by the end of the decade reached the middle of the age continuum and had been followed into the electorate by two younger cohorts in which the attitudes of class politics were much less strong. These cohorts indeed supplied a large part of the fuel for the volatilizing of electoral support in the 1960s.

Replacement also changed the composition of the electorate through differentials in fertility and mortality and through external migration. But these effects were relatively slight. When the parties are evenly matched, even trace effects can decide which shall form the government. But in quantitative terms the altered composition of the electorate due to differential birth rates and selective death as well as to emigration and immigration was overshadowed by other changes. Death hurt the Conservative Party more than Labour during the 1960s. Indeed, several decades have still to elapse before elderly voters will be equally drawn from the two parties. The fact that men and the working class have rather shorter expectation of life than women and the middle class only partially offsets the greater losses suffered by the Conservatives due to the concentration of their support in the upper age cohorts.

The gains to Labour from differential birth rates have been correspondingly slight. Fertility has consistently been greater in the working class and, on the evidence of our research and other studies, has been greater in the Labour than in the Conservative segment of the working class. But Labour has profited more handsomely from generational effects not dependent on differential fertility as new cohorts have entered the electorate. In the 1960s, for the first time, those coming into the electorate had a greater chance of having been born into a Labour than a Conservative household, since the parties came into relative equality only in the 1940s. The coming of age of new electors added a further increment to Labour's support in 1970 when the age of voting was lowered to 18. Other things being equal, this change in the franchise alone cut Mr Heath's overall majority by more than 30 seats.

Party strength in the 1960s was also marginally affected by migration. It is difficult to assess the volume of the triangular trade by which native-born British have emigrated to the older Commonwealth nations as well as to the United States and South Africa; immigrants from the 'new' Commonwealth, especially the Indian sub-continent and the West Indies, have entered Britain and taken up mainly unskilled jobs; and many of the native born who formerly held these jobs have moved upward to skilled or non-manual occupations. The first leg of this triangle, emigration, benefited neither party. The second leg, immigration, benefited Labour, although this advantage was more than offset by the electorate's response to immigration as a political issue. The political effects of the third leg, upward mobility induced among the native born, are more problematic. It is clear that an upward change of occupational status will tend to move those who experience it towards the Conservatives. But we can only speculate as to how much of the upward mobility observed during the 1960s would have been absent if the coloured immigrants had never arrived.

The replacement of voters through migration, death and enfranchisement must have produced, without a single individual changing his or her allegiance, the equivalent of a swing of almost 2 per cent from the Conservatives to Labour during the 1960s. The fact that, with this handicap, the Conservatives stayed in the race and indeed won in 1970 draws us on to the third type of change, the conversion of those who remained in the electorate in these years.

We have said that transient conversion in the 1960s was conditioned by the weakening of the class alignment. An electorate which saw politics less in class terms could respond to other issues and events. The realignment – and replacement – of the electorate therefore had much to do with the amplitude of conversion. But to explain the direction and timing of particular shifts of party strength we must look to the attitudes and perceptions that surrounded particular issues.

Given the myriad issues present in politics during any period, we have sought to distinguish from the rest the issues of genuine impact on the electorate by applying the threefold test of the analytic framework developed in Chapter 13. Such an issue must be one on which the electorate has real and strongly held views; these views must not be evenly divided; and the parties must be differently linked to the issue in the electorate's mind. Fewer of the issues which preoccupy governments pass the first of these tests than is often supposed. But the number passing the second is increased by the presence of 'valence' issues on which the electorate displays virtual consensus about certain values or goals. The third test is, however, most likely to account for short-term shifts in an issue's impact as the electorate alters its judgment of the position or performance of government and opposition.

The evidence from the early 1960s shows that one area of policy dispute had strongly altered the balance of strength between the parties. The electorate had strongly formed views about social and economic welfare policies, believed overwhelmingly that these policies ought to be strengthened, and perceived Labour as much the likelier of the two parties to achieve this result. These beliefs comprised an important element of Labour's return to power in 1964.

The evidence from the early part of the decade also indicates that another area of policy dispute, coloured immigration, had high potential but failed in that period to alter the party balance because the electorate saw no real difference between the policies of the two parties. The issue of coloured immigration passed the tests of strongly formed attitude and of overwhelmingly preponderant views in one direction – in this case, overwhelming support for reducing the flow of immigrants. But apart from localities in which there was a high concentration of coloured immigrants, the electorate did not see one party as likely to shut off the flow, the other not. Where this third element was added, as it undoubtedly was in Smethwick in 1964, the issue's potential became very real indeed.

The impact of both these issues changed as the decade passed. Our evidence suggests that the early action of the Labour Government in raising pensions and other social benefits markedly reduced the demand for increases in the social services. Hence, the views of the electorate on what ought to be done became more divided. Moreover, the Conservatives towards the end of the decade came to appear to the electorate more like Labour on social welfare policy.

The transformation of the immigration issue was equally striking and went largely unrecognized in political commentaries. The issue continued to attract intense feeling, which lay overwhelmingly on the side of shutting off the flow of immigrants. But the difference of stand which had been attributed to the parties early in the decade only by the limited part of the electorate which lived in areas of high immigrant concentration was by the end of the decade perceived by the electorate as a whole. As a result, the immigration issue had a substantial though largely unseen impact on the party balance over the 1966 Parliament. The role played by this issue in the Conservative victory in 1970 may well have been missed, in part because most observers still expected to find its influence confined to constituencies with high immigrant concentration or candidates of Powellite sympathies.

This framework helps to explain the role of economic change in shifts of party support. The electorate can be counted on to have genuine attitudes on the 'valence' issue of economic well-being. Clearly, those who perceive governments as affecting their individual economic position do tend to vote accordingly. But there was remarkably little variation over the decade in the fraction of the electorate which formed such perceptions. The great majority of the electorate did not feel that its lot had been worsened by the Conservatives in 1963. Neither did it feel that its lot had been improved by Labour in 1966 or worsened by Labour in 1968 and 1969. To be sure, there was some variation of this sort, but it could not account for more than a part of the impact of economic change.

The economy is, however, a collective or national issue as well as an individual issue, and governments gain or lose support according to their perceived success in dealing with the economy as a whole. For this reason, the political translation of economic change can itself change in a few short years. During the early and middle 1960s governments tended, as we have seen, to gain or lose support as the level of employment rose or fell (although the number of electors who changed party far exceeded the number who went on or off the rolls of the unemployed). As Britain's trading position moved to the centre of economic debate, the relationship between employment and party support weakened. Instead, the fluctuations of party strength in the later part of the decade were, as we have also seen, more closely related to changes in the balance of payments. Indeed, Labour's demonstration that it could produce a surplus and the doubt cast on its performance by the last trade figures before the 1970 election hold a major clue as to the reasons both for the party's recovery between January and June of 1970 and for its failure in the end to secure the victory that the polls had led it to expect.

Popular images of the parties and their leaders were also an important source of transient conversions in the 1960s. We can be sure that the parties are differently linked to the 'issues' which they or their leading personalities pose for the electorate: a disastrous leader will be a liability only to his own party. Hence, the influence of the images of the parties or leaders will depend on their salience to the electorate and on whether they are positively or negatively toned. Our reading of popular feeling about the leaders in the early 1960s show Macmillan to be by no means a liability to his party. His popularity may by 1963 have receded from the heady days of 'Super-mac' in 1959. But he remained for the electorate a salient leader, who attracted as much favourable as unfavourable feeling. Wilson's salience was much less as a new leader, but he was in the beginning seen much more favourably than unfavourably.

Macmillan's successors did less well in popular esteem. Douglas-Home in 1964 and Heath in 1966, 1969 and 1970 were on balance unfavourably seen and cost their party a competitive advantage. Wilson's image fluctuated more widely. By 1964 he had gained in salience without being less favourably seen, and he made a substantial personal contribution to Labour's triumph in 1966. The cloud which passed over his leadership in later years was evident in popular feeling by 1969. But by 1970 he was again more favourably than unfavourably seen, even in the aftermath of his surprise defeat at the hands of the Conservatives.

Politics are not, of course, a detached part of the country's life. The changes in attitude and behaviour we have traced in the 1960s, and in prior decades, must be seen as part of the general transformation of British society and institutions. In summarising the political change of one decade we should draw special attention to four background factors whose effects, as we have tried to show, have been especially important.

The first of these is the way the country is housed. Since the First World War, a mixture of public policy and private initiative has profoundly altered the nation's stock of dwellings. The realisation by Lloyd George, and by his political heirs in all parties, that public housing programmes could have wide appeal to the mass of people paved the way for the provision of public housing by local governments on a grand scale. While private development dispersed much of the middle class into owner-occupied housing before and after the Second World War new concentrations of working class housing were being provided by public initiative. We saw in Chapter 5 how strongly this dual trend continued in the 1960s.

Many of the detailed implications of these changes can only be guessed at. But we cannot doubt that housing policy, through its immense impact on the shape of everyday life, has also transformed political anxieties and attitudes. There was nothing inevitable about the direction of this change. Other countries in Europe, as well as in the English-speaking world overseas, have developed very different patterns of housing finance and ownership with different consequences for the dispersion of voters into single class milieux, as well as for the anxieties which the elector looks to the state to satisfy. Our evidence suggests that Britain has been rehoused in a way that has tended to conserve the basic class alignment in our politics.

A second type of institutional change that has made a major contribution to political change is the remaking of the educational system. The Education Act of 1944 was intended to put more nearly equal educational opportunities within reach of the whole population. The Act was a powerful expression of egalitarian ideals, or in a more pejorative phrase, of meritocratic ideals. Its consequences were far-reaching – yet our evidence suggests that they left the alignment of class and party surprisingly intact. The streaming of pupils that was such a prominent feature of the new educational order did not lead to a major alteration in the class pattern of education. Our evidence shows clearly how grammar school places tended to be taken up either by middle-class children or by children from homes which had absorbed middle-class aspirations – and political attitudes. The movement between classes helped to minimize the impact of the new educational order on the party system.

Experience under the 1944 Act encouraged demands for further reform. But the coming of comprehensive schools did not mean the end of streaming, nor by 1970 was there time for it to have great impact on the overall composition of the electorate. Moreover, the middle-class streaming of children by geographic area, not to mention the removal of children to the private sector, tended to leave the meritocratic framework of the educational order remarkably intact – and with it the prevailing social and political alignment.

A third institutional element in recent political change lies in the structure and performance of the British economy. In Britain, as in other mature industrial nations, the contraction in the proportion of the workforce employed in primary industry has been linked with a steady rise in the proportion in non-manual occupations. This rise has induced a net upward mobility in the electorate. The fact that this mobility is capable of making middle-class Conservatives out of the children of working-class Labour parents is plainly shown by our evidence. But our evidence also shows that since the root of this mobility between generations lies in the educational system, its political effects were again discounted by the fact that in the working class it was the Conservative families whose children were most likely to take advantage of the new educational gateways to the middle class. Paradoxically this historical legacy of working-class conservatism diminished the larger gain the Conservatives would have made from the tilt of the economy towards non-manual occupations.

The political effects of economic growth have been mixed. On the one hand, it seems clear that the rising affluence of the postwar period, especially in the 1950s, eroded class antagonisms left by the interwar depression. The marked equalization in after-tax incomes that had come in the 1940s continued (though with no comparable change in the distribution of wealth) and all economic strata shared in the general increment in prosperity as new goods and services came for the first time within reach of a mass market. All this in our view must be included among the factors that tended to weaken the class alignment in the 1960s.

On the other hand it is clear that the rate at which the British economy has grown is moderate by contrast with a number of the countries of the developed world. If Britain's rate of economic growth had kept pace with those of Western Europe the resulting political transformation might have been much more marked. Although the class alignment weakened in Britain in the 1960s, as we have seen, fragmentary evidence from Europe suggests that the depolarization of politics by class was happening there too. In this sense the sluggish performance of the British economy has tended to conserve the prevailing political alignment.

The fourth institutional change with a major relevance to political change is the transformation of the communications media. The high level of literacy, the survival of a number of politically differentiated newspapers in a compact national market, and the skill of newspapermen in reaching out for a mass readership combined to make the British public of a generation ago more habituated to the printed media than the electorate of any other large democracy. The national morning newspapers held strong partisan commitments and these were closely reflected in the party affiliations of their readers. If readers were not in the first place converted by their newspapers their continued exposure to a heavy flow of politically slanted information helped to reinforce existing party alignments.

But this pattern has been sharply altered by the transformation of the media themselves. The monopoly of a partisan press, weakened by the coming of radio, was broken completely by television which for the mass of the people became the prime source of political information. British governments, unlike some others, felt constrained not to exploit the air waves for party advantages, and the broadcasting authorities have broadly sought to be politically neutral. Thus as television reached saturation coverage by the end of the 1950s, the British electorate became exposed to a quite different kind of political information. The public showed that it clearly perceived the difference in bias between the broadcast and the printed media.

There can hardly be any doubt that this revolution in the media helped to prepare the way for the much more fluid changes of party preference in recent years. The electorate by no means stopped reading newspapers. But the angling of politics by the press was somewhat muted and was now over-shadowed by a treatment of events on television and radio that was almost ostentatious in its presentation of the several sides of any issue. It should occasion no surprise that the years just after television had completed its conquest of the national audience were the years in which the electoral tides began to run more freely.

There are subtleties here which it is difficult to treat by more than conjectures. Television may well have wielded an influence on the electorate not only by exposing many voters to the other side for the first time. It may also have insulated part of the electorate from the type of social interaction which had fostered party solidarities. Some of the many hours the electorate now give to television viewing used to be spent in pubs or other social contacts. The emergence of the new medium may thus have removed electors from a type of neighbourhood contact which reinforced party ties to a home viewership which loosened them. Thus the long-term change in the structure of mass communication, unlike those in housing, education, and the economy may have fed the volatility that has been so increasingly evident in the electorate's behaviour.

Comparative Perspectives

This has been a book about British politics. Yet each of our main themes is of central relevance to the student of comparative government. Our frameworks are general ones and many of our specific findings involve analyses that might be applied elsewhere. Indeed, we would argue that intensive work within one system may at times contribute more to the comparative study of politics than work that is explicitly comparative in scope, simply because it can focus more intensively on change and the processes which underlie it.

Consider, for example, the process of political mobilization – the recruitment, in very different societies, of mass publics into political activities, especially participation in popular elections. Many writers have theorized that urbanization, literacy and the use of mass media have been the critical elements in this process and have sought empirical evidence for whether urban, literate, high-media countries also have high participation and rural, illiterate, low-media countries do not.[1]

It requires only a moment's reflection to see that such a test matches a dynamic theory to static measures. This simple theory of mobilization posits that *changes* in urbanization, literacy, and media usage will induce *changes* in political participation. But the test we have described is made in terms of the levels of these social and political characteristics found in a collection of countries at a given period of time. A dynamic element is introduced only by assuming that a common process of mobilization underlies the experience of these countries, which are at demonstrably different 'stages' of the process. But the test which depends on this assumption can have little to say about the accuracy of the assumption itself.

There is no way round this difficulty except to measure change. To do so will require sustained observation of particular political systems, including careful efforts to reconstruct what was true in the past. The task is alive

[1] For a sampling of this flourishing body of literature, see Daniel Lerner, *The Passing of Traditional Society*, Glencoe, Ill., 1958, pp. 56–65; Seymour Martin Lipset, *Political Man: The Social Bases of Politics*, New York, 1959, pp. 27–63; Daniel Lerner, 'Toward a Communication Theory of Modernization', in Lucien W. Pye, ed., *Communications and Political Development*, Princeton, N.J., 1963, pp. 327–50; Phillips Cutright, 'National Political Development: Its Measurement and Social Correlates', *American Sociological Review* (April 1963); Hayward R. Alker, Jr., 'Causal Inference and Political Analysis', in Joseph L. Bernd, ed., *Mathematical Applications in Political Science, II*, Dallas, Tex., 1966, pp. 7–43; Donald J. McCrome and Charles F. Cnudde, 'Toward a Communications Theory of Democratic Political Development: A Causal Model', *American Political Science Review*, **61**, 1 (March 1967), pp. 72–9; and Deane Neubauer, 'Some Conditions of Democracy', *American Political Science Review*, **61** (December 1967), pp. 1002–9.

with difficulties. Indeed, snapshots from a number of political systems have been treated as if they were successive frames of a moving picture of one system precisely because we so rarely have the frames that describe the state of a single system at successive points in time. The studies that yield them can make a signal contribution to comparative inquiry.

Such work can set the stage for a deeper comparative inquiry. If more adequate models suggest differences between political systems, comparative analysis can show whether these appear in the actual experience of different countries. In our own work we have sensed the opportunities for such further inquiry in treating each of the three main types of change we have identified in British electoral politics.

There have been a number of comparative analyses of the bases of party alignment. Less attention has been given the process of realignment, of the displacement of certain grounds of party cleavage by others. Comparative analysis could define more clearly the conditions and stages of realignment. We have felt particularly that comparison with other systems would help explore the importance of events at the level of elites, on the one hand, and dispositions among the mass electorate, on the other, in carrying through the great realignments of party support. In some sense Britain must have been readier than any of the other English-speaking countries for a realignment of politics on class lines early in this century in view of the greater importance of class in Britain's social structure. Certainly the contrast with America, where regional, racial and religious bases of social identification competed with class, makes plausible the fact that Americans should have been less disposed even in the heyday of the Roosevelt New Deal to divide between the parties along class lines.

But we are also impressed by the importance of circumstances at the level of elites for the realignment which took place in British politics. Especially important was the ruinous split in the Liberal Party, which gave Labour the priceless asset of becoming the Conservatives' main opponent after the First World War. Had the Liberals remained at anything like their prewar strength, it is far from clear that the grounds of party alignment in the past forty years would have been less mixed than in America, with the passions aroused by the Anglican-nonconformist split and by Ireland still taking their place alongside class among the major bases of party support. We have indeed cited evidence in Chapter 9 that the lessening class distance between the parties, especially at the leadership level, has in recent years allowed other ancient passions, including nationalist sentiment in Scotland and Wales, to draw off supporters that, on class grounds, Labour and the Conservatives could expect to have.

One other finding on prevailing party attachments set us thinking in a strongly comparative vein. Chapter 2 gives evidence of the greater tendency of generalized partisan self-images in America to hold fast in the face of deviating behaviour at the polls by those who hold them. We ascribed this difference to the differing structure of the choices which are set before the British and the American voter. At each election the British voter chooses among candidates only for a single office, whereas the American is obliged to choose among candidates for a bewildering array of offices spanning several levels of government. Since a large number of these carry a partisan designation American voters are encouraged by this process of choice to go through an additional stage of concept formation about their relationship to party in a generalized sense, even if they reach the view that they are 'independents' with no party tie. It is plausible to think that such a tie, once formed in the mind of American voters, is less likely to be eroded away by defection at a given election, whereas British voters who change their support are likely to change their partisan self-image as well. The truth of this supposition, which has obvious implications for the process of realignment, would be clearer if we were able to examine the link between self-image and current behaviour where the voter is faced with still other patterns of choice.

The effects of the replacement of the electorate through the vital processes of birth and death are the least explored of any we have considered in this work. There are of course cases in which the political consequences of fertility and mortality could scarcely be missed. General de Gaulle was by no means the only observer to appreciate the way the French in Canada by a heroic feat of fertility had for two hundred years kept themselves from being overwhelmed by English Canada. The Nazis' genocidal policies towards the Jews transformed the societies of central Europe by the end of the Second World War. Our evidence suggests, however, that birth and death may have political effects which are by no means negligible under far less dramatic circumstances than these. We would indeed suppose that their cumulative effects have been substantial in several party systems where they have not been seen as major factors in shifts of party support.

We felt most clearly drawn in a comparative direction by the possibility of extending this type of demographic analysis to take account of the influence of public policy on births and deaths. Governments rarely think of themselves as shaping the physical composition of the electorate by the policies they adopt. But in this they are quite mistaken. Health and welfare policies can have a marked influence on rates of fertility and mortality across parts of the population that are of widely divergent political views.

Hence, this type of analysis would define a new class of policy issues, as well as explore one of the subtlest of the 'feedback loops' between policy outputs and political supports.

The sources of transient conversion of party support present a rich field for comparative inquiry. The classificatory scheme we have set out in Chapter 13 is a general one that could be applied to the politics of any competitive party system. Comparisons between systems could give further insight into the factors that influence the salience of issues or the extent to which they set the parties apart. Such comparisons could also give insight into the circumstances under which more embracing ideologies give structure to the public's perceptions of the parties and responses to several issues at once. Our studies indicate that the ideological schema of left and right is of trifling importance in shifts of party strength in contemporary Britain. But there is evidence that this framework looms much larger in the sources of change in some party systems. Sustained observation within various countries can help define this difference and probe the reasons behind it.

One possible extension of the approaches in this book would lie in a more intensive examination of the interplay between party leaders and the mass electorate. This interplay is fundamental to many of the analyses we have attempted. We have emphasized the importance of events at the elite level in the decline of the Liberals and the rise of the Labour Party. But we have also asserted the importance of the actions and identities of political leaders in the weakening that has begun to be apparent in the class alignment. The possible reasons for erosion of the class alignment are complex and much is due to the passing of an era when class hatred could feed on severe economic deprivation in much of the working class. Yet some part of the weakening of this cleavage may be due to Labour's having turned to a more middle class leadership and having presented the country in power with policies that strongly converged towards those of the Conservatives, especially, perhaps, in asserting national interests against those of the Trade Unions.

An interest in interactional frameworks, in the mutual impact of leaders and led, has rightly provided a major element in recent theoretical and empirical work on political change. This aspect is fundamental to the models which Downs and others have abstracted from economic theory, and the refinement of spatial models of political competition offers a further instance of how an interactional emphasis can extend what we know of political change. We have seen in Chapter 15 that no single dimension of left and right organized the attitudes of the British electorate in the early

1960s. But this is far from saying that the Labour Government did not give evidence of the sort of convergent behaviour that models of this kind would under many circumstances predict. During the 1964–6 Parliament electoral considerations undoubtedly entered into the Wilson government's attempts to assume the Tories' clothes on nuclear weapons, the control of immigration and the defence of sterling (and even on a British presence east of Suez before the party reverted to a more traditional attitude when the costs of such a presence proved high). Only on the issue of nationalizing the steel industry did the Labour Party stake out a position that was strongly discrepant from that of the Conservatives – and the calculations that actuated the Labour Cabinet certainly had more to do with placating left wing M.P.s at Westminster rather than with winning votes in the country.

Although voting by secret ballot is so remarkably diffused across the world the public's intervention in the affairs of government through popular elections is far from a settled matter. Indeed, in the liberal democracies themselves the institutions of regular elections are under sharper attack than at any time since the rise of the fascist challenge between the wars. The alienation of people from the forms of parliamentary democracy or popular government is a familiar theme of current political commentary.

The focus of this book has been analytic rather than evaluative or reformative. It has not sought to describe how the system of popular involvement in government ought in ideal circumstances to work or how it ought to be changed. We have sought primarily to develop and apply to British politics a series of frameworks for the analysis of political change. But we also believe that these frameworks can help to provide the empirical evidence which would be required as a basis for informed judgments upon the adequacy of the system.

Appendices

APPENDIX A

The Samples

Background. This book has depended largely on information derived from interview surveys of people selected to represent the adult population of England, Wales and Scotland. Northern Ireland was left out partly because, having had its own parliament at Stormont, it is deliberately under-represented at Westminster, but mainly because it lies outside the main-stream of British party competition. A separate and special questionnaire would have been needed. Moreover, unless we had increased our sampling fraction in Northern Ireland, the three dozen interviews we might have expected there would have been too few for reliable statistical analysis.

Our first round of interviews took place between 24 May and 13 August 1963, with 90 per cent of a total of 2009 interviews completed by the end of June. The second round took place between 18 October and 4 December 1964, with 95 per cent of a total of 1828 interviews completed by 7 November. The third round took place between 4 April and 4 June 1966, with 90 per cent of a total of 2082 interviews completed by 2 May. The fourth round of interviews took place between 9 June and 31 July 1969 with 90 per cent of a total of 1114 interviews completed by 28 June. The final round of interviews took place between 19 June and 31 July 1970 with 95 per cent of a total of 3242 interviews completed by 21 July.

The interviews were undertaken by the field staff of the British Market Research Bureau Ltd. At each of the first two rounds and at the fourth round they averaged a little more than an hour in length, at the third and fifth rounds a little less than an hour. The response rates are dis-cussed below and the questionnaires are set out in summary form. The replies were coded by a team of graduates in Oxford and punched into Hollerith cards from which the data files necessary for the sub-sequent analysis were organized. Each respondent who was interviewed four times provided more than 1500 distinct items of information ranging from attributes such as sex or age to complex beliefs as to the relationship of class to party or the extent to which British politics con-formed to a model of responsible party government.

Sample design. Our initial sample was a self-weighting, multi-stage, stratified sample of the adult population of England, Wales and Scotland living in private households or institutions. Parliamentary constituencies served as the primary sampling units. The 618 constituencies of Great Britain were arrayed into 40 strata (80 half-strata) on the basis of region, relative Conservative and Labour strength in 1959, the presence of a Liberal candidate in 1959 and of a prospective Liberal candidate in the forthcoming election, urban or rural character, and level of unemployment. Two constituencies were chosen within each stratum (one within each half-stratum) with probability proportionate to size of electorate.

The sample design within each of the eighty chosen constituencies depended on the density of population.

1. Within forty-three borough constituencies and three geographically compact county constituencies a systematic sample was taken from a random start without further clustering.

2. Within sixteen county constituencies in which an urban core contained at least 40 per cent of the population the core was represented by a systematic sample selected from a random start without clustering; the rest of the constituency was represented by a systematic sample selected from a random start within a single polling district that was chosen with probability proportionate to size of electorate.

3. Within eighteen county constituencies of low population density the polling districts were arrayed into two strata on the basis of relative proportions of jurors.[1] Within each such stratum a systematic sample was selected from a random start within a single polling district chosen with probability proportionate to size of electorate.

By these procedures thirty-two names were selected from the electoral register of each sample constituency at the first round of interviews – 2560 names in all. For two reasons, however, we chose to regard this sample partly as a sample of households rather than as a sample of individuals. In the first place, by May of 1963 the register which had been compiled in October of 1962 and which had come into force in February of 1963 was already seven months out of date. By re-enumerating the sample house-

[1] All electors qualified for jury service used to be marked with a J in the electoral register. The J-index (the ratio of J's to the electorate) therefore provided a rough means of stratifying polling districts in economic terms since the qualifications for jury service involved basically the paying of local taxes on property valued at more than £10 per annum. This figure may have been low enough to include the great majority of dwellings, but it has been common in cheaper rented property for the landlord rather than the tenant to pay the rates.

holds we could impose a sampling frame closer to the register that was to be compiled in October of 1963, and upon which a 1964 General Election would be fought. In the second place, the register compiled in October of 1962 had excluded some 4 per cent or so of the adult population which escapes being registered in a given year[1] and the twenty-year-olds coming of age between 2 June 1963 and 2 June 1964, who would be included either as Y voters[2] or as full electors on the register in force at the time of a 1964 General Election.

Interviewers were therefore instructed to enumerate the persons over 20 living in the sample households and if this enumeration disclosed names not included on the electoral register to select an additional respondent for interview by a predetermined random procedure. In every case an interview was also sought with the originally selected sample elector if he still lived at the sample address. No effort was made, however, to follow electors who had moved away from these addresses prior to the first round.[3]

This sample of households remained our essential device for representing the qualified electorate at the second and third rounds of interviews seventeen and thirty-four months later. To keep the group of households representative of all households in Britain a fresh sample of names was drawn from the electoral register in force at the time of each of these later rounds and the addresses associated with these names were cancelled against the register in force at the time of the prior round to give a sample of 'new' households. To keep our sample of respondents representative of all adults living in these households we also examined the electoral registers in force at each of the later rounds to see what 'new' names had appeared at existing sample addresses. Within each household in which one or more new names had appeared an additional respondent was selected for interview by a procedure analogous to that used for the supplementary selec-

[1] See P. Gray and T. Corlett, *The Electoral Register as a Sampling Frame*, Central Office of Information, 1950, and P. Gray and F. A. Gee, *Electoral Registration for Parliamentary Elections*, H.M.S.O., London, 1967.

[2] Under the electoral law then in force, twenty-year-olds who came of age between 10 October, the date of compilation of the register, and 2 June were entered on the register with a Y against their names and were entitled to vote in any election after the following 2 October.

[3] Under these procedures the probability of our selecting a given 'new' respondent varied about the probability of selection of those whose names were drawn from the electoral register as the ratio of the number of electors who had been registered at the address to the number of unregistered adults which the interviewer found to be living at the address. The inverse of this ratio is therefore an appropriate 'weight' which might be applied to the information gathered from such a new respondent. We have found, however, that the application of such weights has negligible effects.

tions at the first round. Respondents from prior rounds who were no longer registered at sample addresses in effect dropped out of our sample of the current electorate, although they were still sought for interview in order to keep our panels as near to full strength as possible.

In 1969 we approached an entirely new sample of electors in the original eighty constituencies. Because of the impending change in the franchise we sought to draw into our sample everyone who would conceivably be of voting age at the next election, that is to say who would be 18 by 8 May 1971.

In 1970 we undertook our largest set of surveys; we endeavoured, first, to contact anyone of those interviewed in 1963 to 1966 whom we could still trace; second, to reinterview our 1969 respondents; and, third, to complete an entirely new sample. Using the same procedures as before we sought out new households and endeavoured to see that those whom we first interviewed in 1969 or 1970 together constituted a microcosm of the electorate.

The four waves of interviewing with the panel that was basically first approached in 1963 yielded fourteen overlapping but analytically distinct samples:

1. A sample of the adult population in the early summer of 1963.
2. A sample of the electorate qualified to vote in the General Election of 1964.
3. A sample of the electorate qualified to vote in the General Election of 1966.
4. A panel of respondents originally interviewed in 1963 and re-interviewed in 1970.
5. A panel of respondents originally interviewed in 1963 and re-interviewed both in 1964 and 1970.
6. A panel of respondents originally interviewed in 1963 and re-interviewed in both 1966 and 1970.
7. A panel of respondents originally interviewed in 1963 and re-interviewed in 1964 and 1966 and 1970.
8. A panel of respondents originally interviewed in 1964 and re-interviewed in 1970.
9. A panel of respondents originally interviewed in 1964 and re-interviewed in both 1966 and 1970.
10. A panel of respondents originally interviewed in 1966 and re-interviewed in 1970.
11. A panel of respondents originally interviewed in 1963 and re-interviewed in 1966.

12. A panel of respondents originally interviewed in 1963 and re-interviewed in both 1964 and 1966.
13. A panel of respondents originally interviewed in 1963 and re-interviewed in 1964.
14. A panel of respondents originally interviewed in 1964 and re-interviewed in 1966.

A further three samples were produced by the new samples approached in 1969 and 1970:

15. A sample of the population over $16\frac{1}{2}$ years old in midsummer 1969.
16. A sample of the electorate qualified to vote in the General Election of 1970.
17. A panel of respondents originally interviewed in 1969 and re-interviewed in 1970.

Figure A1 on the next page shows the number of respondents falling into each of these seventeen categories. This sketch sets out a number of points about the fieldwork and sample design. To begin with, the five distinct interviewing periods are represented here by the years in which they occurred: 1963, 1964, 1966, 1969 and 1970. A new set of respondents (New R) was interviewed in each of these periods and in all but 1963 and 1969 interviews were also taken with respondents who had been interviewed before.

The arrows connecting a sequence of boxes identify the respondents who share the same fieldwork history in terms of when they were interviewed and whether they were registered at their original sample addresses when they were. For example, the sequence of boxes at the extreme left represents the 633 respondents who were interviewed at their original sample addresses in 1963, 1964, 1966 and 1970; the sequence at the upper right, the solitary respondent who was interviewed at his original address in 1963, not interviewed in 1964, interviewed in 1966 but not registered at his original address, and not interviewed thereafter. As these examples suggest, the number of respondents who shared to the end a common field history is given by the frequency which appears (typically more than once) in the final box of a sequence. Thus, of the respondents who were interviewed for the first time in 1964 (see 'New R' for that year), 112 were re-interviewed at their original sample addresses both in 1966 and 1970, as shown by the frequency in the box at the foot of the chart.

The interviewing done in each period completed the information required for one or more of the samples. Thus, the interviewing in 1963

A.1 Size of Samples, 1963–70

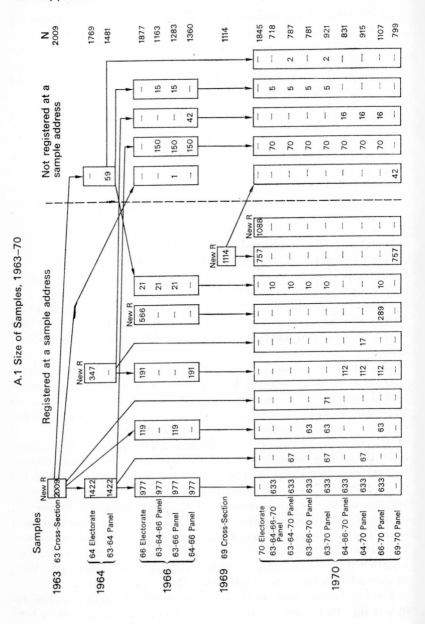

completed the information required for the '1963 cross-section' sample; the interviewing of hold-over respondents and newly selected respondents in 1964 completed the information required for the '1964 electorate' and '1963–64 panel' samples; and so on. In all cases except the 1963 and 1969 cross-section samples, the interviews needed in a given year to complete the information for a particular sample came from two or more distinct sets of respondents, as the chart indicates. For example, the information for the '1964 electorate' sample came both from respondents newly chosen in 1964 and from re-interviews of respondents who had been interviewed in 1963 and were still registered at their original sample addresses. And the information required to complete the '1963–64 panel' sample came both from the re-interviews of 1963 respondents who in 1964 were still registered at their original addresses and from the re-interviews of those who were not still registered at these addresses.

The contribution that each of several distinct sets of respondents makes to the size of a given sample can be seen at once by locating the row for the sample under the 'end year' in which the information for the sample was completed and looking at the frequencies which appear in this row within the several boxes to the right. The total size of the sample is given by the frequency in the column of N's at the extreme right. For example, the information for the '1964–66–70 panel' sample came from four sets of respondents with distinct interview histories: (1) 633 interviewed in 1963, 1964, 1966 and 1970 at their original sample addresses; (2) 112 newly chosen in 1964 and interviewed in 1964, 1966 and 1970 at their original addresses; (3) 70 interviewed at their original sample address in 1963 but re-interviewed in 1964, 1966 and 1970 at another address; and (4) 16 respondents newly chosen and interviewed at an original sample address in 1964 and re-interviewed at a different address in 1966 and 1970.

Response rates. No survey of a large national population ever achieves an interview with each of the people with whom it is wished to make contact. This fact matters little if the fraction of the sample which escapes interview is small. But as the fraction increases the possibility of serious bias must always be considered. If the persons who have not granted an interview differ from those who have, and if they constitute a substantial part of the whole, the findings obtained from the part of the sample interviewed will not be fully representative.

We therefore took steps to ensure as high a rate of response as was reasonably possible. The original interviewer was instructed to call at a sample address at least three times before accepting a failure to contact a respondent. Many interviews were in fact successfully made at a fourth or subsequent call. In addition, after an appreciable lapse of time, new interviewers were sent into areas in which non-response, either from refusal or non-contact, was relatively high. On the first round of interviews alone, this supplementary technique yielded more than one hundred and fifty respondents who had previously refused or who had not yet been contacted.

Table A.2 gives the proportion of our initial sample [1] which was interviewed in 1963, or interviewed for the first time in 1964 or 1966, as well as the proportion not interviewed in 1963, distributed across the several

A.2 Rate of Response with Original Sample

Names issued in May 1963		2560	
Dead by May 1963	30		
Premises empty or demolished	54		
Had moved away before contacted	165	249	
Interviews attempted with electors whose names had been issued		2311	
Interviews attempted with persons selected by enumeration process		218	
Total interviews attempted		2529	100·0%
Reasons for non-response in 1963			
Temporarily away	126		
Out or no reply	133		
Refused	217		
Too old or ill	33		
Other	11	520	
Total interviews obtained in 1963		2009	79·4%
Additional first interviews obtained in 1964		207	
Additional first interviews obtained in 1966		47	
Additional first interviews sought in 1970		—	
Total interviews obtained		2263	89·5%

possible reasons for non-response. For a non-governmental survey of a nationwide random sample involving interviews of an hour's length this rate of response is extraordinarily high. Indeed, the eventual response rate was only slightly below 90 per cent, although part of this total represents respondents who were originally selected in 1963 but not successfully interviewed until 1964 or 1966.

Substantially lower rates of response were achieved with the samples of the electorate qualified to vote in 1964 and 1966 [2 and 3], owing in part to the complexities of our longitudinal design. In 1969 when we approached an entirely fresh sample and in 1970 when once again we approached a new sample and the only re-interviews included in our electorate sample were from our 1969 respondents, the response rate rose. Presumably the bias which may have been introduced by the lessened response in 1964 and 1966 (and to a smaller extent in 1970) was partially offset by introduction of weights to eliminate in the panel element of these electorate samples the known effects of panel mortality. The basis and construction of these weights are explained below. The relative rates of response in our five electorate samples are shown in Table A.3.

A.3 Rates of Response with Electorate Samples

	1963	1964	1966	1969	1970
Total interviews attempted	2529	2590[a]	2682[a]	1425	2645
Total interviews obtained	2009	1769	1877	1114	1845[a]
Proportion obtained	79·4%	68·3%	70·0%	78·2%	69·8%

· [a] These totals include some potential respondents with whom interviews were not in fact sought for reasons of ill health or prior record of refusal.

Our panel samples [4 to 14 and 17] were subject to an additional source of non-response, the drop-out of respondents who could not be re-interviewed. No longitudinal study of a dispersed and mobile population escapes losses of this kind. By the standards of other national studies which have extended over comparable periods ours were not excessive. A nationwide re-interview study undertaken by the Oxford University Institute of Statistics in 1953–4 reported a panel survival rate of 66·1 per cent after a year's time, although that study made less effort than ours to trace people who had moved more than a short distance from their original addresses.[1] A national re-interview study of American electoral behaviour undertaken by the Survey Research Center of the University of Michigan achieved a survival rate of 70 per cent after twenty-six months and of 61 per cent after fifty months. A study of consumer behaviour undertaken by the Survey Research Center achieved a survival rate of 61 per cent after twenty-one months.[2]

[1] See P. Vandome, 'Aspects of the Dynamics of Consumer Behaviour', *Bulletin of the Oxford Institute of Statistics*, **20** (1958), 65–105 and T. P. Hill, L. R. Klein, and K. H. Straw, 'The Savings Survey 1953: Response Rates and Reliability of Data', Ibid., **17** (1955), 89–126.

[2] See Philip E. Converse, Angus Campbell, Warren E. Miller and Donald E. Stokes, 'Stability and Change in 1960: A Reinstating Election', *American Political Science Review*, **55** (1961), 269–80, and Marion Sobol, 'Panel Mortality, Panel Bias', *Journal of the American Statistical Association*, **54** (1959), 52–68.

The survival rates of four main interlocking panels of our own study are shown by Table A.4. Since anyone who drops out of a panel has given at least one interview we are able to study the bias due to this source by comparing the information given by the surviving panel and the full sample when the drop-outs were still in the project. In the case of our own panels, the results of such a comparison are distinctly reassuring. Over a wide range of characteristics the full sample interviewed in 1963 looked remarkably like the sub-sample of respondents who would survive the 1964 and 1966 interviews. For example, the proportion of men was 44·6 per cent in the full 1963 sample and 46·4 per cent in the 1963–4–6 panel; the proportion who had left school at age 15 or earlier was 81·9 per cent in the full

A.4 Survival Rates of Panels

	Original Sample[a]	Surviving Panel	Percent Surviving
1963–4 Panel	1982	1481	74·7%
1963–4–6 Panel	1945	1163	59·9%
1963–4–6–70 Panel	1722	718	41·7%
1969–70 Panel	1095	799	73·0%

[a] These base figures have been reduced by the number of initial respondents who were known to have died before the time of re-interview since this type of shrinkage affects population and sample alike and introduces no bias.

sample and 80·8 per cent in the panel; the proportion intending to vote Labour at the forthcoming General Election was 43·6 per cent in the full sample and 44·1 per cent in the panel. The clearest tendency towards bias appeared in the possession of political information. For example, the proportion who knew the name of their M.P. in the summer of 1963 was 50·9 per cent in the full sample but 56·3 per cent among those who were to survive in the three-year panel.

Over a seven-year period panel wastage may involve more serious biases. We therefore took comfort that the 921 survivors of the 1963 interviews whom we managed to contact in 1970 were within 3 per cent of the original sample in terms of sex, schooling and party allegiance.

This sort of diagnosis also supplies a partial cure. If we know how a panel differed from a full sample at some initial time we can apply weights to remove these known differences and, with them, many of the unknown but correlated differences which would appear at later interviews if the drop-outs remained in the study. Three initial differences are the basis of the weights we have applied. In the first place, we have taken account of the difference of survival rate between those who did and those who did not know at least three items of information in 1963 which seemed to form a cumulative scale in Guttman's sense. Next, we took account of the difference of survival rate between those who did and did not answer 'Don't know' to at least one of the issue questions which we put to our respondents in 1963. Finally, we took account of a very slight remaining difference of survival rate between men and women within the classes formed by crossing the first and second of these dimensions.

These differences of survival are summarized in Table A.5. The bias due to the factors which have defined the cells of the table can be removed by

A.5 Proportion of Original Sample Surviving
by Characteristics in 1963

	Knowledge of items of information			
	Knew three or more		Knew less than three	
	Replied to all questions on issues	Said don't know to at least one issue	Replied to all questions on issues	Said don't know to at least one issue
Men	70%	62%	61%	51%
Women	69%	64%	58%	50%

applying to the panel respondents a set of weights that is proportional to the inverse of these rates of survival. For this purpose we set the weight for men of high information and high attitude formation equal to 1·0 and have set the weight for each of the other groups proportionately higher. The weight for women of low information and low attitude formation, for example, was set at 1·4 since the proportion of this group surviving three interviews was only five-sevenths that of men with both high information and high attitude formation.

Table A.6 on the next page compares our three-interview panel with the full original sample before and after the application of these weights. The first two columns of the table make clear how remarkably little bias across a wide range of characteristics was introduced by the removal of 40 per cent of our initial respondents from the surviving panel. The third column shows the effect of the application of our weights in bringing the panel more nearly in line with the original sample. A weighting procedure exactly analogous to this was applied to each of our panels, with comparable results.

A.6 Comparison of Characteristics of Original Sample
with Unweighted and Weighted 1963–4–6 Panel

Characteristics in 1963	Original Sample[a]	Unweighted Panel	Weighted Panel
Social grades I–III	27·7%	28·2%	27·5%
Social grades IV–VI	69·7	69·3	70·2
Men	44·6	46·4	44·9
Left school before age 16	81·9	80·8	81·4
Follows politics very or fairly closely	47·8	50·5	48·2
Knows M.P.'s name	50·9	56·3	51·2
Read or heard about M.P.	30·0	33·0	30·0
Favours entry into Common Market	31·8	33·6	32·3
Favours more nationalization	24·2	25·3	24·7
Voted in 1959	78·6	80·6	79·6
Intending to vote Conservative	32·4	34·8	34·2
Intending to vote Labour	43·6	44·1	44·7
Labour 'lead' over Conservative	11·2	9·3	10·5

[a] Original sample reduced by removal of respondents who had died before 1966.

The weights calculated to reduce bias due to panel drop-out were allowed to influence the analysis of the 1964, 1966 and 1970 electorate samples as well. Since these electorate samples included parts of various of our panels, some of the non-response of these samples was comprised of people whom we had interviewed before. By applying the appropriate panel weights to the surviving panel element of these samples we could in effect weight those whom we did interview in the later year to represent those whom we did not. This is the sense in which we noted above that the somewhat higher non-response of the 1964, 1966 and 1970 electorate samples had been partially offset.

Repeated interviewing of the same respondents raises the possibility of 'contamination' of the panel, as well as of bias due to panel drop-out. The evidence on this sort of learning in comparable studies has, however, been generally negative.[1] Our design permitted us to compare our four-wave panel, weighted to correct for panel mortality, with the half-sample of the electorate we selected anew in 1970. Companions of the political interest and other characteristics of these two groups lent very little support to the idea that we had contaminated our long-term panelists by

[1] The most elaborate study of possible contamination in a political survey, one whose findings were also negative, is P. F. Lazarsfeld, B. Berelson and H. Gaudet, *The People's Choice*, New York, 1944.

repeated interviewing. How large the experience of being interviewed looms in the life of the average respondent is easily exaggerated. Many vignettes from what our respondents said illustrate how trifling an element of seven years of life four hours of casual conversation with one of our interviewers constituted.

Sampling error. A sample survey is liable to many errors which have nothing to do with sampling. Errors which arise from the failure to contact all potential respondents or from misleading answers being given to certain questions may indeed be far more serious than those which arise from choosing a sample to represent the population from which it is drawn. Nonetheless, those who report sample estimates owe their readers the means of judging the reliability of these estimates in a sampling sense. Explicit sample designs are meant not only to minimize sampling error; they are meant to furnish explicit estimates of its probable magnitude as well.

Unfortunately the estimation of sampling error is greatly complicated by modern developments of sample design. If we had drawn a simple random sample of the British electorate any reader acquainted with the formulas of an elementary statistics text could calculate the probable error of many of the figures reported in this book. But we should have paid dearly for such a simplification, since a simple random sample of the same cost would have to be much smaller in size and would yield sampling errors much larger than those of the multistage stratified design that we actually employed. The effects of the 'clustering' of respondents under such a design are mildly paradoxical. On the one hand, the sampling errors of a clustered design will in general be larger than those of a simple random sample of equal size.[1] But, on the other hand, the sampling errors of a clustered design will in general be smaller than those of a simple random sample of equal cost. The reason this is true is of course that an appropriate clustered design for sampling a large and dispersed population vastly reduces the unit cost of interviewing, yielding a larger sample and smaller sampling error for the same outlay of resources.

The formulas for sampling error under complex sample designs are, however, unfamiliar and difficult to apply. We therefore have set out in Tables A.7 and A.8 on the next three pages some average values of the sampling errors of percentage and differences of percentages calculated from the exact formulas appropriate to our design. Table A.7 gives the average value of the sampling error associated with percentages according to the

[1] See Leslie Kish, 'Confidence Intervals for Clustered Samples', *American Sociological Review,* **22** (1957), 154–65.

A.7 Approximate Sampling Error of Percentages[a]
(expressed in percentages)

Reported Percentages	Number of Interviews									
	2000	1500	1000	700	500	400	300	200	100	50
50	3·0	3·3	3·8	4·4	5·1	5·6	6·4	7·7	11	15
30 or 70	2·7	3·0	3·5	4·0	4·6	5·1	5·8	7·1	9·8	14
20 or 80	2·4	2·6	3·0	3·5	4·0	4·5	5·1	6·2	8·6	12
10 or 90	1·8	1·9	2·3	2·6	3·0	3·3	3·8	4·6	6·4	9·1
5 or 95	1·3	1·4	1·6	1·9	2·2	2·4	2·8	3·4	4·7	6·6

[a] The figures in this table represent *two* standard errors. Hence, for most items the chances are 95 out of 100 that the value being estimated lies within a range equal to the reported percentages, plus or minus the sampling error.

magnitude of the percentage and the size of the sample on which it is based, since the sampling error varies with both of these things. Under the assumption that the sample estimates are normally distributed, an assumption that is quite appropriate with samples of this size, an interval the width of the sampling error (two standard errors) on each side of the sample estimate has a chance of 19 in 20 of including the true value in the underlying population. Let us suppose that 50 per cent of 1000 newspaper readers within the sample are found to be 'very much' interested in politics and that we wish to know how much this sample estimate may vary around the percentage of newspaper readers who would be found to be very much interested in politics if we were able to interview all readers in Britain rather than a sample of 1000. By inspecting the row of Table A.7 for percentages of 50 and the column for samples of 1000 we find that the average sampling error associated with this combination is 3·8 per cent. Therefore, we may say that the interval from 46·2 to 53·8 has a chance of 19 in 20 of including the percentage of newspaper readers in the underlying population that would be found to be very much interested in politics.

Table A.8 gives the average value of the sampling error associated with a difference of two percentages according to the magnitude of the percentages and the size of the samples on which each percentage is based, since the sampling error varies with each of these things. Under the assumption that our sample estimates of these differences are normally distributed, an observed difference that is as large as the given value of the sampling error (two standard errors) has a chance of at least 19 in 20 of reflecting a real

A.8 Approximate Sampling Error of Differences[a]
(in percentages)

For Percentages from 35% to 65%

	2000	1500	1000	700	500	400	300	200	100	50
2000	4·2	4·4	4·8	5·3	5·9	6·3	7·0	8·3	11	16
1500		4·6	5·0	5·4	6·0	6·5	7·1	8·4	11	16
1000			5·3	5·8	6·3	6·7	7·4	8·6	11	16
700				6·2	6·7	7·1	7·7	8·9	12	16
500					7·1	7·5	8·1	9·2	12	16
400						7·9	8·5	9·5	12	16
300							9·0	10	12	17
200								11	13	17
100									15	19
50										22

For Percentages around 20% and 80%

	2000	1500	1000	700	500	400	300	200	100	50
2000	3·3	3·5	3·8	4·2	4·7	5·0	5·6	6·6	8·9	12
1500		3·7	4·0	4·3	4·8	5·2	5·7	6·7	9·0	12
1000			4·3	4·6	5·0	5·4	5·9	6·9	9·1	13
700				4·9	5·3	5·7	6·2	7·1	9·3	13
500					5·7	6·0	6·5	7·4	9·5	13
400						6·3	6·8	7·6	9·7	13
300							7·2	8·0	10	13
200								8·7	11	14
100									12	15
50										17

difference in the underlying populations rather than being a reflection of nothing more than the accidents of sampling. Let us suppose that we are interested in the difference between the 50 per cent of 1000 newspaper

A.8—continued

For Percentages around 10% and 90%

	2000	1500	1000	700	500	400	300	200	100	50
2000	2·5	2·6	2·9	3·2	3·5	3·8	4·2	4·9	6·7	9·3
1500		2·7	3·0	3·3	3·6	3·9	4·3	5·0	6·7	9·4
1000			3·2	3·5	3·8	4·0	4·4	5·1	6·8	9·4
700				3·7	4·0	4·2	4·6	5·3	7·0	9·5
500					4·3	4·5	4·9	5·5	7·1	9·6
400						4·7	5·1	5·7	7·3	9·7
300							5·4	6·0	7·5	9·9
200								6·5	7·9	10
100									9·1	11
50										13

For Percentages around 5% and 95%

	2000	1500	1000	700	500	400	300	200	100	50
2000	1·8	1·9	2·1	2·3	2·5	2·8	3·1	3·6	4·9	6·8
1500		2·0	2·2	2·4	2·6	2·8	3·1	3·6	4·9	6·8
1000			2·3	2·6	2·7	2·9	3·2	3·7	5·0	6·9
700				2·7	2·9	3·1	3·3	3·8	5·1	6·9
500					3·1	3·3	3·5	4·0	5·2	7·0
400						3·4	3·7	4·1	5·3	7·1
300							3·9	4·4	5·4	7·2
200								4·7	5·8	7·4
100									6·6	8·1
50										9·3

[a] The values shown are the differences required for significance (two standard errors) in comparisons of percentages derived from two *different* subgroups of the population.

readers who are very much interested in politics and the 35 per cent of 500 non-readers who are very much interested. By inspecting the part of Table A.8 that gives the sampling errors for the difference of two percentages that are in the 35–65 per cent range we find that the value in the row for one group of 1000 and the column for a second group of 500 is 6·3 per cent. Since the observed difference of 15 per cent is larger than this we may say that the chance is at least 19 in 20 that the observed difference reflects a greater interest on the part of readers that we would find if we interviewed all readers and non-readers rather than drawing a sample of 1000 of one and of 500 of the other.

We also give in Figure A.9 on the next page a graph of the relationship between the ratio of the sampling errors obtained from our actual sample and those from a simple random sample of equal size according to the size of the groups on which sample estimates are based. It will be observed that the magnitude of this ratio increases with the size of the group; the practical significance of the clustering of our observations becomes greater as the number of observations per cluster is greater.[1] The relationship between the value k of this ratio and the magnitude n of the group on which the sample estimate is based is fitted best in a least-squares sense by the line whose equation is

$$k = 1 \cdot 062 + 0 \cdot 000132 n. \tag{1}$$

This relationship provides a basis for interpolating sampling errors for cases which are intermediate between the values given by Tables A.7 and A.8. For a single percentage p based on a group of size n the mean sampling error of p is given by

$$2k \sqrt{\frac{p(1 - p)}{n - 1}} \tag{2}$$

Similarly, for a difference of two percentages p_1 and p_2 based on groups of size n_1 and n_2 the mean sampling error of $p_1 - p_2$ is given by

$$2k \sqrt{\frac{p_1(1 - p_1)}{n_1 - 1} + \frac{p_2(1 - p_2)}{n_2 - 1}}. \tag{3}$$

Explicit formulas are not available and new methods are only now emerging for calculating the sampling errors of more refined statistics such as correlation and regression coefficients under complex sample designs. Fortunately there is evidence that the errors of these statistics are less

[1] This assumes that the observations of a part-sample are distributed fairly well over all primary sampling units, rather than being concentrated in a restricted subset of the primary sampling units.

A.9 Ratio of Actual Mean Sampling Errors to Sampling Errors under Simple Random Sampling by Size of Groups on Which Estimates Are Based

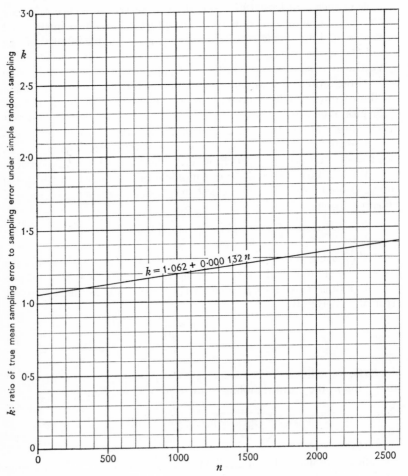

$k = 1.062 + 0.000\,132\,n$

n: Size of group on which sample estimate based

likely to be inflated by clustering than are the errors of ratio estimates.[1] Therefore, the reader is better able to apply the conventional formulas to the occasional values of such statistics that have entered our report, and we have in some cases given in the footnotes our own estimates of these errors.

[1] L. Kish and M. Frankel, 'Balanced Repeated Replications for Analytical Statistics', *Proceedings of the Social Statistics Section of the American Statistical Association, 1968*, Washington D.C., pp. 2–10.

APPENDIX B

Survey Questions 1963–70

IN the pages that follow we set out all the questions asked in our five surveys, indicating the years in which the questions were posed and the parts of the sample involved. The questions are arranged in subject groups and are not, for the most part, in the same order as they appeared in the original questionnaires. Those whom we first sought to interview in 1963 or 1969 but did not reach until 1964 or 1966 or until 1970 had some of the 1963 or 1969 questions put to them only and these are not recorded here.

Wherever possible we have interspersed the percentage distributions of replies in the text of the questions or below them. Since vastly more space would be required to give the distributions of replies coded from the 'free answer' questions, we have limited the percentages to the replies to the 'closed' questions in each questionnaire. In each case the distribution refers to the replies given by the sample of the electorate then qualified to vote (denoted as 1, 2, 3, 15 and 16 on pp. 432–3 and in Figure A.1 in the sampling appendix) rather than by any of the panels. We have not, for example, included responses from the 1963–70 panel in the 1970 percentages. In forming the percentage distributions we have deleted all cases which could not be coded as either a specific response or as 'don't know'. The base of any percentage is the part of the sample which replied to the question: either the whole sample (less those 'not ascertained') in the case of a question put to everyone, or the part-sample to which the question was put in the case of questions which were asked only of those who had given a specified reply to certain prior questions.

The questions are indexed under the following 52 heads:

1. Newspapers
2. Television, radio and conversation
3. Interest in politics
4. Party qualities
5. Party difference
6. Leader qualities
7. Secondary leaders

8. Party images
9. Feeling thermometer
10. Most important problems
11. Party competence
12. Economic competence
13. Economic problems
14. Economic well-being
15. Taxes, pensions, social services
16. Business power
17. Trade unions
18. Strikes
19. Nationalization
20. Immigration
21. Common Market
22. America
23. Empire
24. Nuclear weapons
25. Rhodesia
26. Death penalty
27. Queen
28. Railways
29. Housing
30. London
31. Modernity
32. Democratic responsiveness
33. Left and right
34. Political antecedents
35. Partisanship of associates
36. Party identification
37. Past voting
38. Current voting
39. Voting intention
40. Local election voting
41. Expectations about result
42. Political activity
43. Knowledge of M.P./candidates
44. Social class
45. Union membership
46. Parental background
47. Personal background
48. Religion
49. Education
50. Emigration
51. Personal housing
52. Household composition and occupational details

The surveys in which any question was asked are indicated by the following superscripts.

63 64 66 69 70 – asked of all respondents.
63a 64a 66a 69a 70a – asked of one of two random halves of all respondents.
70b – asked only of panel respondents first interviewed 1963–6.
70c – asked of all except 1963–6 panel.
70d – asked only of 1963–6 panel if they had said Government made a difference to well-being.
70e – asked only of 1969–70 panel.
70f – asked of random half of new 1970 sample.
70g – asked of all except random half of new 1970 sample.
70h – asked only of new 1970 sample.
70i – asked only of random half of panel respondents first interviewed 1963–6.

Index of Questions

Wording and Responses

1. *Newspapers*

a. Do you read a morning newspaper regularly? *If yes* Which newspaper is that? Are there any other morning newspapers you read regularly?[63 64 66 69 70]

b. Do you follow news about politics much in [name of newspaper]?[63 69]

c. Did you follow the election campaign in [name of newspaper]?[64 66 70]

d. Did you follow the election campaign in any other newspaper? What newspaper was that?[63 66 70]

	63	69	64	66	70
Reads paper	77	72	81	78	71
Follows politics/campaign	49	43	72	64	70
Follows campaign in other paper	—	—	27	28	31

e. When did you begin to read [name of newspaper] regularly?[63] Did you stop reading [name of newspaper] any time after that?[63] What do you especially like in [name of newspaper]?[63] Do you like the way news about politics is handled in [name of newspaper], do you dislike it, or doesn't it make much difference to you?[63] Do you think that [name of newspaper] tends to favour any particular party? What party is that?[63]

f. If stopped reading newspaper at any time When was that?[63] When was the last time you weren't reading [name of newspaper] regularly?[63]

g. If second morning newspaper mentioned. When did you begin to read [name of newspaper] regularly?[63] Did you stop reading [name of newspaper] any time after that?[63]

h. What do you especially like in [name of newspaper]?[63] Do you follow news about politics much in [name of newspaper]?[63] Do you like the way news about politics is handled in [name of newspaper], do you dislike it, or doesn't it make much difference to you?[63] Do you think that [name of newspaper] tends to favour any particular party? What party is that?[63]

i. If stopped reading newspaper at any time When was that?[63] When was the last time you weren't reading [name of newspaper] regularly?[63]

j. Do you follow news about politics much in any evening or Sunday newspaper? (Yes 26%) *If yes* Which is that? Any others?[63]

2. *Television, Radio and Conversation*

a. Do you follow news about politics much on television? (Yes 55%[63], 49%[69])

b. Did you follow the election campaign on television? (Yes 75%[64], 72%[66], 66%[70]) *If yes*[64] [66] Were there any programmes about the election campaign which you found specially interesting? Which were they?

c. Do you follow news about politics much on the radio? (Yes 19%[63], 17%[69])

d. Did you follow the election campaign on the radio? (Yes 24%[64], 20%[66], 24%[70])

e. Do you talk much about politics to other people (Yes 27%[63], 32%[69]) *If yes* [63]Who do you talk to about politics? Anyone else?

f. Did you talk to other people about the election campaign? (Yes 59%[64], 63%[66], 70%[70]) *If yes* [64]Who do you talk to about the campaign? Anyone else?

    g. If follows politics[63] (*campaign*[64]) *by more than one medium* [63] [64]Of all the ways that you follow[63] (followed[64]) news about politics, which one would you say you got the most information from?

3. *Interest in Politics*

a. How much interest do you generally have in what's going on in politics – a good deal, some, or not much?[63] [69] How much interest did you have in the campaign – a good deal, some, or not much?[64] [66] [70]

	63	69	64	66	70
Good deal	16	17	34	31	38
Some	37	39	36	36	33
Not much	47	44	30	33	29

b. How much attention do you generally pay to what's going on in politics when there isn't an election? Would you say you generally follow politics very closely (11%), fairly closely (37%), or not much at all (52%)?[63]

c. Would you say that you usually care a good deal which party wins a general election (66%) or that you don't care very much which party wins (31%)? (DK 3%)[69]

4. *Party Qualities*

a. Is there anything in particular that you like about the Conservative Party? What is that? Anything else?[63] [64] [66] [69] [70]

b. Is there anything in particular that you don't like about the Conservative Party? What is that? Anything else?[63] [64] [66] [69] [70]

c. Is there anything in particular that you like about the Labour Party? What is that? Anything else?[63 64 66 69 70]

d. Is there anything in particular that you don't like about the Labour Party? What is that? Anything else?[63 64 66 69 70]

e. Is there anything in particular that you like about the Liberal Party? What is that? Anything else?[63]

f. Is there anything in particular that you don't like about the Liberal Party? What is that? Anything else?[63]

5. *Party Difference*

a. Considering everything the parties stand for, would you say that there is a good deal of difference between the parties, some difference, or not much difference?[63 64 66 69 70]

	63	64	66	69	70
Good deal	36	46	42	29	32
Some	20	23	26	22	27
Not much	34	26	29	44	38
DK	10	5	3	5	3

b. *If has opinion* Do you think that there's more difference between the Labour and Conservative parties than a few years ago, less difference, or about the same difference?[69 70]

	More	Same	Less	DK
69	28	27	33	12
70	20	37	33	10

c. Do you think there once was a time when there was more of a difference between the parties than there is now? (Yes 48%, No 27%, DK 25%)[63] *If thinks there was more of a difference than now*[63] When was that? And when do you think the parties came closer together?

6. *Leader Qualities*

a. Now I would like to ask you about the good and bad points of the party leaders.[63 64 66 69 70]

b. Is there anything in particular that you like about Harold Macmillan[63] (Sir Alec Douglas-Home[64]) (Edward Heath[66 69 70])? Anything else?

c. Is there anything in particular that you don't like about Harold Mac-Millan[63] (Sir Alec Douglas-Home[64]) (Edward Heath[66 69 70])? Anything else?

d. Is there anything in particular that you like about Harold Wilson? Anything else?[63] [64] [66] [69] [70]

e. Is there anything in particular that you don't like about Harold Wilson? Anything else?[63] [64] [66] [69] [70]

f. Is there anything in particular that you like about Jo Grimond? Anything else?[63]

g. Is there anything in particular that you don't like about Jo Grimond? Anything else?[63]

h. Would you like to see Mr Heath replaced as leader of the Conservative Party?[69] (Yes 41%)

i. Would you like to see Mr Wilson replaced as leader of the Labour Party?[69] (Yes 24%)

7. *Secondary Leaders*

a. Apart from Macmillan[63] (Home[64], Heath[70b]), how do you feel about the other Conservative leaders? Do you generally like them, dislike them, or don't you have much feeling about them?

b. Apart from Wilson, how do you feel about the other Labour leaders? Do you generally like them, dislike them, or don't you have much feeling about them?[63] [64] [70b]

	Con. Leaders			Lab. Leaders		
	63	64	70b	63	64	70b
Like	21	28	36	23	27	30
Dislike	11	10	7	13	16	17
Indifferent	59	54	53	55	47	49
DK	9	8	4	9	10	4

c. Apart from Heath, do you happen to remember the names of any other leading Conservative figures active today? Anyone else?[69] [70e]

d. Apart from Wilson, do you happen to remember the names of any other leading Labour figures active today? Anyone else?[69] [70e]

8. *Party Images*

a. Here is a list of twelve pairs of words and phrases you might use to describe political parties, and between each pair is a measuring stick of seven squares. Taking the first pair of words – i.e. 'Out of date/ Modern' – as an example, the square on the extreme left would mean that the party concerned is very out of date, the next square would mean it was fairly out of date, and so on. The words at the top of your card will help you to choose the square you think is appropriate. Now will you tell me which square you would use to describe the (Conservative Party) (Labour Party) (Liberal Party)?[63a 64a 66a 69a 70a]

	Very	Fairly	Slightly	Neither	Slightly	Fairly	Very	
Out of date	☐	☐	☐	☐	☐	☐	☐	Modern
Expert	☐	☐	☐	☐	☐	☐	☐	Clumsy
Powerful	☐	☐	☐	☐	☐	☐	☐	Weak
Foolish	☐	☐	☐	☐	☐	☐	☐	Wise
Middle class	☐	☐	☐	☐	☐	☐	☐	Working class
United	☐	☐	☐	☐	☐	☐	☐	Split
Bad	☐	☐	☐	☐	☐	☐	☐	Good
Left wing	☐	☐	☐	☐	☐	☐	☐	Right wing
Weak-minded	☐	☐	☐	☐	☐	☐	☐	Strong-minded
Honest	☐	☐	☐	☐	☐	☐	☐	Dishonest
Dull	☐	☐	☐	☐	☐	☐	☐	Exciting
Young	☐	☐	☐	☐	☐	☐	☐	Old

9. *Feeling Thermometer*

a. There is a slightly different way that I want to ask you how you feel towards certain places or people. This card has what we call a 'feeling thermometer'. (*Interviewer hands card to respondent.*) If you don't know too much about one of the places or people that I'm going to ask you about, or don't feel particularly warm or cold towards them, then you should place them in the middle, at the 50° mark. If you have warm

		Average temperature 1969	1970
(i)	The Queen and Royal Family	77	78
(ii)	Unofficial strikers	20	22
(iii)	The B.B.C.	63	—
(iv)	The Common Market	46	38
(v)	Harold Wilson	45	56
(vi)	The Liberal Party	48	53
(vii)	The upper classes	50	—
(viii)	Coloured immigrants	54	38
(ix)	Edward Heath	53	58
(x)	Scottish Nationalists	42	41
(xi)	Barbara Castle	45	—
(xii)	Civil servants	51	—
(xiii)	The Commonwealth	65	65
(xiv)	The working classes	74	74
(xv)	Enoch Powell	57	59
(xvi)	America	58	—
(xvii)	The Conservative Party	61	61
(xviii)	Trade unions	49	50
(xix)	Roy Jenkins	46	—
(xx)	Comprehensive schools	61	62
(xxi)	The Labour Party	48	57
(xxii)	The police	79	82
(xxiii)	The middle classes	63	65
(xxiv)	London	67	—
(xxv)	Jeremy Thorpe	—	58
(xxvi)	Parliament	—	73
(xxvii)	Other Labour leaders	—	51
(xxviii)	Other Conservative leaders	—	56

feeling towards them, you should give them a score somewhere between 50° and 100° depending on how warm your feeling is. On the other hand, if you don't feel very favourable towards them you should place them somewhere between the 0° and 50° mark. First of all, I would like to ask you your feeling towards the Queen and Royal Family. Where would you place the Queen and the Royal Family on the thermometer according to your feeling towards it?[69 70]

10. *Most Important Problems*

a. What do you yourself feel are the most important problems the Government should do something about? Anything else?[63 69 70c]

b. First problem mentioned. What would you like to see the Government do about that? Which party would be the most likely to do what you want on this, the Conservatives, Labour, the Liberals, or wouldn't it make much difference?

c. Second problem mentioned. What would you like to see the Government do about that? Which party would be the most likely to do what you want on this, the Conservatives, Labour, the Liberals, or wouldn't it make much difference?

d. Third problem mentioned. What would you like to see the Government do about that? Which party would be the most likely to do what you want on this, the Conservatives, Labour, the Liberals, or wouldn't it make much difference?

e. What issues did you yourself feel were most important in this election?[66]

11. *Party Competence*

a. Which party would be[64 66] (is generally[69 70]) better able to handle foreign affairs, the Conservatives, Labour, or wouldn't there be[64 66] (isn't there[69 70]) any difference between them on this?

	64	66	69	70
Conservatives	46	38	50	46
Labour	16	22	8	16
No difference	20	29	29	28
DK	18	11	13	10

b. Which party would be[64 66] (is generally[69 70]) better able to handle problems here at home, the Conservatives or Labour, or wouldn't there be[64 66] (isn't there[69 70]) any difference between them on this?

	64	66	69	70
Conservatives	27	24	38	34
Labour	44	46	22	28
No difference	17	24	31	31
DK	12	6	9	7

12. *Economic Competence*

a. Speaking (more[66] [70]) generally, how satisfied are you with the (Labour[70]) Government's handling of Britain's economic affairs?

	66	69	70
Satisfied	50	23	47
Neutral/DK	28	18	22
Dissatisfied	22	59	31

b. Do you think that Britain's economic difficulties are mainly the fault of the Labour Government or of the last Conservative Government?[66] [69] [70] *Unless DK* In what way?[69]

	66	69	70
Labour	13	29	25
Both equally	30	38	29
Conservative	43	21	33
DK	14	12	13

13. *Economic Problems*

a. Britain has had a lot of economic difficulties in the last few years. What measures do you think are needed to put the country right economically? Anything else?[69]

b. What do you think Britain has to do to pay her way internationally? Is there anything else?[69]

c. Some people say that prices will go on rising no matter who's in power. Others think that the Government can do a lot to check rising prices. What do you think?[70c] (Go on rising 40%, Government can do a lot 55%, DK 5%)

d. Which party would you say would be best at keeping prices steady, the Conservatives or Labour, or wouldn't there be any difference between them on this?[70c] (Con 41%, Lab. 12%, no difference 41%, DK 6%)

e. People talk about unemployment. Have you or anyone in your immediate family been worried about losing their job in the last year or so? (Yes 19%[69] 16%[70c])

f. Would you say unemployment is a special problem in this area? (Yes 22%[69] 24%[70c])

g. Some people say that if you have full employment you can't keep prices steady. That is, the country can have full employment or steady prices but not both. Do you think this is true?[69] [70g]

	Yes	No	DK
69	22	52	26
70g	25	60	15

If has opinion Why is that?[69]

h. Suppose it were true, that you couldn't keep unemployment down and keep prices steady, which of the two would you rather have?[69] [70g]

	Unemployment down	*Steady prices*	*Both*	*DK*
69	48	38	9	5
70g	48	41	6	5

i. We'd also like your opinion about handling the problems of unemployment and rising prices. Do you think that having everyone employed makes it more difficult to hold prices steady, or don't you think that having everyone employed makes it more difficult to hold prices steady? If you don't have an opinion about this just say so.[70f] (More difficult 28%, not more difficult 44%, DK 28%)

j. Suppose the Government had to choose between keeping everyone in employment and holding prices steady, which do you think it should choose?[70f] (Full employment 49%, steady prices 41%, DK 10%)

k. Some people say there's got to be some control over wage and salary increases if the national economy is to be got right. Others are against any control of wages and salaries. Which do you tend to agree with?[69] [70c]
If has opinion Why do you feel that way?[69]

	Some control	*No control*	*DK*
69	66	26	8
70c	75	19	6

14. *Economic Well-Being*

a. We are also interested in how well off people are these days. How about you? Compared with three or four years ago[63] (a year ago[64] [66]) (two or three years ago[69] [70]), are you and your family better off now, worse off, or have you stayed about the same?

	63	*64*	*66*	*69*	*70*
Better off	33	22	22	28	29
About the same	46	61	55	40	44
Worse off	21	17	23	32	27

If better or worse off Why is that?[63]

b. Now looking ahead over the next three or four years[63] [64] [66] (next year or two[69] [70]) do you think that you will be better off, worse off, or will you stay about the same?

	63	64	66	69	70
Better off	24	30	26	21	31
About the same	48	40	45	44	45
Worse off	9	11	19	24	14
DK	19	19	10	11	10

If better or worse off Why is that?[63]

c. Do you think that what the Government does makes any difference to how well off you are?

	63	66	69	70
Makes difference	62	70	67	71
Does not make difference	28	26	28	25
DK	10	4	5	4

If yes[63] [66] *All respondents*[69] [70]

d. Has (did[70]) the Conservative[63] (Labour[66] [69] [70]) Government made (make[70]) you better or worse off or hasn't it made much difference?

	63	66	69	70
Better off	27	18	10	17
Worse off	17	24	34	29
No difference	51	56	52	52
DK	5	2	4	2

If government makes a difference[63] [66] [70d]

e. If a Labour Government comes in would you be better or worse off, or won't it make much difference?[63] Looking ahead, do you think that the Labour Government will make you better or worse off or won't it make much difference?[66]

f. If a Conservative Government had come in would it have made you better or worse off or wouldn't it have made much difference?[66]

  All respondents[69] [70c]

g. If a Conservative Government came in, would it make you better or worse off or wouldn't it make much difference?[69]

h. Now that a Conservative Government has come in, do you think that it will make you better or worse off or won't it make much difference?[70c]

	63 Lab.	66 Lab.	66 Con.	69 Con.	70c Con.
Better off	22	30	18	22	32
Worse off	18	29	18	7	8
No difference	36	30	53	52	47
DK	24	11	11	19	13

i. Do you think the fact that Labour won the election will make any difference to how well off you are?[64] (Yes 38% No 47% DK 15%)

15. *Taxes, Pensions, Social Services*

a. If the Government had a choice between reducing taxes and spending more on the social services, which should it do?[63 66 69 70]

	63	66	69	70
Tax cuts	52	55	69	65
Social service increases	41	36	21	27
DK	7	9	10	8

b. Do you feel that the Government should spend more on pensions and social services or do you feel that spending for social services should stay about as it is now?[64 66 69 70g]

	64	66	69	70g
More	77	55	(43)	(56)*
As now	20	41	(52)†	(40)‡
DK	3	4	(5)	(4)

* More 39%, more on pensions 17%.
† As now 44%, less 8%.
‡ As now 36%, less 4%.

c. If has opinion[64 66 69 70g] Which party would be more likely to spend more on pensions and social services, the Conservatives or Labour, or wouldn't there be any difference between them on this?[64 66 69 70g]

	64	66	69	70g
Conservatives more	8	7	18	17
Labour more	69	64	46	48
No difference	16	23	29	29
DK	7	6	7	6

d. Do you feel that the Government should spend more on old-age pensions (77%) or do you feel that spending on pensions should stay about as it is (19%) (spend less 1%, DK 4%)[70f]

e. Which party would be more likely to spend more on old-age pensions, the Conservatives (19%), or Labour (39%), or wouldn't there be any difference between them (31%)? (DK 11%)[70f]

f. Do you feel that the Government should spend more on other social services (36%) or do you feel that spending on other social services should stay about as it is (48%)? (spend less 9%, DK 7%)[70f]

g. Which party would be more likely to spend more on other social services, the Conservatives (14%), or Labour (41%), or wouldn't there be any difference between them (32%)? (DK 13%)[70f]

16. *Business Power*

a. Do you think that big business has too much power in this country (or don't you think it has too much power[63]) or not ?[64] [66] [70]

	63	64	66	69	70
Too much	59	54	55	48	48
Not too much	25	29	32	37	38
DK	16	17	13	15	14

17. *Trade Unions*

a. Do you think that the trade unions have too much power or not ?[63] [64] [66] [69] [70]

	63	64	66	69	70
Too much	53	54	64	64	66
Not too much	31	32	25	25	24
DK	16	14	11	11	10

b. Do you think that the trade unions should have close ties to the Labour Party or do you think that the trade unions should stay out of politics ?[63] [64] [66] [69] [70g]

	63	64	66	69	70g
Close ties	25	19	16	16	17
Stay out of politics	60	69	74	72	72
DK	15	12	10	12	11

c. Do you think the trade unions should have close ties to the Labour Party (17%) or do you think the trade unions shouldn't have ties to a party (69%)? (DK 14%)[70f]

18. *Strikes*

a. How serious a problem do you think strikes are, very serious, fairly serious, or not very serious ?[64] [66] [69] [70]

	64	66	69	70
Very serious	78	77	81	84
Fairly	14	16	14	12
Not very serious	6	6	4	3
DK	2	1	1	1

b. When you hear of a strike are your sympathies generally for or against the strikers ?[64] [66] [69] [70]

	64	66	69	70
For	13	15	14	11
Against	47	60	56	46
Depends/DK	40	25	30	43

c. Which party do you think has the better approach to strikes, the Conservatives, or Labour, or don't you think there is much difference between them on this?[64] [66] [69] [70]

	64	66	69	70
Conservatives	10	11	22	23
Labour	32	31	20	20
No difference	43	51	49	45
DK	15	7	9	12

19. *Nationalization*

a. There's a lot of talk about nationalizing industry. Which of these statements comes closest to what you yourself feel should be done? If you don't have an opinion about this, just say so.[63] [64] [66] [70b]

	63	64	66	70b
(i) A lot more industries should be nationalized	10	8	8	10
(ii) Only a few more industries, such as steel, should be nationalized	14	17	17	9
(iii) No more industries should be nationalized but the industries that are nationalized now should stay nationalized	36	45	42	40
(iv) Some of the industries that are nationalized now should be denationalized	22	18	19	29
(v) No opinion/don't know	18	12	14	12

If has opinion Which party would be more likely to nationalize some more industry, the Conservatives ($4\%^{63}$, $6\%^{64}$) or Labour ($90\%^{63}$, $90\%^{64}$) or wouldn't there be any difference between them on this ($4\%^{63}$, $2\%^{64}$)? (DK $2\%^{63}$, $2\%^{64}$)

20. *Immigration*

a. Do you think too many immigrants have been let into this country or not?[63] [64] [66] [69] [70g]

	63	64	66	69	70g
Too many	83	81	81	87	85
Not too many	12	13	14	10	10
DK	5	6	5	3	5

b. If yes too many[64] [66] *If has opinion*[69] [70g]. How strongly do you feel about this? Very strongly, fairly strongly, or not very strongly?[64] [66] [69] [70g]

	64	66	69	70g
Very strongly	52	54	56	50
Fairly strongly	34	33	30	34
Not very strongly	14	13	14	16

c. Is it a problem around this neighbourhood?[64 66 69 70e] (around here[70h])?

	64	66	69	70e	70h
Yes	14	13	12	12	12

d. Which party is more likely to keep immigrants out, the Conservatives, or Labour, or don't you feel there is much difference between them on this?[64 66 69 70]

	64	66	69	70
Conservatives	26	26	50	57
Labour	19	13	6	4
No difference	41	53	36	33
DK	14	8	8	6

e. Do you think that the number of immigrants that have been let into this country is all right or not? Have there been too many or too few let in?[70f] (All right 22%, too many 74%, too few 1%, DK 3%)

f. If has opinion[70f] How strongly do you feel about this? Very strongly (49%), fairly strongly (34%), or not very strongly (15%). DK (2%)

g. Do you generally approve (49%) or disapprove (29%) of laws to prevent discrimination against coloured immigrants, or don't you have an opinion on this (22%)?[69]

h. If has opinion Which party do you think is more likely to support laws to prevent discrimination against coloured immigrants, the Conservatives (21%) or Labour (28%), or don't you think there is much difference between them on this (42%)? DK (9%)[69]

i. There are 50 million people living in this country. Do you know how many of them are coloured?[70h] (Under 1m. (6%), 1m.–2·5m. (15%), 2·5m.–10m. (13%), over 10m. (15%), other reply (2%), DK (49%))

j. Looking back over the past ten years, do you think that the presence of coloured people in this country has brought any changes in our national way of life? (Yes 39%) What changes?[70h]

k. Which of these statements comes closest to what you yourself feel should be done about immigrants?[70h]

(*Show card*)

Britain should:

(i) Assist in sending immigrants home (20%).

(ii) Stop further immigration but allow immigrants already here to stay (50%).

(iii) Allow in immediate families of immigrants already here and a few skilled workers only (22%).

(iv) Allow in new workers and their families (4%).

(v) Allow free entry (2%).
    DK, no opinion (2%).

l. Which of these statements do you think comes closest to the Labour Party's position?[70h]
(*Show card*)
   Britain should:
   (i)   Assist in sending immigrants home (4%).
   (ii) Stop further immigration but allow immigrants already here to stay (19%).
   (iii) Allow in immediate families of immigrants already here and a few skilled workers only (30%).
   (iv) Allow in new workers and their families (23%).
   (v)   Allow free entry (10%).
         DK, no opinion (14%).

m. Which of these statements do you think comes closest to the Conservative Party's position?[70h]
(*Show card*)
   Britain should:
   (i)   Assist in sending immigrants home (22%).
   (ii) Stop further immigration but allow immigrants already here to stay (36%).
   (iii) Allow in immediate families of immigrants already here and a few skilled workers only (19%).
   (iv) Allow in new workers and their families (6%).
   (v)   Allow free entry (2%).
         DK, no opinion (15%).

n. Have you heard anything about Enoch Powell's proposals on immigration?[70h] (Yes 75%) *If yes*

o. Which of these statements do you think comes closest to his position?
(*Show card*)
   Britain should:
   (i)   Assist in sending immigrants home (76%).
   (ii) Stop further immigration but allow immigrants already here to stay (20%).
   (iii) Allow in immediate families of immigrants already here and a few skilled workers only (2%).
   (iv) Allow in new workers and their families (0%).
   (v)   Allow free entry (0%).
         DK, no opinion (2%).

p. Were you glad (78%) or sorry (16%) Powell spoke out on immigration?[70h] (DK 6%).

21. *Common Market*

a. Were you generally glad (30%) or sorry (26%) that Britain didn't go into the Common Market, or don't you have an opinion on that (44%)?[63]

b. If the question of going into the Common Market comes up again, do you think that Britain should go in, stay out, or don't you have an opinion on that?[63 64 66 69]
Do you think that Britain should go into the Common Market, stay out, or don't you have an opinion on that?[70]

	63	64	66	69	70
Go in	32	33	54	34	18
Stay out	29	32	17	41	58
DK	39	35	29	25	24

c. If has opinion Which party would be more likely to take Britain into the Common Market, if the question comes up again, the Conservatives or Labour, or would there be any difference between them on this?[64 66 70]
d. Which party do you feel is most in favour of taking Britain into the Common Market, the Conservatives or Labour, or isn't there any difference between them on that?[69]

	64	66	69	70
Conservative	44	57	22	38
Labour	22	16	32	13
No difference	21	23	39	42
DK	13	4	7	7

e. If stay out or don't know[70c] Do you think it's right for Britain to negotiate to find out what the terms are? (Yes 83% No 11% DK 6%)

22. *America*

a. How close do you feel Britain's ties with America should be, very close, fairly close, not very close?[63 66 70b]

	63	66	70b
Very close	36	38	38
Fairly close	38	47	43
Not very close	19	12	15
DK	7	3	4

23. *Empire*

a. Do you think Britain gave up her Empire too fast, or not?[63 66 70b]

	63	66	70b
Too fast	41	43	52
Not too fast	38	38	31
DK	21	19	17

24. *Nuclear Weapons*

a. There's a lot of talk these days about[63] [64] [66] (We're interested in your views about 70b) nuclear weapons. Which of these statements comes closest to what you yourself feel should be done? If you don't have an opinion (about this[63]) just say so.[63] [64] [66] [70b]

	63	64	66	70b
(i) Britain should keep her own nuclear weapons, independent of other countries	34	40	33	26
(ii) Britain should have nuclear weapons only as a part of a western defence system	42	42	46	50
(iii) Britain should have nothing to do with nuclear weapons under any circumstances	15	10	14	16
(iv) No opinion/don't know	9	8	7	8

b. If has opinion Which party would be more likely to keep nuclear weapons for Britain, the Conservatives ($72\%^{64}$ $42\%^{66}$), or Labour ($8\%^{64}$ $10\%^{66}$), or wouldn't there be any difference between them on this ($13\%^{64}$ $36\%^{66}$)? (DK $7\%^{64}$ $12\%^{66}$)

25. *Rhodesia*

a. Which of these statements comes closest to what you yourself feel should be done about Rhodesia? If you don't have an opinion just say so.[66] [70b] (*Show card*)

	66	70b
(i) Grant independence on the terms Ian Smith wants	5	9
(ii) Negotiate a settlement with Smith's Government	40	47
(iii) Go on using economic sanctions until Smith gives in	29	19
(iv) Use force against Smith's Government	8	7
(v) No opinion/Don't know	18	18

b. If has opinion[66] Which of these statements do you think comes closest to the Labour Party's position?[66] Which of these statements comes closest to the Conservative Party's position?[66]

26. *Death Penalty*

a. Would you like[63] (did you want[66] [69] [70]) to see the death penalty kept or abolished?

	63	66	69	70
Kept	71	77	74	69
Abolished	20	17	19	16
DK	9	6	7	15

27. *Queen*

a. How important do you yourself feel the Queen and Royal Family are to Britain – very important, fairly important, or not very important?[63] [64] [66] [69] [70]

	63	64	66	69	70
Very important	63	61	58	54	55
Fairly important	22	25	26	18	27
Not very important	14	13	16	27	18
DK	1	1	—	1	—

28. *Railways*

a. Have you heard anything about Dr Beeching's proposals for changing the railways?[63] (Yes 91%) *If yes* Do you think these changes should be made in the railways (52%) or not (39%)?[63] (Mixed 3%, DK 6%) Why is that?

29. *Housing*

a. Some people say that council house tenants get things too easy; others disagree. Which do you think?[69] (Too easy 26%, Disagree 60%, DK 14%)

30. *London*

a. Some people think that government is too much centralized in London. Others are quite content with things as they are. What do you think?[69] [70]

	69	70
Too centralized	36	36
Content	55	58
DK	9	6

31. *Modernity*

a. Do you generally like to see things modern and up to date (67%) or do you think that well-tried, traditional things (22%) are generally better?[63] (Half and half 3%, DK 8%)

32. *Democratic Responsiveness*

a. Over the years how much do you feel the government pays attention to what people think when it decides what to do?[63] [69] Why is that?[63]

	Good deal	Some	Not much	DK
63	8	20	50	22
69	9	19	61	11

b. Over the years do you think that having political parties makes the government pay attention to what people think?[63] [64] [66] [69] Why is that?[63] [64] [69]

	Good deal	Some	Not much	DK
63	21	29	16	34
64	17	16	28	39
66	19	30	40	11
69	23	25	26	26

c. (Over the years[64] [66]) how much do you think that having elections makes government pay attention to what the people think?[63] [64] [66] [69] [70]. Why is that?[63] [64] [69]

	Good deal	Some	Not much	DK
63	46	26	9	19
64	35	18	22	25
66	42	24	26	8
69	46	26	16	12

d. Over the years do you think that control of government should pass from one party to another every so often or do you think that its all right for one party to have control for a long time? [63] [64] [66] [69] [70]

	Alternate	One party	DK
63	54	32	14
64	58	30	12
66	54	36	10
69	56	34	10
70	59	34	7

How strongly do you feel about this?[63] [69]

	Very strongly	Fairly strongly	Not very strongly
63	45	43	12
69	44	42	14

e. Did you feel before this election that the Labour Government had been in office long enough to have had a fair trial?[66] (Yes 26%, No 71%, DK 3%)

f. How much attention do you think most M.P.s pay to the people who elect them when they decide what to do in Parliament?[63] [69]

	Good deal	Some	Not much	DK
63	14	27	32	27
69	18	32	36	14

33. *Left and Right*

a. Do you ever think of yourself as being to the left, the centre or the right in politics or don't you think of yourself in this way? *If yes* Where would you say you are?

	63	64	66
Thinks in these terms	25	28	27
Does not think in these terms	69	65	66
DK	6	7	7
Left	33	32	29
Centre	33	40	44
Right	33	28	26
(Other)	1	—	1

b. *If yes* Do you think you have moved to the left or right recently or don't you think of yourself as having moved? (Has moved 33%[64] 21%[66])

c. Do you ever think of the parties as being to the left, the centre, or to the right in politics, or don't you think of the parties that way?[63] [64] [66] (*If yes*) Which party would you say is farthest to the left?[63] And which party is farthest to the right?[63] *If two parties now named* And where would you put the [party not yet named]. Would you say the [third party just named] is closer to [first party named] or [second party named]?[63]

d. *If thinks of parties in this way* What do you have in mind when you say a party is to the left or to the right?[63] What is it about a party that would make you think of it as to the left or to the right?[64]

e. Do you think of any party as having moved to the left or right recently (48%[64] 55%[66]) or don't you think of any party as having moved in this way? *If party has moved* Which party is that? How has it moved?

f. Do you think of any other party as having moved in this way[64] (to the left or right recently[66])? Which party is that?[64] [66] How has it moved?[64] [66] When would you say it moved?[66]

34 *Political Antecedents*

a. Do you remember when you were young whether your father was very much interested in politics, somewhat interested, or didn't he pay much attention to it? Did he have any particular preference for one of the parties when you were young? Which party was that?[63] [69] [70] What was the main reason he felt that way?[63] [69] [70]

	Very int.	Fairly	Not very	DK	Con.	Lab.	Lib.	0th	None	DK
63	30	28	26	16	27	31	13	1	7	21
69	27	31	30	12	29	37	10	1	7	16
70	32	31	25	12	27	39	12	1	4	17

b. How about your mother? When you were young, was she very much interested in politics, somewhat interested, or didn't she pay much attention to it? Did she have any particular preference for one of the parties when you were young? Which party was that?[63] [69] [70] What was the main reason she felt that way?[63]

	Very int.	Fairly	Not very	DK	Con.	Lab.	Lib.	0th	None	DK
63	8	22	56	14	25	21	8	—	21	25
69	13	26	52	9	28	31	10	1	14	16
70	20	30	41	9	28	34	11	1	9	17

c. About how old were you when you first began to have likes and dislikes about the parties? Which party did you like best then?[63] [69] [70]

	Con.	Lab.	Lib.	0th	DK
63	38	46	9	1	6
69	39	44	9	2	6
70	32	47	9	2	10

35. *Partisanship of Associates*

a. How would you describe the politics of people who live around here? Would you say they are mainly Conservative, mainly Labour, or what? [69] [70]

	Con.	Lab.	Lib./Other	Divided	DK
69	33	32	2	15	18
70	30	37	2	21	10

b. How about other members of your family[69] (your near relations[70])? Are they mainly Conservative, mainly Labour, or what?

	Con.	Lab.	Lib./Other	DK/None
69	39	36	4	21
70	37	43	4	16

c. Are you single or married? *Unless single* How about [husband/wife]? Is he/she Conservative, Labour, Liberal, or what?[69] [70h]

	Single	Married	Widowed	Separated	Con.	Lab.	Lib./Other	DK/None
69	24	65	9	2	41	34	9	16
70h	18	72	9	1	38	40	8	14

d. Do you currently have a job? (Yes 64%[69], 61%[70c]) *If yes* How would you describe the party preference of the people at your place of work? Would you say they are mainly Conservative, mainly Labour, mainly Liberal, or what?

	Con.	Lab.	Lib./Other	Mixed	DK
69	29	32	2	12	25
70	26	37	1	20	16

36. *Party Identification*

a. Generally speaking do you usually think of yourself as Conservative, Labour or Liberal[63] (or what[64] [66] [69] [70])? *Unless none/DK* How strongly [chosen party] do you generally feel – very strongly, fairly strongly, or not very strongly?[63] [64] [66] [69] [70]

	63	64	66	69	70
Con.	36	39	35	42	40
Lab.	44	42	46	32	42
Lib.	10	12	10	9	8
None	8	5	7	10	8
DK/Other[69]	2	2	2	7	2
Very strongly	36	47	48	32	47
Fairly strongly	43	41	42	44	41
Not very strongly	21	12	10	24	12

b. Was there ever a time when you thought of yourself as [first party not chosen] or [second party not chosen] rather than [chosen party]? Which was that? *If reports previous affiliation* When did you change from [former party] to [present party]? What was the main thing that made you change from [former party] to [present party]?[63] [64] [66] [69] [70]
c. *If does not accept party affiliation* Do you generally feel[63] (think of yourself as[64] [66] [69] [70]) a little closer to one of the parties than to the others? Which party is that?

	63	64	66	69	70
Yes	49	44	44	43	39
Con.	36	36	36	41	47
Lab.	42	37	51	48	47
Lib.	22	27	13	11	6

d. If does not feel closer Was there ever a time when you did feel[63] (think of yourself as[64] [66] [69] [70]) closer to one of the parties than the others? Which (party) was that? When was that[63] (did you move away from [former party][64] [66] [69] [70])? What made you[63] (was the main thing that made you[64] [66] [69] [70]) move away from [former party]?

37. *Past Voting*

a. (Do you remember[63]) what was the first General Election you voted in? [64] [69] [70] Which party did you vote for then[63] (in that election[64] [69] [70])?

b. Now think of the General Election in the autumn of 1959 when the Conservatives were led by Macmillan and Labour by Gaitskell. Do you remember for certain whether you voted then?[63] [64] [66] *If did not vote* Do you remember whether you (would have[63]) preferred one of the parties to the others then? Which party was that?[63] [64] [66]

c. Now think of[66] (How about[69] [70c]) the General Election in the autumn of 1964 when the Conservatives were led by (Sir Alec Douglas-[69] [70c]) Home and Labour by (Harold[69] [70c]) Wilson. Do you remember for certain whether you voted then?[66] [69] [70b] Which party did you vote for then?[66] [69] [70b] *If did not vote* Do you remember whether you preferred one of the parties to the others then? Which party was that?[66] [69] [70b]

d. Think back to the General Election in 1966 when the Conservatives were led by Heath and Labour by Wilson. Do you remember for certain whether you voted then?[69] [70] Which party did you vote for then?[69] [70] *If did not vote* Do you remember whether you preferred one of the parties to the other then?[69] [70] Which party was that?[69] [70]

e. Can you tell me which General Elections seem to you to have been especially important? Any others? Did you vote in that election? Which party did you vote for in that election?[64]

f. In the General Elections since you have been old enough to vote, have you always voted for the same party or have you voted for different parties?[63] *If same party* Which party is that? *If different parties* Which parties were they? Taking just the General Elections since the end of the Second World War, have you voted for the same party or for different parties? *If same party* Which party is that?[63]

38. *Current Voting*

a. We find many people around the country who have good reasons for not voting. How about you? Did you vote in the General Election this year (or did something prevent you from voting)?[64][66][70] Did you vote in person or by post?[64][66][70] (At what hour did you vote?[64]) Which party did you vote for?[64][66][70]

b. How long ago did you decide to vote that way?[64][66][70]

c. What would you say is the main reason you voted [chosen party]?[64][66][70]

d. Would you say that you preferred [chosen party] *very* strongly, *fairly* strongly, or *not very* strongly?[64][66][70]

e. Did you think of voting for any other party? Which party is that?[64][66][70]

f. *If voted Conservative or Labour* Suppose you had thought the Conservative/Labour couldn't win. Would you rather have seen Labour/the Conservatives, or the Liberals form the new Government?[64][66][70]

g. *Ask if no Liberal stood* Would you have voted Liberal if a Liberal candidate had stood in this constituency?[64][66][70]

h. *If voted Liberal or (Other[70])* Would you have voted for another party if you had felt that the Liberal/(Other[70]) candidate hadn't much chance of winning in this constituency? *If would still have voted Liberal or (Other[70])* Would you rather have seen the Conservatives or Labour win the election?

i. *If did not vote*[64][66][70] What would you say is the main reason you didn't vote?

j. If you had voted, which party would you probably have voted for? *If don't know*[64][66][70] Were you a little more inclined to one of the parties than the others? Which party is that?

39. *Voting Intention*

a. There will be a General Election some time this year or next[63] (in the next year or two[69]). How likely would you say it is that you will vote in that election – quite certain, very likely, fairly likely, or not very likely?

b. If the General Election were held[63] (If you were voting in a General Election[69]) tomorrow, which party would you vote for?[64][69]

	Voting quite certain	Very likely	Fairly likely	Not very likely	DK	Con.	Lab.	Lib.	Other	Wouldn't vote	DK
63	71	14	7	6	2	33	44	12	—	3	8
69	67	12	8	10	3	49	27	9	2	5	8

c. *If vote Conservative or Labour*[63] Would you prefer [chosen party] very strongly (60%), fairly strongly (32%), or not very strongly (8%)?[63] If [chosen party] wasn't successful, would you rather see a [first party not chosen] or a [second party not chosen] government?[63] (Con. 15%, Lab. 9%, Lib. 60%, DK 16%)

d. If vote Liberal[63] Would you prefer the Liberals very strongly (51%), fairly strongly (42%) or not very strongly (7%)?[63] If you thought the Liberals had a chance of winning in this constituency but not in the country as a whole, how would you vote?[63] (Con. 5%, Lab. 3%, Lib. 88%, wouldn't vote 1%, DK 3%) (*If would still prefer Liberals*) And if you thought that the Liberals hadn't much chance of winning in this constituency either, how would you vote? (Con. 7%, Lab. 4%, Lib. 81%, Other 1%, wouldn't vote 5%, DK 2%) (*If would still prefer Liberals*) Suppose there was a straight fight between the Conservatives and Labour in this constituency, how would you vote? (Con. 36%, Lab. 31%, wouldn't vote 25%, DK 8%)

e. If don't know which party to vote for[63] Well, are you leaning towards one of the parties? Which party is that? (Con. 20%, Lab. 12%, Lib. 16%, No 40%, DK 12%)

f. If not Conservative or Labour[69] If you had to chose between Conservative and Labour, which would you choose? (Con. 32%, Lab. 31%, Neither 13%, DK 24%)

40. *Local Election Voting*

a. Talking to people around the country, we've found that a great many people weren't able to vote in the local elections early this May[63] (earlier this spring.[64]) How about you? Did you vote in the local elections this year or did something prevent you from voting? *If voted* How did you vote?

	Voted	Con.	Lab.	Lib.	Ind.	Other
63	49	34	48	11	5	2
64	62	38	45	8	8	1

b. If voted Do you always vote that way in local elections?[63] (Yes 80%) Were there any issues in the local elections this year that were especially important to you?[63] (Yes 20%) What were they?[63]

41. *Expectations about Result*

a. Regardless of your own preference, which party do you think has the best chance of winning the next election?[63] Regardless of your preference, which party did you think would win the election?[64] [66] [70]

b. How about here in this constituency? Which party has[63] (did you think had[64] [66] [70]) the best chance of winning in this constituency[63] (would win here[64] [66] [70])?

	Nationally				Locally		
	Con.	Lab.	Lib.	DK	Con.	Lab.	Lib.	DK
63	20	63	1	16	35	49	2	14
64	33	56	—	11	47	47	2	4
66	12	85	—	3	43	52	1	4
70	33	64	—	3	44	51	1	4

c. (*To first question if Liberals*) Do you feel very sure of this, fairly sure, or not very sure?[63] (*If Con. or Lab.*) How close do you think the Liberals could come to winning?[62] (Could win 1%, fairly close 28%, not very close 64%, DK 7%) (*If Lib.*) Have you changed your mind about this during the past year or so?[63]

d. (*To constituency question*) (*If Con. or Lab.*) How good a chance do you think the Liberals have of winning here in this constituency?[63] (If says Libs don't stand here) How good a chance would they have if they did stand here?[63] (*If Libs stood*) How close did you think the Liberals would come to winning in this constituency, fairly close, not very close, not at all close? (Fairly close 21%[64] 17%[66] 10%[70])

e. Would you say that you usually care[63] (cared) a good deal which party wins a General Election[63] (won the election[64] [66] [70]) or that you don't (didn't) care very much which party wins (won)? (Care a good deal 65%[63] 69%[64] 71%[66] 69%[70])

42. *Political Activity*

a. Have you paid a subscription to any political party in the last year? *If yes* Which party was that?[63] [64] [69] [70e] *If Labour* Was that as a member of the local party or through a trade union?[63] [64] [69] [70e]

	63	64	69	70e
Yes	12	14	10	10
Con.	45	53	38	44
Lab. (local)	20	15	10	10
(T.U.)	29	25	41	39
Lib.	5	6	6	2
Other	1	1	5	5

b. *If yes* Do you take an active part in party work?[63] (Yes 17%) What is that?[63]

c. Have you attended any public political meetings during the past year?[63] (Yes 4%) What meetings were those?

d. Did you suggest to anyone how they should vote?[64] (Yes 12%) Who was that? Anyone else?

e. Did you attend any political meetings during the campaign?[64] (Yes 8%) *If yes* Were those indoor (83%) or outdoor (13%) meetings? (Both 4%)

f. Did you do any party work during the election campaign?[64] (Yes 3%) *If yes* What was that? Which party was that?

g. Did any of the parties canvass at your home during the election campaign?[64] (Yes 33%) *If yes* Which parties called?

43. *Knowledge of M.P./Candidates*

a. Do you happen to remember (your M.P.'s name[63]) (the name of the candidate who was elected to Parliament from this constituency[64]) (who was the Member of Parliament for this constituency before the election [66] [70]) (the name of the Member of Parliament for this constituency[69])? Do you happen to remember which party he/she belongs to?[63] [69] Do you happen to know which party he/she is?[64] Do you happen to remember his/her party?[66] [70] Do you happen to know whether he/she stood for Parliament again in this election?[66] [70]

	63	64	66	69	70
Correct on name	55	85	79	49	73
Correct on Party	79	94	91	75	86
Correct on standing again	—	—	—	—	88

b. Have you read or heard anything about [name of M.P.[63] [64]] [name of M.P. before election[66] [70]]? Have you ever seen him/her in person?[63] [64] [66] [70]

	63	64	66	70
Heard or read something	30	66	47	60
Seen in person	35	35	37	37

c. Do you remember the names of any other candidate standing for Parliament from this constituency?[64] [66] [70]

d. Now take [name of Conservative] the Conservative candidate. Have you read or heard anything about him/her?[64] [66] Have you ever seen him/her in person?[64] [66]

e. How about [name of Labour candidate] the Labour candidate. Have you read or heard anything about him/her?[64] [66] Have you ever seen him/her in person?

f. How about [name of Liberal, if one stood] the Liberal candidate. Have you read or heard anything about him/her?[64] [66]

g. If has read or heard anything of M.P. Can you tell me anything in particular about what [name of M.P.] has done in Parliament?[63] Anything else?[63]

Do you know if [name of M.P.] has held any special position in Parliament or in the Government?[63] What is that?[63]

Do you know of any problems facing the Government that [name of M.P.] has taken a stand on?[63] What is that? Do you know what stand [name of M.P.] has taken on that?[63]

Have you heard anything about [name of M.P.]'s opinion on the Common Market?[63] What is that?[63] Do you think he/she favours Britain going into the Common Market?[63]

Have you heard anything about [name of M.P.]'s opinion on defence, disarmament or nuclear weapons?[63] What is that?[63] Do you think he/she favours Britain having her own nuclear weapons or not?[63]

Have you heard anything about [name of M.P.]'s opinion on public ownership or nationalizing industry?[63] What is that?[63] Do you think he/she favours nationalizing more industry or not?[63]

Do you happen to remember anything that [name of M.P.] has done for the people of this constituency?[63] What is that?[63]

Has he/she ever done anything for you or your family personally?[63] What is that?

Can you tell me what sort of person he/she is?[63]

Would you say that he/she is upper class, middle class or working class?[63]

Do you know if he/she has any business or trade union connection or any other connection of that kind? What sort of connection is that?[63]

On the whole, do you feel that [name of M.P.] is doing a good job as a Member of Parliament, a fair job, or only a poor job? Why do you feel that way?[63]

44. *Social Class*

a. Most people say they belong either to the middle class or to the working class.[63] [64a] [66a] [70i] Do you ever think of yourself as being in one of these classes?[63] [64a] [66a] [70i] Which class is that? *If not middle class or working class* If you had to make a choice would you call yourself middle class or working class?

Thinks in class terms	63 66	64a 60	66a 66	70i 66
Middle	27	27	28	28
Working	73	73	72	72

b. Do you ever think of yourself as belonging to a particular social class? (Yes 50%[64a], 40%[66a], 30%[69], 43%[70hi]) Which class is that? *Unless says middle class or working class* Most people say they belong either to the middle class or to the working class. If you had to make a choice would you call yourself middle class or working class?

c. Would you say you are about average [chosen class] or that you are in the upper or lower part of [chosen class]?[63 64 66 69]

d. What would you say the main social classes are?[70e] Which class would you put yourself in?[70e] (Middle 30%, Working 47%, Other 14%, DK 9%)

e. What would you say your family was when you were young, middle class or working class?[63 66 69 70e]

f. What would you say your father's family were when he was young, middle class or working class?[69 70e]

g. What would you say your mother's family was when she was young, middle class or working class?[69 70e]

	% middle class			
	63	66	69	70
Family	23	23	22	24
Father	—	—	20	21
Mother	—	—	21	22
Neighbours	—	—	23	23

h. What social class would you say most of the people living round here belong to?[69] *If not middle class or working class* If you had to make a choice between saying people round here were mainly middle class and saying they were mainly working class, which would you say?[69] Would you say that most of the people living round here are middle class or working class?[70]

i. On the whole do you think there is bound to be some conflict between different social classes or do you think they can get along together without any conflict?[63 64 66 69 70e]

	63	64	66	69	70e
Bound to be conflict	34	42	41	33	32
Can get along	57	52	54	61	64
DK	9	6	5	6	4

j. What sort of people would you say belong to the middle class?[63] What sort of jobs do middle class people have?[63]

k. What sort of people would you say belong to the working class?[63] What sort of jobs do working class people have?[63]

l. How difficult would you say it was for people to move from one class to another?[63] (Very 24%, fairly 22%, not very 33%, DK 21%) Why is that?[63]

m. How often would you say people move from one class to another, very often (4%), fairly often (16%), not very often (61%)?[64] (Not at all 7%, DK 12%) Under what circumstances do you think a person could move from the working class to the middle class?[64]

n. Some people feel they have a lot in common with other people of their own class but others don't feel this way so much. How about you? Would you say you feel pretty close to other [chosen class] people (55%) or that you don't feel much closer to them than to people in other classes (37%)?[63] (DK 8%)

o. How much interest would you say you have in how [chosen class] people as a whole are getting along in this country? Do you have a good deal of interest in it (36%), some interest (40%), or not much interest at all (20%)?[63] (DK 4%)

p. Do you think that middle class people vote mainly for one party (37%) or are they fairly evenly divided between the parties (48%)?[63] (DK 15%) (*If mainly for one*) Which party is that? (Con. 94%) Why do you think they vote mainly for that party?[63] How about working class people? Do they vote mainly for one party (62%) or are they fairly evenly divided between the parties (31%)?[63] (DK 7%) *If mainly for one* Which party is that (Lab. 99%)? Why do you think they vote mainly for that party?[63]

q. How wide are the differences between social classes in this country, do you think?[70e] Do you think these differences have become greater (11%) or less (56%) or have remained about the same (26%)? (DK 7%)

45. *Union Membership*

a. Does anyone in this household belong to a trade union?[63] *If yes* Who is it that belongs? Which trade union is that?[63] About how long has member belonged to this trade union?[63]

b. Some members of trade unions feel they have a lot in common with other members, but others don't feel this way so much. How about [member]? Would you say that [member] feels pretty close to trade union members in general (37%) or that [member] doesn't feel much closer to them than to other kinds of people (49%)[63] (DK 14%)

c. How much interest would you say that [member] has in how trade union people are getting along in this country? Does [member] have a good deal of interest in it (33%), some interest (34%) or not much interest (33%)?[63]

d. Do you think that trade union members vote mainly for one party (54%) or are they fairly evenly divided between the parties (46%)? *If one* Which party is that? (Lab. 98%) Why do you think they vote mainly for that party?[63]

e. Do you currently have a job? *If yes* Are you a member of a trade union? Which trade union is that?[64] [69] [70c]

f. *If a member* At your place of work how many people who are doing your kind of job are members of a trade union – all of them, most of them, or only some of them? *If all or most* At your place of work do you have to be a trade union member to do your job?[64] [69] [70]

	64	69	70
All	58	59	66
Most	30	30	24
Some	11	9	9
DK	1	2	1
Membership compulsory	50	47	54

g. Do you see any trade union magazines or journals?[64] (Yes 65%) What is it that you see? How much attention do you pay to it – a good deal (31%), some (33%) or not much (36%)?[64] Do you recall seeing any articles or discussions on political questions? (Yes 30%) *If yes* What was that?

h. Did a shop steward or other trade union representative approach you during the election campaign and ask you to vote?[64] (Yes 2%) Who was that? What position did he have?[63]

i. *If not a member* At your place of work are any of the people who are doing your kind of job members of a trade union?[64] (Yes 18%, No 74%, DK 8%) *If yes* How many of them are members of a trade union – most of them (39%), some of them (24%), or only a few of them (31%)?[64] (DK 6%) Have you been asked to join a trade union since you have been at your present place of work? (Yes 13%[64] 11%[69] 16%[70c]) *If yes* Can you tell me why you didn't join?[64] *If no* Would you join if asked? (Yes 24%[64] 26%[67] 33%[70]) Why is that?[64]

If does not have a job Does anyone in this household belong to a trade union? (Yes 32%[64] 27%[69] 27%[70]) Who is it that belongs? Which trade union is that?

46. *Parental Background*

a. Can you tell me where your parents were living when you were born? Were your parents brought up there or did they come from somewhere else? *If either parent from somewhere else* Where exactly did they come from?[63] [70c] (Both always there 52%,[63] 42%,[70c] one always there 22%,[63] 28%,[70c] neither 25%,[63] 28%,[70c] DK 1%[63] 2%)[70c]

b. Can you tell me where your father was brought up?[64]

c. Can you tell me where your mother was brought up?[64]

d. What was your father's occupation when you were a child? What sort of job did he actually do?[64] [69]

e. Did he have any qualification (such as apprenticeship, professional qualification, university degree, diploma, etc.)? What was that?[64] [69]

f. What type of firm or organization did he work for?[64] [69]
If in civil service, forces, police, etc. What was his rank or grade when you were a child?[64] [69]
If in any other type of organization Did he hold any particular positions in this organization when you were a child?[64] [69] (e.g. foreman, typing supervisor, office manager, company secretary, etc.[69]) *If yes* What was that?[64] [69] *If proprietor or manager* About how big an organization was that? For instance, roughly how many people worked there?[64] [69]

g. Can you tell me if your father stayed on in school after he had reached the minimum age for leaving? (Yes 6%[69] 7%[70h])

h. Can you tell me if your mother stayed on in school after she had reached the minimum age for leaving? (Yes 8%[69] 7%[70h])

i. What was your father-in-law's occupation when your husband/wife was a child? What sort of job did he actually do?[69]

j. Did he have any qualification? What was that?[69]

k. What type of organization did he work for?[69]

47. *Personal Background*

a. About how old was your father when you were born?[69]

b. What year was your father born?[70]

c. What year was your mother born?[70]

d. How many brothers and sisters do/did you have?[70]

e. Were you ever in the forces[64] (Yes 61% of men) *If yes* When was that? Did you ever serve overseas?

f. Do you hold a public library ticket? (Yes 36%[69] 41%[70])

48. *Religion*

a. What is your religion?[63 69 70h]
b. When you were young what was your parents' religion?[63 69 70] *Unless 'no religion'* How often do you attend church (chapel, synagogue)?

49. *Education*

a. Can you tell me how old you were when you left school?[63] What kind of a school was that[63] (did you go to[69 70h])?
b. Did you stay on at school after the minimum leaving age? (Yes 29%[69] 29%[70h]) *If yes* How old were you when you left school?[69 70h]
c. Did you have any full- or part-time education after leaving school? (Yes 32%[63]) Did you have any further education after that? (Yes 33%[69] 30%[70h]). *If yes* What was that?[63 69 70h]

50. *Emigration*

a. Have you ever thought of emigrating from Britain to another country?[70] (Yes 35%) *If yes* What country is that?
b. Have any of your brothers or sisters emigrated from Britain to another country?[70] (Yes 11%) *If yes* How many have emigrated? What country/countries did they go to?

51. *Personal Housing*

a. How long have you lived in your present home?[63 64 69 70]
b. Do you or your family rent or own your own home?

	63	64	69	70
Own	43	46	46	50
Rent (council)	29	28	29	29
Rent (private)	25	22	23	19
Other	3	4	2	2

c. Do you expect to move in the next year or two? (Yes 19%[69] 19%[70]) *If yes* Where do you think you will be moving?
d. Do you have a telephone in your home? (Yes 35%[69] 39%[70])

52. *Household Composition and Occupational Details*

[There were slight differences between surveys in the order or form in which these personal questions were asked. However, this summary, taken from the 1964 survey, is a fairly exact representation of the questions covered on each occasion.]

- Can you tell me who else there is in your household besides yourself? (List, showing relationship to respondent, sex, age, marital status)
- Which member of your family living here actually is the owner/is responsible for the rent?
- What type of firm or organization does (householder) work for?
- What job does (householder) actually do? Does he/she hold any particular position in the organization?

(If in public service) What is his/her rank or grade?

(If proprietor or manager) How many employees?

- Has (householder) any qualification? (e.g., apprenticeship or degree).
- Would you mind telling me which of these income groups (householder) belongs to?

(If respondent is not householder) Do you have a paid job?

(If yes, repeat householder's occupational questions.)

APPENDIX C

Differences from First Edition

ALTHOUGH many of the sections of the first edition survive in this book, none has escaped small editorial changes and updating. In many sections where the central argument survives the illustrations are altered. We have also transformed the structure of the book. Our first edition was arranged according to two interlocking dualisms: one, that between the construction and application of analytic frameworks; the other, that between long-term and short-term sources of electoral change. Its part fell into this pattern:

	Changes of alignment	Transient variations
Construction	Part One	Part Two
Application	Part Three	Part Four

We have reordered our material here by relaxing the distinction between construction and application and promoting 'replacement' to a status co-ordinate with 'realignment' and 'short-term conversions'. These three types of change and the factors in 'continuities of alignment' define the four parts of this revised edition.

The reader who wishes to see the detailed relationship between the two editions may consult the guide below. It lists the contents of the first edition and, where any significant part of the contents of a section has survived in this edition, indicates the chapter in which it is now located.

INTRODUCTION

1 Approaches to Change
Types of Change (1); Elector and Electorate (1); The Electorate and Political Leaders (1); The Context of Research (1); Traditions of Electoral Research (omitted); Elements of Design (1); Plan of the Book (1)

10   The Flow of Political Information
The Sources of Information (omitted); Exposure to Communication and Partisan Change (omitted); Partisan Dispositions and the National Press (omitted); The Press and Partisan Change (omitted)

PART III

11   The Evolution of Party Strength
The Decline of the Liberals (7); The Making of the New Alignment (8); Generations and Political Change (10)

12   Partisan Change 1959–66
Pathways to Change (12); Conservative Decline 1959–63 (12); Conservative Recovery 1963–4 (12); Change 1959–64 (12); Labour Consolidation 1964–6 (12); Change 1959–66 (12)

13   Patterns in Change
The Cumulation of Change (12); Sources of Traditional Behaviour (omitted); The Sources of Uniform Swing (6)

14   The Liberal Presence
The Circulation of Liberal Strength (omitted); Dispositions towards Liberalism (omitted); Constraints on Liberal Voting (omitted); The Liberal Presence and the Strength of the Larger Parties (omitted)

PART IV

15   Issues and Change
A Framework of Issues (13); Issues of Strongest Impact (14); Issues of High Potential (14); Issues of Less Potential (14)

16   Images of the Parties
The Nature of Party Images (16); Themes Associated with the Parties (16); The Image of Newness (16)

17   The Pull of the Leaders
The Salience of the Leaders (17); The Content of Leader Images (17); The Net Direction of Attitudes towards Leaders (17); The Electoral Impact of the Leaders (17)

18   The Economic Context
The Economy as an Issue (18); The State of the Economy 1959–66 (18); Perceptions of Individual Well-Being (18); The Parties and the Economy (18)

19   The Final Choice of Government

CONCLUSIONS

20   Analytic Perspectives

Sources

APART from our own survey, discussed at length in Appendix A, we have drawn extensively on the work of others. Many of our debts are implicit in our footnotes. Here we merely acknowledge some of the principal sources on which we have drawn.

(a) *Election statistics*. Since British law makes no acknowledgement of parties, it has never been possible for official sources to publish any return of votes that makes political sense. We are much indebted to the Home Office returns, to the Registrar General's Annual Reports and to individual registration officers for statistics about the electorate. But we have naturally turned to the invaluable *Times House of Commons* for much of our data on votes; for the pre-war period successive editions of the *Constitutional Year Book* have provided our main source although F. W. S. Craig has since assembled this material in a more convenient and authoritative form.

Local election returns have been far more frustrating. Nowhere are these collected centrally. Our debt to the diligence and expertise of Mr Michael Steed of Manchester University is enormous. He has assembled large bodies of returns from all kinds of sources both in connection with the local elections of our period and on a historical basis.

(b) *Opinion polls*. Anyone working in the field of recent British politics and elections must owe a lot to the data assembled over the past thirty years by Dr Henry Durant and the Gallup Poll. In all sorts of areas he has provided data where none existed before. In the 1960s, his findings on the standings of parties and leaders, published since the demise of the *News Chronicle* in the *Daily Telegraph*, had increasing impact on the politicians themselves. The voter's fever chart, published weekly or monthly, helped to shape party strategy and election timing. But in the files of the Gallup Poll there exist more fundamental data on the composition and attitude of the electorate over time which has been a major quarry for many beside ourselves.

Since 1957 and more particularly since 1961 the findings of National Opinion Polls, published in the *Daily Mail*, have provided a rival source to Gallup. Since September/October 1963, when National Opinion Polls switched from quota sampling to probability sampling, their findings have been of particular interest to academic students and, as has been evident, we have drawn heavily on their findings at the time of the 1964 and 1966 elections. (A summary of the election polls can be found in *The British General Election of 1964* and *The British General Election of 1966*.)

A third polling organization, Research Services, Ltd., under the guidance of Dr Mark Abrams, did much stimulating research, some privately on behalf of the Labour Party, some published in the *Observer* and some in the *Public Opinion Quarterly* and elsewhere.

Since 1965 the Opinion Research Centre under Humphrey Taylor has provided one more very valuable source of polling data and since 1969 the Louis Harris organization has joined the field.

Our debt to all these polling organizations is a personal one and extends far beyond the figures cited in the text.

(*c*) *Election studies*. The pioneer survey studies of elections were in the United States and the American literature on voting research is now prodigious. Here we can only list a few major works.

P. F. Lazarsfeld, B. Berelson and H. Gaudet, *The People's Choice*, New York, 1944.

B. Berelson, P. F. Lazarsfeld and W. N. McPhee, *Voting*, Chicago, 1954.

A. Campbell, G. Gurin and W. E. Miller, *The Voter Decides*, Evanston, 1954.

A. Campbell, P. E. Converse, W. E. Miller and D. E. Stokes, *The American Voter*, New York, 1960.

A. Campbell, P. E. Converse, W. E. Miller and D. E. Stokes, *Elections and the Political Order*, New York, 1966.

N. Polsby and A. Wildavsky, *Presidential Elections*, New York, 1964.

G. M. Pomper, *Elections in America: Control and Influence in Democratic Politics*, New York, 1968.

W. D. Burnham, *Critical Elections and the Mainsprings of American Politics*, New York, 1970.

S. Verba and N. Nie, *Participation in America: Political Democracy and Social Equality*, New York, 1972.

W. H. Flanigan, *Political Behavior of the American Electorate*, 2nd ed., Boston, 1972.

In Britain, the only books involving substantial local surveys are:[1]

M. Benney, R. H. Pear and A. H. Gray, *How People Vote*, London, 1956.

[1] Two other local surveys are reported in articles: A. H. Birch and P. Campbell, 'Voting Behaviour in a Lancashire Constituency', *British Journal of Sociology*, 1 (1950), 197–208; P. Campbell, A. H. Birch and D. Donnison, 'Voting Behaviour in Droylesden in October 1951', *Manchester School*, 20 (1952), 57–65.

R. S. Milne and H. C. Mackenzie, *Straight Fight*, London, 1954.
—— and ——, *Marginal Seat*, London, 1958.
A. H. Birch, *Small Town Politics*, Oxford, 1959.
F. Bealey, J. Blondel and W. J. McCann, *Constituency Politics*, London, 1965.
I. Budge and D. W. Urwin, *Scottish Political Behaviour*, London, 1966.
J. Trenaman and D. McQuail, *Television and the Political Image*, London, 1961.
J. G. Blumler and D. McQuail, *Television in Politics*, London, 1968.

Some other books which draw together a large amount of data should also be noted:

M. Abrams, R. Rose and R. Hinden, *Must Labour Lose?* London, 1960.
R. R. Alford, *Party and Society*, Chicago, 1963 and London, 1964.
A. J. Allen, *The English Voter*, London, 1964.
G. Almond and S. Verba, *The Civic Culture*, Princeton, 1963.
J. Blondel, *Voters, Parties and Leaders*, London, 1963.
J. Bonham, *The Middle Class Vote*, London, 1954.
D. E. Butler, *The British General Election of 1951*, London, 1952.
——, *The British General Election of 1955*, London, 1955.
—— and R. Rose, *The British General Election of 1959*, London, 1960.
—— and A. S. King, *The British General Election of 1964*, London, 1965.
—— and A. S. King, *The British General Election of 1966*, London, 1966.
—— and J. Freeman, *British Political Facts 1900–1968*, London, 1969.
——, *The Electoral System in Britain Since 1918*, 2nd edn., Oxford, 1963,
—— and M. Pinto-Duschinsky, *The British General Election of 1970*, London, 1971.
F. W. S. Craig, *British Parliamentary Election Statistics 1918–1970*, Chichester, 1970.
——*British Parliamentary Election Results 1918–49* (1969); *1950–70* (1971).
J. H. Goldthorpe, D. Lockwood, F. Bechhofer and J. Platt, *The Affluent Worker*, 3 vols. Cambridge, 1968–70.
M. Kinnear, *The British Voter*, London, 1968.
R. L. Leonard, *Elections in Britain*, London, 1968.
R. B. McCallum and A. Readman, *The British General Election of 1945*, Oxford, 1947.
R. T. McKenzie, *British Political Parties*, 3rd edn., London, 1964.
—— and A. Silver, *Angels in Marble*, London, 1968.
H. G. Nicholas, *The British General Election of 1950*, London, 1951.

E. A. Nordlinger, *The Working-Class Tories*, London, 1967.

H. Pelling, *Social Geography of British Elections, 1885–1910*, London, 1967.

P. G. J. Pulzer, *Political Representation and Elections*, London, 1967.

R. Rose, *Politics in England*, London, 1965.

W. G. Runciman, *Relative Deprivation and Social Justice*, London and Berkeley, 1967.

Index

Index

DATE			
FAC SPR 89	NOV 1 9 1993		
DEC 1 0 1993			

© THE BAKER & TAYLOR CO.